WINNING RECIPES

More Than 300 Delicious Recipes,
Tips, and Tricks from America's
Favorite Cooking Contest

Back cover recipes: *(top, left)* Mozzarella and Pesto Crescent Tarts, page 112; *(top, center)* Oatmeal Cookie Granola Berry Parfaits, page 33; *(top, right)* Creamy Bean Soup with Taquito Dippers, page 201; *(bottom, left)* Cream-Filled Strawberry-Brownie Cake, page 382; *(bottom, center)* Spicy Citrus Shrimp and Black Bean Tacos, page 280; and *(bottom, right)* Carrot Cake Tart, page 408

Book design by Christina Gaugler

Library of Congress Cataloging-in-Publication Data is on file with the publisher.

ISBN 978–1–62336–566–0

4 6 8 10 9 7 5 3 direct mail hardcover

We inspire and enable people to improve their lives and the world around them.
For more of our products, visit rodalestore.com or call 800–848–4735.

Contents

GRAND PRIZE–WINNING MOMENT

Carolyn Gurtz, Gaithersburg, Md., was named the 43rd Pillsbury Bake-Off® Contest grand prize winner Tuesday, April 15, 2008. She received $1 million and a complete set of kitchen appliances valued at $10,000 for Double-Delight Peanut Butter Cookies.

MALE BONDING

Eight men were among the 100 finalists competing in Dallas for the $1 million grand prize, awarded April 15, 2008. Left to right: Will Sperry, Bunker Hill, W. Va.; Bob Gadsby, Great Falls, Mont.; Mike Briggs, Arlington, Va.; Chris Batton, North Irwin, Pa.; David Dahlman, Chatsworth, Calif.; Scott Hatfield, Grove City, Pa.; Edgar Rudberg, St. Paul, Minn.; and Harrison Carpenter, Longmont, Colo.

Introduction

"The newest $1 million Pillsbury Bake-Off® Contest winner is . . . ."

With that dramatic announcement, another talented amateur cook earns a place of honor in America's most prestigious culinary competition. Since it began in 1949, long before today's reality TV shows and chef competitions, the Pillsbury Bake-Off® Contest has been giving real people a chance to be recognized and rewarded for their unique skill—cooking creativity. The rest of America wins, too, with innovative and delectable new recipes to make meal times special for family and friends.

The Experience of a Lifetime

For every Bake-Off® Contest grand prize winner, the experience starts with the spark of a creative cooking idea, a new recipe innovative enough to earn them a trip to the contest finals. With tens of thousands of entries for each Bake-Off® Contest, the competition for one of the 100 coveted finalist spots is intense. Once those 100 best recipes are chosen, the 100 talented cooks who submitted them are off on an amazing adventure.

Each of the 100 finalists wins an all expense-paid trip to the Bake-Off® Contest finals, held in appealing destinations around the country, like Nashville, Las Vegas, Orlando, Hollywood, Phoenix, or Dallas. While the location changes, every contest finals offers fun-filled activities, the camaraderie of 99 other cooking enthusiasts and the thrill of the competition and awards ceremony.

Let the Contest Begin!

First items on the agenda for finalists are a contest orientation and enjoying the local sights. Then the cooking contest itself kicks off with a lively grand march of all the finalists onto the competition floor. Within minutes, the first whiffs of sautéing garlic and onions start to fill the air. The sound of chopping knives provides a counterpoint to the whir of mixers, as the temperature in the room (which had been chilled in advance) rises from the heat of 100 ranges and overhead banks of camera lights.

Contest sponsors have transformed a hotel ballroom into the competition arena, with 100 mini kitchens set up in rows across the floor. Each finalist has a range and a small countertop area to prepare their recipe, with ingredients and utensils to make their recipe three times—once for the judges and the other two for sampling to guests on the contest floor or as a backup. While the contest work station may not have all the conveniences of a home kitchen, it does have an extra benefit, a "runner." That's what contest sponsors call the floor assistants who aid Bake-Off® Contest finalists, running to bring ingredients from the refrigerators and freezers at the edge of the competition floor, escorting finalists to the judges or photography area, whisking away dirty dishes and generally helping to make the contest day go smoothly. Runners help with lots of things but one thing they don't do is help the contestants prepare their recipes.

Visitors in the Kitchen

Pillsbury Bake-Off® Contest finalists also share their mini kitchens with guests, like food reporters curious about the recipe and what inspired its creation, supermarket representatives and sponsor hosts. Photographers and video crews maneuver their way through the work stations, trying to capture all the action of 100 cooks in the midst of the competition.

CATEGORY WINNER: SWEET TREATS
Sue Compton reacts after Oprah Winfrey announces the Delanco, N.J., woman's recipe for Mini Ice Cream Cookie Cups as the grand prize winner of the 44th Pillsbury Bake-Off® Contest Wednesday, April 14, 2010, live on *The Oprah Winfrey Show*. Compton received a $1 million prize and a GE Profile™ Induction Free-Standing Range and $7,000 worth of GE Profile™ kitchen appliances.

Often famous faces are spotted on the competition floor, too, as the celebrity host or another well-known guest stops to get a cooking tip from a finalist or nibble a finished dish. The roster of Bake-Off® Contest attendees includes celebrities from each decade of its history, ranging from Art Linkletter and Eleanor Roosevelt to Ronald Reagan, Bob Barker, Dick Clark, Willard Scott, Alex Trebek, Marie Osmond, Joy Behar, and Martha Stewart.

Of course, the 100 finalists are the most important stars at each competition, because their creative genius makes the contest possible. While there were three men competing at the first contest in 1949, most of the 100 finalists were homemakers, reflecting the predominant role of women in the years following World War II. As more women joined the workforce, the number of Bake-Off® Contest finalists who worked outside the home grew also. The list of professions from recent contests reflects the diversity of women's jobs today, with college professor, physician, business owner, portrait photogra-

A MOMENT OF PRIDE

Shana Butler feels the emotion of the 45th Pillsbury Bake-Off® Contest, Monday, March 26, 2012, at the Peabody Orlando Hotel in Florida. Finalists from across the country competed for a $1 million grand prize. The grand prize winner was announced live Tuesday, March 27, on Hallmark Channel's *The Martha Stewart Show.*

pher and financial controller among the many career choices of finalists. With more men cooking in the home, more males have captured a finalist slot, too, with as many as fourteen men among the 100 finalists at one competition.

Judging the Contest

One group of important Bake-Off® Contest guests isn't ever spotted on the competition floor—the official contest judges. To protect the contest's integrity, they are sequestered behind closed doors near the cooking area, to ensure that they do not know which finalist has created any of the recipes. As the finalists deem their dish ready for judging, they deliver their food to the judging room door, where it's quickly whisked from sight to the judges. The panel of food expert judges score the recipes using the official judging criteria, then work in jury-room secrecy to deliberate on their final selection of the prize-winning recipes. How can they choose from among 100 spectacular dishes? As one newspaper food editor exclaimed about her judging role, "We're looking for something that makes you say 'Wow!' when you bite into it."

While the judges continue their deliberation—often for hours after the competition's end—contest sponsors dismantle the mini kitchens and wash mountains of dirty dishes. As the contest staff finishes last-minute preparations for the exciting awards ceremony, the 100 finalists wait in suspense to learn which recipes have earned prize money.

The Winner Is . . .

The Bake-Off® Contest has always had a lucrative prize pool, awarding a grand prize plus additional category prizes. For the first contest, originally called the Grand National Recipe and Baking Contest, the grand prize was $25,000. Then it grew to $40,000, then $50,000. In 1996, the grand prize jumped to an amazing $1 million.

As the contest's celebrity host announces each of the category prize winners, the tension builds for the final announcement. The grand prize-winning recipe is revealed with an envelope containing the name of the winning recipe—the recipe that has earned the latest $1 million prize. Imagine the thrill for the

HAULING HARVEST
Bake-Off® Kitchens staff members Kathy Saatzer and Diane Carlson move produce to the kitchens where they will be divided for finalists' recipes during the preparation for the 45th Pillsbury Bake-Off® Contest, held Monday, March 26, 2012, at the Peabody Orlando Hotel in Florida. Finalists from around the country competed for a $1 million grand prize. The grand prize winner was announced live Tuesday, March 27, on Hallmark Channel's *The Martha Stewart Show.*

finalist whose recipe name is in that envelope!

For the finalist who earns the top prize, the next days are a whirlwind of activity. Recent grand prize winners were whisked away for appearances on one of the network morning shows, then later prepared their recipe for the country's most popular daytime talk show. Their recipe and photo appeared in newspapers around the country, and local television news shows shared video of the cooking action and dramatic awards announcement.

Everyone Wins!

Whether or not finalists win prize money, they all take home great memories of the event. Some leave having made cherished new friends from among the other finalists after sharing the Bake-Off® Contest experience. Finalists often become celebrities in their home cities, too, as a result of their Bake-Off® Contest participation. They report being recognized in the grocery store by someone who's seen news coverage of the Bake-Off® Contest. Others enjoy being able to use their notoriety to help gain attention for local charitable activities. Finalists may even hear from people around the country who have tried their winning recipe and want to share their pleasure with the dish.

What's Cooking in America's Kitchens

The recipes in each competition reflect what's cooking in contemporary American kitchens. While the early contests featured "from scratch" ideas, today's contest offers quicker, easier recipes. As more convenience products made their way into shopping carts, creative cooks used them as the starting point for Bake-Off® Contest entries. Bake-Off® Contest recipes also introduced America's cooks to new flavors and ingredients, helping to broaden the reach of emerging cooking trends.

Today's Bake-Off® Contest recipes often pack more flavor punch than cooking did in the '50s

WAVES AND SMILES

Finalists enter the 45th Pillsbury Bake-Off® Contest, Monday, March 26, 2012, at the Peabody Orlando Hotel in Florida. Finalists from across the country competed for a $1 million grand prize. The grand prize winner was announced live Tuesday, March 27, on Hallmark Channel's *The Martha Stewart Show.*

PREP WORK

Christine Field prepares her recipe at the 45th Pillsbury Bake-Off® Contest, Monday, March 26, 2012, at the Peabody Orlando Hotel in Florida. Finalists from across the country competed for a $1 million grand prize. The grand prize winner was announced live Tuesday, March 27, on Hallmark Channel's *The Martha Stewart Show.*

and '60s, reflecting the growing diversity of America's cuisine and a new interest in spicier flavors. Entrants are using the wealth of choices in today's supermarkets, like an expanded variety of ethnic ingredients, new produce selections and shortcut convenience items, to add originality to their entries.

You Can Be a Bake-Off® Contest Finalist!

Home cooks who'd like to become a Bake-Off® Contest finalist can look to some of these new cooking ideas for inspiration for their entries. The official contest rules provide all the requirements for each event, including recipe categories that define what kinds of creations should be entered and eligible products that must be included in entries. For the first contest, all recipes had to use Pillsbury™ flour; now eligible products include a long list of ingredients, including many items

FROM 1 TO 100

The 100 finalists display their recipes at the 45th Pillsbury Bake-Off® Contest, Monday, March 26, 2012, at the Peabody Orlando Hotel in Florida. Finalists from across the country competed for a $1 million grand prize. The grand prize winner was announced live Tuesday, March 27, on Hallmark Channel's *The Martha Stewart Show.*

SPECIAL AWARD: JIF® PEANUT BUTTER

Sandra Hilbert won the $5,000 Jif® Peanut Butter Award at the 45th Pillsbury Bake-Off® Contest, Tuesday, March 27, 2012, at the Peabody Orlando Hotel in Florida. The announcement came as part of a special live broadcast of Hallmark Channel's *The Martha Stewart Show*. Her recipe was for Chewy Peanut Butter-Caramel Bars.

that allow for quick-to-prepare recipes. Rules also include the judging criteria—appropriate use of eligible products, taste, appearance, creativity, and crowd appeal—which are used in selecting the 100 final recipes and by the judging panel at the event. Reading and following the contest rules are an important first step in preparing to enter the contest.

Bake-Off® Contest hopefuls submit their complete recipe online. All recipe entries first go to an independent judging agency, where the entrants' identifying information is removed. Recipes are screened to check that they meet the contest requirements, and the home economists read them to select the most appealing. These are forwarded to the Bake-Off® Contest kitchens, where they are prepared for evaluation by taste panels of home economists. Additional kitchen testing to ensure recipes will work consistently in home kitchens and a search process to verify originality further narrow the field of entries. Then the Bake-Off® Contest home economists

SETTING THE SCENE

The contest floor awaits the 100 finalists at the 46th Pillsbury Bake-Off® Contest, held Monday, November 11, 2013, in Las Vegas. Finalists from around the country competed for a $1 million grand prize.

THE 100 FINALISTS

The 100 finalists join the Pillsbury Doughboy™ for a group photo at the 46th Pillsbury Bake-Off® Contest, held Monday, November 11, 2013, at Aria Resort & Casino in Las Vegas. Finalists from around the country competed for a $1 million grand prize.

MEET THE CATEGORY WINNERS
(Right to left) Beth Royals, Courtney Sawyer, Jody Walker, and Megan Beimer pose at the 47th Pillsbury Bake-Off® Contest.

complete the difficult task of choosing just 100 recipes to compete at the finals.

What does it take to become one of the elite 100? Some entrants, like grand prize winner Suzanne Conrad of Findlay, Ohio, make it to the competition the first time they submit a recipe. Others, like Michael Weaver of San Francisco, tried for 30 years before finally winning a trip to compete in 2006. But essential for any Bake-Off® Contest hopeful is a great-tasting original recipe.

A Collection of Memorable Bake-Off® Recipes

You can try some of the many wonderful Bake-Off® Contest recipes in this collection that spans more than 60 years of American cooking traditions. Within this cookbook, you'll find favorites from throughout the contest's history. All the million-dollar grand prize winners are here, along with many of the Bake-Off® Contest classics and newer recipes destined to become favorites in home cooks' recipe repertoires. As you enjoy making dishes you've prepared in the past or trying new ideas, remember that behind each dish is a home cook, just like you and your neighbors, who was inspired to try something new.

The Bake-Off® Through the Years

Imagine that first contest. The year was 1949. President Harry Truman had a plan to lead the world to peace and prosperity. Soldiers had returned from the war in the Pacific and Europe. Women moved from their wartime jobs to full-time homemaking. Wartime sugar rationing had finally ended, and home cooks were baking up a storm: cookies, cakes, pies, and brownies. There was a spirit of celebration in the air—and why not? The nation had made a transition from a period of terrible adversity to a time of prosperity. The postwar economy was thriving and people had time and money again to enjoy good food and entertaining. At Pillsbury, President Philip Pillsbury felt like celebrating, too; he wanted to recognize the achievements of those unsung heroes of the dining room and cookie jar—home cooks.

What was missing from the life of devoted, industrious home cooks? Public recognition, glamour, and rewards for their culinary talents. Where was the most glamorous place in the country? The ballroom of the Waldorf-Astoria Hotel in New York City. So, what if 100 of the best home cooks were gathered together, treated like royalty and rewarded for their efforts? Wouldn't that bring excitement and respect to kitchens from the shores of Florida to the mountains of Alaska? A competition was announced, an avalanche of entries arrived and what was to become Pillsbury's Bake-Off® Contest was born.

Those first years of the Bake-Off® Contest were amazing. Contestants from all over the country and from every walk of life were showered with luxury to convey the message that the quiet work they did daily—the cooking, the baking, the serving, the planning, the attention to detail—was appreciated and esteemed. Many contestants had never been on a train or stayed in a hotel before. And they certainly had never met the likes of former first lady and nationally syndicated columnist Eleanor Roosevelt, or television and radio personality Art Linkletter. These celebrities were at the first event, then known as the Grand National Recipe and Baking Contest. Contestants were served breakfast in bed, treated to a luncheon that included pheasant under glass, and pampered with the kind of admiring attention formerly reserved for captains of industry and film stars. In retrospect, those first Bake-Off® Contests could be read as a sign of the changes that would transform American society over the next sixty years. Women would soon begin to extend their activities outside the home again, to pursue professional achievements and professional status. Is it any wonder that the Smithsonian Institution recently accepted Pillsbury contest memorabilia into their permanent collection?

In fact, the recipes popularized through the Bake-Off® Contest have become a part of our culture. No collection of the favorite recipes of the last century would be complete without a nod to Peanut Blossoms, cookies made with a chocolate kiss baked in a peanut-butter thumbprint. For that timeless cookie, thank Freda Smith, who invented them for Bake-Off® Contest 9, in 1957. French Silk Chocolate Pie has become such an American icon it can be found from the humblest diners to the fanciest restaurants—Betty Cooper worked up the recipe for Bake-Off® Contest 3, in 1951. And the Tunnel of Fudge Cake? Millions of these cakes have been served since Ella Rita Helfrich invented it for Bake-Off® Contest 17, in 1966.

The Bake-Off® Contest was held annually until 1976 and then changed to an every-other-year schedule. Now, more than 60 years later, the contest is back to a yearly event and it remains popular as it continues to reflect the changing food needs and interests. Recipes entered in the Pillsbury Bake-Off® Contest through the years reveal what flavors were popular, the ingredients found in most pantries, the changing demographics of our country and what was happening in households nationwide. Bake-Off® recipes are special because they are a reflection of how Americans are living and eating. These are not recipes created by a master chef, or the thoughts of a single company, but are the accumulated wisdom and experience of hundreds of thousands of cooks. The Bake-Off® recipes are a testament to how, what and sometimes even why Americans cook.

1950s

The first Pillsbury Bake-Off® Contest spurred a phenomenon that many copied but few have perfected over the years. Throughout the '50s, the

Laura Rott, Theodora Smafield, and Mrs. Richard Sprague, grand prize winners of the first Pillsbury Bake-Off® Contest in New York City in 1949.

annual Bake-Off® Contest showcased the creativity of America's best home cooks and their favorite new flavors in the kitchen. The fictitious everywoman Ann Pillsbury—aka the Pillsbury Lady—presided over the contest and its innovative magazines. Ann encouraged cooks young and old to share a "love of good baked things that is so very strong in our country." Reflecting mid-century interest in the glamorous home, the contest was held at New York City's Waldorf-Astoria Hotel, where it resided for many years. The contest showcased kitchen innovations, including a white General Electric four-burner, double-oven. By the late '50s, electric mixers, another labor- and time-saving device, were introduced in each cook's "kitchen" at the contest.

In early Bake-Off® Contests, the one ingredient required for entry was at least one-half cup of Pillsbury™ BEST™ enriched flour, so it's not surprising that baked goods—specifically scratch cakes—represented the largest category of entries during the contest's first decade. Most women worked in the home and in the kitchen. Homemakers didn't have the kind of access to supermarkets we enjoy today, so most of these early baking recipes called for ordinary pantry ingredients. Recipes like "My Inspiration" Cake, with its layers of pecans and chocolate, were destined as the finale for a dinner party, while whimsical Snappy Turtle Cookies would be taken to a social gathering or school event.

Entrées have been a Bake-Off® Contest category since the very first contest, and the most popular entrées were casseroles. The main dishes of this era could best be described as hearty and satisfying. The first time an entrée recipe was awarded the grand prize was at the 8th Bake-Off® Contest held in 1956. California Casserole, a veal casserole topped with dumplings, was the winning recipe.

1960s

During the 1960s, women led busy lives at home, in their communities and in leisure activities. More women joined the workforce and began making strides in their professional careers. They had less time to spare in the kitchen and eagerly turned to convenience foods, like cake mixes, and time-saving appliances for help in making easy but delicious meals for their families. In 1966, the "Busy Lady" Bake-Off® theme recognized the growing trend of convenience cooking with simplified recipes. Bake-Off® recipes were "shortcutted, streamlined and up-to-dated for you" by Pillsbury. In 1967, the official Bake-Off® magazine featured shortcuts to prize reci-

TV host Art Linkletter congratulated Mrs. Alice Reese when she won the $25,000 top prize in the 13th Pillsbury Bake-Off® Contest in Los Angeles in 1961. Her winning recipe was Candy Bar Cookies.

pes and offered "homemade goodness with hurry-up timing" to the average family cook.

At the Bake-Off® Contest, the self-cleaning oven made its debut, and fresh refrigerated biscuit and crescent roll doughs were used as key ingredients in baking and main dish entries, like Crafty Crescent Lasagna, for the first time. In 1969, the contest changed forever when it introduced "three divisions"—flour, mix and fresh refrigerated

Kurt Wait prepares his grand prize–winning Macadamia Fudge Torte at the 37th Pillsbury Bake-Off® Contest in Dallas in 1996. Kurt was the first male finalist ever to win the grand prize. He also won the first million-dollar grand prize.

Mary Lou Warren (second from right), expressed delight when she was named the $40,000 grand prize winner in the 32nd Pillsbury Bake-Off® Contest. Cheering for her were (left to right) Karen Everly, $15,000 cake mix category winner; Laurene Harschutz, $15,000 flour category winner, and Debi Wolf, $15,000 refrigerated dinner roll category winner. The 32nd Bake-Off® Contest was held in 1986 in Orlando, Florida.

dough—each with a $10,000 grand prize. The best recipe won a $25,000 cash prize. That year, for the first time ever, a dessert recipe made with fresh refrigerated dough (Magic Marshmallow Crescent Puffs) won the grand prize.

1970s

By 1972, Ann Pillsbury had disappeared from the Bake-Off® Contest, but a new icon had taken her place. The Pillsbury Doughboy, in a cowboy hat, graced the cover of the 1972 Bake-Off® recipe collection. His friendly face would remain a standing symbol of the contest for some time to come. The Doughboy's cowboy hat symbolized more than a friendly demeanor. It signaled the Bake-Off® Contest was on the move. Houston, New Orleans, San Diego, and San Francisco were new sites for the contest and reflected America's growing diversity and shifts in population away from the East Coast. Celebrity hosts and judges awarded prizes on Bake-Off® day.

By the early 1970s, the "health" food craze was recognizable in the Bake-Off® Contest and nutrition occupied the minds of home cooks. "Natural" ingredients were buzzwords, homey cakes made with ingredients like molasses, bananas, and oats gained in popularity, and many recipes featured apples, carrots, whole wheat, and granola. There was a definite trend to include broccoli, zucchini, spinach, carrots and every kind of bean in main dish recipes. But most contestant recipes reflected a lack of time for cooking. Pie baking as a whole was on the decline—but pie-like bar cookies, or "squares," such as Pecan Pie Surprise Bars, were becoming increasingly common. Overall, casserole recipes, such as Zesty Italian Crescent Casserole, were inexpensive to make and streamlined steps made them easy to prepare. In the mid-1970s, the Bake-Off® recipe collection cost around a dollar and included recipes developed for the newest kitchen innovation, the microwave oven.

During the days preceding the 30th Pillsbury Bake-Off® Contest in 1982, the banquet hall of the San Antonio Convention Center was transformed into 100 mini kitchens. On the contest day, the hall was a maze of activity as finalists baked, food editors interviewed, photographers snapped pictures and the telecast crew shot footage for the awards show.

1980s

In the mid-1980s, the Bake-Off® Contest offered a fast-forward cuisine of quick and easy recipes (with simple main dish recipes in demand as two-paycheck families became a necessity), snacks and a new entrant to the arena, ethnic recipes. Competitors brought a wide variety of ethnic backgrounds to the contest. Wontons and Mexican-style recipes popped on the Bake-Off® scene for the first time, while Italian-inspired recipes continued to be popular. In ethnic entries, such as Mushroom Piroshki Appetizers, traditional ingredients were used with a convenience product that replaced made-from-scratch dough or pastry. Chicken became more common than red meat in main dish recipes. The microwave acquired a place in almost every home in the '80s, and many finalists used a microwave to prepare part or all of their entries in a matter of minutes. A microwave category was a new category at the contest.

The '80s were also a decade of decadence and the Bake-Off® dessert entries from that time mimic this trend. Fancy, indulgent desserts, like Chocolate Praline Layer Cake, were popular and cooks turned to Europe for inspiration. Pie baking, which had declined during the '70s, was revived with the invention of refrigerated pie crust. Time continued to be a precious commodity and consumers made desserts for entertaining rather than everyday meals. Four of the five grand prize–winning recipes of this decade were cakes or tarts.

High-spending style was a hallmark of the '80s, and the Bake-Off® Contest followed suit. The grand prize increased to $40,000, and first-place winners in each of five categories won $15,000 for their favorite family recipes. Celebrities continued to be featured hosts, and in 1984, Bob Barker, longtime host of the TV show *The Price is Right*, awarded more than $130,000 in cash prizes in San Diego.

From left to right: In 1971, Mrs. Kirsten H. Rindon, Mrs. Judith Soden, and Mrs. Reta Martens pose with the GE range on which they will bake their original recipes in the 22nd Pillsbury Bake-Off® Contest in Honolulu, Hawaii.

1990s

Although the theme "quick and easy" had been a staple at past Bake-Off® Contests, for the first time in 1998, Quick & Easy was its own category in the contest, increasing the number of categories to five. The categories—30-Minute Main Dishes, Simple Side Dishes, Fast and Easy Treats, and Quick Snacks and Appetizers—all reflected the changing nature of the American kitchen. What changed in the kitchen? Time, more than ever, was in short supply for families with jobs, hobbies and kids, but a desire to give families the best food that mom—or dad—could make was never compromised by Bake-Off® finalists.

In the '90s, recipes reflected our increasingly global community with the most diverse ethnic cuisines ever. Pantries were more internationalized, stocked with ingredients once considered exotic, like coconut milk, 5-spice powder, couscous, and sun-dried tomatoes, and gave rise to prize-winning dishes such as Salsa Couscous Chicken. Consumers discovered the health benefits of legumes, and by the late '90s, a popular vegetable was black beans. There also was an increase in vegetarian main dishes like Bean Picadillo Tortillas.

Gourmet ingredients became mainstream and cooks displayed increased sophistication by combining the best of European and American traditions. The Chocolate Mousse Fantasy Torte combined an American original—brownies—with a European classic—chocolate mousse. Dessert recipes were inspired by the explosion in availability and variety of products, such as candy bars and ice cream topping (as used in Chocolate Chip, Oats, and Caramel Cookie Squares). Pies showed a complex exploration and adaptation of U.S. regional favorites, like Pennsylvania Dutch Cake and Custard Pie, a twist on traditional shoofly pie.

The contest entered the modern era on February 26, 1996, when more than $1,054,000 in cash and prizes were awarded for the first time. The

Eleanor Roosevelt and Art Linkletter look on as Philip Pillsbury presents a check for $10,000 to Laura Rott at the first Pillsbury Bake-Off® Contest. The first Pillsbury Bake-Off® Contest was held in 1949 at the Waldorf-Astoria Hotel in New York City. Miss Rott won second place for her recipe, Starlight Mint Surprise Cookies.

T.O. Davis was among three men who competed in the first Pillsbury Bake-Off® Contest in 1949 in New York City.

first million-dollar winner was Macadamia Fudge Torte, a recipe developed by Kurt Wait of California, one of 14 men whose recipes were chosen for the contest.

2000s and Today

At the turn of the century, the Bake-Off® Contest turned 50! After all these years, the contest is still about creating great food while reflecting the changing nature of American society. In the first decade of the new century, the Bake-Off® Contest offered adventurous flavors that blurred ethnic boundaries in entries like Blueberry Burrito Blintzes and Chutney Pizza with Turkey, Spinach and Gorgonzola. For the first time, recipes could be entered in the contest in Spanish. Savvy and sophisticated trendsetters reflected major changes in food and culture as Americans enjoyed easy access to the Internet and cable television. At the Bake-Off® Contest, the growth of cooking shows and the popularity of food-oriented Web sites was reflected in artful garnishes, expert cooking techniques, and true "foodie" language previously used only by professional chefs. Bolder, even exotic, flavors came to the forefront as American cooks encountered a variety of cooking styles both at home and in travels around the world. Bake-Off® Contest entries ranged from long and involved to quick and easy. To save time, many main dish recipes used quick and easy ingredients, like rotisserie chicken and pre-washed and cut produce.

In the 2000s, the number of Bake-Off® categories increased to six. Dinner Made Easy, Wake Up to Breakfast, Simple Snacks, Weekends Made Special, the empty-nest direction of Cooking for Two and a healthy cooking category, Brand New You, reflected a trend set by health-conscious American cooks. In 2006 and 2008, a new Bake-Off® prize was added—America's Favorite Recipe. Consumers voted online for their favorite recipe among the final 100 recipes. The recipe that received the most online votes received the America's Favorite Recipe Award as well as a cash prize.

In 2013, the Bake-Off® Contest embraced change in a big way. The contest streamlined to three categories with separate entry periods, and, to ensure quick and easy recipes, entries were capped at seven ingredients and 30 minutes or less of active prep time. Also new: America was invited to cast votes to determine which 100 recipes would vie for the sweet $1 million grand prize. The 2014 contest in Nashville welcomed entries in four recipe categories—Simply Sweet Treats, Savory Snacks & Sides, Weekend Breakfast Wows, and Amazing Doable Dinners—and intro- duced new special awards, including a prize to recognize the best finalist recipe utilizing a Pills- bury™ Gluten Free refrigerated dough. In an exciting and groundbreaking twist, the Bake-Off® Contest judges determined the best finalist in each of the four categories and America was given the chance to vote online for their favorite recipe to help determine the grand prize winner The four finalists are featured in this book. Go to pillsbury.com/bakeoff to meet the grand prize winner.

Mrs. Dorothy DeVault, winner of the 10th Pillsbury Bake-Off® Contest, holds aloft her check for $25,000. Looking on are (left to right) Miss Irene Dunne, guest of honor; Mrs. Eleanor Pillsbury and Art Linkletter. [New York, 1958]

Pillsbury Bake-Off® Contest Chronology

YEAR & LOCATION	GRAND PRIZE WINNER	RECIPE & DESCRIPTION	CONTEST NOTES
1949 New York	Theodora Smafield Rockford, Illinois	**No-Knead Water-Rising Twists** (p. 75) Nut sweet roll raised under water.	Mrs. Eleanor Roosevelt attended as a guest.
1950 New York	Lily Wuebel Redwood City, California	**Orange Kiss-Me Cake** (p. 371) Loaf cake topped with orange juice and nuts; no frosting.	The Duke and Duchess of Windsor were guests of honor.
1951 New York	Helen Weston La Jolla, California	**Starlight Double-Delight Cake** (p. 372) Chocolate cake with cream cheese frosting—half of which goes into cake batter.	First male prize winner was Jack Meili, Minneapolis, Minnesota.
1952 New York	Beatrice Harlib Lincolnwood, Illinois	**Snappy Turtle Cookies** (p. 312) Brown sugar cookie, cleverly shaped in a chocolate shell.	Self-frosted cakes made a strong appearance.
1953 New York	Lois Kanago Denver, Colorado	**"My Inspiration" Cake** (p. 368) Quick-mix white cake with nut crust and chocolate in middle of layers.	Maryknoll sister traveled from Hawaiian convent to compete and won 3rd prize.
1954 New York	Dorothy Koteen Washington, D.C.	**Open Sesame Pie** (p. 417) Combines a toasted sesame seed crust with date chiffon filling.	Stores reported a "run" on sesame seeds after the Bake-Off® Contest. Sesame seeds became a regularly stocked item after that.

YEAR & LOCATION	GRAND PRIZE WINNER	RECIPE & DESCRIPTION	CONTEST NOTES
1955 New York	Bertha Jorgensen Portland, Oregon	**Ring-A-Lings** (p. 64) No-knead sweet roll with nut filling and orange glaze.	A no-knead yeast dough is named the big winner.
1956 New York	Margaret Hatheway Santa Barbara, California	**California Casserole** (p. 246) Veal casserole topped with crumb-covered dumplings.	Gourmet main dishes starred at the Bake-Off® Contest.
1957 Los Angeles	Gerda Roderer Berkeley, California	**Accordion Treats** (p. 297) Alsatian-type cookie baked in pleated aluminum foil.	A family cookie recipe from Alsace-Lorraine won $25,000 for a new resident of the U.S.
1958 New York	Dorothy DeVault Delaware, Ohio	**Spicy Apple Twists** (p. 407) Spicy-flavored apple roll-up.	Ninety-nine contestants competed, while the 100th stayed home to have her baby.
1959 Los Angeles	Eunice Surles Lake Charles, Louisiana	**Mardi Gras Party Cake** (p. 366) Southern-style buttermilk cake with sea foam icing.	Greer Garson was guest of honor. Rich treats were featured among 100 recipes.
1960 Washington, D.C.	Leona Schnuelle Crab Orchard, Nebraska	**Dilly Casserole Bread** (p. 52) Casserole bread made with cottage cheese, seasoned with dill.	Chief submarine steward took best-of-class prize for his Sub-Meringue Pie.
1961 Los Angeles	Alice Reese Minneapolis, Minnesota	**Candy Bar Cookies** (p. 310) Shortbread wafer with caramel filling and chocolate topping.	Convenience ingredients and methods make first strong appearance.
1962 New York	Julia Smogor Cedar Rapids, Iowa	**Apple Pie '63** (p. 402) All-American pie featuring favorite flavors: apples, caramel and cheese.	Mamie Eisenhower was guest of honor; 12-year-old boy won first prize in junior division with Cheeseburger Casserole.
1963 Los Angeles	Mira Walilko Detroit, Michigan	**Hungry Boys' Casserole** (p. 232) Biscuits are cut with doughnut cutter to create a unique topping.	Man from Oakland, California, won best-of-class with his cake.

YEAR & LOCATION	GRAND PRIZE WINNER	RECIPE & DESCRIPTION	CONTEST NOTES
1964 Miami	Janis Risley Melbourne, Florida	**Peacheesy Pie** (p. 410) Pie with peach-flavored crust plus peaches and cheesecake filling.	Teenager developed recipe as class assignment and won the grand prize.
1966 San Francisco	Mari Petrelli Ely, Nevada	**Golden Gate Snack Bread** (p. 142) Shortcut yeast bread flavored with cheese spread and onion soup mix.	Bake-Off® Contest recognized growing trend to convenience cooking with "Busy Lady" theme.
1967 Los Angeles	Maxine Bullock Spring City, Tennessee	**Muffin Mix Buffet Bread** (p. 53) Cream of vegetable soup and corn muffin mix in a yeast bread.	Convenience cooking continued to play a prominent role at the Bake-Off® Contest.
1968 Dallas	Phyllis Lidert Fort Lauderdale, Florida	**Buttercream Pound Cake** (p. 363) Lightly lemon-flavored cake with an unusual poppy seed filling.	Two new categories used convenience mixes and refrigerated fresh dough.
1969 Atlanta	Edna M. Walker Hopkins, Minnesota	**Magic Marshmallow Crescent Puffs** (p. 68) Hollow-centered sweet roll made with refrigerated crescent dough and marshmallow that melts during baking.	For the first time, a recipe made with refrigerated fresh dough won the grand prize.
1970 San Diego	Nan Robb Huachuca City, Arizona	**Onion Lover's Twist** (p. 140) A creative shape for a yeast onion bread made by braiding three dough strips.	$1,000 nutrition award was given for the most nutritious recipe, chosen by computer.
1971 Honolulu	Pearl Hall Snohomish, Washington	**Pecan Pie Surprise Bars** (p. 323) A new easy-to-do bar form of popular caramel pecan pie.	Best Consumer Value Award $1,000 for most economically nutritious recipe, chosen by computer.

YEAR & LOCATION	GRAND PRIZE WINNER	RECIPE & DESCRIPTION	CONTEST NOTES
1972 Houston	Isabelle Collins Ramona, California (Refrigerated Winner)	**Quick and Chewy Crescent Bars** (p. 330) Bar cookie uses just seven ingredients.	For the first time, two $25,000 grand prizes were offered.
	Rose DeDominicis Verona, Pennsylvania (Grocery Winner)	**Streusel Spice Cake** (p. 360) A pound cake made from yellow cake mix with a spiced streusel filling and topping.	
1973 Beverly Hills	Albina Flieller Floresville, Texas (Refrigerated Winner)	**Quick Crescent Pecan Pie Bars** (p. 324) Quick and easy bars with the taste of pecan pie.	"Bake-It-Easy" theme stressed need for simple recipes with high family appeal.
	Bonnie Brooks Salisbury, Maryland (Grocery Winner)	**Banana Crunch Cake** (p. 356) A banana and sour cream-flavored yellow cake with a crunchy coconut topping.	
1974 Phoenix	Doris Castle River Forest, Illinois (Refrigerated Winner)	**Savory Crescent Chicken Squares** (p. 168) Crescent sandwich with a delightfully seasoned chicken filling.	The Bake-Off® Contest celebrated its silver anniversary.
	Francis Jerzak Porter, Minnesota (Grocery Winner)	**Chocolate Cherry Bars** (p. 354) An easy bar or dessert square made with chocolate cake and cherry pie filling.	

YEAR & LOCATION	GRAND PRIZE WINNER	RECIPE & DESCRIPTION	CONTEST NOTES
1975 San Francisco	Barbara Gibson Ft. Wayne, Indiana (Refrigerated Winner)	**Easy Crescent Danish Rolls** (p. 63) Large, attractive rolls filled with cream cheese and preserves.	Refrigerated's casual entertaining category and Grocery's family category stressed the "Easy Idea" contest theme.
	Luella Maki Ely, Minnesota (Grocery Winner)	**Sour Cream Apple Squares** (p. 432) Apples and cinnamon flavor this moist, cake-like bar or dessert.	
1976 Boston	Lois Ann Groves Greenwood Village, Colorado (Refrigerated Winner)	**Crescent Caramel Swirl** (p. 355) A dessert coffee cake made with crescent rolls and a homemade caramel sauce.	The Bicentennial Year set the theme for America's Bake-Off® Contest, and Boston was a fitting city for the event.
	Lenora Smith Baton Rouge, Louisiana (Grocery Winner)	**Whole Wheat Raisin Loaf** (p. 54) A hearty whole wheat bread with oatmeal and raisins.	
1978 New Orleans	Linda Wood Indianapolis, Indiana (Refrigerated Winner)	**Chick-n-Broccoli Pot Pies** (p. 254) Nutritious individual pies with flaky biscuit crust.	Ingredients in prize-winning recipes reflected consumer interest in nutrition.
	Esther Tomich San Pedro, California (Grocery Winner)	**Nutty Graham Picnic Cake** (p. 359) A hearty cake made with graham cracker crumbs and orange juice and topped with brown sugar glaze.	

YEAR & LOCATION	GRAND PRIZE WINNER	RECIPE & DESCRIPTION	CONTEST NOTES
1980 Miami	Millicent (Caplan) Nathan Boca Raton, Florida	**Italian Zucchini Crescent Pie** (p. 285) A meatless main dish featuring Muenster cheese and zucchini.	$40,000 grand prize awarded.
1982 San Antonio	Elizabeth Meijer Tucson, Arizona	**Almond-Filled Cookie Cake** (p. 365) A rich, crisp almond dessert adapted from a Dutch pastry.	A 10-year-old girl from West Virginia was the youngest finalist ever to compete in the contest. Eleven of the contestants were under age 19.
1984 San Diego	Susan Porubcan Jefferson, Wisconsin	**Country Apple Coffee Cake** (p. 97) An apple coffee cake made with refrigerated biscuits and flavored with a hint of whiskey.	Microwave category recognized growing consumer interest in microwave cooking.
1986 Orlando	Mary Lou Warren Medford, Oregon	**Apple Nut Lattice Tart** (p. 406) An updated apple pie made with apples, golden raisins, nuts and a lattice top.	A wide variety of ethnic entries reflected increasingly diverse national tastes.
1988 San Diego	Julie Bengtson Bemidji, Minnesota	**Chocolate Praline Layer Cake** (p. 380) A chocolate cake featuring praline filling baked with the cake layers—topped with whipped cream.	Contest categories were expanded to include Green Giant® canned and frozen vegetables.
1990 Phoenix	Linda Rahman Petaluma, California	**Blueberry Poppy Seed Brunch Cake** (p. 95) A coffee cake featuring a refreshing blend of blueberry, lemon and poppy seed flavors.	Contest featured 12 male finalists, a new record. Three men were prize winners.
1992 Orlando	Gladys Fulton Summerville, South Carolina	**Pennsylvania Dutch Cake and Custard Pie** (p. 418) A contemporary dessert with roots in an old-fashioned regional favorite.	$50,000 grand prize awarded. Contestants included a grandmother and granddaughter. Both were cash prize winners.

YEAR & LOCATION	GRAND PRIZE WINNER	RECIPE & DESCRIPTION	CONTEST NOTES
1994 San Diego	Mary Anne Tyndall Whiteville, North Carolina	**Fudgy Bonbons** (p. 317) Soft, fudgy miniature cookies with a truffle-like center.	Recipes reflected our global community with the most diverse ethnic cuisines and ingredients ever.
1996 Dallas	Kurt Wait Redwood City, California	**Macadamia Fudge Torte** (p. 390) A moist chocolate cake with pockets of rich fudge and a macadamia nut streusel topping.	The first $1 million grand prize and the first male winner.
1998 Orlando	Ellie Mathews Seattle, Washington	**Salsa Couscous Chicken** (p. 253) North African-style dish with complex flavors used salsa to shorten preparation and cooking time.	For the first time ever, only quick and easy recipes with limited preparation time or ingredients. Fourteen men, the most ever, were finalists.
2000 San Francisco	Roberta Sonefeld Hopkins, South Carolina	**Cream Cheese Brownie Pie** (p. 415) Layers of brownie and cream cheese in a piecrust, topped with pecans and hot fudge.	50th anniversary of the Pillsbury Bake-Off® Contest. A Hall of Fame honored outstanding classic recipes.
2002 Orlando	Denise Yennie Nashville, Tennessee	**Chicken Florentine Panini** (p. 172) Refrigerated pizza crust creates panini filled with chicken breasts, frozen spinach, caramelized onions and provolone cheese.	Entry in category for lighter recipes took grand prize. Entries reflect consumer interest in bolder flavors and appeal of ethnic and fusion dishes.
2004 Hollywood	Suzanne Conrad Findlay, Ohio	**Oats and Honey Granola Pie** (p. 420) Reminiscent of pecan pie, this pie has crushed granola bars in its flavorful filling. It's made with refrigerated pie crust.	The finalists' aprons were styled by designer Isaac Mizrahi. A feature documentary, *The Million Dollar Recipe*, captured the contest excitement.

YEAR & LOCATION	GRAND PRIZE WINNER	RECIPE & DESCRIPTION	CONTEST NOTES
2006 Orlando	Anna Ginsberg Austin, Texas	**Baked Chicken and Spinach Stuffing** (p. 249) Familiar freezer foods—spinach and waffles—are creatively used in a stuffing that's served with glazed chicken.	Consumers selected America's Favorite Recipe via online voting. Designer Todd Oldham created the official apron. A Cooking for Two category reflected the growing number of small households.
2008 Dallas	Carolyn Gurtz Gaithersburg, Maryland	**Double-Delight Peanut Butter Cookies** (p. 306) A twist on the classic peanut butter cookie with a crunchy outside, creamy inside and a hint of cinnamon.	Two new categories celebrated America's love for pizza and Mexican-flavored foods. Celebrity chef Sandra Lee announced winners.
2010 Orlando	Sue Compton Delanco, New Jersey	**Mini Ice Cream Cookie Cups** (p. 439) An easy, make-ahead recipe with a beautiful presentation, these are a fun, impressive dessert for any occasion.	Category winners were flown to Chicago, where the winning moment was aired live on *The Oprah Winfrey Show.*
2012 Orlando	Christina Verrelli Devon, Pennsylvania	**Pumpkin Ravioli with Salted Caramel Whipped Cream** (p. 434) A sweet twist on pumpkin ravioli with flaky crescent dough, cream cheese and caramel sauce.	*The Martha Stewart Show* hosted a special broadcast to reveal the $1 million grand prize winner, live from Orlando.
2013 Las Vegas	Glori Spriggs Henderson, Nevada	**Loaded Potato Pinwheels** (p. 136) A cheesy bacon and potato mix rolled up in crescent dough creates an awesome appetizer.	Contest was held in Las Vegas for the first time. Grand prize winner appeared on *The Queen Latifah Show.* The most interesting contest note for this year is that for the first time, an appetizer won the grand prize.

YEAR & LOCATION	GRAND PRIZE WINNER	RECIPE & DESCRIPTION	CONTEST NOTES
2014 Nashville	Beth Royals Richmond, Virginia	**Peanutty Pie Crust Clusters** (p. 316) A delicious treat with flaky pie crust squares, peanut butter and toffee.	For the first time ever, the public voted online to help choose the grand prize winner.

Hall of Fame

To celebrate its 50th Anniversary in 1999, the Bake-Off® Contest created a Hall of Fame to recognize some of the competition's most popular recipes. Contest home economists pored over nearly 4,000 recipes to select those that should be honored. They considered classic Bake-Off® Contest recipes and the ones most requested by consumers, finally narrowing their choices to the best ten recipes. Four more recipes won a place of honor through special consumer voting.

Black and White Brownies (page 342) by Penelope Weiss, Bake-Off® Contest 35, 1992.

Broccoli-Cauliflower Tetrazzini (page 284) by Barbara Van Itallie, Bake-Off® Contest 33, 1988.

Chocolate Praline Layer Cake (page 380) by Julie Bengtson, Bake-Off® Contest 33, 1988.

Crescent Caramel Swirl (page 355) by Lois Ann Groves, Bake-Off® Contest 27, 1976.

Dilly Casserole Bread (page 52) by Leona Schnuelle, Bake-Off® Contest 12, 1960.

French Silk Chocolate Pie (page 428) by Betty Cooper, Bake-Off® Contest 3, 1951.

Ham and Cheese Crescent Snacks (page 128) by Ronna Sue Farley, Bake-Off® Contest 26, 1975.

Italian Zucchini Crescent Pie (page 286) by Millicent (Caplan) Nathan, Bake-Off® Contest 29, 1980.

Magic Marshmallow Crescent Puffs (page 68) by Edna M. Walker, Bake-Off® Contest 20, 1969.

Peanut Blossoms (page 307) by Freda Smith, Bake-Off® Contest 9, 1957.

Poppin' Fresh™ Barbecups (page 242) by Peter Russell, Bake-Off® Contest 19, 1968.

Salted Peanut Chews (page 328) by Gertrude M. Schweitzerhof, Bake-Off® Contest 29, 1980.

Tunnel of Fudge Cake (page 374) by Ella Rita Helfrich, Bake-Off® Contest 17, 1966.

Zesty Italian Crescent Casserole (page 237) by Madella Bathke, Bake-Off® Contest 28, 1978

Better Than Ever

Most of the recipes will look familiar to Bake-Off® Contest followers, although many have been updated to conform to currently available products or to eliminate any food-safety concerns that the original recipes might have raised. These pages hold the benefit of all these cooks' experiences and accumulated cooking wisdom: their practical time-saving tips, their heirloom recipes, their diversity of background and taste and, above all, their prize-winning recipes.

Rise & Dine Breakfasts and Brunches

Renee Heimerl of Oakfield, Wisconsin, places the finishing touches on her Quick and Fruity Crescent Waffles (page 82) at the 43rd Bake-Off Contest held in Dallas, Texas.

KIWI-PINEAPPLE YOGURT PARFAITS

Try this breakfast treat that layers fresh tropical fruit, creamy yogurt and crunchy granola.

PREP TIME: 15 MINUTES
TOTAL TIME: 15 MINUTES

MAKES 2 SERVINGS

Sherri King-Rodrigues, Warren, Rhode Island
Bake-Off® Contest 41, 2004

GRANOLA MIXTURE

4 granola bars, unwrapped, broken into pieces

12 to 14 whole macadamia nuts

YOGURT MIXTURE

1 container (6 oz) fat-free vanilla yogurt

½ cup frozen (thawed) reduced-fat whipped topping

1 tablespoon shredded coconut

1 tablespoon finely grated white chocolate baking bar

FRUIT MIXTURE

½ cup coarsely chopped peeled kiwifruit (1½ medium)

½ cup coarsely chopped drained fresh pineapple or well-drained canned pineapple tidbits

1½ teaspoons honey

GARNISH, IF DESIRED

White chocolate baking bar curls or shavings

2 kiwifruit slices

1. In food processor or gallon-size re-sealable food-storage plastic bag, place granola bars and nuts; process or crush with meat mallet until chopped.

2. In small bowl, mix yogurt mixture ingredients until well blended; set aside. In another small bowl, gently toss fruit mixture ingredients until coated; set aside.

3. In each of 2 (12- to 14-oz) tulip-shaped parfait glasses, alternately spoon about 3 tablespoons granola mixture, ¼ cup yogurt mixture and ¼ cup fruit mixture; repeat layers. Top each parfait with a sprinkle of remaining granola mixture. Garnish each with white chocolate curls and kiwifruit slice. Serve immediately.

CLEVER IDEA: *Any 12- to 14-oz tall parfait, dessert or wine glasses can be used.*

1 Serving: Calories 550 (Calories from Fat 220); Total Fat 24g; Saturated Fat 7g; Trans Fat 0g; Cholesterol 0mg; Sodium 230mg; Total Carbohydrate 72g; Dietary Fiber 6g; Sugars 46g; Protein 11g

OATMEAL COOKIE GRANOLA BERRY PARFAITS

PREP TIME: 30 MINUTES
TOTAL TIME: 30 MINUTES

MAKES 8 SERVINGS

April Timboe, Siloam Springs, Arkansas
Bake-Off® Contest 46, 2013

1 package Pillsbury™ Big Deluxe™ refrigerated oatmeal raisin cookies

½ cup finely chopped pecans

½ cup shredded unsweetened coconut

3 cups plain fat-free Greek yogurt

¾ cup blueberry preserves

80 fresh raspberries (about 12-oz.)

16 fresh mint leaves

1. Heat oven to 325°F. Line 2 large cookie sheets with parchment paper. Let cookie dough stand at room temperature 10 minutes to soften. In large bowl, mix cookie dough, pecans and coconut with wooden spoon or knead with hands until well blended. Crumble mixture evenly on cookie sheets.

2. Bake both cookie sheets at the same time 18 to 28 minutes, stirring every 5 minutes and rotating cookie sheets halfway through baking, until golden brown. Cool completely, about 20 minutes. Break granola into smaller pieces.

3. Meanwhile, in medium bowl, mix yogurt and blueberry preserves until well blended. Refrigerate.

4. To assemble parfaits, spoon ¼ cup of the granola into each of 8 (8 oz) glasses. Top each with 3 heaping tablespoons of the yogurt mixture and 7 raspberries. Repeat with remaining granola and yogurt mixture. Top each with remaining raspberries and fresh mint leaves.

CLEVER IDEA: *Granola can be made ahead of time. Store in large re-sealable food-storage plastic bag up to 3 days.*

1 Serving: Calories 460 (Calories from Fat 160); Total Fat 17g; Saturated Fat 6g; Trans Fat 0g; Cholesterol 0mg; Sodium 200mg; Total Carbohydrate 63g; Dietary Fiber 6g; Sugars 48g; Protein 12g

PEANUT BUTTER COOKIE GRANOLA

Pillsbury™ refrigerated peanut butter cookie dough gives a tasty new twist to this simple granola mix that makes a perfect snack, breakfast on the go or topping for yogurt or ice cream.

PREP TIME: 15 MINUTES
TOTAL TIME: 1 HOUR 10 MINUTES
MAKES 22 SERVINGS

Wanda Riley, Roxie, Mississippi
Bake-Off® Contest 44, 2010

1 roll (16.5 oz) Pillsbury™ refrigerated peanut butter cookies

½ teaspoon ground cinnamon

2½ cups old-fashioned oats

1 cup sliced almonds

1 cup chopped pecans

1 cup flaked coconut

⅓ cup raisins

⅓ cup sweetened dried cranberries

½ cup mini chips semi-sweet chocolate

½ cup peanut butter chips

1. Let cookie dough stand at room temperature 10 minutes to soften.

2. Meanwhile, heat oven to 325°F. Line 2 large cookie sheets with sides with nonstick foil or cooking parchment paper. In large bowl, mix cookie dough and cinnamon. Add oats, almonds, pecans, coconut, raisins and cranberries; knead into dough until well blended. Crumble mixture evenly on cookie sheets.

3. Bake both cookie sheets at the same time 17 to 22 minutes, stirring every 5 minutes and rotating cookie sheets halfway through baking, until light golden brown. Cool completely on cookie sheets, about 30 minutes.

4. Break granola into smaller pieces if necessary. In large bowl, mix granola, chocolate chips and peanut butter chips. Store in large re-sealable food-storage plastic bag, or store in ½-cup amounts in small food-storage bags for ready-to-go snacks. Store up to 3 days.

1 Serving: Calories 250 (Calories from Fat 120); Total Fat 13g; Saturated Fat 3.5g; Trans Fat 0.5g; Cholesterol 0mg; Sodium 110mg; Total Carbohydrate 27g; Dietary Fiber 2g; Sugars 13g; Protein 4g

HAM AND EGGS FRITTATA BISCUITS

Fresh herbs enhance the delicate flavors baked in a biscuit that holds a veggie-packed egg topping.

PREP TIME: 15 MINUTES
TOTAL TIME: 35 MINUTES

MAKES 8 SERVINGS

Sandy Bradley, Bolingbrook, Illinois
Bake-Off® Contest 40, 2002

1 can (16.3 oz) Pillsbury™ Grands!™ refrigerated buttermilk or Southern style biscuits

3 eggs

1¼ to 1½ teaspoons Italian seasoning

½ cup diced cooked ham

1 cup shredded Italian cheese blend (4 oz)

¼ cup roasted red bell peppers (from a jar), drained, chopped

½ cup diced seeded plum (Roma) tomatoes

2 tablespoons thinly sliced fresh basil leaves

Fresh basil sprigs

Cherry tomatoes

1. Heat oven to 375°F. Spray large cookie sheet with no-stick cooking spray. Separate dough into 8 biscuits; place 3 inches apart on cookie sheet. Press out each biscuit to form 4-inch round with ¼-inch-high rim around outside edge.

2. In small bowl, beat 1 of the eggs. Brush over tops and sides of biscuits. Sprinkle with 1 teaspoon of the Italian seasoning.

3. In another small bowl, beat remaining 2 eggs and remaining ¼ to ½ teaspoon Italian seasoning. Spoon egg mixture evenly into indentations in each biscuit. Top with ham, ½ cup of the cheese, the roasted peppers, tomatoes, sliced basil and remaining ½ cup cheese.

4. Bake 15 to 20 minutes or until biscuits are golden brown and eggs are set. Garnish with basil sprigs and cherry tomatoes.

1 Serving: Calories 290 (Calories from Fat 140); Total Fat 16g; Saturated Fat 6g; Trans Fat 3g; Cholesterol 100mg; Sodium 840mg; Total Carbohydrate 25g; Dietary Fiber 0g; Sugars 6g; Protein 12g

VEGGIE FRITTATA BREAKFAST SANDWICHES

PREP TIME: 20 MINUTES

TOTAL TIME: 60 MINUTES

MAKES 8 SERVINGS

Jon Winkeller, Gilbert, Arizona
Bake-Off® Contest 46, 2013

1 can (13.8 oz) Pillsbury™ refrigerated classic pizza crust

¾ cup shredded Italian cheese blend (3 oz)

½ cup finely chopped kalamata olives

1 bag (11.8 oz) frozen Mediterranean blend

6 eggs

6 teaspoons basil pesto

2 large roasted red bell peppers (from a jar), cut in half, patted dry

1. Heat oven to 400°F. Spray 8-inch square (2-quart) glass baking dish with no-stick cooking spray.

2. Unroll dough on large cookie sheet; press dough into 16x8-inch rectangle. Cut into 8 squares; do not separate. Top 4 of the squares with ¼ cup of the cheese and ¼ cup of the olives; press into dough. Bake 12 to 16 minutes or until edges are golden brown.

3. Meanwhile, microwave frozen vegetables on High 5 minutes. Cool 3 minutes; coarsely chop. In large bowl, beat eggs, remaining ¼ cup of the olives and 2 teaspoons of the pesto with wire whisk until well blended. Stir in vegetables; pour mixture into baking dish. Bake 22 to 25 minutes or until eggs are set. Top with remaining ½ cup of the cheese. Cut into 4 squares.

4. To assemble, separate bread into 8 squares. Spread 1 teaspoon pesto on bottom of each un-topped square. Top with one frittata square, one roasted red bell pepper half and olive-topped bread square. Cut each sandwich in half diagonally.

1 Serving: Calories 290 (Calories from Fat 110); Total Fat 13g; Saturated Fat 4g; Trans Fat 0g; Cholesterol 150mg; Sodium 680mg; Total Carbohydrate 33g; Dietary Fiber 2g; Sugars 2g; Protein 12g

CHEESY FLORENTINE BISCUIT CUPS

Healthful spinach is combined with a cheesy filling in a tender biscuit cup.

PREP TIME: 20 MINUTES
TOTAL TIME: 50 MINUTES
MAKES 8 SERVINGS

Theresa D'Amato, York, Pennsylvania
Bake-Off® Contest 43, 2008

2 tablespoons unsalted or salted butter

1 box (9 oz) frozen chopped spinach

½ teaspoon salt

¼ teaspoon pepper

1 can (16.3 oz) Pillsbury™ Grands!™ Flaky Layers refrigerated original biscuits (8 biscuits)

4 oz thick-cut slices Canadian bacon, cut into ¼-inch cubes

8 eggs

2 cups shredded mild Cheddar cheese (8 oz)

1. Heat oven to 350°F. Spray 8 jumbo muffin cups or 8 (6-ounce) glass custard cups with no-stick cooking spray.

2. In 10-inch skillet, melt butter over medium heat. Stir in spinach, salt and pepper. Cook 5 to 7 minutes, stirring occasionally and breaking up spinach if necessary, until spinach is hot. Remove from heat; set aside.

3. Separate dough into 8 biscuits. Place 1 biscuit in each muffin cup, pressing dough ¾ of the way up sides of cups. Place heaping 1 tablespoon bacon on dough in bottom of each cup. Top each with spinach mixture. Using finger or end of wooden spoon handle, make 1½-inch-wide indentation in center of each cup. Break 1 egg into each cup. Top each egg with ¼ cup cheese (cups will be full). (If using custard cups, place on large cookie sheet with sides.)

4. Bake 20 to 25 minutes or until centers feel firm when touched and biscuits are golden brown. Cool 5 minutes. Remove from pan to serving plates. Serve warm.

1 Serving: Calories 420 (Calories from Fat 240); Total Fat 26g; Saturated Fat 11g; Trans Fat 4g; Cholesterol 225mg; Sodium 1130mg; Total Carbohydrate 26g; Dietary Fiber 0g; Sugars 6g; Protein 21g

CHEESY FLORENTINE BISCUIT CUPS *(page 37)*

TOMATO-BASIL EGGS ALFREDO IN BREAD BASKETS *(opposite)*

TOMATO-BASIL EGGS ALFREDO IN BREAD BASKETS

Pillsbury™ refrigerated breadsticks make individual bread baskets that are filled with a delicious pesto, tomato and egg mixture for a complete breakfast in an edible bowl!

PREP TIME: 25 MINUTES
TOTAL TIME: 25 MINUTES

MAKES 6 SERVINGS

Niki Plourde, Gardner, Massachusetts
Bake-Off® Contest 44, 2010

1 medium tomato

1 can (11 oz) Pillsbury™ refrigerated original breadsticks (12 breadsticks)

½ cup basil pesto

¼ teaspoon salt

⅛ teaspoon black pepper

6 eggs

2 tablespoons half-and-half or milk

⅛ teaspoon salt

1½ tablespoons chopped fresh basil leaves

2 tablespoons unsalted or salted butter

⅓ cup Alfredo pasta sauce (from 16-oz jar)

1. Heat oven to 375°F. Spray large cookie sheet with no-stick cooking spray. Cut 6 thin slices from tomato; finely dice remaining tomato for garnish. Set aside.

2. Unroll dough; separate into 12 breadsticks. Shape each of 6 breadsticks into a coil; place 2 inches apart on cookie sheet. Starting at center, press out each coil into 3½-inch round. Twist remaining breadsticks; wrap 1 twisted breadstick around edge of each round to make ½-inch rim; press edges to seal.

3. Spread 1 rounded teaspoon of the pesto in bottom of each round; top with tomato slice. Sprinkle with ¼ teaspoon salt and pepper. Bake 10 to 15 minutes or until edges are golden brown.

4. Meanwhile, in medium bowl, beat eggs and half-and-half with wire whisk until well blended. Add ⅛ teaspoon salt. Stir in 1 tablespoon of the basil. Heat 12-inch nonstick skillet over medium heat. Melt butter in skillet; add egg mixture. Cook 4 minutes, gently lifting cooked portions with spatula so that thin, uncooked portion can flow to bottom, until eggs are thickened but still slightly moist. Stir in pasta sauce.

5. Divide egg mixture evenly among bread baskets. Garnish with diced tomato and remaining ½ tablespoon basil.

1 Serving: Calories 350 (Calories from Fat 190); Total Fat 21g; Saturated Fat 8g; Trans Fat 0g; Cholesterol 200mg; Sodium 710mg; Total Carbohydrate 28g; Dietary Fiber 0g; Sugars 4g; Protein 12g

HAM AND EGGS CRESCENT BRUNCH PIZZA

Combine two breakfast favorites, fresh vegetable frittata and flaky crescents, and you've got the idea behind this cheesy dish.

PREP TIME: 30 MINUTES
TOTAL TIME: 1 HOUR 10 MINUTES

MAKES 8 SERVINGS

Bobby Braun, Marietta, Georgia
Bake-Off® Contest 32, 1986

1 can (8 oz) Pillsbury™ refrigerated crescent dinner rolls

4 eggs

½ teaspoon Italian seasoning

½ teaspoon salt, if desired

1 to 1¼ cups cubed, cooked ham

1 to 1¼ cups shredded mozzarella cheese (4 to 5 oz)

1 box (9 oz) frozen cut broccoli, thawed, drained

1 jar (4.5 oz) sliced mushrooms, drained

2 tablespoons chopped green bell pepper

1 large tomato, peeled, seeded, diced (about 1 cup)

2 tablespoons grated Parmesan cheese

1. Heat oven to 350°F.

2. Separate dough into 8 triangles. Place triangles in ungreased 12-inch pizza pan or 13x9-inch pan; press over bottom and ½ inch up sides to form crust. Seal perforations. Beat eggs, Italian seasoning and salt with fork or wire whisk; pour into dough-lined pan. Top with ham, mozzarella cheese, broccoli, mushrooms, bell pepper and tomato; sprinkle with Parmesan cheese.

3. Bake 30 to 40 minutes or until eggs are set and crust is golden brown.

CLEVER IDEAS:

• *To seed a tomato, cut the tomato crosswise in half and squeeze each half gently over a bowl to remove the seeds.*

• *Add a little kick, and use shredded pepper Jack cheese instead of the mozzarella.*

1 Serving: Calories 240 (Calories from Fat 120); Total Fat 14g; Saturated Fat 5g; Trans Fat 1.5g; Cholesterol 125mg; Sodium 670mg; Total Carbohydrate 15g; Dietary Fiber 2g; Sugars 2g; Protein 15g

HUEVOS RANCHEROS PIZZA

Bring the traditional Mexican breakfast to the dinner table in a delightful new way.

PREP TIME: 25 MINUTES
TOTAL TIME: 45 MINUTES

MAKES 8 SERVINGS

Pamela Tapia, Smyrna, Georgia
Bake-Off® Contest 43, 2008

1 lb uncooked chorizo sausage links (casings removed) or bulk chorizo sausage

1 can (4.5 oz) chopped green chiles

½ cup salsa

1 chipotle chile, chopped, plus 2 tablespoons adobo sauce (from 7-oz can chipotle chiles in adobo sauce)

1 can (13.8 oz) Pillsbury™ refrigerated classic pizza crust

¾ cup crumbled cotija cheese or shredded mozzarella cheese

1 to 2 tablespoons butter

8 eggs

2 to 3 tablespoons chopped fresh cilantro

2 ripe medium avocados, pitted, peeled and sliced

1. Heat oven to 425°F.

2. In 12-inch nonstick skillet, cook chorizo over medium heat 8 to 10 minutes, stirring occasionally, until no longer pink. Remove chorizo with slotted spoon; drain on paper towels. Drain all but 1 tablespoon drippings from skillet. Place chorizo in medium bowl; add green chiles, salsa, chipotle chile and adobo sauce; stir until well mixed. Set aside.

3. Spray 13x9-inch pan with no-stick cooking spray. Unroll pizza crust dough in pan; press dough to edges of pan. Prick pizza crust thoroughly with fork. Brush reserved 1 tablespoon chorizo drippings evenly over crust. Bake 8 to 9 minutes or until edges are light golden brown.

4. Spread chorizo mixture over partially baked crust. Sprinkle with cheese. Bake 8 to 10 minutes longer or until crust is deep golden brown.

5. Meanwhile, wipe out skillet. In skillet, melt 1 to 2 tablespoons butter over medium-high heat until hot. Break eggs and slip into skillet. Immediately reduce heat to low. Cover; cook 7 to 10 minutes or until whites and yolks are firm, not runny (eggs will cook together in skillet).

6. Cut pizza into 8 pieces. Separate eggs. Top each serving with 1 fried egg; sprinkle with cilantro. Serve with avocado slices.

1 Serving: Calories 590 (Calories from Fat 350); Total Fat 39g; Saturated Fat 14g; Trans Fat 0g; Cholesterol 245mg; Sodium 1470mg; Total Carbohydrate 31g; Dietary Fiber 3g; Sugars 5g; Protein 27g

HUEVOS RANCHEROS PIZZA *(opposite)*

SPINACH, SAUSAGE AND FETA QUICHE *(page 44)*

SPINACH, SAUSAGE, AND FETA QUICHE

Greek flavors blend deliciously in a classic quiche that's easy as pie.

PREP TIME: 30 MINUTES
TOTAL TIME: 1 HOUR 45 MINUTES

MAKES 8 SERVINGS

Kathleen Haller, Baltimore, Maryland
Bake-Off® Contest 43, 2008

- 1 box Pillsbury™ refrigerated pie crusts, softened as directed on box
- ½ cup finely crushed garlic and butter croutons
- 1 cup shredded Cheddar cheese (4 oz)
- 4 oz smoked turkey sausage, sliced
- 1 box (9 oz) frozen chopped spinach, thawed, squeezed to drain and chopped
- 2 tablespoons finely chopped onion
- 1 cup crumbled feta cheese (4 oz)
- 4 eggs
- 1½ cups half-and-half
- ¼ teaspoon salt, if desired
- ⅛ teaspoon pepper
- 8 cherry tomatoes, cut into quarters

1. Heat oven to 350°F. Place pie crust in 9-inch glass pie plate or quiche pan as directed on box for One-Crust Filled Pie.

2. Cover bottom of pie crust with crushed croutons; sprinkle with Cheddar cheese. Layer sausage slices on cheese; top with spinach, onion and feta cheese.

3. In large bowl, beat eggs, half-and-half, salt and pepper with wire whisk until well blended; slowly pour into pie crust.

4. Bake 45 minutes. Cover crust edge with strips of foil. Bake 5 to 15 minutes longer or until knife inserted in center comes out clean. Let stand 15 minutes before serving. Garnish with tomatoes.

1 Serving: Calories 280 (Calories from Fat 160); Total Fat 18g; Saturated Fat 8g; Trans Fat 0g; Cholesterol 130mg; Sodium 530mg; Total Carbohydrate 18g; Dietary Fiber 1g; Sugars 3g, Protein 10g

HAM AND CHEESE OMELET BAKE

Here's a brunch bake that has it all, from ham and cheese to veggies, with a biscuit crust.

PREP TIME: 15 MINUTES

TOTAL TIME: 1 HOUR 15 MINUTES

MAKES 8 SERVINGS

Julie Amberson, Browns Point, Washington
Bake-Off® Contest 41, 2004

1 (10-oz.) box frozen broccoli & cheese flavored sauce

1 (10.2-oz.) can (5 biscuits) Pillsbury™ Grands!™ Flaky Layers refrigerated original biscuits

10 eggs

1½ cups milk

1 teaspoon dry ground mustard

Salt and pepper, if desired

2 cups diced cooked ham

⅓ cup chopped onion

4 oz. (1 cup) shredded Cheddar cheese

4 oz. (1 cup) shredded Swiss cheese

1 (4.5-oz.) jar sliced mushrooms, drained

1. Heat oven to 350°F. Cut small slit in center of broccoli and cheese sauce pouch. Microwave on High for 3 to 4 minutes, rotating pouch ¼ turn once halfway through microwaving. Set aside to cool slightly.

2. Meanwhile, spray bottom only of 13x9-inch (3-quart) glass baking dish with cooking spray. Separate dough into 5 biscuits. Cut each biscuit into 8 pieces; arrange evenly in sprayed dish.

3. In large bowl, beat eggs, milk, mustard, salt and pepper with wire whisk until well blended. Stir in ham, onion, both cheeses, mushrooms and cooked broccoli and cheese sauce. Pour mixture over biscuit pieces in dish. Press down with back of spoon, making sure all biscuit pieces are covered with egg mixture.

4. Bake at 350°F for 40 to 50 minutes or until edges are deep golden brown and center is set. Let stand 10 minutes before serving. Cut into squares.

1 Serving: Calories 462 (Calories from Fat 253); Total Fat 28g; Saturated Fat 13g; Trans Fats 0g; Cholesterol 298mg; Sodium 778mg; Total Carbohydrate 23g; Dietary Fiber 1g; Sugars 7g; Protein 29g

ITALIAN BRUNCH TORTA

This breakfast or brunch pie filled with hearty Italian ingredients tastes and looks like a gourmet dish. Just don't tell them how easy it was with Pillsbury™ refrigerated pie crusts!

PREP TIME: 20 MINUTES
TOTAL TIME: 1 HOUR 35 MINUTES

MAKES 8 SERVINGS

Loretta Torrens, Gilbert, Arizona
Bake-Off® Contest 44, 2010

1 box Pillsbury™ refrigerated pie crusts, softened as directed on box

1 tablespoon olive oil

2 cloves garlic, sliced

1 box (9 oz) frozen chopped spinach, thawed, squeezed to drain

1 cup shredded Parmesan cheese

¼ lb provolone cheese, thinly sliced

4 thin slices Genoa salami (1½ oz)

1 jar (15 or 16 oz) roasted red bell peppers, drained, patted dry

¾ cup olive tapenade (about 5-oz jar), drained

½ lb capicollo ham, thinly sliced

3½ oz dry-pack sun-dried tomatoes, coarsely chopped

1 egg, beaten

½ teaspoon oregano leaves

1. Place cookie sheet in oven (torta will bake on heated cookie sheet). Heat oven to 375°F. Make pie crusts as directed on box for Two-Crust Pie using 9-inch glass pie plate.

2. In 10-inch skillet, heat oil over medium heat. Add garlic; cook 30 seconds, stirring constantly. Stir in spinach until well combined.

3. Spread ½ of spinach mixture in crust-lined plate. Reserve 2 tablespoons of the Parmesan cheese. Layer spinach with provolone cheese, salami, red peppers, tapenade, ham, sun-dried tomatoes, remaining Parmesan cheese and remaining spinach mixture. Top with second crust; seal edges and flute.

4. Brush egg on top crust; sprinkle with reserved 2 tablespoons Parmesan cheese and oregano. Cut 4 small slits in top. Place on cookie sheet in oven.

5. Bake 50 to 55 minutes, covering edge of crust with strips of foil after 15 to 20 minutes, until golden brown. Cool 20 minutes before serving. If desired, serve torta with fresh fruit on plates lined with romaine lettuce.

1 Serving: Calories 470 (Calories from Fat 28g); Total Fat 28g; Saturated Fat 12g; Trans Fat 0g; Cholesterol 65mg; Sodium 1360mg; Total Carbohydrate 36g; Dietary Fiber 3g; Sugars 8g; Protein 18g

TEX-MEX BREAKFAST BAKE

Biscuit bites flavored with spicy enchilada sauce form the base for this bold breakfast bake.

PREP TIME: 20 MINUTES
TOTAL TIME: 1 HOUR 15 MINUTES
MAKES 6 SERVINGS

Lynne Milliron, Austin, Texas
Bake-Off® Contest 41, 2004

¼ lb. bulk lean breakfast sausage

1 (10-oz.) can red enchilada sauce

2½ oz. (½ cup) crumbled queso fresco (Mexican cheese) or farmer cheese

⅓ cup sour cream

¼ cup chopped green onions (4 medium)

1 (16.3-oz.) can Pillsbury™ Grands!™ Flaky Layers refrigerated original or buttermilk biscuits

5 oz. (1¼ cups) shredded Colby-Monterey Jack cheese blend

¼ cup chopped fresh cilantro

1. Heat oven to 350°F. Spray 8x8- or 11x7-inch (2-quart) glass baking dish with cooking spray. In 10-inch skillet, cook sausage over medium-high heat, stirring frequently, until no longer pink.

2. Meanwhile, in small bowl, mix ¼ cup of the enchilada sauce, the queso fresco, sour cream and onions; set aside. Pour remaining enchilada sauce into medium bowl. Separate dough into 8 biscuits; cut each into 8 pieces. Gently stir dough pieces into enchilada sauce to coat. Spoon mixture into sprayed dish; spread evenly.

3. Drain sausage on paper towels. Sprinkle sausage evenly on top of biscuit pieces. Spread sour cream mixture evenly over top.

4. Bake at 350°F for 30 to 35 minutes or until center is set and edges are deep golden brown. Remove from oven. Sprinkle Colby-Monterey Jack cheese over top.

5. Return to oven; bake an additional 10 minutes or until cheese is bubbly. Sprinkle with cilantro. Let stand 5 minutes before serving. Cut into squares.

1 Serving: Calories 468 (Calories from Fat 270);
Total Fat 30g; Saturated Fat 14g; Trans Fats 0g;
Cholesterol 61mg; Sodium 1030mg;
Total Carbohydrate 37g; Dietary Fiber 1g;
Sugars 6g; Protein 14g

SUNRISE PIZZA SUPREME

PREP TIME: 20 MINUTES
TOTAL TIME: 35 MINUTES

MAKES 12 SERVINGS

Nikki LoRe, Rochester, New York
Bake-Off® Contest 46, 2013

1 can Pillsbury™ refrigerated thin pizza crust

1 bag (11.8 oz) frozen grilled potatoes

1 box (7 oz) frozen broccoli, carrots and sweet peppers

12 oz hot Italian bulk sausage

1 cup shredded Italian 5-cheese blend with cream cheese (4 oz)

4 eggs

½ cup grated Parmesan cheese

½ teaspoon salt

½ teaspoon pepper

1. Heat oven to 400°F. Spray 15x10-inch pan with sides with no-stick cooking spray. Unroll dough in bottom and ¼ inch up sides of pan. Bake 5 minutes.

2. Meanwhile, microwave frozen potatoes on High 6 minutes. Cool 3 minutes; chop larger pieces. Microwave frozen vegetable blend on High 4 minutes. Set aside.

3. In 12-inch skillet, crumble sausage. Cook over medium-high heat 4 minutes or until sausage is no longer pink, stirring occasionally; drain. Stir in vegetables.

4. Spread sausage mixture over partially baked crust to within ½ inch of edges. Top with ½ cup of the shredded cheese.

5. In medium bowl, beat eggs, Parmesan cheese, salt and pepper with wire whisk until well blended. Drizzle over cheese. Top with remaining ½ cup shredded cheese. Bake 12 to 15 minutes or until cheese is melted and edges are golden brown.

1 Serving: Calories 260 (Calories from Fat 130); Total Fat 14g; Saturated Fat 5g; Trans Fat 0g; Cholesterol 85mg; Sodium 660mg; Total Carbohydrate 20g; Dietary Fiber 1g; Sugars 0g; Protein 12g

SAUSAGE APPLE AND BRIE STROMBOLI

PREP TIME: 25 MINUTES
TOTAL TIME: 60 MINUTES

MAKES 6 SERVINGS

Mary Jo Fletcher LaRocco, North Kingstown, Rhode Island
Bake-Off® Contest 46, 2013

1 lb bulk pork sausage

1 can (13.8 oz) Pillsbury™ refrigerated classic pizza crust

½ cup orange marmalade medley

1 small Granny Smith apple, cored, sliced ⅛-inch thick

8 oz Brie cheese, cut in ¼-inch slices

5 tablespoons chopped pecans

5 tablespoons sweetened dried cranberries

1. Heat oven to 375°F. Line 15 x 10-inch nonstick pan with sides with parchment paper. Spray parchment paper with no-stick cooking spray.

2. In 12-inch nonstick skillet, cook sausage over medium-high heat 10 to 15 minutes, stirring frequently, until sausage is no longer pink; drain.

3. Unroll dough in pan. Press dough almost to edges of pan. Spread ⅓ cup of the marmalade down center of dough in 4-inch-wide strip. Top with apple slices, half of the cheese slices, the sausage, remaining half cheese slices, 3 tablespoons of the pecans and 3 tablespoons of the cranberries.

4. Using kitchen scissors or sharp knife, make cuts 1 inch apart on long sides of dough to within ½ inch of filling. Fold strips of dough diagonally over filling, alternating from side to side, stretching dough as needed. Bake 15 minutes.

5. Meanwhile in small bowl, mix remaining marmalade, 2 tablespoons pecans and 2 tablespoons cranberries. Spread marmalade mixture over top and sides of partially baked stromboli. Bake an additional 10 to 15 minutes longer or until golden brown. Loosen stromboli from parchment paper; let stand 5 minutes.

6. Serve with additional apple slices, pecans and cranberries, if desired. Serve warm.

1 Serving: Calories 550 (Calories from Fat 240); Total Fat 27g; Saturated Fat 11g; Trans Fat 0g; Cholesterol 70mg; Sodium 970mg; Total Carbohydrate 58g; Dietary Fiber 2g; Sugars 7g; Protein 20g

APPLE BACON BREAKFAST FLATBREAD

PREP TIME: 25 MINUTES
TOTAL TIME: 50 MINUTES

MAKES 12 SERVINGS

Jenny Downey, Delaware, Ohio
Bake-Off® Contest 46, 2013

1 can (8 oz) Pillsbury™ Crescent Recipe Creations™ refrigerated seamless dough sheet

12 slices bacon, chopped

4 oz (half of 8-oz package) cream cheese, softened

¼ cup red raspberry preserves

1 cup shredded pepper Jack cheese (4-oz)

1 large apple, peeled, chopped

1 cup shredded sharp Cheddar cheese (4-oz)

1. Heat oven to 375°F. Spray 15x10-inch nonstick pan with sides with original no-stick cooking spray. Unroll dough in pan; press dough to edges of pan. Bake 8 to 12 minutes or until golden brown.

2. Meanwhile, in 10-inch skillet, cook bacon over medium-high heat 5 minutes or until crisp. Drain on paper towels; set aside.

3. Spread cream cheese over partially baked crust to within $^1/_2$ inch of edges. Spread preserves over cream cheese. Top with pepper Jack cheese, bacon, apple and Cheddar cheese. Bake 5 to 10 minutes longer or until thoroughly heated and cheese is melted.

1 Serving: Calories 240 (Calories from Fat 140); Total Fat 16g; Saturated Fat 8g; Trans Fat 0g; Cholesterol 40mg; Sodium 480mg; Total Carbohydrate 15g; Dietary Fiber 0g; Sugars 2g; Protein 9g

CHEESE STEAK CRESCENT BRAIDS

Weave a pretty breakfast with refrigerated crescent roll dough wrapped around steak, peppers and cheese.

PREP TIME: 35 MINUTES

TOTAL TIME: 60 MINUTES

MAKES 6 SERVINGS

Cindy Joy, Alameda, California
Bake-Off® Contest 33, 1988

1 tablespoon butter or margarine

4 portions thinly sliced frozen sandwich steaks (from 12.25-oz box), cut crosswise into ½-inch strips

1 large green bell pepper, cut into thin bite-sized strips (1½ cups)

1 medium onion, chopped (½ cup)

2 cans (8 oz each) Pillsbury™ refrigerated crescent dinner rolls

1 cup shredded mozzarella cheese (4 oz)

1 egg, beaten, if desired

1. Heat oven to 350°F. In 10-inch skillet, melt butter over medium-high heat. Add steak strips; cook 8 to 10 minutes, stirring frequently, until no longer pink. Remove steak from skillet; place on plate. Add bell pepper and onion to skillet; cook about 5 minutes, stirring occasionally, until crisp-tender. Return cooked steak to skillet; mix well. If desired, add salt and pepper to taste.

2. Unroll 1 can of dough onto ungreased cookie sheet, firmly pressing perforations and edges to seal. Press or roll into 13x7-inch rectangle.

3. Spoon heaping cup of steak mixture in 2-inch-wide strip lengthwise down center of dough to within $1/4$ inch of each end. Sprinkle $1/2$ cup of the cheese over steak mixture.

4. Make cuts 1 inch apart on long sides of rectangle just to edge of filling. For braided appearance, fold strips of dough at an angle halfway across filling with ends slightly overlapping, alternating from side to side. Fold ends of braid under to seal. On second ungreased cookie sheet, repeat with remaining can of dough, steak mixture and cheese. Brush braids with beaten egg.

5. Bake 16 to 22 minutes or until golden brown, switching position of cookie sheets in oven halfway through baking. Cool 1 minute; remove braids from cookie sheets. Let stand 5 minutes before serving. Cut into slices.

CLEVER IDEA: *For a small family, cut the recipe in half and use one can of crescent rolls.*

1 Serving: Calories 410 (Calories from Fat 210); Total Fat 23g; Saturated Fat 9g; Trans Fat 4g; Cholesterol 35mg; Sodium 710mg; Total Carbohydrate 32g; Dietary Fiber 1g; Sugars 7g; Protein 19g

DILLY CASSEROLE BREAD

Classic Bake-Off® Contest recipes have permeated our culture so thoroughly that many families think of them as family heirlooms. People who have found this particularly good herbed bread over the years don't know it's Leona Schnuelle's grand prize–winning Dilly Casserole Bread—they only know it's delicious.

PREP TIME: 20 MINUTES

TOTAL TIME: 3 HOURS

MAKES 1 LOAF (18 SLICES)

Hall of Fame

Leona Schnuelle, Crab Orchard, Nebraska

Bake-Off® Contest 12, 1960 Grand Prize Winner and Hall of Fame

2 to 2⅔ cups Pillsbury™ BEST™ All Purpose Flour

2 tablespoons sugar

2 to 3 teaspoons instant minced onion

2 teaspoons dill seed

1 teaspoon salt

¼ teaspoon baking soda

1 pkg. active dry yeast

¼ cup water

1 tablespoon margarine or butter

1 cup small curd creamed cottage cheese

1 egg

2 teaspoons margarine or butter, melted

¼ teaspoon coarse salt, if desired

1. In large bowl, combine 1 cup flour, sugar, onion, dill seed, 1 teaspoon salt, baking soda and yeast; mix well.

2. In small saucepan, heat water, 1 tablespoon margarine and cottage cheese until very warm (120 to 130°F). Add warm liquid and egg to flour mixture; blend at low speed until moistened. Beat 3 minutes at medium speed.

3. By hand, stir in remaining 1 to 1⅔ cups flour to form a stiff batter. Cover loosely with greased plastic wrap and cloth towel. Let rise in warm place (80 to 85°F) until light and doubled in size, 45 to 60 minutes.

4. Generously grease 1½ or 2-quart casserole. Stir down batter to remove all air bubbles. Turn into greased casserole. Cover; let rise in warm place until light and doubled in size, 30 to 45 minutes.

5. Heat oven to 350°F. Uncover dough. Bake 30 to 40 minutes or until loaf is deep golden brown and sounds hollow when lightly tapped. If necessary, cover with foil to prevent overbrowning. Remove from casserole; place on wire rack. Brush loaf with melted margarine; sprinkle with coarse salt. Cool 15 minutes. Serve warm or cool.

1 Serving: Calories 84 (Calories from Fat 18); Total Fat 2g; Saturated Fat 1g; Trans Fats 0g; Cholesterol 12mg; Sodium 206mg; Total Carbohydrate 13g; Dietary Fiber 1g; Sugars 2g; Protein 3g

MUFFIN MIX BUFFET BREAD

The original recipe called for cream of vegetable soup, which is no longer available, so we now use Cheddar cheese soup to make the bread. Updated and revised, this moist batter bread is slightly sweet, perfect as part of the brunch selection, and just as delicious as the original was in 1967.

PREP TIME: 25 MINUTES
TOTAL TIME: 1 HOUR 20 MINUTES
MAKES 16 SERVINGS

Maxine Bullock, Spring City, Tennessee
Bake-Off® Contest 18, 1967 Grand Prize Winner

1 (8½-oz.) pkg. corn muffin mix

2 pkg. active dry yeast

¾ cup warm water

4 cups Pillsbury™ BEST™ All Purpose, Unbleached or Self Rising Flour

1 (10¾-oz.) can condensed Cheddar cheese soup

½ cup butter or margarine, melted

1. Grease two 8- or 9-inch square pans. Set aside 2 tablespoons of the dry muffin mix. In large bowl, dissolve yeast in warm water (105 to 115°F). Lightly spoon flour into measuring cup; level off. Add remaining dry muffin mix, 2 cups of the flour, soup and ¼ cup of the melted butter; mix just until dry ingredients are moistened. Gradually stir in remaining 2 cups flour to form a stiff dough. Knead on floured surface until smooth, about 1 minute. Cover; let rest 15 minutes.

2. Heat oven to 375°F. Divide dough in half; press each half into greased pan. Cut each into 8 strips. Drizzle remaining ¼ cup melted butter over loaves; sprinkle with reserved muffin mix. Cover; let rise in warm place 12 to 15 minutes or until light.

3. Bake at 375°F for 18 to 25 minutes or until golden brown. Immediately remove from pans. Break apart or cut with knife. Serve warm.

1 Slice: Calories 250 (Calories from Fat 80); Total Fat 9g; Saturated Fat 5g; Trans Fat 1.5g; Cholesterol 20mg; Sodium 370mg; Total Carbohydrate 36g; Dietary Fiber 2g; Sugars 1g; Protein 5g

WHOLE WHEAT RAISIN LOAF

As a grand prize winner in 1976, this hearty loaf introduced thousands to the joys of making their own whole-grain bread. You'll find the raisins and spices have a natural affinity with the nut-like flavors of rolled oats and whole wheat.

Enjoy the goodness of oats and whole wheat flour in this delicious yeast bread flavored with raisin and spice—a wholesome breakfast or tea-time snack.

PREP TIME: 30 MINUTES
TOTAL TIME: 4 HOURS
MAKES 32 SERVINGS

Lenora Smith, Baton Rouge, Louisiana
Bake-Off® Contest 27, 1976 Grand Prize Winner

2 to 3 cups Pillsbury™ BEST™ All Purpose or Unbleached Flour

½ cup sugar

3 teaspoons salt

1 teaspoon cinnamon

½ teaspoon nutmeg

2 pkg. active dry yeast

2 cups milk

¾ cup water

¼ cup oil

4 cups Pillsbury™ BEST™ Whole Wheat Flour

1 cup rolled oats

1 cup raisins

1 tablespoon margarine or butter, melted

1 teaspoon sugar, if desired

1. In large bowl, combine 1½ cups all purpose flour, ½ cup sugar, salt, cinnamon, nutmeg and yeast; mix well. In medium saucepan, heat milk, water and oil until very warm (120 to 130°F). Add warm liquid to flour mixture; blend at low speed until moistened. Beat 3 minutes at medium speed. By hand, stir in whole wheat flour, rolled oats, raisins and an additional ¼ to ¾ cup all purpose flour until dough pulls cleanly away from sides of bowl.

2. On floured surface, knead in remaining ¼ to ¾ cup all purpose flour until dough is smooth and elastic, about 5 minutes. Place dough in greased bowl; cover loosely with greased plastic wrap and cloth towel. Let rise in warm place (80 to 85°F) until light and doubled in size, 20 to 30 minutes.

3. Grease two 9x5 or 8x4-inch loaf pans. Punch down dough several times to remove all air bubbles. Divide dough in half; shape into loaves. Place in greased pans. Cover; let rise in warm place until light and doubled in size, 30 to 45 minutes.

4. Heat oven to 375°F. Uncover dough. Bake 40 to 50 minutes or until loaves are deep golden brown and sound hollow when lightly tapped. If loaves become too brown, cover loosely with foil during last 10 minutes of baking. Immediately remove from pans; cool on wire racks for 1½ hours or until completely cooled. Brush tops of loaves with margarine; sprinkle with sugar.

1 Slice: Calories 160 (Calories from Fat 25); Total Fat 3g; Saturated Fat 1g; Trans Fat 0g; Cholesterol 0mg; Sodium 210mg; Total Carbohydrate 29g; Dietary Fiber 3g; Sugars 7g; Protein 5g

GRAHAM CRACKER BROWN BREAD

The secret ingredient in this unusual bread is graham crackers—they add color, texture and flavor appeal. The recipe makes two loaves. Have one now and freeze one to serve later.

PREP TIME: 20 MINUTES
TOTAL TIME: 2 HOURS
10 MINUTES

MAKES 2 LOAVES
(16 SLICES EACH)

Grace M. Kain, West Boothbay Harbor, Maine
Bake-Off® Contest 10, 1958

2 cups graham cracker crumbs or finely crushed graham crackers (30 squares)

½ cup shortening

1¾ cups buttermilk

¾ cup molasses

2 eggs slightly beaten

1¾ cups Pillsbury™ BEST™ All Purpose Flour

2 teaspoons baking soda

1 teaspoon salt

¼ to ½ teaspoon ground nutmeg

1 cup raisins

1. Heat oven to 375° F. Grease and flour bottoms only of two 8 x 4-inch loaf pans. In large bowl, beat graham cracker crumbs and shortening with electric mixer on medium speed until well blended. Add buttermilk, molasses and eggs; beat well.

2. In small bowl, mix flour, baking soda, salt and nutmeg. Add to graham cracker mixture; beat at low speed until well blended. Fold in raisins. Pour batter into pans.

3. Bake 35 to 40 minutes or until toothpick inserted in center comes out clean. Cool 10 minutes. Remove from pans to cooling rack. Cool completely, about 1 hour.

CLEVER IDEA: *To substitute for buttermilk, use 5 teaspoons vinegar or lemon juice plus milk to make 1¾ cups.*

1 Slice: Calories 120 (Calories from Fat 40); Total Fat 4.5g; Saturated Fat 1g; Trans Fat 0.5g; Cholesterol 15mg; Sodium 200mg; Total Carbohydrate 19g; Dietary Fiber 0g; Sugars 11g; Protein 2g

LEMON NUT ROLLS

Flour still was the only eligible product in the 1958 contest, and recently married women between ages nineteen and thirty-one could enter a special Bride Award Category. These light, tender potato rolls won first prize for a newly married contestant.

PREP TIME: 30 MINUTES
TOTAL TIME: 2 HOURS
10 MINUTES

MAKES 16 SERVINGS
(1 ROLL PER SERVING)

Betty May, Sykesville, Maryland
Bake-Off® Contest 10, 1958

ROLLS

2½ to 3½ cups all-purpose flour

⅓ cup mashed potato flakes

⅓ cup sugar

1 teaspoon salt

½ teaspoon grated lemon peel

1 pkg. active dry yeast

¾ cup water

½ cup milk

⅓ cup margarine or butter

1 tablespoon lemon juice

1 egg

FILLING

2 tablespoons margarine or butter, softened

¾ cup sugar

½ cup chopped pecans

1 teaspoon grated lemon peel

GLAZE

½ cup powdered sugar

½ teaspoon grated lemon peel

½ teaspoon lemon juice

2 to 3 teaspoons milk or half-and-half

1. In large bowl, combine 1 cup flour, potato flakes, ⅓ cup sugar, salt, ½ teaspoon lemon peel and yeast; blend well. In small saucepan, heat water, milk and ⅓ cup margarine until very warm (120 to 130°F). Add warm liquid, lemon juice and egg to flour mixture. Blend at low speed until moistened; beat 2 minutes at medium speed. By hand, stir in remaining 1½ to 2½ cups flour to form a stiff dough. Cover loosely with plastic wrap and cloth towel. Let rise in warm place (80 to 85°F) until light and doubled in size, about 1 hour.

2. Grease two 8- or 9-inch round cake pans. On floured surface, toss dough until no longer sticky. Roll into 16 x 12-inch rectangle; spread with 2 tablespoons margarine. In small bowl, combine remaining filling ingredients; sprinkle over dough. Starting with 16-inch side, roll up tightly, pressing edges to seal. Cut into 16 slices; place in greased pans. Cover; let rise in warm place (80 to 85°F) until light and doubled in size, 30 to 40 minutes.

3. Heat oven to 375°F. Uncover dough. Bake 20 to 30 minutes or until lightly golden brown. Immediately remove from pans; cool on wire racks. In small bowl, blend glaze ingredients and enough milk to drizzle over warm rolls.

1 Roll: Calories 250 (Calories from Fat 80); Total Fat 9g; Saturated Fat 1.5g; Trans Fat 1g; Cholesterol mg; Sodium 210mg; Total Carbohydrate 40g; Dietary Fiber 1g; Sugars 18g; Protein 3 g

LICKITY QUICK LEMONADE BREAD

PREP TIME: 15 MINUTES

TOTAL TIME: 1 HOUR 30 MINUTES

MAKES 1 LOAF (12 SLICES)

Mrs. Joseph Pellecchia, East Boston, Massachusetts

Bake-Off® Contest 18, 1967

1 cup sugar

½ cup shortening

½ cup milk

1½ cups Pillsbury™ BEST™ All Purpose Flour

2 teaspoons baking powder

2 eggs

1 tablespoon plus ⅓ cup frozen lemonade concentrate, thawed

1. Heat oven to 350° F. Grease 9x5-inch loaf pan.

2. In large bowl, beat all ingredients except the ⅓ cup lemonade concentrate with electric mixer on low speed 30 seconds; beat 3 minutes at medium speed. Pour in pan.

3. Bake 50 to 60 minutes or until toothpick inserted in center comes out clean. Loosen bread from edges of pan. Pour ⅓ cup concentrate over bread. Cool in pan on cooling rack 15 minutes; remove from pan.

CLEVER IDEA: *If using self-rising flour, omit baking powder.*

1 Slice: Calories 240 (Calories from Fat 90); Total Fat 10g; Saturated Fat 2.5g; Trans Fat 1.5g; Cholesterol 35mg; Sodium 95mg; Total Carbohydrate 34g; Dietary Fiber 0g; Sugars 22g; Protein 3g

A Peek Inside the Bake-Off® Contest:

There's a story behind every recipe. What makes a memory? Grandma's rhubarb pie or Aunt Rafina's family favorite—a curry sauce she makes every Thanksgiving. Food is a link to our family and friends. It becomes part of our family history and memories. "Remember when Dad made . . ." sets the stage for family stories.

Bake-Off® recipes are family stories, too. Every one of the recipes in this book was created by an ordinary woman or man who wanted to create a special moment and memory for family and friends.

Add your memories to the Bake-Off® family album. To create your own special moments, enjoy the homemade goodness of these winning recipes. Throughout this cookbook, you'll find a variety of recipes to make for your family and friends, whether it's a weeknight meal, a holiday dinner or a casual weekend get-together. They reflect the tastes and trends of American homes just like yours. Each time you prepare a recipe, jot down a notation about when you served it and the occasion, and this cookbook will become a family keepsake. Pick your favorites to make again and again for family and friends.

Whether you're a finalist at a Pillsbury Bake-Off® Contest or simply a star in your own kitchen, you share something special. Both you and Bake-Off® contestants know the food you developed with love for your family will become treasured family recipes in someone's home.

HONEY SESAME BAGELS

PREP TIME: 15 MINUTES
TOTAL TIME: 45 MINUTES

MAKES 6 SERVINGS

Kellie White, Valley Park, Missouri
Bake-Off® Contest 46, 2013

¼ cup seedless blackberry spreadable fruit

¼ cup unsalted butter, softened

½ cup honey

1 can Pillsbury™ refrigerated classic pizza crust

¼ cup sesame seed

1 egg white

1. Heat oven to 450°F. Line cookie sheet with parchment paper; spray with no-stick cooking spray. In small bowl, gently swirl spreadable fruit into butter. Set aside.

2. In 4-quart saucepan or Dutch oven, bring honey and 10 cups water to a boil over medium-high heat. Reduce heat to medium-low.

3. Meanwhile, remove dough from package; but do not unroll. Cut dough crosswise into 6 pieces; shape each piece into a ball. Using your finger, form a 1-inch diameter hole in center of each ball to resemble a bagel. Gently add 3 bagels at a time to water for 1 minute. Using tongs or slotted spoon, turn bagels over; simmer an additional 1 minute. Place on cooling rack.

4. Sprinkle 2 tablespoons of the sesame seed on small plate. Dip bottom of each bagel in seed; place 3 inches apart on cookie sheet. In small bowl, beat egg white and 1 tablespoon water; brush on top of bagels. Sprinkle with remaining sesame seed.

5. Bake 15 to 18 minutes or until golden brown. Remove from cookie sheet to cooling rack. Serve with blackberry butter.

1 Serving: Calories 400 (Calories from Fat 120), Total Fat 14g; Saturated Fat 6g; Trans Fat 0g; Cholesterol 20mg; Sodium 480mg; Total Carbohydrate 64g; Dietary Fiber 2g, Sugars 23g, Protein 7g

BEEHIVE BUNS

These honey-flavored raisin buns are shaped like miniature beehives. Serve them fresh from the oven with butter.

PREP TIME: 45 MINUTES
TOTAL TIME: 2 HOURS
45 MINUTES

MAKES 24 SERVINGS
(1 ROLL PER SERVING)

Janis Chudleigh, Bethany, Connecticut
Bake-Off® Contest 32, 1986

ROLLS

2 cups whole wheat flour

2 pkg. active dry yeast

1 teaspoon salt

1 cup raisins

1 cup very hot water

1 cup milk

⅓ cup honey

⅓ cup margarine or butter

2 eggs

2 to 3¼ cups all-purpose flour

GLAZE

3 tablespoons honey

3 tablespoons margarine or butter

1¼ cups powdered sugar

1 teaspoon vanilla

1. In large bowl, combine whole wheat flour, yeast and salt; set aside. Cover raisins with water for 1 minute; drain. In small saucepan heat milk, ⅓ cup honey and ⅓ cup margarine until very warm (120 to 130°F). Add warm mixture to flour mixture. Beat in eggs 1 at a time; stir in drained raisins. By hand, stir in 1½ to 2 cups all-purpose flour until dough pulls cleanly away from sides of bowl.

2. On floured surface, knead in an additional ½ to 1¼ cups all-purpose flour until dough is smooth and elastic, about 5 minutes. Place dough in greased bowl; cover loosely with plastic wrap and cloth towel. Let rise in warm place (80 to 85°F) until light and doubled in size, 45 to 60 minutes.

3. Grease 24 muffin cups. Punch down dough several times to remove all air bubbles. Divide dough into 24 pieces. (Cover dough pieces with inverted bowl to prevent drying out.) Using 1 piece of dough at a time, roll to form 10- to 12-inch rope. Coil rope in muffin cup, tucking end into top center to form beehive shape. Repeat with remaining pieces. Cover; let rise in warm place until light and doubled in size, about 30 to 40 minutes.

4. Heat oven to 350°F. Uncover dough. Bake 15 to 20 minutes or until golden brown. Immediately remove from muffin cups; place on wire racks. In small saucepan, heat 3 tablespoons each honey and margarine. Stir in powdered sugar and vanilla until smooth. Drizzle over warm rolls.

1 Slice: Calories 210 (Calories from Fat 45); Total Fat 5g; Saturated Fat 1g; Trans Fat 0.5g; Cholesterol 17mg; Sodium 146mg; Total Carbohydrate 33g; Dietary Fiber 2g; Sugars 16g; Protein 4g

APRICOT-GINGER CHEESE DANISH

Convenient Pillsbury™ crescent rounds make quick work of an impressive breakfast Danish with double toppings—spicy apricot and cream cheese.

PREP TIME: 20 MINUTES
TOTAL TIME: 45 MINUTES
MAKES 4 SERVINGS

Marla Clark, Moriarty, New Mexico
Bake-Off® Contest 44, 2010

1 can (8-oz.) Pillsbury™ Place 'N Bake™ refrigerated crescent rounds (8 rounds) or
1 can (8-oz.) Pillsbury™ refrigerated crescent dinner rolls

¼ cup apricot preserves

½ teaspoon finely chopped crystallized ginger

2 -oz. cream cheese, softened (¼ cup)

1 tablespoon sugar

1½ teaspoons Pillsbury™ BEST™ All Purpose Flour

¼ teaspoon pure vanilla extract

1 egg

1 tablespoon water

¼ cup natural sliced almonds

1. Heat oven to 375°F. If using crescent rounds, remove from package, separate into 8 rounds. If using crescent rolls, remove from package, but do not unroll. Using serrated knife, cut roll into 8 rounds; carefully separate rounds. On ungreased large cookie sheet, place 2 rounds side by side; press joining edges together to form figure-eight shape. Press each round until 3 inches in diameter and about ¼ inch thick. Press 1½-inch indentation in center of each round. Repeat with remaining rounds to make 4 figure-eights, placing 3 inches apart on cookie sheet.

2. In small bowl, mix preserves and ginger. In another small bowl, stir cream cheese, sugar, flour and vanilla until smooth.

3. Fill 1 indentation on each figure-eight with 1 tablespoon preserves mixture. Fill other indentation on each figure-eight with 1 rounded tablespoon cheese mixture.

4. In small bowl, beat egg and water with wire whisk or fork until well blended. Carefully brush edge of dough with egg mixture; sprinkle with almonds. Bake 10 to 14 minutes or until light golden brown. Cool 10 minutes before serving.

1 Serving: Calories 390 (Calories from Fat 190); Total Fat 21g; Saturated Fat 7g; Trans Fat 3g; Cholesterol 60mg; Sodium 510mg; Total Carbohydrate 42g; Dietary Fiber 1g; Sugars 18g; Protein 7g

APRICOT-GINGER CHEESE DANISH (*page 61*)

EASY CRESCENT DANISH ROLLS (*opposite*)

EASY CRESCENT DANISH ROLLS

Crescent rolls are the starting point for these plump homemade Danish rolls with a cream-cheese filling. These pastries can be made to suit everyone's taste by just changing the flavor of preserves.

PREP TIME: 20 MINUTES
TOTAL TIME: 45 MINUTES

MAKES 8 SERVINGS

Barbara Gibson, Ft. Wayne, Indiana
Bake-Off® Contest 26, 1975 Grand Prize Winner

ROLLS

1 package (8 oz) cream cheese, softened

½ cup sugar

1 tablespoon lemon juice

2 cans (8 oz each) Pillsbury™ refrigerated crescent dinner rolls or 2 cans (8 oz each) Pillsbury™ Crescent Recipe Creations™ refrigerated seamless dough sheet

4 teaspoons preserves or jam

GLAZE

½ cup powdered sugar

1 teaspoon vanilla

2 to 3 teaspoons milk

1. Heat oven to 350°F. In small bowl, beat cream cheese, sugar and lemon juice until smooth.

2. If using crescent dough, separate dough into 8 rectangles; firmly press perforations to seal. If using dough sheet, cut dough into 8 rectangles. Spread each rectangle with about 2 tablespoons cream cheese mixture. Roll up each, starting at longest side; firmly pinch edges and ends to seal. Gently stretch each roll to about 10 inches.

3. On ungreased large cookie sheet, coil each roll into a spiral with seam on the inside, tucking end under. Make deep indentation in center of each roll; fill with ½ teaspoon preserves.

4. Bake 20 to 25 minutes or until deep golden brown. In small bowl, mix glaze ingredients, adding enough milk for desired drizzling consistency. Drizzle over warm rolls.

1 Serving: Calories 400 (Calories from Fat 200); Total Fat 22g; Saturated Fat 10g; Trans Fat 3.5g; Cholesterol 30mg; Sodium 530mg; Total Carbohydrate 45g; Dietary Fiber 0g; Sugars 26g; Protein 6g

RING-A-LINGS

Bertha Jorgensen's method of filling, twisting and shaping her orange-flavored yeast rolls has been copied in many recipes since 1955. Judges that year were so impressed with the eating quality of her hazelnut-filled rolls and innovative shaping, they picked hers as the best recipe in America's premier cooking event. They're perfect for a special breakfast or brunch.

PREP TIME: 40 MINUTES
TOTAL TIME: 2 HOURS 25 MINUTES
MAKES 22 SERVINGS

Bertha Jorgensen, Portland, Oregon
Bake-Off® Contest 7, 1955 Grand Prize Winner

DOUGH

4 to 4½ cups Pillsbury™ BEST™ All Purpose or Unbleached Flour

⅓ cup sugar

2 teaspoons salt

2 teaspoons grated orange peel

2 pkg. active dry yeast

1 cup milk

⅓ cup margarine or butter

2 eggs

FILLING

1 cup powdered sugar

⅓ cup margarine or butter, softened

1 cup filberts, pecans or walnuts, ground

GLAZE

3 tablespoons sugar

¼ cup orange juice

1. Lightly spoon flour into measuring cup; level off. In large bowl, combine 2 cups of the flour, ⅓ cup sugar, salt, orange peel and yeast; mix well.

2. In small saucepan, heat milk and ⅓ cup margarine until very warm (120 to 130°F). Add warm liquid and eggs to flour mixture; blend at low speed until moistened. Beat 3 minutes at medium speed. By hand, stir in remaining 2 to 2½ cups flour to form a stiff dough. Place dough in greased bowl; cover loosely with plastic wrap and cloth towel. Let rise in warm place (80 to 85°F) until light and doubled in size, 35 to 50 minutes.

3. In small bowl, blend powdered sugar and ⅓ cup margarine until smooth. Stir in filberts; set aside. In second small bowl, blend glaze ingredients; cover and set aside.

4. Grease 2 large cookie sheets. Stir down dough to remove all air bubbles. On floured surface, roll dough to 22x12-inch rectangle. Spread filling mixture lengthwise over half of dough. Fold dough over filling. Cut crosswise into 1-inch strips; twist each strip 4 to 5 times. To shape rolls, hold folded end of strip down on greased cookie sheet to form center; coil strip around center. Tuck loose end under. Repeat with remaining twisted strips. Cover; let rise in warm place until light and doubled in size, 30 to 45 minutes.

5. Heat oven to 375°F. Uncover dough. Bake 9 to 12 minutes or until light golden brown. Brush tops of rolls with glaze. Bake an additional 3 to 5 minutes or until golden brown. Immediately remove from cookie sheets; cool on wire racks. Serve warm.

1 Roll: Calories 210 (Calories from Fat 77); Total Fat 9g; Saturated Fat 2g; Trans Fats 1g; Cholesterol 18mg; Sodium 275mg; Total Carbohydrate 29g; Dietary Fiber 1g; Sugars 11g; Protein 4g

A Peek Inside the Bake-Off® Contest:

Most people hear about Roberta (Bobbie) Sonefeld's 2000 Bake-Off® Contest win and immediately zero in on the $1 million grand prize she was awarded for her decadently rich Cream Cheese Brownie Pie. But Bobbie says the richest part of the experience was the Bake-Off® weekend itself, a dazzling trip she and her husband, Steve, have christened their "second honeymoon."

The 2000 Bake-Off® Contest took place in the San Francisco Marriott, an opulent hotel in downtown San Francisco. "Neither of us had ever been to the West Coast," recalled Bobbie. "The way Pillsbury treated us was just great: Three gourmet meals a day plus all kinds of tours and sightseeing." An added benefit, said Bobbie, was that "all the activity had a calming effect." When the day of the cooking contest rolled around, "I was used to the idea." Didn't she get nervous? "Well, yes," she admits, "but I didn't get the butterflies bad until the night before. The next morning—once I was done baking and there wasn't anything I could do about it—I was fine. Then I thought, 'Wow, I already feel like a winner, it doesn't matter what happens next.'"

What happened next is part of history: Bobbie's Cream Cheese Brownie Pie, entered in the Fast & Fabulous Desserts & Treats category, won the grand prize. The Sonefelds' second honeymoon became even more extravagant, as they jetted to New York City for a whirlwind round of television and radio appearances. They also went to Philadelphia to appear on QVC. Bobbie remembers New York as another great restaurant town where she had meals she never even dreamed of two weeks before.

After an amazing week traveling the country together, Bobbie and Steve returned home to Hopkins, South Carolina, their full-time jobs and their family. And that's when the trip stopped being a honeymoon and turned into a homecoming, as Bobbie and Steve returned to the loving arms of their very excited sons.

ORANGE DATE CRESCENT CLAWS

Like bakery bear claws with a moist date-nut filling, these rolls are fun to shape and a treat to eat.

PREP TIME: 25 MINUTES
TOTAL TIME: 40 MINUTES

MAKES 8 ROLLS

Barbara Rhea, Beavercreek, Ohio
Bake-Off® Contest 33, 1988

½ cup chopped walnuts or pecans

¼ cup sugar

1 teaspoon grated orange peel

½ cup chopped dates

1 (8-oz.) can refrigerated crescent dinner rolls

2 tablespoons margarine or butter, melted

1. Heat oven to 375°F. In small bowl, combine walnuts, sugar and orange peel; blend well. Reserve ¼ cup of mixture for topping. Stir dates into remaining mixture; set aside.

2. Separate dough into 4 rectangles; firmly press perforations to seal. Cut each rectangle in half crosswise; press or roll out each to form eight 4-inch squares. Brush each with margarine. Spoon about 2 tablespoons date mixture across center ⅓ of each square to within ¼ inch of edges. Fold sides of dough over filling; pinch center seam and ends to seal. Place seam side down on ungreased cookie sheet.

3. Using scissors or sharp knife, make three ½-inch cuts in one folded edge. To form claws, separate cut sections of each roll by gently curving into crescent shape. Brush top of each claw with remaining margarine; sprinkle with reserved sugar-nut mixture. Bake at 375°F for 8 to 12 minutes or until golden brown.

1 Roll: Calories 235 (Calories from Fat 120); Total Fat 14g; Saturated Fat 3g; Trans Fat 2g; Cholesterol 0mg; Sodium 249 mg; Total Carbohydrate 25g; Dietary Fiber 1g; Sugars 14g; Protein 3g

ORANGE-CHERRY-ALMOND PINWHEELS

Start with a Pillsbury™ refrigerated dough sheet layered with white baking chips, dried cherries and almonds, then slice and bake for easy breakfast rolls that taste like they're from a pastry shop!

PREP TIME: 20 MINUTES

TOTAL TIME: 1 HOUR 5 MINUTES

MAKES 8 SERVINGS

JoAnne Rademacher, Berthold, North Dakota
Bake-Off® Contest 44, 2010

¼ cup unsalted or salted butter, softened

1 tablespoon almond paste

1 egg

⅛ teaspoon ground nutmeg

1 tablespoon Pillsbury BEST™ All Purpose Flour

1 can (8 oz) Pillsbury™ Crescent Recipe Creations™ refrigerated seamless dough sheet

½ cup dried tart cherries

⅓ cup white baking chips

Grated peel of 1 large orange (about 1 tablespoon)

¼ cup plus 1 tablespoon sliced almonds

½ cup powdered sugar

2 tablespoons whipping cream

⅛ teaspoon pure almond extract

1. In small bowl, beat butter, almond paste and egg with electric hand mixer until mixture is smooth. Beat in nutmeg and flour.

2. On work surface, unroll dough sheet; press into 14x8-inch rectangle. Spread butter mixture over dough, leaving ½ inch of 1 short end uncovered. Sprinkle cherries, baking chips, 2 teaspoons of the orange peel and ¼ cup almonds over butter mixture to edges of dough; press in lightly.

3. Starting at short end covered with butter mixture, roll up dough. Pinch and press uncovered end into roll to seal. Reshape roll with hands. Wrap roll in waxed paper; refrigerate 30 minutes.

4. Heat oven to 375°F. Lightly spray cookie sheet with original no-stick cooking spray, or line with cooking parchment paper. Using serrated knife, cut roll into 8 slices; place cut sides up and 3 inches apart on cookie sheet. Bake 13 to 17 minutes or until golden brown.

5. Meanwhile, in small bowl, mix powdered sugar, cream and almond extract with spoon until smooth; spoon and spread over hot rolls on cookie sheet. Sprinkle with remaining 1 tablespoon almonds and 1 teaspoon orange peel. Remove from cookie sheet to cooling rack. Serve warm or cool.

1 Serving: Calories 300 (Calories from Fat 150); Total Fat 16g; Saturated Fat 8g; Trans Fat 0g; Cholesterol 45mg; Sodium 240mg; Total Carbohydrate 35g; Dietary Fiber 1g; Sugars 22g; Protein 4g

MAGIC MARSHMALLOW CRESCENT PUFFS

"Such a simple way to get great taste," people exclaim when they try this Bake-Off® Contest classic recipe. It is created by wrapping refrigerated crescent-roll dough around cinnamon-sugar-coated marshmallows. The marshmallows melt during baking, forming a sweet, hollow puff.

PREP TIME: 35 MINUTES
TOTAL TIME: 35 MINUTES
MAKES 16 SERVINGS

Hall of Fame

Edna M. Walker, Hopkins, Minnesota
Bake-Off® Contest 20, 1969 Grand Prize Winner and Hall of Fame

ROLLS

¼ cup granulated sugar

2 tablespoons Pillsbury™ BEST™ All Purpose Flour

1 teaspoon ground cinnamon

2 cans (8 oz each) Pillsbury™ refrigerated crescent dinner rolls

16 large marshmallows

¼ cup butter or margarine, melted

GLAZE

½ cup powdered sugar

½ teaspoon vanilla

2 to 3 teaspoons milk

¼ cup chopped nuts

1. Heat oven to 375°F. Spray 16 medium muffin cups with no-stick cooking spray. In small bowl, mix granulated sugar, flour and cinnamon.

2. Separate dough into 16 triangles. For each roll, dip 1 marshmallow into melted butter; roll in sugar mixture. Place marshmallow on shortest side of triangle. Roll up, starting at shortest side and rolling to opposite point. Completely cover marshmallow with dough; firmly pinch edges to seal. Dip 1 end in remaining butter; place butter side down in muffin cup.

3. Bake 12 to 15 minutes or until golden brown. (Place foil or cookie sheet on rack below muffin cups to guard against spills.) Cool in pan 1 minute. Remove rolls from muffin cups; place on cooling racks set over waxed paper.

4. In small bowl, mix powdered sugar, vanilla and enough milk for desired drizzling consistency. Drizzle glaze over warm rolls. Sprinkle with nuts. Serve warm.

1 Roll: Calories 200 (Calories from Fat 90); Total Fat 10g; Saturated Fat 4g; Trans Fat 1.5g; Cholesterol 10mg; Sodium 250mg; Total Carbohydrate 25g; Dietary Fiber 1g; Sugars 13g; Protein 2g

COOKIES AND CRESCENT SWEET ROLLS

For the sweetest of mornings, try this special treat that intertwines refrigerated dinner rolls and refrigerated cookies!

PREP TIME: 30 MINUTES
TOTAL TIME: 1 HOUR 5 MINUTES
MAKES 12 SERVINGS

Robert Holt, Mendota Heights, Minnesota
Bake-Off® Contest 37, 1996

ROLLS

1 can (8 oz) Pillsbury™ refrigerated crescent dinner rolls or 1 can (8 oz) Pillsbury™ Crescent Recipe Creations™ refrigerated seamless dough sheet

6 inches Pillsbury™ refrigerated chocolate chip cookies (from 16.5-oz roll)

¼ cup chopped pecans

GLAZE

⅔ cup powdered sugar

¼ teaspoon vanilla

3 to 4 teaspoons milk

1. Heat oven to 350°F. Lightly spray 9-inch round cake pan or glass pie plate with cooking spray.

2. If using crescent rolls: Unroll dough; separate into 2 long rectangles. Overlap long sides ½ inch to form 1 large rectangle. Press seam and perforations to seal. If using dough sheet: Unroll dough.

3. Spoon small amounts of cookie dough evenly over crescent dough; press or pat to evenly cover. Sprinkle with pecans. Starting at long side, roll up; pinch seam to seal. Cut into 12 pieces. Arrange cut side up in pan.

4. Bake 28 to 35 minutes or until crescent dough is golden brown. Cool 15 minutes.

5. Meanwhile, in small bowl, mix glaze ingredients, adding enough milk for desired drizzling consistency. Drizzle over warm rolls. Serve warm.

1 Serving: Calories 220 (Calories from Fat 90); Total Fat 10g; Saturated Fat 2.5g; Trans Fat 2g; Cholesterol 0mg; Sodium 220mg; Total Carbohydrate 29g; Dietary Fiber 0g; Sugars 17g; Protein 2g

"PEANUT BUTTER-LICIOUS" RING-A-ROUNDS

Peanut butter meets chocolate with a hint of banana in a scrumptious breakfast treat.

PREP TIME: 25 MINUTES
TOTAL TIME: 50 MINUTES

MAKES 12 SERVINGS

Erika Couch, Frederick, Maryland
Bake-Off® Contest 43, 2008

ROLLS

⅓ cup powdered sugar

¼ cup creamy peanut butter

2 tablespoons butter, softened

½ teaspoon banana extract

2 cans (11 oz each) Pillsbury™ refrigerated original breadsticks (12 breadsticks each)

GLAZE

½ cup milk chocolate baking chips

3 tablespoons butter

2 teaspoons light corn syrup

⅛ teaspoon vanilla

⅛ teaspoon banana extract

¼ cup pecan chips

1. Heat oven to 375°F. Spray large cookie sheet with no-stick cooking spray. In small bowl, stir powdered sugar, peanut butter, 2 tablespoons butter and ½ teaspoon banana extract until smooth; set aside.

2. Unroll both cans of dough on cutting board; divide into 4 equal sections along center perforations. Spread about ¼ cup peanut butter mixture over each of 2 dough sections. Place remaining dough sections over filling. Using sharp knife, cut along perforations into 12 strips. Gently stretch each strip until about 10 inches long. Twist each strip 4 or 5 times. Coil each strip into pinwheel shape; tuck end under. Place 2 inches apart on cookie sheet.

3. Bake 12 to 18 minutes or until golden brown. Remove rolls from cookie sheet to cooling rack placed on waxed paper. Cool 10 minutes.

4. Meanwhile, in 2-quart saucepan, melt chocolate chips, 3 tablespoons butter and the corn syrup over medium heat, stirring occasionally, until chocolate chips are melted and mixture is smooth. Stir in vanilla and ⅛ teaspoon banana extract.

5. Drizzle glaze over warm rolls. Sprinkle each with 1 teaspoon pecan chips. Serve warm or at room temperature.

1 Serving: Calories 290 (Calories from Fat 120); Total Fat 14g; Saturated Fat 6g; Trans Fat 0g; Cholesterol 15mg; Sodium 400mg; Total Carbohydrate 35g; Dietary Fiber 0g; Sugars 11g; Protein 6g

"PEANUT BUTTER-LICIOUS" RING-A-ROUNDS (*opposite*)

ESPRESSO HAZELNUT BEIGNETS (*page 76*)

NO-KNEAD WATER-RISING TWISTS

This first Bake-Off® Contest winner originally had a unique rising method. In that procedure, the dough was wrapped in a tea towel and submerged in warm water to rise. In this updated version, we have streamlined the preparation of the dough and the rising method.

PREP TIME: 40 MINUTES
TOTAL TIME: 1 HOUR 35 MINUTES
MAKES 12 SERVINGS

Theodora Smafield, Rockford, Illinois
Bake-Off® Winner 1, 1949 Grand Prize Winner

2½ to 3½ cups Pillsbury™ BEST™ All Purpose or Unbleached Flour

1 cup sugar

1 teaspoon salt

1 pkg. active dry yeast

¾ cup milk

½ cup margarine or butter

1 teaspoon vanilla

2 eggs

½ cup chopped nuts

1 teaspoon cinnamon

1. Lightly spoon flour into measuring cup; level off. In large bowl, combine 1 cup flour, ½ cup of the sugar, salt and yeast; blend well.

2. In small saucepan, heat milk and margarine until very warm (120 to 130°F). Add warm liquid, vanilla and eggs to flour mixture; blend at low speed until moistened. Beat 2 minutes at medium speed. By hand, stir in remaining 1½ to 2½ cups flour to form a soft dough. Cover loosely with greased plastic wrap and cloth towel. Let rise in warm place (80 to 85°F) until light and doubled in size, 30 to 40 minutes. (Dough will be sticky.)

3. Grease 2 large cookie sheets. In small bowl, combine nuts, remaining ½ cup sugar and cinnamon; blend well. Drop about ¼ cup dough into nut mixture; thoroughly coat. Stretch dough to about 8 inches in length; twist into desired shape. Place on greased cookie sheets. Repeat with remaining dough. Cover; let rise in warm place, about 15 minutes.

4. Heat oven to 375°F. Uncover dough. Bake 8 to 16 minutes or until light golden brown. Immediately remove from cookie sheets; cool on wire racks. Serve warm.

1 Serving: Calories 280 (Calories from Fat 110); Total Fat 12g; Saturated Fat 2.5g; Trans Fat 1.5g; Cholesterol 35mg; Sodium 290mg; Total Carbohydrate 39g; Dietary Fiber 1g; Sugar 18g; Protein 5g

ESPRESSO HAZELNUT BEIGNETS

Enjoy bakery shop beignets from buttermilk biscuits in just minutes!

PREP TIME: 25 MINUTES
TOTAL TIME: 25 MINUTES

MAKES 8 SERVINGS

Karyn Hentz, Arlington, Virginia
Bake-Off® Contest 46, 2013

4 cups canola oil

¼ cup sugar

½ teaspoon instant espresso powder

1 can Pillsbury™ Grands!™ Homestyle refrigerated buttermilk biscuits (8 ct)

½ cup mocha cappuccino flavored hazelnut spread

1. In 3-quart heavy saucepan, heat oil to 375°F. In shallow bowl or plate, mix sugar and espresso powder. Set aside.

2. Separate dough into 8 biscuits. Press each biscuit into 4-inch round. Spoon 1 tablespoon of the mocha cappuccino hazelnut spread on each biscuit. Fold dough over filling; press edges to seal.

3. Gently place 3 biscuits in hot oil. Cook 1½ minutes or until deep golden brown. Using tongs, gently turn over. Cook 1½ minutes or until deep golden brown. Remove to paper towels to drain. Roll in sugar mixture. Repeat with remaining biscuits, cooking 2 or 3 at a time. Serve warm.

1 Serving: Calories 464 (Calories from Fat 271); Total Fat 31g; Saturated Fat 5g; Trans Fat 0g; Cholesterol 2mg; Sodium 568mg; Total Carbohydrate 42g; Dietary Fiber 1g; Sugars 21g; Protein 4g

BLUEBERRY BURRITO BLINTZES

In this triple-blueberry-flavored version of classic blintzes, the creamy filling is conveniently tucked in a flour tortilla—simply delicious!

PREP TIME: 30 MINUTES
TOTAL TIME: 30 MINUTES

MAKES 8 SERVINGS

Kathy Anne Sepich, Gresham, Oregon
Bake-Off® Contest 42, 2006

1 bag (10 oz) frozen blueberries

½ cup small-curd 2% reduced-fat cottage cheese

2 tablespoons granulated sugar

½ teaspoon grated lemon peel

¼ to ½ teaspoon ground nutmeg

¼ to ½ teaspoon ground cinnamon

4 oz reduced-fat cream cheese (Neufchâtel), softened

1 container (6 oz) fat free blueberry patch yogurt

1 package (11 oz) flour tortillas for burritos, 8 inch (8 tortillas)

1 tablespoon butter or margarine

¼ cup blueberry syrup

Powdered sugar, if desired

Lemon slices, if desired

1. Thaw blueberries as directed on bag; drain, reserving liquid. In medium bowl, mix cottage cheese, sugar, lemon peel, nutmeg, cinnamon, cream cheese and yogurt until well blended. Gently stir in drained blueberries.

2. Place large sheet of waxed paper on work surface. For each blintz, place 1 flour tortilla on waxed paper. Spoon about ⅓ cup yogurt mixture in center. With pastry brush, moisten outer edge of tortilla with reserved blueberry liquid. Fold opposite sides of tortilla over filling, ends meeting in center; fold remaining 2 sides of tortilla over each other.

3. In 12-inch nonstick skillet, melt ½ tablespoon of the butter over medium heat. Cook 4 blintzes at a time, seam side down, about 2 minutes on each side until golden brown. Place blintzes, seam side down, on serving platter; drizzle with syrup. Sprinkle with powdered sugar; garnish with lemon slices.

1 Serving: Calories 268 (Calories from Fat 80); Total Fat 9g; Saturated Fat 4g; Trans Fat 0g; Cholesterol 15mg; Sodium 562mg; Total Carbohydrate 40g; Dietary Fiber 2g; Sugars 13g; Protein 8g

BLUEBERRY BURRITO BLINTZES (*page 77*)

BANANA-FILLED CARAMEL CHOCOLATE CREPES (*opposite*)

BANANA-FILLED CARAMEL CHOCOLATE CREPES

Heavenly! Enjoy a restaurant-fancy brunch entrée at home.

PREP TIME: 1 HOUR 25 MINUTES
TOTAL TIME: 1 HOUR 25 MINUTES

MAKES 12

Sherry Smith, Bunker Hill, West Virginia
Bake-Off® Contest 43, 2008

CREPES

- 1 box (18.4 oz) Pillsbury™ Family Size Chocolate Fudge Brownie Mix
- 1 cup Pillsbury BEST™ All Purpose Flour
- 3 eggs, beaten
- 1½ cups milk
- ½ cup vegetable oil

FILLING

- 1 cup butter
- ½ cup granulated sugar
- 2 teaspoons vanilla
- 1 tablespoon finely grated lemon peel
- 6 large firm ripe bananas, cut into ¼-inch slices

TOPPINGS

- ½ cup caramel ice cream topping
- ¾ cup frozen (thawed) whipped topping
- 2 tablespoons powdered sugar
- ¼ cup chopped walnuts

1. In large bowl, stir together brownie mix, flour, eggs, milk and oil until smooth.

2. Spray 10-inch skillet with no-stick cooking spray; heat over medium heat. Pour about ¼ cup batter onto center of skillet. Immediately rotate skillet until thin layer of batter covers bottom. Cook over medium heat about 1 minute, turning once, until top appears slightly dry.

3. Remove crepe to cutting board, flipping crepe over so first cooked side is facing up. Immediately roll up crepe; place on plate to cool. Cover with kitchen towel. Repeat with remaining batter.

4. In large saucepan, cook butter and granulated sugar over medium heat, stirring frequently, until sugar is dissolved. Stir in vanilla and lemon peel until well mixed. Add banana slices; gently toss until coated and slightly softened.

5. Fill 1 crepe at a time, keeping remaining crepes covered. Gently unroll crepe; fill with slightly less than ¼ cup banana filling. Reroll crepe; place seam side down on platter. Repeat with remaining crepes. Top crepes with drizzle of caramel topping and dollop of whipped topping. Sprinkle tops lightly with powdered sugar; sprinkle with walnuts. Serve immediately.

1 Serving: Calories 490 (Calories from Fat 270); Total Fat 30g; Saturated Fat 13g; Trans Fat 0.5g; Cholesterol 90mg; Sodium 190mg; Total Carbohydrate 47g; Dietary Fiber 2g; Sugars 22g; Protein 5g

STRAWBERRIES AND CHOCOLATE SUGAR COOKIE CREPES

Turn sugar cookie dough into melt-in-your-mouth crepes.

PREP TIME: 25 MINUTES
TOTAL TIME: 25 MINUTES

MAKES 8 SERVINGS

Juliette Smith, Houston, Texas
Bake-Off® Contest 46, 2013

1 cup milk

1 roll Pillsbury™ refrigerated sugar cookie dough

2 eggs

3 tablespoons butter, melted

¼ cup chocolate flavored hazelnut spread

2 cups quartered fresh strawberries

2 cups whipped cream topping (from aerosol can)

1. Pour milk into microwavable measuring cup. Microwave 60 seconds or until warm. In medium bowl, break up cookie dough. Add milk. Beat 30 seconds with electric mixer on medium speed. Add eggs. Beat 30 seconds longer or until batter is smooth.

2. Heat 10-inch nonstick skillet over medium-high heat. Add 1 teaspoon of the melted butter. Lift and tilt pan in circular motion to coat bottom. Pour ⅓ cup of the crepe batter into pan. Quickly lift and tilt pan in circular motion to spread batter evenly over bottom. Cook 30 seconds to 1 minute. Slide large spatula under crepe and carefully turn over, smoothing crepe with tip of spatula if necessary. Cook 30 seconds to 1 minute longer. Remove from heat and gently slide crepe onto flat plate. Repeat with remaining butter and batter to make 8 crepes, adjusting temperature as needed. Stack crepes to keep warm.

3. Meanwhile, in small microwavable bowl, microwave chocolate hazelnut spread 15 to 20 seconds until of drizzling consistency. Stir in remaining 1 teaspoon melted butter.

4. To serve, fold crepes in quarters; arrange one crepe on each dessert plate. Top each serving with ¼ cup strawberries. Drizzle with chocolate hazelnut spread mixture. Serve with whipped cream.

1 Serving: Calories 370 (Calories from Fat 180); Total Fat 20g; Saturated Fat 9g; Trans Fat 3.5g; Cholesterol 75mg; Sodium 280mg; Total Carbohydrate 43g; Dietary Fiber 0g; Sugars 5g; Protein 5g

TROPICAL SUNSHINE FLATCAKES WITH ORANGE CREAM

Tired of the same old pancakes? Head for the tropics with a unique and tasty breakfast.

PREP TIME: 30 MINUTES
TOTAL TIME: 40 MINUTES

MAKES 8 SERVINGS

Audrey Madyun, Toledo, Ohio
Bake-Off® Contest 43, 2008

FLATCAKES

1 tablespoon vegetable oil

½ cup pecan chips

1 can (13.9 oz) Pillsbury™ refrigerated orange flavor sweet rolls with icing (8 rolls)

TOPPING

2 tablespoons butter

2 firm ripe medium bananas, sliced (2 cups)

2 tablespoons lime juice

1 cup fresh or canned, drained, pineapple tidbits

1 jar (12 oz) pineapple ice cream topping

1 can (15 oz) mandarin orange segments in light syrup, drained

ORANGE CREAM

1¼ cups whipping cream

Icing from can of sweet rolls

1. Heat oven to 400°F. Generously brush 1 tablespoon oil on 1 large cookie sheet or 2 small cookie sheets.

2. Cut waxed paper or cooking parchment paper into 16 (6-inch square) sheets. Sprinkle about 1½ teaspoons pecans on 1 sheet. Place 1 orange roll on pecans; sprinkle 1½ teaspoons pecans on top of roll. Top with another waxed paper square. Using rolling pin, roll evenly until orange roll is 4½ inches in diameter; remove waxed paper. Place roll on cookie sheet. Repeat with remaining rolls, placing 1 inch apart on cookie sheet. Set icing aside.

3. Bake 8 to 10 minutes or until golden brown.

4. Meanwhile, in 10-inch skillet, melt butter over medium-high heat. Add bananas, lime juice and pineapple; cook 1 minute, stirring frequently. Reduce heat to medium-low. Gently stir in pineapple topping; cook 3 to 4 minutes, stirring occasionally, until warmed. Gently stir in orange segments.

5. In medium bowl, beat whipping cream and icing with electric mixer on high speed until soft peaks form.

6. To serve, top flatcakes with warm pineapple topping and orange cream.

1 Serving: Calories 560 (Calories from Fat 250); Total Fat 28g; Saturated Fat 11g; Trans Fat 2.5g; Cholesterol 50mg; Sodium 380mg; Total Carbohydrate 72g; Dietary Fiber 2g; Sugars 46g; Protein 4g

QUICK AND FRUITY CRESCENT WAFFLES

Waffles without the batter?
It's easy with Pillsbury™
crescents.

PREP TIME: 25 MINUTES
TOTAL TIME: 25 MINUTES

MAKES 4 SERVINGS

Renee Heimerl, Oakfield, Wisconsin
Bake-Off® Contest 43, 2008

¼ cup pecan pieces

1 can (8 oz) Pillsbury™ refrigerated crescent dinner rolls (8 rolls)

½ cup blueberry spreadable fruit

1 container (6 oz) 99% fat free blueberry yogurt

1 firm ripe banana, cut into ¼-inch slices

½ cup whipped cream from aerosol can

¼ teaspoon ground cinnamon

Fresh blueberries, if desired

1. Heat oven to 200°F. Heat square or rectangular waffle maker. Spray with original no-stick cooking spray.

2. Meanwhile, in 8-inch nonstick skillet, toast pecans over medium heat 5 to 7 minutes, stirring frequently, until lightly browned. Remove from skillet; set aside.

3. Separate crescent dough into 8 triangles. Place 2 or 3 triangles at a time on waffle maker, leaving at least ½ inch of space around each triangle. Close lid of waffle maker; cook 1 to 2 minutes or until golden brown. Place cooked waffles on cookie sheet in oven to keep warm.

4. In 1-quart saucepan, heat spreadable fruit and yogurt over medium heat 2 to 3 minutes, stirring occasionally, until hot.

5. To serve, stack 2 crescent waffles, slightly overlapping, on each of 4 serving plates. Spoon ¼ of the fruit sauce over each serving; top each serving with ¼ of the banana slices and 1 tablespoon of the pecans. Top with whipped cream; sprinkle lightly with cinnamon. Garnish with blueberries.

1 Serving: Calories 450 (Calories from Fat 170); Total Fat 19g; Saturated Fat 6g; Trans Fat 3g; Cholesterol 10mg; Sodium 470mg; Total Carbohydrate 63g; Dietary Fiber 5g; Sugars 35g; Protein 7g

A Peek Inside the Bake-Off® Contest:

A pink stove might seem like an odd lucky charm, but it worked wonders for 1955 Bake-Off® Finalist Rosemary Sport. "At the time, we were living in a housing project. When I won, what I actually won was the trip and the range, but nobody made me an offer to buy the range at a fair price. So I kept that pink range in the living room in a crate."

The prize range "was the pivotal point in our lives," she says today. "We had wanted to buy a house anyway, but the motivation hadn't shown up—and the baby had." Motivation arrived after Rosemary's Bake-Off® trip, in the form of the pink electric range and the prestige of having been a Bake-Off® Contest finalist. "I went to work as a chef in a restaurant in Newton Highlands. I said 'I am a Bake-Off® finalist,' and that made everybody think I could do anything. That's how I got the job in the restaurant. I worked nights and my husband worked days—and we saved my money to buy a house to put the range in!" Two years later Rosemary and her family were the proud owners of a house in Abington, Massachusetts. What happened to the pink electric range? "I bought a pink refrigerator and painted my kitchen in pink tones."

Rosemary raised her family in that house with a pink kitchen, cooking up quite a few batches of her tasty, Bake-Off® prize-winning Peach Elizabeth for dessert. A few years later Rosemary returned to school and won a prestigious Fulbright scholarship. Rosemary credits her Pillsbury recognition with starting her on "an uphill spiral," which, when paired with her hard work, created great success. When the spark of inspiration comes—even in the form of a pink electric range—anything is possible.

SAUSAGE STUFFED WAFFLES WITH BLACKBERRY SAUCE

PREP TIME: 10 MINUTES

TOTAL TIME: 30 MINUTES

MAKES 8 SERVINGS

Sherry Ricci, Mendon, New York
Bake-Off® Contest 46, 2013

8 pork sausage patties

1 can Pillsbury™ Grands!™ Flaky Layers Original refrigerated biscuits

1 jar (12 oz) blackberry jam

1 tablespoon powdered sugar

1 pint fresh blackberries

8 sprigs fresh mint leaves

1. Heat waffle maker. Spray with original no-stick cooking spray. Meanwhile, heat sausage patties in microwave as directed on package. Drain on paper towels. Cool about 10 minutes.

2. Separate dough into 8 biscuits. Slit each biscuit on side, forming a deep pocket. Place sausage patty in each pocket. Press edges to seal.

3. Place 2 to 4 biscuits in waffle maker; close lid. Cook 4 to 5 minutes or until golden brown. Remove from waffle maker and cover with foil to keep warm. Repeat with remaining biscuits.

4. Meanwhile, in 1-quart saucepan, mix jam and 2 tablespoons water. Cook over low heat, stirring occasionally, until smooth and thoroughly heated.

5. To serve, sprinkle biscuits with powdered sugar. Drizzle with blackberry sauce; garnish with blackberries and mint leaves. Serve with remaining sauce.

1 Serving: Calories 420 (Calories from Fat 160); Total Fat 18g; Saturated Fat 5g; Trans Fat 2g; Cholesterol 20mg; Sodium 740mg; Total Carbohydrate 57g; Dietary Fiber 2g; Sugars 3g; Protein 7g

LEMON-BLUEBERRY MACADAMIA WAFFLES

Waffles made with Pillsbury™ refrigerated sugar cookie dough—yes! Enjoy this decadent breakfast treat anytime—topped with fresh blueberry sauce, whipped cream and macadamia nuts. Yum!

PREP TIME: 20 MINUTES
TOTAL TIME: 40 MINUTES

MAKES 4 SERVINGS

David Dahlman, Chatsworth, California
Bake-Off® Contest 46, 2013

1 roll Pillsbury™ refrigerated sugar cookie dough

¾ cup blueberry preserves

1½ cups fresh or frozen (thawed and drained) blueberries

1 cup whipping cream

2 eggs

2 teaspoons grated lemon peel

½ cup chopped roasted unsalted macadamia nuts

1. Let cookie dough stand at room temperature 10 minutes to soften. In 1-quart saucepan, mix blueberry preserves and blueberries. Cook over medium heat, stirring occasionally, until thoroughly heated. Set aside; keep warm.

2. In small bowl, beat ½ cup of the cream with electric mixer on medium-high speed 1 to 2 minutes or until stiff peaks form; refrigerate.

3. Heat oven to 200°F. Heat waffle maker. (Waffle makers without a nonstick coating may need to be brushed with vegetable oil or sprayed with no-stick cooking spray.)

4. In large bowl, break up cookie dough; add eggs and lemon peel. Beat with electric mixer on medium speed 1 minute or until smooth. Beat in remaining ½ cup of the cream and 3 tablespoons water until smooth; stir in nuts.

5. Pour ⅓ cup batter onto each waffle section. (Check manufacturer's directions for recommended amount of batter.) Close lid of waffle maker. Cook 4 to 6 minutes or until waffles are golden brown. Carefully remove waffles to heatproof plate; keep warm in oven. Repeat with remaining batter.

6. To serve, top each waffle with blueberry mixture and whipped cream.

1 Serving: Calories 1030 (Calories from Fat 500); Total Fat 55g; Saturated Fat 22g; Trans Fat 7g; Cholesterol 185mg; Sodium 430mg; Total Carbohydrate 123g; Dietary Fiber 2g; Sugars 6g; Protein 10g

BLUEBERRY MUFFIN TOPS

Pillsbury™ refrigerated sugar cookie dough gives these muffin tops a head start for an easy blueberry breakfast treat that's delicious served warm or cool.

PREP TIME: 20 MINUTES
TOTAL TIME: 45 MINUTES

MAKES 28 SERVINGS

Susan Spicko, Newton Falls, Ohio
Bake-Off® Contest 44, 2010

1 roll (16.5 oz) Pillsbury™ refrigerated sugar cookies

1¼ cups Pillsbury™ BEST™ All Purpose Flour

¼ cup sugar

2 tablespoons butter

½ teaspoon baking powder

¼ teaspoon baking soda

1 package (3 oz) cream cheese, softened

1 egg

⅓ cup milk

2 to 3 teaspoons grated lemon peel

2 tablespoons lemon juice

1¼ cups fresh or frozen (thawed) blueberries

1. Let cookie dough stand at room temperature 10 minutes to soften. Meanwhile, heat oven to 350°F. Line 2 cookie sheets with cooking parchment paper. In small bowl, mix ¼ cup of the flour, sugar and butter with fork until crumbly; set aside to use for topping. In another small bowl, mix remaining 1 cup flour, baking powder and baking soda; set aside.

2. In medium bowl, beat dough and cream cheese with electric mixer on medium speed until blended. On low speed, beat in egg, milk, lemon peel and lemon juice until well blended. Stir in flour mixture just until combined (do not over-mix; mixture will be a thick batter). Carefully fold in blueberries. (If using thawed berries, rinse and pat dry with paper towel before adding.)

3. Drop batter by heaping tablespoonfuls 1 to 2 inches apart onto cookie sheets, using rubber spatula to scrape batter from tablespoon. Bake 3 minutes; remove from oven. Sprinkle each muffin top with about 1 teaspoon crumb topping; immediately return to oven.

4. Bake 16 to 20 minutes longer or just until edges begin to brown. Cool on cookie sheets 2 to 3 minutes before removing to cooling racks. Serve warm or cool.

1 Serving: Calories 120 (Calories from Fat 45); Total Fat 5g; Saturated Fat 2g; Trans Fat 1g; Cholesterol 15mg; Sodium 95mg; Total Carbohydrate 18g; Dietary Fiber 0g; Sugars 9g; Protein 1g

BOSTON CREAM FRENCH TOAST

PREP TIME: 20 MINUTES

TOTAL TIME: 1 HOUR 25 MINUTES

MAKES 10 SERVINGS

Kristen Abbott, Paoli, Pennsylvania

Bake-Off® Contest 46, 2013

1 can Pillsbury™ refrigerated crusty French loaf

1 can (14 oz) sweetened condensed milk

1¼ cups whipping cream

2 egg yolks

2 teaspoons vanilla

¾ cup chocolate flavored hazelnut spread

1. Heat oven to 350°F. Bake crusty French loaf as directed on can. Cool 10 minutes.

2. Meanwhile, spray 13x9-inch pan (dark pan not recommended) with no-stick cooking spray. In large bowl, beat sweetened condensed milk, 1 cup of the cream, the egg yolks and vanilla with wire whisk until well blended. Pour half of mixture into pan.

3. Trim ends of bread; cut into 20 (about ¾-inch) slices. Place slices over egg mixture. Pour remaining egg mixture over bread slices. Bake 30 to 33 minutes or until light golden brown.

4. In medium microwaveable bowl, microwave remaining ¼ cup cream on High 20 to 30 seconds or until hot. Stir in hazelnut spread until smooth.

5. For each serving, with spatula, remove 1 piece French toast and place custard side up on serving plate. Top with another piece of French toast, custard side down, forming a sandwich with custard in the center. Drizzle each serving with 1 tablespoon chocolate hazelnut sauce.

1 Serving: Calories 460 (Calories from Fat 220); Total Fat 25g; Saturated Fat 12g; Trans Fat 0.5g; Cholesterol 90mg; Sodium 270mg; Total Carbohydrate 50g; Dietary Fiber 0g; Sugars 22g; Protein 8g

CHOCOLATE DOUGHNUT POPPERS

Baked doughnuts, not fried, have an ooey, gooey chocolate center to discover. A sweet glaze ups the irresistible.

PREP TIME: 20 MINUTES
TOTAL TIME: 40 MINUTES
MAKES 9 SERVINGS

Megan Beimer, Alexandria, Virginia
Bake-Off® Contest 47, 2014

1 can Pillsbury™ Crescent Recipe Creations™ refrigerated seamless dough sheet

5 tablespoons chocolate flavored hazelnut spread

1 tablespoon butter, melted

½ cup powdered sugar

3 to 4 teaspoons milk

¼ cup finely chopped nuts

1. Heat oven to 350°F. Lightly sprinkle work surface with Pillsbury™ BEST™ All Purpose or Unbleached Flour. Unroll dough on work surface; press to form 12x9-inch rectangle. With pizza cutter or sharp knife, cut into 3 rows by 3 rows to make 9 rectangles.

2. Spoon rounded teaspoonful hazelnut spread onto center of each rectangle. Brush edges of rectangles with melted butter. Bring dough up around filling to cover completely. Pinch edges together to seal; shape into ball. Place seam side down, 2 inches apart, on ungreased cookie sheet.

3. Bake 12 to 15 minutes or until golden brown. Remove from cookie sheet to cooling rack. Cool 5 minutes.

4. Meanwhile, in small bowl, mix powdered sugar and milk with whisk until smooth and thin enough to glaze. Dip top of each doughnut popper into glaze; place on parchment paper. Let stand about 1 minute or until glaze is set. Place nuts in small bowl. Dip each popper into glaze again, then into nuts. Serve warm.

1 Serving: Calories 210 (Calories from Fat 100); Total Fat 11g; Saturated Fat 3.5g; Trans Fat 0g; Cholesterol 0mg; Sodium 220mg; Total Carbohydrate 24g; Dietary Fiber 0g; Sugars 7g; Protein 2g

MIDDLEBERRY SCONES

PREP TIME: 15 MINUTES

TOTAL TIME: 35 MINUTES

MAKES 8 SERVINGS
(1 SCONE PER SERVING)

Lisa Keys, Middlebury, Connecticut
Bake-Off® Contest 36, 1994

SCONES

1½ cups Pillsbury™ BEST™ all-purpose flour

½ cup Pillsbury™ BEST™ whole wheat flour

2 tablespoons sugar

1 tablespoon baking powder

½ teaspoon salt

½ teaspoon ground cinnamon

1 teaspoon grated orange peel

¼ cup butter or margarine

⅔ cup half-and-half

1 egg

⅓ cup raspberry or strawberry preserves

1 teaspoon sugar

SPREAD AND GARNISH

1 package (3 oz) cream cheese, softened

16 fresh raspberries or strawberries, if desired

1 teaspoon grated orange peel, if desired

1. Heat oven to 425°F. Lightly grease cookie sheet. In large bowl, mix flours, 2 tablespoons sugar, the baking powder, salt, cinnamon and 1 teaspoon orange peel. With fork or pastry blender, cut in butter until mixture looks like coarse crumbs.

2. In small bowl, mix half-and-half and egg. Add to flour mixture; stir just until dry ingredients are moistened. Place dough on well-floured surface; knead lightly 4 times. Divide in half; pat each half into 8-inch circle. Place 1 circle on cookie sheet; spread preserves to within 1 inch of edge. Place remaining circle over preserves; pinch edges to seal. Sprinkle top with 1 teaspoon sugar. Cut into 8 wedges; do not separate.

3. Bake 15 to 18 minutes or until edges are golden brown. Cut through scones. Serve warm with cream cheese; garnish with remaining ingredients.

1 Scone: Calories 282 (Calories from Fat 110); Total Fat 13g; Saturated Fat 7g; Trans Fat 0g; Cholesterol 60 mg; Sodium 431mg; Total Carbohydrate 38g; Dietary Fiber 2g; Sugars 12g; Protein 5g

CHOCOLATE CRESCENT TWIST

With a nod to European bakeries, this streusel-topped cinnamon-chocolate pastry is a divine companion to a cup of coffee!

PREP TIME: 15 MINUTES
TOTAL TIME: 1 HOUR 15 MINUTES
MAKES 6 SERVINGS

Steve Grieger, Oceanside, California
Bake-Off® Contest 38, 1998

STREUSEL

3 tablespoons all-purpose flour

3 tablespoons sugar

1 tablespoon butter or margarine

TWIST

1 can (8 oz) Pillsbury™ refrigerated crescent dinner rolls or 1 can (8 oz) Pillsbury™ Crescent Recipe Creations™ refrigerated seamless dough sheet

⅔ cup semisweet chocolate chips

1 tablespoon sugar

1 to 3 teaspoons ground cinnamon

1 tablespoon butter or margarine, melted

1 tablespoon semisweet chocolate chips

1. Heat oven to 375°F. Grease and flour 8x4- or 7x3-inch loaf pan. In small bowl, mix flour and 3 tablespoons sugar. With fork, cut in 1 tablespoon butter until crumbly.

2. If using crescent rolls: Unroll dough; press to form 12x8-inch rectangle. Firmly press perforations to seal. If using dough sheet: Unroll dough; press to form 12x8-inch rectangle.

3. Sprinkle dough rectangle with ⅔ cup chocolate chips, 1 tablespoon sugar, the cinnamon and half of the streusel mixture.

4. Starting at long side, roll up; pinch edge to seal. Join ends to form ring; pinch to seal. Gently twist ring to form figure 8; place in pan. Brush with melted butter; sprinkle with remaining half of streusel. Sprinkle with 1 tablespoon chocolate chips; press lightly into dough.

5. Bake 30 to 40 minutes or until deep golden brown. Cool on cooling rack 20 minutes. Remove from pan. Serve warm.

1 Serving: Calories 330 (Calories from Fat 160); Total Fat 18g; Saturated Fat 9g; Trans Fat 2g; Cholesterol 10mg; Sodium 320mg; Total Carbohydrate 39g; Dietary Fiber 1g; Sugars 22g; Protein 4g

MOCHA LATTE BACON DANISH

PREP TIME: 20 MINUTES
TOTAL TIME: 45 MINUTES

MAKES 8 SERVINGS

Marla Clark, Albuquerque, New Mexico
Bake-Off® Contest 46, 2013

6 oz cream cheese, softened

¼ cup powdered sugar

1 can Pillsbury™ Grands!™ Big & Flaky refrigerated crescent dinner rolls

1 egg, beaten

6 slices bacon, chopped

½ cup chocolate flavored hazelnut spread

2 teaspoons instant espresso powder

1. Heat oven to 350°F. Line large cookie sheet with parchment paper. In small bowl, beat cream cheese and powdered sugar with electric mixer on medium speed until smooth.

2. Remove dough from can; do not unroll. Cut into 8 slices. Place cut side down 2 inches apart on cookie sheet. Press each slice into 3-inch round. Press 1½-inch-wide indentation in center of each round. Spoon tablespoons cream cheese mixture into each indentation. Brush edges with beaten egg.

3. Bake 15 to 20 minutes or until golden brown. Cool 10 minutes.

4. Meanwhile, in 10-inch nonstick skillet, cook bacon over medium heat 15 minutes, stirring frequently, until crisp. Drain well.

5. In small microwavable bowl, mix chocolate hazelnut spread and espresso powder. Microwave on High 30 seconds; stir. Drizzle over rolls. Sprinkle with bacon.

1 Serving: Calories 370 (Calories from Fat 220); Total Fat 24g; Saturated Fat 9g; Trans Fat 2g; Cholesterol 55mg; Sodium 510mg; Total Carbohydrate 31g; Dietary Fiber 0g; Sugars 5g; Protein 7g

DOUBLE CHOCOLATE-ORANGE SCONES

Sweetened with mini chocolate chips and orange marmalade, then drizzled with chocolate when cooled, these easy breakfast scones are a special treat any time of the day!

PREP TIME: 30 MINUTES
TOTAL TIME: 1 HOUR 15 MINUTES
MAKES 12 SERVINGS

Michelle Gauer, Spicer, Minnesota
Bake-Off® Contest 44, 2010

SCONES

2 cups Pillsbury BEST™ All Purpose Flour

½ cup granulated sugar

⅓ cup baking cocoa

2 teaspoons baking powder

½ teaspoon salt

⅓ cup cold butter, cut into ½-inch pieces

¾ cup whipping cream

¼ cup sweet orange marmalade

1 teaspoon pure vanilla extract

1 cup mini chips semi-sweet chocolate

1 tablespoon raw sugar (turbinado sugar), if desired

2 oz semi-sweet baking chocolate or ⅓ cup mini chips semi-sweet chocolate

ORANGE BUTTER

½ cup butter, softened

¼ cup powdered sugar

2 tablespoons sweet orange marmalade

1. Heat oven to 375°F. Line large cookie sheet with cooking parchment paper. In large bowl, mix flour, granulated sugar, cocoa, baking powder and salt. Cut in ⅓ cup cold butter, using pastry blender or fork, until mixture looks like coarse crumbs.

2. In small bowl, gently stir cream, ¼ cup marmalade and vanilla until mixed. Make a well in center of crumb mixture; add cream mixture to well. Stir with fork until crumb mixture is moistened and dough is sticky. Gently stir in 1 cup mini chocolate chips. Form dough into a ball.

3. On well-floured surface, roll or pat dough into 9-inch round, ¾ inch thick. Using knife dipped in flour, cut round into 12 wedges. Place 1 inch apart on cookie sheet. Sprinkle with raw sugar. Bake 14 to 18 minutes or until edges are set. Remove from cookie sheet to cooling rack. Cool 30 minutes.

4. In small microwavable bowl, microwave baking chocolate uncovered on High 30 seconds until softened; stir until smooth. Drizzle diagonally over scones.

5. In small bowl, beat ½ cup butter and powdered sugar with fork until light and fluffy. Stir in 2 tablespoons marmalade. Serve with scones.

1 Serving: Calories 420 (Calories from Fat 25g); Total Fat 25g; Saturated Fat 15g; Trans Fat 0.5g; Cholesterol 50mg; Sodium 280mg; Total Carbohydrate 46g; Dietary Fiber 3g; Sugars 24g; Protein 4g

DOUBLE CHOCOLATE–ORANGE SCONES *(opposite)*

RASPBERRY NUT DREAMS *(page 94)*

RASPBERRY NUT DREAMS

Don't have a food processor? Use a sharp knife to coarsely chop the nuts for these Hawaiian-inspired sweet rolls.

PREP TIME: 25 MINUTES
TOTAL TIME: 55 MINUTES

MAKES 16 SERVINGS

Kathy Sweeton, Long Beach, California
Bake-Off® Contest 42, 2006

½ cup salted roasted macadamia nuts

⅓ cup packed brown sugar

2 packages (3 oz each) cream cheese, softened

1 cup organic frozen raspberries (from 10-oz bag), thawed as directed on bag, drained and liquid reserved

1 can (16.3 oz) Pillsbury™ Grands!™ Flaky Layers refrigerated buttermilk biscuits

⅓ cup flaked coconut

1. Heat oven to 350°F. Lightly spray 16 regular-size muffin cups with cooking spray. In food processor, process macadamia nuts with on-and-off motions until coarsely chopped. Add brown sugar; process until combined. Place in small bowl; set aside.

2. In same food processor, process cream cheese, 2 tablespoons nut mixture and 1 to 2 tablespoons reserved raspberry liquid until smooth.

3. Separate dough into 8 biscuits; separate each into 2 layers, making a total of 16 rounds. Lightly press each round in bottom and up side of muffin cup. Spoon about ½ tablespoon cream cheese mixture into each dough-lined cup. Top each evenly with raspberries, 1 tablespoon remaining nut mixture and 1 teaspoon coconut.

4. Bake 14 to 22 minutes or until coconut is lightly browned. Cool in pan 5 minutes before serving.

1 Serving: Calories 190 (Calories from Fat 100); Total Fat 11g; Saturated Fat 4g; Trans Fat 2g; Cholesterol 10mg; Sodium 320mg; Total Carbohydrate 19g; Dietary Fiber 2g; Sugars 8g; Protein 3g

BLUEBERRY POPPY SEED BRUNCH CAKE

Blueberry topping and a luscious lemon-poppy seed cake are a winning combination in a Bake-Off® Contest grand prize recipe.

PREP TIME: 30 MINUTES
TOTAL TIME: 1 HOUR 35 MINUTES
MAKES 16 SERVINGS

Linda Rahman, Petaluma, California
Bake-Off® Contest 34, 1990 Grand Prize Winner

CAKE

⅔ cup sugar

½ cup margarine or butter, softened

2 teaspoons grated lemon peel

1 egg

1½ cups Pillsbury™ BEST™ All Purpose or Unbleached Flour

2 tablespoons poppy seed

½ teaspoon baking soda

¼ teaspoon salt

½ cup sour cream

FILLING

2 cups fresh or frozen blueberries, thawed, drained on paper towels

⅓ cup sugar

2 teaspoons Pillsbury™ BEST™ All Purpose or Unbleached Flour

¼ teaspoon nutmeg

GLAZE

⅓ cup powdered sugar

1 to 2 teaspoons milk

1. Heat oven to 350°F. Grease and flour bottom and sides of 9- or 10-inch springform pan. In large bowl, combine ⅔ cup sugar and margarine; beat until light and fluffy. Add lemon peel and egg; beat 2 minutes at medium speed.

2. Lightly spoon flour into measuring cup; level off. In medium bowl, combine 1½ cups flour, poppy seed, baking soda and salt; mix well. Add to margarine mixture alternately with sour cream, beating until well combined. Spread batter over bottom and 1 inch up sides of greased and floured pan, making sure batter on sides is ¼ inch thick.

3. In another medium bowl, combine all filling ingredients; mix well. Spoon over batter.

4. Bake at 350°F for 45 to 55 minutes or until crust is golden brown. Cool 10 minutes; remove sides of pan.

5. In small bowl, blend powdered sugar and enough milk for desired drizzling consistency. Drizzle over warm cake. Serve warm or cool.

1 Roll: Calories 185 (Calories from Fat 70); Total Fat 8g; Saturated Fat 2g; Trans Fat 1g; Cholesterol 15mg; Sodium 139mg; Total Carbohydrate 28g; Dietary Fiber 1g; Sugars 17g; Protein 2g

COUNTRY APPLE COFFEE CAKE

The apple and cinnamon flavors are down-home, but the innovative shaping of this refrigerated biscuit coffee cake gives it a pastry shop look that's easy to duplicate.

PREP TIME: 20 MINUTES
TOTAL TIME: 1 HOUR 10 MINUTES
MAKES 8 SERVINGS

Susan Porubcan, Jefferson, Wisconsin
Bake-Off® Contest 31, 1984 Grand Prize Winner

COFFEE CAKE

2 tablespoons butter or margarine, softened

1½ cups chopped peeled apples

1 can (12 oz) Pillsbury™ Grands!™ Jr. Golden Layers™ refrigerated biscuits

⅓ cup packed brown sugar

¼ teaspoon ground cinnamon

⅓ cup light corn syrup

1½ teaspoons whiskey, if desired

1 egg

½ cup pecan halves or pieces

GLAZE

⅓ cup powdered sugar

¼ teaspoon vanilla

1 to 2 teaspoons milk

1. Heat oven to 350°F. Using 1 tablespoon of the butter, generously grease 9-inch round cake pan or 8-inch square pan. Spread 1 cup of the apples in pan.

2. Separate dough into 10 biscuits. Cut each into quarters. Arrange biscuit pieces, points up, over apples. Top with remaining ½ cup apples.

3. In small bowl, mix remaining 1 tablespoon butter, the brown sugar, cinnamon, corn syrup, whiskey and egg; beat 2 to 3 minutes or until sugar is partially dissolved. Stir in pecans. Spoon over biscuit pieces and apples.

4. Bake 35 to 45 minutes or until deep golden brown. Cool 5 minutes. If desired, remove from pan.

5. In small bowl, mix glaze ingredients, adding enough milk for desired drizzling consistency. Drizzle over warm cake. Serve warm or cool. Cover and refrigerate any remaining coffee cake.

1 Serving: Calories 330 (Calories from Fat 130); Total Fat 14g; Saturated Fat 2g; Trans Fat 3.5mg; Cholesterol 25mg; Sodium 510mg; Total Carbohydrate 47g; Dietary Fiber 2g; Sugars 24g; Protein 4g

CARAMELIZED PEACH UPSIDE-DOWN COFFEE CAKE

Bake up a new sweet peachy coffee cake delight using Pillsbury™ sugar cookie dough.

PREP TIME: 30 MINUTES
TOTAL TIME: 1 HOUR 30 MINUTES

MAKES 8 SERVINGS

Brenda Watts, Gaffney, South Carolina
Bake-Off® Contest 45, 2012

1 roll Pillsbury™ refrigerated sugar cookie dough

¼ cup unsalted or salted butter

⅓ cup packed brown sugar

½ teaspoon ground cinnamon

1½ cups thinly sliced peeled peaches or frozen sliced peaches, thawed

2 teaspoons baking powder

2 eggs

½ cup half-and-half

⅔ cup peach preserves

3 tablespoons orange juice

⅓ cup chopped pecans

1. Let cookie dough stand at room temperature 10 minutes to soften. Meanwhile, heat oven to 350°F. Line 10-inch spring-form pan with foil. Lightly spray bottom and side of foil-lined pan with no-stick cooking spray. In 12-inch skillet over medium heat, melt butter. Stir in brown sugar and cinnamon until blended. Add sliced peaches; cook 4 to 6 minutes or until peaches are tender, stirring occasionally. Spoon and spread peach mixture over bottom of pan.

2. In large bowl, break up cookie dough. Add baking powder and eggs. Beat with electric mixer on medium speed about 1 minute or until well blended. On low speed, beat in half-and-half an additional minute or until cookie dough mixture is smooth and creamy. Pour mixture evenly over peaches in pan.

3. Bake 35 to 50 minutes or until toothpick inserted into center comes out clean. Cool 2 minutes. Place heatproof serving plate upside down over pan; turn plate and pan over. Remove pan. Carefully remove foil. Cool 5 minutes.

4. Meanwhile, in small microwavable bowl, stir peach preserves and orange juice together until blended. Microwave peach mixture on High 30 to 60 seconds or until warm.

5. To serve, drizzle coffee cake with peach mixture and sprinkle with pecans.

1 Serving: Calories 490 (Calories from Fat 299); Total Fat 22g; Saturated Fat 8g; Trans Fat 3.5g; Cholesterol 80mg; Sodium 350mg; Total Carbohydrate 69g; Dietary Fiber 1g; Sugars 48g; Protein 5g

Starters, Appetizers, and Breads

Julie McIntire of Independence, Missouri, presents her Salmon Crescent Sushi Rolls (page 135) at the 45th Bake-Off Contest in Orlando, Florida.

CHAI CRUNCH

All the flavors of exotic chai tea are here in a crunchy snack mix.

PREP TIME: 10 MINUTES
TOTAL TIME: 1 HOUR 25 MINUTES
MAKES 22 SERVINGS

Carol Thoreson, Rockford, Illinois
Bake-Off® Contest 41, 2004

½ cup butter or margarine

½ cup honey

1 teaspoon instant nonfat dry milk or non-dairy original-flavor creamer, if desired

½ teaspoon ground cardamom

½ teaspoon ground ginger

½ teaspoon ground cinnamon

½ teaspoon ground nutmeg

½ teaspoon ground cloves

½ teaspoon dried orange peel

1 teaspoon vanilla

3 cups Corn Chex™ cereal

3 cups Wheat Chex™ cereal

3 cups Honey Nut Cheerios™ cereal

1 cup dried banana chips

1½ cups sliced almonds

1. Heat oven to 300°F. In 1-quart saucepan, melt butter over medium heat. Remove from heat. Stir in honey, dry milk, cardamom, ginger, cinnamon, nutmeg, cloves, orange peel and vanilla until well mixed.

2. In 15x11-inch roasting pan, mix all remaining ingredients. Pour butter mixture over cereal mixture; toss until evenly coated.

3. Bake at 300°F for 45 to 60 minutes or until golden brown, stirring every 15 minutes. Pour mixture onto waxed paper or paper towels. Cool 15 minutes before serving. Store in tightly covered container.

CLEVER IDEA: *For spicy flavor, omit dried milk or creamer. If dried milk is used, flavor will be less spicy and a little sweeter.*

1 Serving: Calories 189 (Calories from Fat 85); Total Fat 10g; Saturated Fat 5g; Trans Fat 0g; Cholesterol 10mg; Sodium 147mg; Total Carbohydrate 26g; Dietary Fiber 3g; Sugars 11g; Protein 3g

SALSA REUBEN DIP

By the time the oven is pre-heated, you can mix up this spread that serves a bunch.

PREP TIME: 15 MINUTES
TOTAL TIME: 45 MINUTES
MAKES 32 SERVINGS

Martha Davis, Inman, South Carolina
Bake-Off® Contest 37, 1996

1 package (8 oz) cream cheese, softened

1 container (8 oz) sour cream

1 cup salsa

4 oz finely chopped cooked corned beef

¾ cup shredded Swiss cheese (3 oz)

½ cup sauerkraut, rinsed, drained and chopped

1 to 2 cloves garlic, minced

Dash salt, if desired

Dash pepper, if desired

Chopped fresh cilantro

Cocktail rye bread slices, tortilla chips or cut-up fresh vegetables

1. Heat oven to 350°F. In large bowl with electric mixer, beat cream cheese, sour cream and salsa on medium speed until well blended. Add all remaining ingredients except cilantro and bread; beat on low speed until thoroughly mixed. Spoon mixture into ungreased 9- or 10-inch pie pan or quiche dish.

2. Bake 20 to 30 minutes or until thoroughly heated. Sprinkle with cilantro. Serve warm with bread slices for dipping. Store in refrigerator.

1 Serving: Calories 100 (Calories from Fat 50); Total Fat 6g; Saturated Fat 3g; Trans Fat 0g; Cholesterol 20mg; Sodium 250mg; Total Carbohydrate 8g; Dietary Fiber 0g; Sugars 1g; Protein 3g

BAKED CLAM DIP WITH CRUSTY FRENCH BREAD DIPPERS

Toast Pillsbury™ French loaf to create the perfect partner for a winning bubbly, triple-cheese clam dip.

PREP TIME: 50 MINUTES
TOTAL TIME: 2 HOURS 30 MINUTES
MAKES 30 SERVINGS

Christine Field, Shillington, Pennsylvania
Bake-Off® Contest 45, 2012

2 cans Pillsbury™ refrigerated crusty French loaf

1 can (18.5 oz) light New England clam chowder soup

1 package (8 oz) ⅓-less-fat cream cheese (Neufchâtel), softened

1 can (10.5 oz) white clam sauce

1 cup shredded mozzarella cheese (4 oz)

½ cup grated Parmesan cheese

1½ cups panko bread crumbs

1 cup butter, melted

¼ teaspoon parsley flakes

1 tablespoon garlic powder

1. Heat oven to 350°F. Spray 1½-quart shallow oven-proof serving dish or 9½-inch glass deep-dish pie plate with no-stick cooking spray.

2. Spray 2 large cookie sheets with no-stick cooking spray. With serrated knife, cut both loaves of dough in half lengthwise. Place 2 pieces of dough, cut sides down, on each cookie sheet; cut 4 or 5 (½-inch-deep) slashes diagonally on top of each loaf.

3. Bake 17 to 20 minutes or until golden brown. Cool on cooling rack.

4. Meanwhile, in food processor bowl, place soup. Cover; process until almost smooth. Add cream cheese; cover and process until well blended. Pour into large bowl; stir in clam sauce, mozzarella cheese, Parmesan cheese and 1 cup of the bread crumbs until well mixed. Pour mixture into serving dish.

5. In small bowl, stir 2 tablespoons of the butter, remaining $\frac{1}{2}$ cup bread crumbs and parsley flakes until well mixed. Sprinkle crumb mixture evenly over clam soup mixture.

6. Bake 35 to 40 minutes or until bubbly and light golden brown around edges. Cool 30 minutes on cooling rack.

7. Meanwhile, in small bowl, stir remaining butter and garlic powder until well mixed. With serrated knife, cut each loaf into $\frac{1}{4}$-inch slices; place on cookie sheets. Brush each slice with garlic-butter mixture (reserve remaining garlic-butter mixture).

8. Bake slices 5 to 8 minutes or until golden brown. Remove from oven; turn slices. Brush with remaining garlic-butter mixture. Bake 5 to 8 minutes or until golden brown and crisp. Cool 5 minutes. Serve bread with warm clam dip. Store any remaining clam dip in refrigerator.

1 Serving: Calories 180 (Calories from Fat 100); Total Fat 11g; Saturated Fat 6g; Trans Fat 0g; Cholesterol 25mg; Sodium 400mg; Total Carbohydrate 16g; Dietary Fiber 0g; Sugars 2g; Protein 5g

A Peek Inside the Bake-Off® Contest:

Challenges are as certain in life as love and taxes. "I like challenges," says Leonard Thompson. Len remembers childhood baking, using a temperamental gasoline stove. "You would have to tiptoe across the floor so the cake wouldn't fall." Len didn't get a chance to perfect his baking back then—the intervening years were dominated by the adventures of raising four children and navigating a successful career. But he always met the demands of making special time for family. "On weekends, usually on Sunday morning, it would be my pancake breakfast day, eggs, bacon, everything . . . the whole family uses my pancake recipe now.

"Since I retired I've gotten back into baking," Len says. The challenges had waited for him. For Thanksgiving he started a pecan pie, "but I made one little mistake, using a pan with holes in the bottom. Everything turned out fine—except there was a black cloud of smoke pouring out of the oven. Half the filling leaked out. And we were supposed to go to Thanksgiving dinner that day! My wife suggested I put chocolate pudding in there, so I did, topped it off with a little whipped cream, and named it 'Disaster Pie.' People really liked it, so I improved it. . . . My wife suggested that I enter it in the Bake-Off® Contest. I only sent in one entry, and lo and behold . . . " Chocolate Silk Pecan Pie was on its way to becoming a Pillsbury classic.

Len considers his journey to the Bake-Off® Contest to have been as rewarding as the outcome. "Getting to the Bake-Off® Contest is a challenge, and if you like challenges, it's a tremendous one, and I do like challenges."

CHEESY CRESCENT NACHOS

Get a jump-start on delicious homemade nachos with Pillsbury™ crescent dinner rolls. A cheesy Mexican appetizer is made spicy with green chiles and salsa.

Gregg Peroutka, Mankato, Minnesota
Bake-Off® Contest 31, 1984

PREP TIME: 15 MINUTES
TOTAL TIME: 45 MINUTES

MAKES 24 SERVINGS

1 can (8 oz) Pillsbury™ refrigerated crescent dinner rolls or 1 can (8 oz) Pillsbury™ Crescent Recipe Creations™ refrigerated seamless dough sheet

3 tablespoons cornmeal

1 can (4.5 oz) chopped green chiles, drained

1 cup shredded Cheddar cheese (4 oz)

1 cup shredded mozzarella or Monterey Jack cheese (4 oz)

Salsa or taco sauce, if desired

1. Heat oven to 350°F. If using crescent rolls: Separate dough into 4 rectangles. If using dough sheet: Cut sheet into 4 rectangles. Coat both sides of each rectangle with cornmeal. Place in ungreased 13x9-inch pan; press over bottom and ½ inch up sides to form crust. Press edges and perforations to seal. Sprinkle with any remaining cornmeal. Top evenly with chiles, Cheddar and mozzarella cheese.

2. Bake at 350°F for 24 to 28 minutes or until crust is golden brown. Cool 5 minutes. Cut into triangles or squares. Serve warm with salsa.

CLEVER IDEAS:

- *Like it spicy? Prepare these nachos with shredded hot-pepper cheese.*

- *Chopped green onions are a colorful, crunchy topping for the salsa.*

- *These crisp nachos go great with bowls of hot chili at lunch or supper. Red and green grapes are a refreshing finish.*

1 Serving: Calories 74 (Calories from Fat 42); Total Fat 5g; Saturated Fat 2g; Trans Fat 0.5g; Cholesterol 10mg; Sodium 153mg; Total Carbohydrate 5g; Dietary Fiber 0g; Sugars 1g; Protein 3g

TEX-MEX APPETIZER TART

Wedge a new appetizer into your plans. Refrigerated pie crust holds a pepped-up cheese filling.

PREP TIME: 10 MINUTES
TOTAL TIME: 55 MINUTES

MAKES 16 SERVINGS

Richard McHargue, Richmond, Kentucky
Bake-Off® Contest 38, 1998

1 box Pillsbury™ refrigerated pie crusts, softened as directed on box

1½ cups shredded Colby-Monterey Jack cheese blend (6 oz)

½ cup roasted red bell peppers (from 7.25-oz jar), drained, chopped

½ cup mayonnaise

1 can (4.5 oz) chopped green chiles

¼ cup chopped fresh cilantro or parsley

1. Heat oven to 375°F. Remove crust from pouch; place flat on ungreased cookie sheet.

2. In medium bowl, mix cheese, roasted bell peppers, mayonnaise and chiles. Spread over crust to within 1 inch of edge. Fold crust edge over filling to form 1-inch border; flute.

3. Bake 25 to 35 minutes or until crust is golden brown. Sprinkle with cilantro. Let stand 10 minutes. Cut into wedges. Serve warm.

1 Serving: Calories 150 (Calories from Fat 110); Total Fat 12g; Saturated Fat 4g; Trans Fat 0g; Cholesterol 15mg; Sodium 200mg; Total Carbohydrate 7g; Dietary Fiber 0g; Sugars 0g; Protein 3g

MANGO SALSA APPETIZER BITES

Party time! Two-bite pie crust appetizers are loaded with a fiesta of flavors.

PREP TIME: 55 MINUTES
TOTAL TIME: 55 MINUTES

MAKES 24 SERVINGS

Judy Mortensen, Antelope, California
Bake-Off® Contest 45, 2012

1 large mango, seed removed, peeled, diced

¼ cup finely chopped red onion

4 teaspoons finely chopped jalapeño chile

½ teaspoon dill weed

½ teaspoon salt

¼ cup finely chopped fresh cilantro

1 teaspoon grated lime peel

2 tablespoons fresh lime juice

1 Pillsbury™ refrigerated pie crust, softened as directed on box

1 large avocado, pitted, peeled and diced

½ cup crumbled chèvre (goat) cheese (2 oz)

Fresh cilantro, if desired

1. In small bowl, combine mango, red onion, jalapeño, dill weed, salt, ¼ cup cilantro, lime peel and 1 tablespoon of the lime juice; mix well. Cover; refrigerate.

2. Heat oven to 450°F. Unroll pie crust. Using 2-inch round cookie cutter, cut 24 rounds from pie crust, rerolling dough if necessary. Press 1 round in bottom and up side of each of 24 ungreased mini muffin cups.

3. Bake 6 to 9 minutes or until golden brown. Cool crusts in cups 15 minutes. Transfer from cups to cooling racks.

4. Meanwhile, in small bowl, combine avocado, goat cheese and remaining 1 tablespoon lime juice. With fork, mash avocado and goat cheese until mixture is smooth. Spoon mixture into small re-sealable food-storage plastic bag; seal bag. Cut off corner of bag.

5. Pipe 1 teaspoon avocado mixture into each cup; top with scant 1 tablespoon of the mango salsa (cups will be full). Garnish with cilantro. Store covered in refrigerator.

1 Serving: Calories 60 (Calories from Fat 35); Total Fat 4g; Saturated Fat 1.5g; Trans Fat 0g; Cholesterol 0mg; Sodium 110mg; Total Carbohydrate 6g; Dietary Fiber 0g; Sugars 1g; Protein 1g

PARTY SPINACH CUPS

PREP TIME: 30 MINUTES

TOTAL TIME: 50 MINUTES

MAKES 20 APPETIZERS

Beverly Ann Crummey, Brooksville, Florida

Bake-Off® Contest 33, 1988

1 tablespoon olive or vegetable oil

⅔ cup chopped onion

1 small clove garlic, finely chopped

1 box (9-oz.) frozen spinach, thawed, well drained

1 can (4-oz.) mushroom pieces and stems, drained, chopped

½ cup Italian-style bread crumbs

½ cup shredded Cheddar cheese (2-oz.)

½ cup plain yogurt

⅛ teaspoon salt

⅛ teaspoon pepper

1 can (12-oz.) Pillsbury™ Golden Layers™ refrigerated flaky biscuits

Sour cream, if desired

1. Heat oven to 375°F. Lightly grease 20 miniature muffin cups.

2. In 10-inch skillet, heat oil over medium heat until hot. Cook and stir onion and garlic in oil until tender. Stir in spinach, mushrooms, bread crumbs, cheese, yogurt, salt and pepper. Separate dough into 10 biscuits; separate each into 2 layers. Place each layer in muffin cup; firmly press in bottom and up side. Spoon generous tablespoonful of spinach mixture into each cup.

3. Bake 15 to 20 minutes or until golden brown. Garnish each with sour cream. Serve warm.

1 Serving: Calories 90 (Calories from Fat 40); Total Fat 4g; Saturated Fat 1.5g; Trans Fat 1g; Cholesterol 0mg; Sodium 310mg; Total Carbohydrate 10g; Dietary Fiber 1g; Sugars 2g; Protein 3g

MUSHROOM PIROSHKI APPETIZERS

Mushroom mixture filled into Pillsbury™ refrigerated pie crusts baked together form tasty appetizers ready to accompany your dinner.

PREP TIME: 50 MINUTES
TOTAL TIME: 1 HOUR 5 MINUTES

MAKES 30 SERVINGS

Marcia L. Gallner, Omaha, Nebraska
Bake-Off® Contest 29, 1980

¼ cup butter or margarine

½ cup finely chopped onion (1 medium)

1 package (8 oz) fresh mushrooms, finely chopped

1 hard-cooked egg yolk, chopped

½ to ¾ teaspoon salt

¼ teaspoon pepper

3 boxes Pillsbury™ refrigerated pie crusts, softened as directed on box

1 egg, beaten, if desired

1. In 10-inch skillet, melt butter over medium heat. Cook and stir onion in butter just until tender. Add mushrooms; cook 3 minutes, stirring frequently. Stir in egg yolk, salt and pepper. Cool 10 minutes.

2. Meanwhile, heat oven to 400°F. Unroll 3 pie crusts. With 2¾-inch round cutter, cut 10 rounds from each crust.

3. Spoon rounded teaspoon of cooled mushroom mixture onto half of each pie-crust round. Fold dough over filling; press edges with fork to seal. Place on ungreased large cookie sheet. Brush with beaten egg.

4. Bake 12 to 15 minutes or until light golden brown. Serve warm.

1 Serving: Calories 60 (Calories from Fat 40); Total Fat 4.5g; Saturated Fat 2g; Trans Fat 0g; Cholesterol 10mg; Sodium 110mg; Total Carbohydrate 6g; Dietary Fiber 0g; Sugars 0g; Protein 0g

MOZZARELLA AND PESTO CRESCENT TARTS

Enjoy all the benefits of this really cool appetizer—it can be served cold, it tastes great and it's easy to make!

PREP TIME: 20 MINUTES
TOTAL TIME: 35 MINUTES

MAKES 16 SERVINGS

Tracie Ojakangas, Springfield, Missouri
Bake-Off® Contest 39, 2000

1 can (8 oz) Pillsbury™ refrigerated crescent dinner rolls or 1 can (8 oz) Pillsbury™ Crescent Recipe Creations™ refrigerated seamless dough sheet

2 tablespoons basil pesto

2 medium tomatoes, seeded, sliced

1 small red onion, thinly sliced

1 to 2 teaspoons chopped fresh rosemary or ½ teaspoon dried rosemary leaves

½ cup diced fresh mozzarella cheese or shredded mozzarella cheese (2 oz)

¼ cup shredded fresh Parmesan cheese (1 oz)

1. Heat oven to 425°F.

2. If using crescent rolls: Unroll dough into 2 long rectangles. Place 3 inches apart on ungreased cookie sheet. Firmly press perforations to seal. If using dough sheet: Unroll dough and cut into 2 long rectangles. Place 3 inches apart on ungreased cookie sheet.

3. Press to form two 10x3-inch strips, forming rim around edge of dough. Spread each strip with 1 tablespoon pesto. Top each with tomatoes, onion and rosemary. Sprinkle each with mozzarella and Parmesan cheese.

4. Bake 10 to 14 minutes or until edges are golden brown and cheese is melted. Cut each into crosswise slices. Serve warm or cool.

CLEVER IDEA: *Four medium plum (Roma) tomatoes can be substituted for the regular tomatoes.*

1 Serving: Calories 90 (Calories from Fat 45); Total Fat 5g; Saturated Fat 2g; Trans Fat 1g; Cholesterol 0mg; Sodium 170mg; Total Carbohydrate 7g; Dietary Fiber 0g; Sugars 2g; Protein 3g

CAPRESE PESTO MARGHERITA STACKERS

These party appetizers taste incredibly upscale, but they are actually easily prepared using mozzarella balls and Pillsbury™ refrigerated breadsticks.

PREP TIME: 30 MINUTES
TOTAL TIME: 55 MINUTES

MAKES 24 SERVINGS

Julie Beckwith, Crete, Illinois
Bake-Off® Contest 44, 2010

1 container (8 oz) fresh mozzarella ciliegine cheese (24 cherry-size balls)

1 can (11 oz) Pillsbury™ refrigerated original breadsticks (12 breadsticks)

3 tablespoons basil pesto

1 tablespoon olive oil

2 tablespoons grated Parmesan cheese

24 frilled toothpicks

24 grape tomatoes

24 fresh basil leaves

1. Heat oven to 375°F. Spray 24 mini muffin cups with no-stick cooking spray. Drain cheese balls; pat dry with paper towels.

2. On work surface, unroll dough; separate into 12 breadsticks. Cut each breadstick in half crosswise; press each half into 3x2-inch rectangle.

3. Spread rounded ¼ teaspoon of the pesto lengthwise down center of each dough rectangle. Place 1 cheese ball on each rectangle. Carefully stretch dough around cheese; pinch edges to seal completely. Place seam sides down in muffin cups. Brush with oil; sprinkle with Parmesan cheese.

4. Bake 14 to 20 minutes or until deep golden brown. Cool in pan 5 minutes. Remove from pan. With each toothpick, spear tomato and basil leaf; insert into cheese ball. Serve warm.

CLEVER IDEA: *For recipe success, use fresh mozzarella cheese balls only.*

1 Serving: Calories 80 (Calories from Fat 40); Total Fat 4.5g; Saturated Fat 2g; Trans Fat 0g; Cholesterol 5mg; Sodium 160mg; Total Carbohydrate 7g; Dietary Fiber 0g; Sugars 1g; Protein 4g

SPINACH-CHEESE BALLS WITH PASTA SAUCE

An electric deep fryer can be used to fry these flavor-packed appetizer balls.

PREP TIME: 60 MINUTES
TOTAL TIME: 60 MINUTES
MAKES 20 SERVINGS

· **Ann Walker**, Conroe, Texas
Bake-Off® Contest 42, 2006

1 box (9 oz) frozen chopped spinach

1 egg, beaten

1 cup shredded Parmesan cheese (4 oz)

1 cup shredded mozzarella cheese (4 oz)

1 teaspoon salt

1 teaspoon onion powder

1 teaspoon garlic powder

1 teaspoon dried oregano leaves

½ cup sour cream

2 tablespoons extra-virgin olive oil

1 container (15 oz) ricotta cheese

2 cups Pillsbury™ BEST™ all-purpose flour

Vegetable oil for deep frying

¾ cup Italian-style bread crumbs

1 jar (25.5 oz) organic garden vegetable pasta sauce, heated

1. Remove frozen spinach from pouch; place in colander. Rinse with warm water until thawed; drain well. Squeeze spinach dry with paper towel.

2. Meanwhile, in large bowl, mix egg, both cheeses, salt, onion powder, garlic powder, oregano, sour cream, oil and ricotta cheese until well blended. Add spinach to cheese mixture; mix well. Stir in flour, 1 cup at a time, until well blended.

3. Fill 10-inch skillet half full with oil; heat over medium heat until candy/deep-fry thermometer reads 350°F. (Or use deep fryer; add oil to fill line and heat to 350°F.)

4. Meanwhile, place bread crumbs in small bowl. Shape spinach-cheese mixture into 1¹/₂-inch balls (about 40), using about 1¹/₂ tablespoons for each; roll in bread crumbs and place on cookie sheet.

5. Fry 6 balls at a time 4 to 6 minutes, turning as necessary, until golden brown. With slotted spoon, remove balls from skillet; place on paper towels to drain. Cool 2 minutes before serving; serve with warm pasta sauce for dipping

1 Serving: Calories 220 (Calories from Fat 110); Total Fat 12g; Saturated Fat 4.5g; Trans Fat 0g; Cholesterol 30mg; Sodium 450mg; Total Carbohydrate 18g; Dietary Fiber 1g; Sugars 2g; Protein 9g

SPINACH CHEESE BALLS WITH PASTA SAUCE (*page 115*)

CHIPOTLE MEATBALL APPETIZERS (*opposite*)

CHIPOTLE MEATBALL APPETIZERS

Cheesy meatballs meet flaky crescents in savory little appetizers.

PREP TIME: 30 MINUTES
TOTAL TIME: 50 MINUTES
MAKES 24 SERVINGS

Carolyn Westerback, Gresham, Oregon
Bake-Off® Contest 46, 2013

1 can Pillsbury™ refrigerated crescent dinner rolls (8 ct)

1 tablespoon vegetable oil

½ cup finely chopped onion

1 chipotle chile in adobo sauce, finely chopped, plus 3 tablespoons adobo sauce (from 7-oz can)

12 frozen Italian-style meatballs (½ oz. each), thawed, halved

2 tablespoons water

4 pieces mozzarella string cheese (1 oz. each)

1 medium avocado, pitted, peeled, cut into 24 small slices

1. Heat oven to 350°F. Spray 24 mini muffin cups with no-stick cooking spray. Separate dough into 4 rectangles; press perforations to seal. Cut each rectangle into 6 squares. Press each square in bottom and up side of mini muffin cup. Bake 6 minutes. Remove from oven. Using handle of wooden spoon, immediately make 1½-inch indentation in center of each cup.

2. Meanwhile, in 10-inch skillet, heat oil over medium heat. Add onion; cook 2 to 3 minutes or until tender. Stir in chipotle chile and the adobo sauce, meatballs and 2 tablespoons water. Cover; reduce heat to low. Cook 3 to 4 minutes, stirring occasionally or until thoroughly heated. Remove meatballs from skillet. Spoon ½ teaspoon of the sauce into each cup. Top each with one meatball half, cut side up.

3. Cut each piece string cheese lengthwise in half; cut each half crosswise into thirds. Top each meatball with 1 piece string cheese. Bake 6 to 10 minutes longer or until edges are golden brown. Cool 1 minute; remove from cups.

4. Top each meatball cup with 1 avocado slice; secure with wooden toothpick. Serve warm.

1 Serving: Calories 90 (Calories from Fat 50); Total Fat 6g; Saturated Fat 2g; Trans Fat 0g; Cholesterol 5mg; Sodium 150mg; Total Carbohydrate 5g; Dietary Fiber 0g; Sugars 0g; Protein 3g

CRESCENT CABBAGE AND BEEF BUNDLES

Relish ground beef and cabbage bundles made using Pillsbury® crescent dinner rolls. Serve these appetizers with a flavorful mayonnaise and horseradish sauce.

PREP TIME: 35 MINUTES
TOTAL TIME: 55 MINUTES

MAKES 8 SERVINGS

Debra Twichell, Valley Falls, Kansas
Bake-Off® Contest 31, 1984

SANDWICHES

1 lb. lean ground beef

⅓ cup chopped onion

2 cups chopped cabbage

½ teaspoon salt

¼ teaspoon pepper

2 oz. (½ cup) shredded Cheddar cheese

2 (8-oz.) cans Pillsbury™ refrigerated crescent dinner rolls

SAUCE

½ cup mayonnaise or salad dressing

3 tablespoons purchased horseradish sauce

1. Heat oven to 375°F. In large skillet, cook ground beef and onion over medium-high heat until beef is thoroughly cooked, stirring frequently. Drain.

2. Add cabbage, salt and pepper; mix well. Reduce heat to medium; cover and cook 10 to 15 minutes or until cabbage is crisp-tender, stirring occasionally. Cool 5 minutes. Stir in cheese.

3. Separate dough into 16 triangles; press or roll each until slightly larger. Spoon about ¼ cup beef mixture on shortest side of each triangle. Roll up, starting at shortest side of triangle, gently wrapping dough around beef mixture and rolling to opposite point. Pinch edges to seal. Place point side down on ungreased large cookie sheet.

4. Bake at 375°F for 15 to 20 minutes or until golden brown. Meanwhile, in small bowl, combine mayonnaise and horseradish sauce; blend well. Serve sauce with sandwiches.

1 Serving: Calories 447 (Calories from Fat 268); Total Fat 30g; Saturated Fat 9g; Trans Fat 3.5g; Cholesterol 46mg; Sodium 750mg; Total Carbohydrate 24g; Dietary Fiber 1g; Sugars 5g; Protein 18g

CREAMY CORN-FILLED SWEET PEPPERS

Perk up your appetizer party with cheesy, corn-stuffed peppers wrapped in flaky crescents.

PREP TIME: 30 MINUTES
TOTAL TIME: 1 HOUR
MAKES 22 APPETIZERS

Jody Walker, Madison, Mississippi
Bake-Off® Contest 47, 2014

1 bag (11 oz) frozen honey roasted sweet corn

1 package (8 oz) cream cheese, softened

1 cup grated Parmesan cheese

1 teaspoon Italian seasoning

11 mini sweet peppers (3 to 4 inches long), cut in half lengthwise leaving stem attached, seeded

1 can Pillsbury™ Crescent Recipe Creations™ refrigerated seamless dough sheet or 1 can Pillsbury™ refrigerated crescent dinner rolls (8 oz)

3 tablespoons butter, melted

1. Heat oven to 375°F. Line large cookie sheet with parchment paper. Microwave corn as directed on bag. Cut open bag; cool 10 minutes.

2. In large bowl, beat cream cheese with electric mixer on medium speed until smooth. Add corn, ½ cup of the Parmesan cheese and ½ teaspoon of the Italian seasoning; mix well. Place cream cheese mixture in large resealable food-storage plastic bag. Cut off ½ inch from corner of bag. Squeeze bag to pipe filling into each pepper half.

3. Unroll dough. (If using crescent roll dough, firmly press perforations to seal.) Press to form 11x9-inch rectangle. With pizza cutter or knife, cut dough into 22 (9x ½-inch) strips.

4. Wrap 1 dough strip around each pepper, from stem to tip. Place filling-side up on cookie sheet, tucking in ends of dough under pepper.

5. Bake 12 to 18 minutes or until golden brown.

6. Meanwhile, in small bowl, mix melted butter and remaining ½ teaspoon Italian seasoning. Remove peppers from oven; brush with butter mixture. Sprinkle remaining ½ cup Parmesan cheese evenly over peppers. Serve warm.

1 Serving: Calories 130 (Calories from Fat 70); Total Fat 8g; Saturated Fat 4.5g; Trans Fat 0g; Cholesterol 20mg; Sodium 250mg; Total Carbohydrate 10g; Dietary Fiber 1g; Sugars 3g; Protein 4g

MEATBALL AND BREADSTICK SUB SKEWERS

Twist an easy 9 ingredients into fun meatball and breadstick skewers begging for a dip in pasta sauce.

PREP TIME: 25 MINUTES
TOTAL TIME: 55 MINUTES

MAKES 6 SERVINGS

Kim Van Dunk, Caldwell, New Jersey
Bake-Off® Contest 46, 2013

1 box (9 oz) frozen chopped spinach

2 slices whole wheat sandwich bread, torn in pieces

¼ cup half-and-half

1 lb ground turkey

¾ teaspoon salt

¼ teaspoon pepper

1 can Pillsbury™ refrigerated original breadsticks

1 cup shredded mozzarella cheese (4 oz)

2 cups tomato pasta sauce

1. Heat oven to 375°F. Line 2 large cookie sheets with parchment paper.

2. Microwave frozen spinach as directed on box; cool slightly. Squeeze dry with paper towels.

3. In medium bowl, mix bread pieces and half-and-half; let stand 1 minute. With fork, mash bread until well blended. Add spinach, turkey, salt and pepper; mix well. Shape mixture into 36 (1½-inch) balls.

4. Unroll dough; separate into 12 breadsticks. Thread one end of a breadstick on 10-inch skewer; add 1 meatball, leaving ¼ inch between dough and meatball. Repeat threading with breadstick and 2 additional meatballs. Place 1 inch apart on cookie sheet. Repeat with remaining breadsticks and meatballs.

5. Bake 18 to 22 minutes, rotating cookie sheets halfway through bake time, or until meatballs are no longer pink in center and meat thermometer in center of meatball reads 165°F. Sprinkle each meatball skewer with about 1 tablespoon cheese. Bake 3 to 4 minutes longer or until cheese is melted.

6. Meanwhile, in 1-quart saucepan, cook sauce over medium-low heat 3 to 4 minutes, stirring occasionally, or until thoroughly heated. Serve with meatball skewers.

CLEVER IDEA: *Use a 1-tablespoon cookie scoop to easily measure and shape meatballs.*

1 Serving: Calories 470 (Calories from Fat 190); Total Fat 21g; Saturated Fat 7g; Trans Fat 0g; Cholesterol 80mg; Sodium 1000mg; Total Carbohydrate 42g; Dietary Fiber 3g; Sugars 8g; Protein 29g

ASIAN-SPICED CASHEW-CHICKEN PIADINIS

Take a shortcut with refrigerated pizza crust in an Italian flatbread appetizer stuffed with Eastern flavors.

PREP TIME: 25 MINUTES
TOTAL TIME: 55 MINUTES

MAKES 12 SERVINGS

Brett Youmans, Reading, Pennsylvania
Bake-Off® Contest 44, 2010

1 package (6 oz) refrigerated grilled chicken breast strips or 6 oz cooked chicken breast, finely chopped

⅓ cup chopped green onions (about 5 medium)

¼ cup chopped cashews, halves and pieces

2 tablespoons teriyaki sauce

1 tablespoon toasted sesame oil

1 tablespoon lime juice

2 teaspoons finely chopped garlic

2 teaspoons grated gingerroot

2 cups coleslaw mix (shredded cabbage and carrots)

⅓ cup loosely packed, chopped fresh cilantro

1 can (11 oz) Pillsbury™ refrigerated thin pizza crust

1 egg

1 teaspoon water

1 tablespoon chopped fresh cilantro, if desired

1. Heat oven to 400°F. Line large cookie sheet with cooking parchment paper or spray with no-stick cooking spray.

2. In 12-inch nonstick skillet, cook chopped chicken, onions, cashews, teriyaki sauce, sesame oil, lime juice, garlic and gingerroot over medium-high heat 2 to 3 minutes, stirring occasionally, until thoroughly heated. Stir in coleslaw mix; cook about 2 minutes or until vegetables are crisp-tender. Stir in ⅓ cup cilantro. Cool completely, about 15 minutes.

3. Unroll pizza crust dough. Starting at center, press dough into 16x12-inch rectangle. Cut rectangle into 12 (4-inch) squares (3 rows lengthwise and 4 rows crosswise).

4. Working with 1 dough square at a time, spoon slightly less than $\frac{1}{4}$ cup chicken mixture onto center. Fold 1 corner of square over filling; bring opposite corner over first corner, tucking under roll to seal. Leave other ends open. Place on cookie sheet. In small bowl, beat egg and water until well blended; lightly brush over piadinis.

5. Bake 9 to 11 minutes or until golden brown. Remove from cookie sheets to cooling racks. Garnish each piadini with $\frac{1}{4}$ teaspoon cilantro. Serve warm.

> **CLEVER IDEA:** *Refrigerated ground fresh ginger in a tube or jar can be substituted for the fresh gingerroot.*

1 Serving: Calories 130 (Calories from Fat 45); Total Fat 5g; Saturated Fat 1g; Trans Fat 0g; Cholesterol 25mg; Sodium 340mg; Total Carbohydrate 15g; Dietary Fiber 1g; Sugars 2g; Protein 6g

A Peek Inside the Bake-Off® Contest:

When Leona Schnuelle captured the grand prize in the 12th Bake-Off® Contest, she suddenly found herself a celebrity in her small town of Crab Orchard, Nebraska. "Everyone seems happier when I arrive, even at the square dances. They say 'Hi, Mrs. Pillsbury!' Even though I miss a *do-si-do* now and then—they think I can bake a dilly of a bread! And the mail I receive! It's exciting to hear from all the different people with all their different ways of life, yet they all seem so interested in a bread recipe." Especially with a loaf like Dilly Casserole Bread to pique their interest.

CHICKEN CURRY CRESCENT SNACKS

Have weekend guests or company stopping by? These tasty snacks fill the bill whether served with a cool drink in the late afternoon or to accompany a chilled summer tomato or cucumber soup for lunch.

PREP TIME: 10 MINUTES
TOTAL TIME: 30 MINUTES

MAKES 8 SERVINGS

Michael Foy, Portland, Oregon
Bake-Off® Contest 38, 1998

1 (4.25-oz.) can chicken spread
¼ cup raisins
¼ cup coarsely chopped salted cashews
½ teaspoon curry powder
1 (8-oz.) can Pillsbury™ refrigerated crescent dinner rolls
Mango chutney, if desired

1. Heat oven to 375°F. In small bowl, combine chicken spread, raisins, cashews and curry powder; mix well.

2. Separate dough into 8 triangles. Spoon about 1 tablespoon chicken mixture on shortest side of each triangle. Roll up, starting at shortest side of triangle and rolling to opposite point. Place rolls, point side down, on ungreased cookie sheet; curve into crescent shape.

3. Bake at 375°F for 8 to 12 minutes or until golden brown. Cool 5 minutes. Serve topped with chutney.

CLEVER IDEA: *If using Pillsbury™ Big & Flaky large refrigerated crescent dinner rolls, make as directed—except fill each triangle with about 2 tablespoons chicken mixture and increase bake time to 11 to 15 minutes.*

1 Serving: Calories 174 (Calories from Fat 97); Total Fat 11g; Saturated Fat 3g; Trans Fat 1.5g; Cholesterol 10mg; Sodium 359mg; Total Carbohydrate 17g; Dietary Fiber 0g; Sugars 5g; Protein 6g

A Peek Inside the Bake-Off® Contest:

Earlier this century the traditional woman's work really was never done. Each week required a full day of baking, of washing and of ironing. Few would return to those days, but it did leave space for quiet family interaction that many feel is unfortunately missing from modern life. "My grandmother had a hearth oven, which she used to bake bread for the week," Gilda Lester recalls. "I helped her, and she always saved a small piece of dough for a pizza for me. I wouldn't give up those days with my grandmother for anything. I helped start the fire, then when the embers had smoldered for just the right amount of time, we cleared the oven for the loaves of bread. Most of my recipes are in my head. They are things that my grandmother, and then my mother, passed on to me." It's this history that helped Gilda create her Spicy Broccoli Aïoli Pizza for the 36th Bake-off Contest.

MEXICAN PARTY WINGS

These wings pack a double punch with sassy flavors in the chicken coating and in the dipping sauce.

PREP TIME: 20 MINUTES
TOTAL TIME: 55 MINUTES

MAKES 24 SERVINGS

Pat Murphy, Modesto, California
Bake-Off® Contest 40, 2002

- 1 cup purchased ranch salad dressing
- 1 (4.5-oz.) can chopped green chiles
- ½ cup Pillsbury™ BEST™ All-Purpose Flour
- 1 (1-oz.) pkg. taco seasoning mix
- 2 teaspoons oil
- 24 chicken drummettes (about 2 lb.)
- Dried parsley flakes

1. Heat oven to 350°F. Spray large cookie sheet with nonstick cooking spray or line with foil. In blender container, combine salad dressing and chiles; cover and blend until smooth. Spoon into small serving bowl. Refrigerate while making drummettes.

2. In shallow dish, combine flour and taco seasoning mix; mix well. Stir in oil with fork until well blended. Coat drummettes with flour mixture. Coat drummettes again to use up flour mixture. Place on sprayed cookie sheet.

3. Bake at 350°F for 15 minutes. Turn drummettes; bake an additional 14 to 17 minutes or until chicken is fork-tender and juices run clear. Sprinkle parsley flakes on salad dressing mixture; serve as dip with warm drummettes.

1 Serving: Calories 110 (Calories from Fat 70); Total Fat 8g; Saturated Fat 1g; Trans Fat 0g; Cholesterol 15mg; Sodium 190mg; Total Carbohydrate 4g; Dietary Fiber 0g; Sugars 2g; Protein 5g

HERB CHICKEN SLIDERS WITH RASPBERRY MUSTARD

Fresh French bread slices hold chicken patties and a hint of raspberry mustard in appetizer sandwiches made easily with refrigerated dough from Pillsbury™.

PREP TIME: 30 MINUTES
TOTAL TIME: 55 MINUTES

MAKES 10 SERVINGS

Laureen Pittman, Riverside, California
Bake-Off® Contest 44, 2010

1 egg

1 teaspoon water

1 can (11 oz) Pillsbury™ refrigerated crusty French loaf

½ cup seedless red raspberry jam

2 tablespoons Dijon mustard

2 teaspoons whole-grain Dijon mustard, if desired

1¼ lb ground chicken or turkey

4 medium green onions, chopped (¼ cup)

2 tablespoons chopped fresh Italian (flat-leaf) parsley

1 teaspoon tarragon leaves

½ teaspoon garlic powder

1 tablespoon canola oil

1 bag (5 oz) mixed baby salad greens

1 medium tomato, thinly sliced

1. Heat oven to 350°F. Spray 10 regular-size muffin cups with no-stick cooking spray. In small bowl, beat egg and water until well blended. Cut loaf of dough crosswise into 10 slices for buns. Place each slice, cut side up, in muffin cup; brush with egg mixture. Bake 16 to 22 minutes or until tops are golden brown. Remove from pan to cooling rack; cool 5 minutes.

2. Meanwhile, in small bowl, beat jam and mustards with fork or wire whisk until smooth; set aside.

3. In medium bowl, mix chicken, green onions, parsley, tarragon and garlic. Shape mixture into 10 patties, about ½ inch thick. In 12-inch nonstick skillet, heat oil over medium-high heat. Add patties; cook 3 to 5 minutes on each side, turning once, until thermometer inserted in center reads 165°F.

4. Cut each bun in half horizontally. Spoon 1 teaspoon raspberry mustard on cut sides of each bun. Place bottoms of buns on large serving platter; top each with burger, small amount of salad greens and top of bun. Garnish platter with salad greens and tomato slices. Serve with remaining raspberry mustard.

1 Serving: Calories 210 (Calories from Fat 60); Total Fat 6g; Saturated Fat 1.5g; Trans Fat 0g; Cholesterol 50mg; Sodium 290mg; Total Carbohydrate 27g; Dietary Fiber 0g; Sugars 10g; Protein 10g

HERB CHICKEN SLIDERS WITH RASPBERRY MUSTARD (*opposite*)

HAM AND CHEESE CRESCENT SNACKS (*page 128*)

HAM AND CHEESE CRESCENT SNACKS

Take a whack at snack attacks with this ham and cheese treat. On-hand ingredients are ready to bake into an effortless appetizer that you can make whenever the urge strikes.

PREP TIME: 15 MINUTES
TOTAL TIME: 40 MINUTES

MAKES 24 SERVINGS

Hall of Fame

Ronna Sue Farley, Rockville, Maryland
Bake-Off® Contest 26, 1975 Hall of Fame

1 can (8 oz) Pillsbury™ refrigerated crescent dinner rolls or 1 can Pillsbury™ Crescent Recipe Creations™ refrigerated seamless dough sheet

2 tablespoons butter or margarine, softened

1 teaspoon yellow mustard

1 cup cubed cooked ham

⅓ cup chopped onion

⅓ cup chopped green bell pepper

1 cup shredded Cheddar or American cheese (4 oz)

1. Heat oven to 375°F.

2. If using crescent rolls: On ungreased cookie sheet, unroll dough. Press or roll dough to form 13x9-inch rectangle, pressing perforations to seal. Form ¼-inch rim around edges. If using dough sheet: On ungreased cookie sheet, unroll dough. Press or roll dough to form 13x9-inch rectangle. Form ¼-inch rim around edges.

3. In small bowl, mix butter and mustard. Spread mixture over dough. Sprinkle with ham, onion, bell pepper and cheese.

4. Bake 18 to 25 minutes or until edges are golden brown. Cut into squares. Serve warm.

> **CLEVER IDEA:** *At end of step 3, recipe can be covered with plastic wrap and refrigerated up to 2 hours. Uncover and bake as directed.*

1 Snack: Calories 70 (Calories from Fat 45); Total Fat 5g; Saturated Fat 2.5g, Trans Fat 0.5g; Cholesterol 10mg; Sodium 200mg; Total Carbohydrate 4g; Dietary Fiber 0g; Sugars 0g; Protein 3g

CHILI DOG BOATS

Hot snacks ready in 30 minutes! Enjoy these appetizers made using hot dogs and Pillsbury™ Grands!™ Jr. Golden Layers™ refrigerated biscuits.

PREP TIME: 15 MINUTES

TOTAL TIME: 30 MINUTES

MAKES 10 SERVINGS

Carole Holt, Mendota Heights, Minnesota
Bake-Off® Contest 33, 1988

1 can (12 oz) Pillsbury™ Grands!™ Jr. Golden Layers™ refrigerated biscuits

10 cocktail-size hot dogs

⅓ cup chili without beans

¼ cup finely chopped onion (½ medium)

¼ cup shredded Cheddar cheese (1 oz)

1 egg

1 tablespoon prepared yellow mustard

1. Heat oven to 400°F. Separate dough into 10 biscuits; press or roll each into 4-inch round. Place hot dog in center of each biscuit round. Top each with about 1 teaspoon each of chili, onion and cheese.

2. Bring sides of dough up to center, forming half circles that stand up. Brush edges of dough with water; pinch edges tightly to seal (as dough bakes, edges will open, forming a boat shape). Place on ungreased cookie sheet.

3. In small bowl with fork, beat egg; stir in mustard. Brush mixture over top and sides of each filled biscuit.

4. Bake 9 to 13 minutes or until light golden brown. Remove from cookie sheet; serve warm or cool.

1 Serving: Calories 180 (Calories from Fat 100); Total Fat 11g; Saturated Fat 3.5g; Trans Fat 2g; Cholesterol 30mg; Sodium 540mg; Total Carbohydrate 15g; Dietary Fiber 0g; Sugars 4g; Protein 5g

CANDIED BACON AND APPLE CANAPÉS

A little time is all it takes to make these impressive appetizers, featuring easy "crackers" made from Pillsbury™ refrigerated pie crust and topped with cheese, apple and candied bacon.

PREP TIME: 60 MINUTES
TOTAL TIME: 60 MINUTES

MAKES 40 SERVINGS

Stephanie Lemus, Westlake Village, California
Bake-Off® Contest 44, 2010

1 box Pillsbury™ refrigerated pie crusts, softened as directed on box

1 egg

1 tablespoon water

1 tablespoon sea salt

⅓ cup packed dark or light brown sugar

½ teaspoon ground red pepper (cayenne)

20 thin slices center-cut bacon (about 12 oz)

½ cup water

1 teaspoon granulated sugar

1 tablespoon lemon juice

2 small Granny Smith apples

4 oz cream cheese (half of 8-oz package), softened

1¼ cups crumbled blue cheese (6 oz)

1. Heat oven to 400°F. Line large cookie sheets with cooking parchment paper. Unroll pie crusts on work surface. Using 2¼-inch round cookie cutter, cut 20 rounds from each crust, rerolling dough if necessary. Place on cookie sheet; prick each round twice with fork. In small bowl, beat egg and 1 tablespoon water until well blended; brush on rounds. Sprinkle with sea salt. Bake 7 to 10 minutes or until golden brown and crisp. Cool while preparing bacon.

2. Line 15x10x1-inch pan with cooking parchment paper. In small bowl, mix brown sugar and red pepper. Place bacon with sides touching in pan; sprinkle with brown sugar mixture. Bake 10 to 15 minutes or until sugar is hot and bubbly. Remove bacon from pan to a plate; let stand 10 to 15 minutes or until cool enough to handle. Using sharp knife, cut each bacon slice into 4 pieces.

3. Meanwhile, in small bowl, mix ½ cup water, granulated sugar and lemon juice until sugar is dissolved. Cut each unpeeled apple into 20 (2x¼-inch) slices; place in water mixture and refrigerate.

4. In another small bowl, mix cream cheese and blue cheese with wooden spoon, leaving small pieces of blue cheese visible. Spoon mixture into pastry bag fitted with ³⁄₄-inch tip; pipe onto each cracker. Drain apple slices; pat dry. For each cracker, place 1 apple slice between 2 bacon pieces; press at an angle into cheese mixture.

> **CLEVER IDEA:** *If a pastry bag is not available, use a 1-gallon re-sealable food-storage plastic bag, cutting a ³⁄₄-inch tip from one corner.*

1 Serving: Calories 90 (Calories from Fat 50); Total Fat 6g; Saturated Fat 2.5g; Trans Fat 0g; Cholesterol 15mg; Sodium 370mg; Total Carbohydrate 8g; Dietary Fiber 0g; Sugars 3g; Protein 2g

CARAMELIZED ONION AND PEPPERED BACON FLATBREAD

Jazzed-up bacon, caramelized onion, fire-roasted tomatoes and cheese? Sounds like delicious toppers to create a cheesy flatbread appetizer.

PREP TIME: 45 MINUTES
TOTAL TIME: 55 MINUTES

MAKES 24 SERVINGS

Dawn Logterman, Janesville, Wisconsin
Bake-Off® Contest 45, 2012

¼ cup firmly packed brown sugar

¼ teaspoon ground black pepper

⅛ teaspoon cayenne pepper

8 slices thick-sliced bacon

4 cups thinly sliced sweet onion (about 1 lb)

2 cloves garlic, minced

2 tablespoons butter

1 can Pillsbury™ refrigerated thin pizza crust

1 can (14.5 oz) diced tomatoes, drained

2 cups (8 oz) shredded mozzarella cheese

½ cup grated Parmesan cheese

¼ cup thinly sliced fresh basil leaves

1. Heat oven to 400°F. Line 15x10-inch pan with sides with aluminum foil. Place cooling rack in pan.

2. In large re-sealable food-storage plastic bag, combine brown sugar, black pepper and cayenne; shake to combine. Separate bacon slices and place in bag; shake to coat. Place bacon on rack in pan.

3. Bake 25 to 30 minutes, turning once halfway through baking, or until bacon is browned and thoroughly cooked. Cool completely. Chop bacon; set aside.

4. Meanwhile, in 12-inch skillet, cook onions and garlic in butter over medium heat 15 to 20 minutes, stirring frequently, or until onions are golden brown. Remove from heat; set aside.

5. Spray 15x10-inch pan with sides with no-stick cooking spray. Unroll pizza crust dough in pan; press dough to edges of pan. Bake 7 minutes. Remove from oven.

6. Spread onion mixture over partially baked crust; top with drained tomatoes. Sprinkle with mozzarella and Parmesan cheeses; top with bacon.

7. Bake 7 to 11 minutes or until crust is golden brown and cheeses are melted.

8. Remove from oven; sprinkle with basil.

1 Serving: Calories 130 (Calories from Fat 60); Total Fat 6g; Saturated Fat 3g; Trans Fat 0g; Cholesterol 15mg; Sodium 300mg; Total Carbohydrate 11g; Dietary Fiber 0g; Sugars 4g; Protein 6g

SALMON CRESCENT SUSHI ROLLS

Roll up salmon and rice in crescent dough to create a yummy appetizer to dip in classic sushi toppers.

PREP TIME: 30 MINUTES
TOTAL TIME: 55 MINUTES

MAKES 24 SERVINGS

Julie McIntire, Independence, Missouri
Bake-Off® Contest 45, 2012

1 can Pillsbury™ Crescent Recipe Creations™ refrigerated seamless dough sheet

8 oz salmon fillet (about 5 x 3 x ¾ inches), skin removed

¾ cup cooked white rice

3 tablespoons sesame seed

½ medium avocado, pitted, peeled, cut into 8 slices

¾ teaspoon wasabi paste

3 teaspoons soy sauce

1. Heat oven to 375°F. Unroll dough sheet; press into 10 x 14-inch rectangle. Cut dough in half lengthwise.

2. Cut salmon lengthwise into 6 pieces. To make each roll, spoon half of rice evenly down 1 long edge of each dough piece in a 1-inch strip to within ¼ inch of edge. Place 3 pieces salmon evenly over rice, overlapping salmon to fit if necessary. Starting at long side topped with salmon, roll up; pinch seam to seal. Sprinkle sesame seed on ungreased cookie sheet; roll and press each log in sesame seed to coat. Place rolls, seam side down, on cookie sheet.

3. Bake 12 to 17 minutes or until golden brown. Cool 5 minutes. Transfer rolls to cutting board. Using serrated knife, cut each roll into 12 slices. Cut each slice of avocado into thirds; place 1 slice on top of each roll. Serve with wasabi and soy sauce.

1 Serving: Calories 60 (Calories from Fat 30); Total Fat 3.5g; Saturated Fat 1g; Trans Fat 0g; Cholesterol 5mg; Sodium 125mg; Total Carbohydrate 6g; Dietary Fiber 0g; Sugars 0g; Protein 3g

LOADED POTATO PINWHEELS

Apps and drinks at home? Roll up a cheesy bacon and potatoes mix in crescents for an awesome appetizer.

PREP TIME: 20 MINUTES
TOTAL TIME: 45 MINUTES
MAKES 28 SERVINGS

Glori Spriggs, Henderson, Nevada
Bake-Off® Contest 46, 2013 Grand Prize Winner

- 1 bag (11.8 oz) frozen grilled potatoes
- 1¼ cups finely shredded sharp Cheddar cheese (5 oz)
- ½ cup cooked real bacon bits (from a jar or package)
- 3 tablespoons milk
- 1 can Pillsbury™ Crescent Recipe Creations™ refrigerated seamless dough sheet or 1 can (8-oz) Pillsbury™ refrigerated crescent dinner rolls
- ⅓ cup sour cream
- 2 tablespoons finely chopped green onion tops (3 medium)

1. Heat oven to 350°F. Spray 2 large cookie sheets with no-stick cooking spray. Microwave frozen potatoes 3 to 4 minutes to thaw. In medium bowl, with fork, mash potatoes, leaving some small pieces. Stir in cheese, ⅓ cup of the bacon bits and the milk until well blended.

2. If using crescent dough sheet, unroll dough on cutting board; press into 14x8-inch rectangle. If using crescent rolls, unroll dough on cutting board, press into 14x8-inch rectangle, firmly pressing perforations to seal. Cut into 2 rectangles, 14x4 inches each. Spread half of the potato mixture on one rectangle to within ¼ inch of long edges. Starting at one long side, tightly roll up dough; pinch seams to seal. Using serrated knife, cut roll into 14 slices. Place slices, cut side up, on cookie sheets. Repeat with remaining dough and filling.

3. Bake 17 to 21 minutes or until golden brown. Immediately, remove from cookie sheets to serving plate. Top each pinwheel with sour cream, remaining bacon bits and the green onions. Serve warm.

1 Serving: Calories 74 (Calories from Fat 35); Total Fat 4g, Saturated Fat 2g; Trans Fat 0g; Cholesterol 10mg; Sodium 168mg; Total Carbohydrate 7g; Dietary Fiber 0g; Sugars 1g; Protein 0g

CRAB CAKES ITALIANO

Pesto easily packs extra flavor into these prize-winning crab cakes. Mamma mia!

PREP TIME: 35 MINUTES
TOTAL TIME: 35 MINUTES

MAKES 8 SERVINGS

Robert Gadsby, Brunswick, Georgia
Bake-Off® Contest 38, 1998

SAUCE

½ cup mayonnaise or reduced-fat mayonnaise

2 tablespoons purchased pesto

CRAB CAKES

1 lb. fresh lump crabmeat, cleaned and rinsed, or imitation crabmeat (surimi), shredded

½ cup Italian-style bread crumbs

⅓ cup mayonnaise or reduced-fat mayonnaise

2 tablespoons purchased pesto

1 egg, beaten

2 tablespoons olive oil

GARNISH, IF DESIRED

Italian plum tomato slices

Fresh basil sprigs

Julienne-cut sun-dried tomatoes

1. In small bowl, combine sauce ingredients; mix well. Cover; refrigerate until serving time.

2. In large bowl, combine all crab cake ingredients except olive oil; mix well. Using ⅓ cup mixture for each, shape into eight 3-inch patties.

3. Heat oil in large nonstick skillet over medium heat until hot. Add patties; cook 4 to 5 minutes on each side or until golden brown and thoroughly cooked. Drain on paper towels. Serve crab cakes topped with sauce. Garnish as desired.

CLEVER IDEA: *To substitute for fresh crabmeat, canned crabmeat, drained, or frozen crabmeat, thawed and drained, can be used.*

1 Serving: Calories 330 (Calories from Fat 234); Total Fat 26g; Saturated Fat 4g; Trans Fat 0g; Cholesterol 92mg; Sodium 538mg; Total Carbohydrate 6g; Dietary Fiber 1g; Sugars 1g; Protein 16g

OLD PLANTATION ROLLS

The first Bake-Off® Contest, in 1949, was called Pillsbury's Grand National Recipe and Baking Contest. It was launched by First Lady Eleanor Roosevelt. These no-knead rolls from more than sixty-five years ago continue to be a natural for today's busy cooks.

PREP TIME: 30 MINUTES
TOTAL TIME: 2 HOURS 30 MINUTES

MAKES 24 SERVINGS (1 ROLL PER SERVING)

Mrs. William Edwin Baker, Colorado Springs, Colorado
Bake-Off® Contest 1, 1949

5 to 6 cups all-purpose flour
¼ cup sugar
1 teaspoon baking powder
1 teaspoon salt
½ teaspoon baking soda

1 pkg. active dry yeast
1 cup water
1 cup milk
½ cup shortening
1 egg

1. Grease 24 muffin cups. In large bowl, combine 3 cups flour, sugar, baking powder, salt, baking soda and yeast; blend well. In small saucepan, heat water, milk and shortening until very warm (120 to 130°F). Add warm liquid and egg to flour mixture. Blend at low speed until moistened; beat 3 minutes at medium speed. By hand, stir in remaining 2 to 3 cups flour to form a stiff dough. Cover loosely with greased plastic wrap and cloth towel. Let rise in warm place (80 to 85°F) until light and doubled in size, about 1 hour.

2. Punch down dough several times to remove all air bubbles. On well-floured surface, toss dough until no longer sticky. Divide dough into 24 equal pieces; shape into balls. Place 1 ball in each greased muffin cup. With scissors or sharp knife, make X-shaped cut in each ball, forming 4 equal pieces. Cover; let rise in warm place until light and doubled in size, 35 to 45 minutes.

3. Heat oven to 400°F. Uncover dough. Bake 13 to 15 minutes or until golden brown. Remove from pans immediately.

CLEVER IDEAS:

- *Rolls can be prepared through the first punch-down in step 2, covered and refrigerated overnight. Increase second rise time to 1¼ hours.*

- *For a more traditional clover-leaf shape, divide dough into 72 pieces; shape into balls. Place 3 balls in each greased muffin cup. Cover; let rise in warm place until light and doubled in size, 35 to 45 minutes. Bake as directed above.*

1 Serving: Calories 150 (Calories from Fat 43); Total Fat 5g; Saturated Fat 2g; Trans Fat 0g; Cholesterol 9mg; Sodium 154mg; Total Carbohydrate 23g; Dietary Fiber 1g; Sugars 3g; Protein 3g

ONION LOVER'S TWIST

This no-knead bread features fresh chopped onions rolled in strips of dough that are braided together to create a light textured onion bread. Serve it warm or cold with a favorite chicken or beef main dish and see why it took top honors.

PREP TIME: 40 MINUTES
TOTAL TIME: 3 HOURS
45 MINUTES

MAKES 32 SERVINGS

Nan Robb, Huachuca City, Arizona
Bake-Off® Contest 21, 1970 $25,000 Grand Prize Winner

BREAD

3½ to 4½ cups Pillsbury™ BEST™ All Purpose or Unbleached Flour

¼ cup sugar

1½ teaspoons salt

1 pkg. active dry yeast

¾ cup water

½ cup milk

¼ cup margarine or butter

1 egg

FILLING

¼ cup margarine or butter

1 cup finely chopped onions or ¼ cup instant minced onion

1 tablespoon grated Parmesan cheese

1 tablespoon sesame or poppy seed

½ to 1 teaspoon garlic salt

1 teaspoon paprika

1. Lightly spoon flour into measuring cup; level off. In large bowl, combine 2 cups flour, sugar, salt and yeast; mix well. In small saucepan, heat water, milk and $\frac{1}{4}$ cup margarine until very warm (120 to 130°F). Add warm liquid and egg to flour mixture; blend at low speed until moistened. Beat 3 minutes at medium speed.

2. By hand, stir in remaining $1\frac{1}{2}$ to $2\frac{1}{2}$ cups flour to form a soft dough. Cover loosely with greased plastic wrap and cloth towel. Let rise in warm place (80 to 85°F) until light and doubled in size, 45 to 60 minutes.

3. Grease large cookie sheet. Melt $\frac{1}{4}$ cup margarine in small saucepan; stir in all remaining filling ingredients. Set aside.

4. Stir down dough to remove all air bubbles. On floured surface, toss dough until no longer sticky. Roll dough into 18x12-inch rectangle. Cut rectangle in half crosswise to make two 12x9-inch rectangles; cut each rectangle into three 9x4-inch strips.

5. Spread about 2 tablespoons onion mixture over each strip to within $\frac{1}{2}$ inch of edges. Bring lengthwise edges of each strip together to enclose filling; pinch edges and ends to seal.

6. On greased cookie sheet, braid 3 rolls together; pinch ends to seal. Repeat with remaining 3 rolls for second loaf. Cover; let rise in warm place until light and doubled in size, 25 to 30 minutes.

7. Heat oven to 350°F. Uncover dough. Bake 27 to 35 minutes or until golden brown and loaves sound hollow when lightly tapped. Immediately remove from cookie sheet; cool on wire racks for 1 hour or until completely cooled.

1 Slice: Calories 91 (Calories from Fat 31); Total Fat 3g; Saturated Fat 1g; Trans Fat 0.5g; Cholesterol 6mg; Sodium 157mg; Total Carbohydrate 13g; Dietary Fiber 1g; Sugars 2g; Protein 3g

GOLDEN GATE SNACK BREAD

The seventeenth Bake-Off® Contest was designated the "Busy Lady Bake-Off®." This streamlined, no-knead cheese bread with its zesty onion filling and easy, innovative shaping still is a big winner with busy people who like to bake.

PREP TIME: 30 MINUTES
TOTAL TIME: 1 HOUR 45 MINUTES
MAKES 16 SERVINGS

Mari Petrelli, Ely, Nevada
Bake-Off® Contest 17, 1966 Grand Prize Winner

BREAD

3½ cups Pillsbury™ BEST™ All Purpose or Unbleached Flour

2 tablespoons sugar

2 pkg. active dry yeast

1 cup water

2 tablespoons margarine or butter

1 (8-oz.) jar pasteurized process cheese spread

FILLING

¼ cup margarine or butter, softened

3 tablespoons dry onion soup mix

1. Lightly spoon flour into measuring cup; level off. In large bowl, combine 1½ cups flour, sugar and yeast; blend well.

2. In small saucepan, heat water and 2 tablespoons margarine until very warm (120 to 130°F). Add warm liquid to flour mixture; blend at low speed until moistened. Beat 2 minutes at medium speed. Beat in cheese until blended. By hand, stir in remaining 2 cups flour to make a stiff dough. Cover loosely with greased plastic wrap and cloth towel. Let rise in warm place (80 to 85°F) until light and doubled in size, about 30 minutes.

3. In small bowl, combine ¼ cup margarine and onion soup mix; blend well. Set aside.

4. Heat oven to 350°F. Grease cookie sheet. Punch down dough. On floured surface, roll out dough to a 20x14-inch rectangle. (Be sure sides are straight before rolling.) Spread with filling. Starting with 14-inch side, roll up, pressing edges and ends to seal. With knife, carefully cut lengthwise down center to form 2 loaves. Place cut side up on greased cookie sheet. Cover; let rise in warm place until light and doubled in size, about 20 minutes.

5. Bake at 350°F for 15 to 25 minutes or until golden brown.

1 Serving: Calories 189 (Calories from Fat 70); Total Fat 8g; Saturated Fat 3g; Trans Fat 1g; Cholesterol 10mg; Sodium 387mg; Total Carbohydrate 25g; Dietary Fiber 1g; Sugars 3g; Protein 5g

CHEDDAR TWISTERS

Cheese and onion get all twisted up in a French-style flaky roll. Mmm!

PREP TIME: 10 MINUTES
TOTAL TIME: 35 MINUTES

MAKES 8 SERVINGS

Karen Kwan, Belmont, California
Bake-Off® Contest 38, 1998

2 cans (8 oz each) Pillsbury™ refrigerated crescent dinner rolls or 2 cans (8 oz each) Pillsbury™ Crescent Recipe Creations™ refrigerated seamless dough sheet

1½ cups finely shredded sharp Cheddar cheese (6 oz)

4 medium green onions, chopped (¼ cup)

1 egg

1 teaspoon water

2 teaspoons sesame seed

½ teaspoon garlic salt with parsley blend (from 4.8-oz jar)

1. Heat oven to 375°F. Lightly grease large cookie sheet with shortening or cooking spray.

2. If using crescent rolls: Unroll both cans of dough; separate into total of 8 rectangles. Firmly press perforations to seal. If using dough sheets: Unroll both cans of dough; cut into total of 8 rectangles.

3. In small bowl, mix cheese and onions. Spoon slightly less than ¼ cup cheese mixture in 1-inch-wide strip lengthwise down center of each rectangle to within ¼ inch of each end. Fold dough in half lengthwise to form long strip; firmly press edges to seal. Twist strip 4 or 5 times; bring ends together to form ring and pinch to seal. Place on cookie sheet.

4. In another small bowl, beat egg and water until well blended; brush over dough. Sprinkle with sesame seed and garlic salt blend.

5. Bake 15 to 20 minutes or until golden brown. Immediately remove from cookie sheet; cool 5 minutes. Serve warm.

CLEVER IDEA: *To substitute for garlic salt with parsley blend, use mixture of ½ teaspoon garlic salt and dash of dried parsley flakes.*

1 Serving: Calories 310 (Calories from Fat 180); Total Fat 20g; Saturated Fat 9g; Trans Fat 3g; Cholesterol 50mg; Sodium 640mg; Total Carbohydrate 23g; Dietary Fiber 0g; Sugars 5g; Protein 10g

ZESTY CHEESE BREAD

Check out this cheese bread made with Pillsbury™ refrigerated pizza crust and sprinkled with chopped green chiles. This zesty appetizer can be made ready in 45 minutes.

PREP TIME: 10 MINUTES
TOTAL TIME: 45 MINUTES

MAKES 10 SERVINGS

Barbara Jones, Norristown, Pennsylvania
Bake-Off® Contest 38, 1998

1 (13.8-oz.) can Pillsbury™ refrigerated classic pizza crust

1 (4.5-oz.) can chopped green chiles, well drained

2 oz. (½ cup) shredded sharp Cheddar cheese

2 oz. (½ cup) shredded hot pepper Monterey Jack cheese

¼ teaspoon garlic powder

1. Move oven rack to highest position. Heat oven to 375°F. Spray cookie sheet with nonstick cooking spray.

2. Do not unroll dough. Place dough on sprayed cookie sheet. Starting at center, press out dough with hands to form 14x5-inch rectangle. Sprinkle chiles and cheeses over dough to within ¹/₂ inch of long sides. Bring long sides up over cheese; pinch to seal. Pinch ends to seal. Sprinkle with garlic powder.

3. Bake at 375°F on highest oven rack for 15 to 20 minutes or until golden brown. Cool 15 minutes. Cut into slices. Serve warm.

1 Serving: Calories 142 (Calories from Fat 44); Total Fat 5g; Saturated Fat 3g; Trans Fat 0g; Cholesterol 11mg; Sodium 382mg; Total Carbohydrate 19g; Dietary Fiber 1g; Sugars 2g; Protein 5g

FEATHERLIGHT CHEDDAR-RANCH PUFFS

Light tender biscuits flavored with Cheddar cheese and ranch dressing mix make a foolproof accompaniment to eggs, soups or salads.

PREP TIME: 25 MINUTES
TOTAL TIME: 60 MINUTES

MAKES 20 SERVINGS

Aimee Hachigian-Gould, Ulm, Montana
Bake-Off® Contest 44, 2010

1 package (¼ oz) active dry yeast (2½ teaspoons)

¼ cup warm water (105°F to 115°F)

3 cups Pillsbury™ BEST™ All Purpose Unbleached or All Purpose Flour

1 tablespoon baking powder

¼ teaspoon baking soda

1 teaspoon salt

1 package (1 oz) ranch dressing mix

½ cup cold butter

½ cup thinly sliced green onions (8 medium)

2 cups shredded Cheddar cheese (8 oz)

1 lb bacon, cooked, crumbled

1¼ cups buttermilk

1. Heat oven to 400°F. Line cookie sheets with cooking parchment paper; spray paper with no-stick cooking spray. In small bowl, mix yeast and warm water; set aside.

2. In large bowl, mix flour, baking powder, baking soda, salt and dressing mix. Cut in butter, using pastry blender or fork, until mixture looks like coarse crumbs.

3. In small microwavable bowl, place onions. Cover with microwavable plastic wrap, folding back one side to vent; microwave on High 30 seconds. Cool slightly, about 2 minutes.

4. Add cheese and bacon to flour mixture; toss until well coated. Stir in yeast mixture, onions and buttermilk all at once until soft dough forms. Drop dough by $\frac{1}{3}$ cupfuls 2 to 3 inches apart onto cookie sheets.

5. Bake 14 to 18 minutes or until puffed and light golden brown. Serve warm with additional butter, if desired.

CLEVER IDEA: *To substitute for buttermilk, place 1 tablespoon lemon juice or white vinegar in 2-cup glass measuring cup and add enough milk to measure $1^1/_4$ cups; let stand a few minutes.*

1 Serving: Calories 200 (Calories from Fat 110); Total Fat 12g; Saturated Fat 7g; Trans Fat 0g; Cholesterol 35mg; Sodium 580mg; Total Carbohydrate 17; Dietary Fiber 0g; Sugars 1g; Protein 8g

Easy Eats
Pizzas, Burgers, Sandwiches and Salads

Susie Littlewood of Royal City, Washington,
prepares her Caramelized Red Onion-Feta Burgers (page 163)
at the 44th Bake-Off Contest held in Orlando, Florida.

5-WAY CINCINNATI PIZZA

Pizza or chili for dinner? You can enjoy both when you top pizza crust with chili. Apple pie spice adds another flavor dimension to the chili mixture; or use ¼ teaspoon cinnamon and ⅛ teaspoon each of ginger and cloves instead.

PREP TIME: 30 MINUTES
TOTAL TIME: 45 MINUTES

MAKES 6 SERVINGS

Melody Levault, Mulkeytown, Illinois
Bake-Off® Contest 40, 2002

1 (13.8-oz.) can Pillsbury™ refrigerated classic pizza crust

½ lb. lean ground beef

½ cup barbecue sauce

1 to 2 teaspoons chili powder

½ teaspoon salt

½ teaspoon cumin

½ teaspoon apple pie spice

2 cups red kidney beans, drained, rinsed (from 19-oz can)

½ cup chopped onion

8 oz. (2 cups) shredded Cheddar cheese

1. Heat oven to 425°F. Spray 12-inch pizza pan or 13x9-inch pan with nonstick cooking spray. Unroll dough; place in sprayed pan. Starting at center, press out dough to edge of pan. Bake at 425°F for 7 to 10 minutes or until light golden brown.

2. Meanwhile, cook ground beef in large skillet over medium-high heat until thoroughly cooked, stirring frequently. Drain. Add barbecue sauce, chili powder, salt, cumin and apple pie spice; mix well. Cook 1 minute, stirring constantly.

3. Remove crust from oven. Spread ground beef mixture over partially baked crust. Top with beans, onion and cheese.

4. Return to oven; bake an additional 11 to 14 minutes or until crust is deep golden brown.

1 Serving: Calories 524 (Calories from Fat 170); Total Fat 19g; Saturated Fat 10g; Trans Fat 0g; Cholesterol 65mg; Sodium 1148mg; Total Carbohydrate 61g; Dietary Fiber 9g; Sugars 14g; Protein 28g

CHICKEN FAJITA PIZZA

Find all the sizzle of a chicken fajita on a tender pizza crust. Simply delicious!

PREP TIME: 20 MINUTES
TOTAL TIME: 40 MINUTES
MAKES 8 SERVINGS

Elizabeth Daniels, Kula, Maui, Hawaii
Bake-Off® Contest 34, 1990

- 1 can (13.8 oz) Pillsbury™ refrigerated classic pizza crust
- 1 tablespoon olive or vegetable oil
- 4 boneless skinless chicken breasts, cut into thin strips
- 1 to 2 teaspoons chili powder
- ½ to 1 teaspoon salt
- ½ teaspoon garlic powder
- 1 cup thinly sliced onions
- 1 cup green or red bell pepper strips (2 x ¼-inch)
- ½ cup salsa
- 2 cups shredded Monterey Jack cheese (8 oz)

1. Heat oven to 425°F. Spray 12-inch pizza pan or 13x9-inch pan with no-stick cooking spray. Unroll dough; place in pan. Starting at center, press out dough with hands to edge of pan.

2. In 10-inch skillet, heat oil over medium-high heat until hot. Add chicken; sprinkle with chili powder, salt and garlic powder. Cook and stir 3 to 5 minutes or until lightly browned. Add onions and bell pepper strips; cook and stir an additional 2 to 3 minutes or until chicken is no longer pink and vegetables are crisp-tender.

3. Spoon chicken mixture evenly over dough. Spoon salsa over chicken. Sprinkle with cheese.

4. Bake 16 to 20 minutes or until crust is golden brown.

> **CLEVER IDEA:** *For a crispier crust, bake crust 7 to 9 minutes or until light golden brown, then add toppings; bake pizza 14 to 18 minutes.*

1 Serving: Calories 300 (Calories from Fat 120); Total Fat 13g; Saturated Fat 6g; Trans Fat 0g; Cholesterol 60mg; Sodium 830mg; Total Carbohydrate 21g; Dietary Fiber 1g; Sugars 4g; Protein 24g

CHICKEN AND BLACK BEAN TOSTIZZAS

It's a pizza . . . it's a tostada . . . it's a tostizza! Pile the fillings on a Grands!™ biscuit in a five-star-rated Bake-Off® Contest chicken recipe.

PREP TIME: 15 MINUTES
TOTAL TIME: 40 MINUTES

MAKES 8 SERVINGS

Karen Durrett, Portland, Oregon
Bake-Off® Contest 36, 1994

1 can (16.3 oz) Pillsbury™ Grands!™ Flaky Layers refrigerated biscuits

1 cup diced cooked chicken

1 cup black beans, drained (from 15- or 19-oz can)

½ cup salsa

2 tablespoons taco seasoning mix (from 1-oz package)

2 green onions, chopped

½ cup bell pepper strips (1 inch long)

1½ cups shredded Cheddar cheese (6 oz)

1. Heat oven to 350°F. Separate dough into 8 biscuits. On ungreased cookie sheets, press or roll each biscuit to form 5½-inch round.

2. In medium bowl, mix chicken, beans, salsa and taco seasoning mix. Spread evenly over biscuits to within ¼ inch of edges. Top evenly with onions, bell pepper and cheese.

3. Bake 20 to 24 minutes or until biscuits are golden brown and cheese is melted, reversing position of cookie sheets halfway through baking time. If desired, garnish with sour cream and guacamole.

1 Serving: Calories 340 (Calories from Fat 150); Total Fat 17g; Saturated Fat 7g; Trans Fat 3.5g; Cholesterol 35mg; Sodium 970mg; Total Carbohydrate 32g; Dietary Fiber 2g; Sugars 6g; Protein 16g

WHITE BEAN SAUSAGE AND VEGGIE PIZZA

Had your veggies today? Savor them on a crispy pizza crust with sausage and lots of melty cheese.

PREP TIME: 20 MINUTES
TOTAL TIME: 40 MINUTES
MAKES 6 SERVINGS

Mary Newell, Romeoville, Illinois
Bake-Off® Contest 46, 2013

1 can Pillsbury™ refrigerated thin pizza crust

1 lb sweet Italian turkey sausage, casings removed

1 box (7 oz) frozen antioxidant blend broccoli, carrots and sweet peppers

1 can (15 oz) cannellini beans, drained, rinsed

1 clove garlic, chopped

¼ cup extra virgin olive oil

¼ teaspoon salt

2 cups shredded Italian 5 cheese blend (8 oz)

1. Heat oven to 400°F. Spray 15x10-inch pan with sides with no-stick cooking spray. Unroll dough in pan; press in bottom and halfway up sides of pan. Bake 8 minutes.

2. Meanwhile, in 10-inch skillet, cook sausage over medium heat, 5 to 7 minutes, stirring occasionally and breaking up sausage, or until no longer pink; drain.

3. Microwave frozen vegetables as directed on box; drain.

4. Meanwhile, place beans, garlic, olive oil and salt in food processor or blender. Cover; process 15 to 20 seconds or until smooth.

5. Spread bean mixture over partially baked crust. Top with sausage, vegetables and cheese. Bake 15 to 18 minutes longer or until crust is golden brown and cheese is melted.

1 Serving: Calories 560 (Calories from Fat 270); Total Fat 31g; Saturated Fat 10g; Trans Fat 0g; Cholesterol 75mg; Sodium 1130mg; Total Carbohydrate 41g; Dietary Fiber 5g; Sugars 0g; Protein 30g

DELUXE TURKEY CLUB PIZZA

PREP TIME: 25 MINUTES

TOTAL TIME: 35 MINUTES

MAKES 6 SERVINGS

Teresa Hannan Smith, Sacramento, California

Bake-Off® Contest 35, 1992

1 can (13.8-oz.) Pillsbury™ refrigerated classic pizza crust

2 teaspoons sesame seed

6 slices bacon, cut into 1-inch pieces

¼ cup light or regular mayonnaise

½ to 1 teaspoon grated lemon peel

1 cup shredded Monterey Jack cheese (4-oz.)

1 tablespoon thinly sliced fresh basil or 1 teaspoon dried basil leaves

¼ lb. cooked turkey breast slices, cut into 1-inch strips

2 small plum (Roma) tomatoes or 1 small tomato, thinly sliced

½ cup shredded Swiss cheese (2-oz.)

Fresh basil leaves, if desired

1. Heat oven to 425°F. Lightly spray 12-inch pizza pan or 13x9-inch pan with cooking spray. Unroll dough; place in pan. Starting at center, press out dough to edge of pan to form crust. Sprinkle sesame seed evenly over dough. Bake 10 to 12 minutes or until crust is light golden brown.

2. Meanwhile, in 10-inch skillet, cook bacon over medium heat until crisp. Remove bacon from skillet; drain on paper towels. In small bowl, mix mayonnaise and lemon peel until well blended.

3. Spread mayonnaise mixture over crust. Top with Monterey Jack cheese, sliced basil, turkey, cooked bacon and tomatoes; sprinkle with Swiss cheese.

4. Bake 7 to 9 minutes longer or until crust is golden brown and cheese is melted. Garnish with fresh basil leaves.

1 Serving: Calories 360 (Calories from Fat 150); Total Fat 17g; Saturated Fat 7g; Trans Fat 0g; Cholesterol 44mg; Sodium 969mg; Total Carbohydrate 34g; Dietary Fiber 1g; Sugars 6g; Protein 19g

POLISH PIZZA

Kielbasa, a smoked pork sausage, is sometimes called Polish sausage. It is delicious in this hearty pizza.

PREP TIME: 20 MINUTES
TOTAL TIME: 35 MINUTES

MAKES 8 SERVINGS

Norma Eckhoff, Cleveland, Ohio
Bake-Off® Contest 36, 1994

CRUST

- 1 tablespoon cornmeal or caraway seed
- 1 (10-oz.) can refrigerated pizza crust
- 4 oz. (1 cup) shredded Swiss cheese

TOPPING

- ½ cup chopped onion
- 3 slices bacon, cut into ½-inch pieces
- 1 (16-oz.) jar or can sauerkraut, well drained
- 1 tablespoon caraway seed
- 1 (4.5-oz.) jar sliced mushroom, well drained
- 6 oz. (1½ cups) shredded Swiss cheese
- ½ lb. Polish kielbasa sausage, cut into ⅛-inch slices
- 1 tablespoon chopped fresh parsley or 1 teaspoon dried parsley flakes

1. Heat oven to 425°F. Lightly grease 13 x 9-inch pan or 12-inch pizza pan; sprinkle with cornmeal. Unroll dough and place in greased pan; starting at center, press out with hands. Sprinkle with 1 cup cheese. Bake at 425°F for 5 to 8 minutes or until light golden brown.

2. Meanwhile, in medium saucepan over medium-high heat, cook onion and bacon until light brown, stirring frequently. Reduce heat to low. Add sauerkraut and 1 tablespoon caraway seed; simmer 3 minutes or until thoroughly heated. Stir in mushrooms. Spread over partially baked crust. Sprinkle with 1½ cups cheese. Top with sausage slices; sprinkle with parsley.

3. Bake at 425°F for 12 to 15 minutes or until edges of crust are deep golden brown and cheese is melted.

1 Serving: Calories 375 (Calories from Fat 210); Total Fat 23g; Saturated Fat 11g; Trans Fat 0.5g; Cholesterol 55mg; Sodium 1054mg; Total Carbohydrate 25g; Dietary Fiber 3g; Sugars 5g; Protein 18g

DEEP-DISH SAUSAGE PATTY PIZZA

An easy homemade sauce tops a convenient refrigerated crust in a pizza you can customize with your favorite kind of sausage.

PREP TIME: 35 MINUTES
TOTAL TIME: 1 HOUR 15 MINUTES
MAKES 8 SERVINGS

Amy Winters, Bartlett, Illinois
Bake-Off® Contest 44, 2010

SAUCE

2 tablespoons olive oil

¼ cup chopped onion

2 teaspoons finely chopped garlic

1 can (28 oz) whole peeled tomatoes, drained, ½ cup juice reserved and tomatoes coarsely chopped

1 teaspoon basil leaves

1 bay leaf

¼ teaspoon salt

2 or 3 dashes black pepper

PIZZA

1 lb bulk sweet Italian pork sausage

2 tablespoons olive oil

1 tablespoon cornmeal

1 can (13.8 oz) Pillsbury™ refrigerated classic pizza crust

4 cups shredded mozzarella cheese (1 lb)

2 teaspoons grated Parmesan cheese

1. Heat oven to 400°F. In 2-quart saucepan, heat 2 tablespoons oil over medium-high heat. Add onion and garlic; cook about 4 minutes, stirring constantly, until onion is tender. Stir in tomatoes, basil, bay leaf, salt and pepper. Reduce heat to medium-low. Simmer uncovered 20 minutes, stirring occasionally. Stir in reserved tomato juice. (Sauce should be thick.) Remove and discard bay leaf.

2. Meanwhile, spray 12-inch skillet with no-stick cooking spray. Spread sausage over bottom of skillet into large patty. Cook over medium-high heat 5 to 8 minutes on each side, turning once, until no longer pink in center. (If necessary, cut patty in half or into quarters to turn.)

3. Coat bottom and side of 12-inch cast-iron skillet or other ovenproof skillet with 1 tablespoon oil; sprinkle with cornmeal. Unroll pizza crust dough in skillet; press on bottom and at least halfway up side. Brush dough with remaining 1 tablespoon oil; prick bottom and sides of dough with fork. Sprinkle mozzarella cheese over dough. Top with sausage patty, keeping patty in one piece.

4. Bake 15 to 18 minutes or until crust is light golden brown. Spread sauce over sausage. Bake 5 to 10 minutes longer or until crust is golden brown. Sprinkle with Parmesan cheese. Let stand 10 minutes before cutting.

CLEVER IDEA: *Did you know? Pillsbury has a gluten free pizza dough.*

1 Serving: Calories 520 (Calories from Fat 280); Total Fat 31g; Saturated Fat 13g; Trans Fat 0g; Cholesterol 55mg; Sodium 1360mg; Total Carbohydrate 33g; Dietary Fiber 2g; Sugars 7g; Protein 27g

CHUTNEY PIZZA WITH TURKEY, SPINACH AND GORGONZOLA

Mild ground turkey and spinach are paired with bold ingredients—mango chutney and Gorgonzola—with great results.

PREP TIME: 25 MINUTES
TOTAL TIME: 40 MINUTES
MAKES 6 SERVINGS

Amy Brnger, Portsmouth, New Hampshire
Bake-Off® Contest 43, 2008

- 2 tablespoons unsalted or salted butter
- 2 cloves garlic, finely chopped
- 1 box (9 oz) frozen chopped spinach, thawed, squeezed to drain
- 1 can (13.8 oz) Pillsbury™ refrigerated classic pizza crust
- 8 oz uncooked ground turkey breast
- ¼ teaspoon salt
- ¼ teaspoon freshly ground pepper
- ¼ cup mango chutney
- ¼ cup slivered blanched almonds
- 1 cup crumbled Gorgonzola cheese (4 oz)
- 2 green onions, thinly sliced (2 tablespoons)

1. Heat oven to 425°F. Spray 13x9-inch pan with no-stick cooking spray.

2. In 10-inch nonstick skillet, melt 1 tablespoon of the butter over low heat. Add garlic; cook, stirring occasionally, until tender. Add spinach. Increase heat to medium; cook 2 to 3 minutes, stirring occasionally, until liquid from the spinach has evaporated and mixture is thoroughly heated. Remove spinach mixture to a bowl.

3. Unroll pizza crust dough in pan; press dough to edges of pan. Bake 7 to 10 minutes or until light golden brown.

4. Meanwhile, add remaining 1 tablespoon butter to skillet; melt over medium heat. Add turkey; cook 4 to 6 minutes, stirring frequently, until no longer pink; drain. Stir in salt and pepper; remove from heat.

5. Cut up large fruit pieces in chutney if necessary. Spread chutney evenly over partially baked crust. Top chutney evenly with turkey and spinach mixture. Sprinkle with almonds and cheese.

6. Bake 10 to 12 minutes longer or until cheese is melted and crust is golden brown. Immediately sprinkle with onions. To serve, cut with serrated knife.

1 Serving: Calories 370 (Calories from Fat 140); Total Fat 16g; Saturated Fat 7g; Trans Fat 0g; Cholesterol 50mg; Sodium 890mg; Total Carbohydrate 38g; Dietary Fiber 2g; Sugars 8g; Protein 20g

CHUTNEY PIZZA WITH TURKEY, SPINACH AND GORGONZOLA *(opposite)*

BUTTERNUT SQUASH-PESTO PIZZA *(page 160)*

BUTTERNUT SQUASH-PESTO PIZZA

Roasted butternut squash adds sweet garden-fresh flavor to this savory pizza. Easy enough for a weeknight meal or special enough for entertaining!

PREP TIME: 35 MINUTES
TOTAL TIME: 50 MINUTES

MAKES 8 SERVINGS

Karen Stuber, Fulton, New York
Bake-Off® Contest 44, 2010

2½ cups diced peeled butternut squash

½ cup chopped onion (about 1 small)

1 tablespoon packed brown sugar

1 teaspoon sea salt or kosher salt

½ teaspoon black pepper

2 tablespoons olive oil

1 can (13.8 oz) Pillsbury™ refrigerated classic pizza crust

4 oz pancetta, diced

3 tablespoons basil pesto

½ cup chopped drained roasted red bell peppers (from 7-oz jar)

⅓ cup chopped walnuts

1 cup shredded Asiago cheese (4 oz)

½ cup crumbled feta cheese (2 oz)

1. Heat oven to 400°F. In medium bowl, mix squash, onion, brown sugar, salt, black pepper and 1½ tablespoons of the oil. Spread mixture in ungreased 13x9-inch (3-quart) glass baking dish. Bake about 20 minutes, stirring occasionally, until squash is tender.

2. Spray large cookie sheet with no-stick cooking spray. Unroll pizza crust dough on cookie sheet into 13x9-inch rectangle. Bake at 400°F for 7 to 10 minutes or until light golden brown.

3. Meanwhile, in 10-inch skillet, heat remaining ½ tablespoon oil over medium heat. Add pancetta; cook 4 minutes, stirring frequently, until lightly browned. Drain.

4. Spread pesto over partially baked crust. Top with squash mixture, pancetta, roasted peppers, walnuts and cheeses. Bake 6 to 8 minutes longer or until edges are golden brown. Let stand 5 minutes before serving.

1 Serving: Calories 360 (Calories from Fat 180); Total Fat 20g; Saturated Fat 7g; Trans Fat 0g; Cholesterol 30mg; Sodium 1070mg; Total Carbohydrate 33g; Dietary Fiber 2g; Sugars 8g; Protein 12g

SPICY BROCCOLI AÏOLI PIZZA

PREP TIME: 15 MINUTES

TOTAL TIME: 45 MINUTES

MAKES 8 SERVINGS

Gilda Lester, Chadds Ford, Pennsylvania
Bake-Off® Contest 36, 1994

CRUST

2 tablespoons cornmeal

1 (10-oz.) can refrigerated pizza crust

TOPPING

¼ cup olive oil or vegetable oil

3 to 4 garlic cloves, chopped

2 tablespoons chopped shallots or onion

1 tablespoon balsamic vinegar or red wine vinegar

⅓ cup grated Romano or Parmesan cheese

½ teaspoon dried basil leaves

½ teaspoon dried thyme leaves

½ teaspoon dried oregano leaves

¼ teaspoon crushed red pepper flakes

6 oz. sliced Havarti or Monterey Jack cheese

1 (1-lb.) pkg. frozen cut broccoli, thawed, well drained

1 (7-oz.) jar roasted red peppers, drained, sliced into 2 x ¼-inch strips

½ cup grated Parmesan or Romano cheese

1. Heat oven to 425°F. Lightly grease 12-inch pizza pan or 13 x 9-inch pan; sprinkle with cornmeal. Unroll dough; press in bottom and up sides of greased pan to form a rim. Bake at 425°F for 5 to 8 minutes or until lightly brown.

2. In food processor bowl with metal blade or blender container, combine oil, garlic, shallots, vinegar, Romano cheese, basil, thyme, oregano and red pepper flakes. Process until smooth; set aside. Arrange Havarti cheese over partially baked crust. Place broccoli evenly over cheese. Dollop oil mixture evenly over top. Arrange pepper strips over broccoli; sprinkle with Parmesan cheese.

3. Bake at 425°F for 17 to 22 minutes or until edges of crust are deep golden brown. Serve immediately.

1 Serving: Calories 319 (Calories from Fat 160); Total Fat 18g; Saturated Fat 8g; Trans Fat 0g; Cholesterol 28mg; Sodium 470mg; Total Carbohydrate 26g; Dietary Fiber 2g; Sugars 3g; Protein 13g

LEBANESE PIZZA

Who needs the corner deli when there's refrigerated pizza crust and a 30-minute recipe like this?

PREP TIME: 20 MINUTES
TOTAL TIME: 35 MINUTES

MAKES 8 SERVINGS

Judy Wood, Birmingham, Alabama
Bake-Off® Contest 38, 1998

CRUST

1 tablespoon cornmeal

1 (13.8-oz.) can Pillsbury™ refrigerated classic pizza crust

2 tablespoons olive or vegetable oil

½ to 1 teaspoon garlic powder

FILLING

2 cups chickpeas (garbanzo beans), drained (from 19-oz can)

½ cup olive or vegetable oil

1 to 2 teaspoons garlic powder

1 tablespoon lemon juice

TOPPINGS

1½ cups chopped Italian plum tomatoes

1 (4¼-oz.) can chopped ripe olives, drained (about 1 cup)

4 oz. (1 cup) feta cheese, crumbled

1. Heat oven to 425°F. Spray 15x10x1-inch baking pan with nonstick cooking spray; sprinkle evenly with cornmeal. Unroll dough; place in greased pan. Starting at center, press out dough with hands. Brush with 2 tablespoons oil; sprinkle with ½ to 1 teaspoon garlic powder. Bake at 425°F for 7 to 9 minutes or until light golden brown.

2. Meanwhile, in blender container or food processor bowl with metal blade, combine all filling ingredients. Blend 1 to 2 minutes or until smooth.

3. Spread filling over partially baked crust. Top with tomatoes, olives and cheese. Return to oven; bake at 425°F for an additional 10 to 12 minutes or until edges of crust are golden brown.

1 Serving: Calories 388 (Calories from Fat 217); Total Fat 24g; Saturated Fat 5g; Trans Fat 0g; Cholesterol 15mg; Sodium 797mg; Total Carbohydrate 35g; Dietary Fiber 4g; Sugars 4g; Protein 9g

CARAMELIZED RED ONION-FETA BURGERS

Make a better burger with awesome additions piled high on freshly baked biscuits.

PREP TIME: 45 MINUTES

TOTAL TIME: 45 MINUTES

MAKES 8 SERVINGS

Susie Littlewood, Royal City, Washington
Bake-Off® Contest 44, 2010

1 large red onion, sliced (2½ cups)

¼ cup red wine vinegar

¼ cup red wine or nonalcoholic red wine

½ cup Concord grape jelly

¼ cup sour cream

½ cup mayonnaise or salad dressing

¾ teaspoon dill weed

½ teaspoon onion powder

¼ teaspoon Beau Monde seasoning, if desired

1 medium English (seedless) cucumber, finely diced (1½ cups)

1 can (16.3 oz) Pillsbury™ Grands!™ Flaky Layers refrigerated original biscuits (8 biscuits)

1 lb lean (at least 80%) ground beef

1 cup crumbled feta cheese (4 oz)

Dash salt

Dash black pepper

8 tomato slices

8 lettuce leaves

1. Heat oven to 350°F. In 10-inch skillet, cook onion, vinegar, wine and jelly over medium heat about 20 minutes, stirring frequently, until onion is tender and sauce is reduced and thickened.

2. Meanwhile, in small bowl, mix sour cream, mayonnaise, dill weed, onion powder, Beau Monde seasoning and cucumber. Refrigerate until ready to serve.

3. Bake biscuits as directed on can. Meanwhile, in large bowl, mix beef, cheese, salt and pepper. Shape mixture into 8 patties, ½ inch thick. Cook patties in grill pan, contact grill or nonstick skillet until meat thermometer inserted in center reads 160°F.

4. Split biscuits. Spread 2 to 3 tablespoons cucumber mixture on bottom of each biscuit. Top with burger, onion mixture and biscuit tops. Serve with tomato, lettuce and remaining cucumber mixture.

CLEVER IDEA: *Beau Monde seasoning is a blend of celery, onion and salt with a touch of sweetness, available on some supermarket shelves. An all-purpose seasoning may be used as a substitute.*

1 Serving: Calories 460 (Calories from Fat 220); Total Fat 24g; Saturated Fat 8g; Trans Fat 2.5g; Cholesterol 55mg; Sodium 800mg; Total Carbohydrate 45g; Dietary Fiber 1g; Sugars 17g; Protein 16g

CARMELIZED RED ONION–FETA BURGERS (*page 163*)

LOADED NACHO BURGERS (*opposite*)

LOADED NACHO BURGERS

Jazz up biscuit buns and fill them with the works including spiced-up burgers, cheesy sauce, bacon, avocado and tomatoes.

PREP TIME: 45 MINUTES
TOTAL TIME: 45 MINUTES

MAKES 8 SERVINGS

Pam Wilkenson, Tracy, California
Bake-Off® Contest 45, 2012

½ cup crushed nacho-flavored tortilla chips (about 25 chips)

1 can (16.3 oz) Pillsbury™ Grands!™ Homestyle refrigerated buttermilk biscuits

¾ cup sliced mild banana pepper rings (from 16-oz jar), drained

1 lb lean (at least 80%) ground beef

¾ cup nacho cheese sauce or dip

¼ teaspoon chili powder

¼ teaspoon ground cumin

2 oz (¼ of 8-oz package) cream cheese, softened

¼ cup finely chopped red onion

⅓ cup diced seeded tomato

¼ cup crumbled cooked bacon

1 medium ripe avocado, pitted, peeled and diced

1. Heat oven to 350°F. Place crushed nacho chips in shallow dish. Press both sides of each biscuit into crushed chips. Bake biscuits on ungreased cookie sheet 13 to 17 minutes or until golden brown. Remove from cookie sheet to cooling rack.

2. Meanwhile, finely chop enough banana pepper rings to equal ¼ cup. In large bowl, mix ground beef, ¼ cup of the nacho cheese sauce, ¼ cup chopped banana peppers, chili powder, and cumin. Shape mixture into 8 patties, 3½ inches in diameter.

3. In nonstick skillet, cook patties over medium-high heat 5 to 7 minutes, turning once, or until meat thermometer inserted in center of patties reads 160°F.

4. In small microwavable bowl, microwave remaining ½ cup nacho cheese sauce on High 30 to 45 seconds or until warm; stir. Split biscuits. Lightly spread cream cheese on cut sides of biscuit halves. Top bottom of each biscuit with burger, nacho cheese sauce, onion, tomato, bacon, avocado, remaining banana pepper rings and biscuit tops.

1 Serving: Calories 455 (Calories from Fat 260); Total Fat 29g; Saturated Fat 9g; Trans Fat 0.5g; Cholesterol 55mg; Sodium 1004mg; Total Carbohydrate 9g; Dietary Fiber 3g; Sugars 6g; Protein 16g

SLOPPY JOE LOAF

Meatloaf baked between layers of French loaf dough makes a delicious hot supper sandwich.

PREP TIME: 20 MINUTES
TOTAL TIME: 50 MINUTES

MAKES 6 SERVINGS

Helena Crutcher, Hazel Green, Alabama
Bake-Off® Contest 40, 2002

- 1 lb. extra-lean ground beef
- 1 small onion, chopped
- 1 (8-oz.) can tomato sauce
- 1 tablespoon Pillsbury™ BEST™ All Purpose or Unbleached Flour
- ¼ teaspoon dried basil leaves
- ¼ teaspoon dried oregano leaves
- ¼ teaspoon fennel seed
- 1 (11-oz.) can Pillsbury™ Refrigerated Crusty French Loaf
- 4 oz. (1 cup) shredded mozzarella cheese

1. Heat oven to 350°F. Spray cookie sheet and large skillet with nonstick cooking spray. In sprayed skillet, combine ground beef and onion; cook until beef is thoroughly cooked, stirring frequently. Drain.

2. Add tomato sauce, flour, basil, oregano and fennel seed; mix well. Reduce heat to medium-low; simmer 5 minutes. Remove from heat.

3. Meanwhile, remove dough from can; place on lightly floured surface. Cut loaf in half lengthwise. Roll each half to form 16x4-inch rectangle. Place 1 dough rectangle on sprayed cookie sheet, being careful not to change shape.

4. Stir ½ cup of the cheese into ground beef mixture. Spoon and spread mixture over dough rectangle on cookie sheet. Sprinkle with remaining ½ cup cheese. Top with remaining dough rectangle.

5. Bake at 350°F for 25 to 30 minutes or until golden brown. Cut into slices.

1 Serving: Calories 296 (Calories from Fat 86); Total Fat 10g; Saturated Fat 5g; Trans Fat 0g; Cholesterol 62mg; Sodium 670mg; Total Carbohydrate 28g; Dietary Fiber 2g; Sugars 4g; Protein 25g

CRESCENT SAMOSA SANDWICHES

Samosas are fried triangular pastries filled with vegetables or meat. This version is prepared quickly and easily with crescent rolls.

PREP TIME: 30 MINUTES
TOTAL TIME: 50 MINUTES

MAKES 16 SERVINGS;
½ CUP SAUCE

Elisabeth Crawford, San Francisco, California
Bake-Off® Contest 36, 1994

FILLING

1 tablespoon oil

½ cup finely chopped onion

2 garlic cloves, minced

¼ lb. lean ground beef

1 cup diced cooked potato

½ cup diced cooked carrot

½ cup frozen sweet peas (from 1-lb. pkg.), thawed

5 tablespoons soy sauce

1 teaspoon curry powder

½ teaspoon cumin

¼ teaspoon coriander

¼ teaspoon ginger

¼ teaspoon turmeric

Dash crushed red pepper flakes

CRESCENTS

2 (8-oz.) cans refrigerated crescent dinner rolls

HONEY DIPPING SAUCE

⅓ cup honey

1 tablespoon lime juice

1 tablespoon soy sauce

¼ teaspoon crushed red pepper flakes

2 garlic cloves, minced

1. Heat oven to 375°F. Heat oil in large skillet over medium heat. Add onion and 2 minced garlic cloves; cook and stir about 5 minutes or until onion is tender. Remove from skillet. Add ground beef; cook and stir 3 to 5 minutes or until browned. Drain. Stir in onion mixture and remaining filling ingredients. Season to taste with salt, if desired.

2. Separate 1 can of dough into 4 rectangles; firmly press perforations to seal. (Keep remaining can refrigerated until ready to use.) Cut rectangles in half crosswise to form 8 squares. Spoon 1 heaping tablespoon of filling in center of each square. Fold 1 corner of dough over filling to form a triangular packet; firmly press edges to seal. Repeat with remaining can of dough and filling. Place on ungreased cookie sheets. If desired, sprinkle triangles with cumin.

3. Bake on middle oven racks at 375°F for 10 to 15 minutes or until golden brown, switching positions of sheets halfway through baking. Meanwhile, in small bowl combine all sauce ingredients; mix well. Serve warm sandwiches with dipping sauce.

1 Serving: Calories 181 (Calories from Fat 70); Total Fat 8g; Saturated Fat 2.5g; Trans Fat 1.5g; Cholesterol 5mg; Sodium 566mg; Total Carbohydrate 22g; Dietary Fiber 1g; Sugars 9g; Protein 4g

SAVORY CRESCENT CHICKEN SQUARES

PREP TIME: 20 MINUTES

TOTAL TIME: 50 MINUTES

MAKES 4 SERVINGS

Doris Castle, River Forest, Illinois

Bake-Off® Contest 25, 1974 Grand Prize Winner

1 package (3 oz) cream cheese, softened

1 tablespoon butter softened

2 cups cubed cooked chicken

1 tablespoon chopped fresh chives or onion

¼ teaspoon salt

⅛ teaspoon pepper

2 tablespoons milk

1 tablespoon chopped pimientos, if desired

1 can (8 oz) Pillsbury™ refrigerated crescent dinner rolls or 1 can (8 oz) Pillsbury™ Crescent Recipe Creations™ refrigerated seamless dough sheet

1 tablespoon butter, melted

¾ cup seasoned croutons, crushed

1. Heat oven to 350°F. In medium bowl, mix cream cheese and 1 tablespoon softened butter; beat until smooth. Add chicken, chives, salt, pepper, milk and pimientos; mix well.

2. Separate or cut dough into 4 rectangles. If using crescent dough, firmly press perforations to seal. Spoon ½ cup chicken mixture onto center of each rectangle. Pull 4 corners of dough to center of chicken mixture; twist firmly. Pinch edges to seal. Place on ungreased cookie sheet. Brush tops of sandwiches with 1 tablespoon melted butter; sprinkle with crushed croutons.

3. Bake 25 to 30 minutes or until golden brown.

1 Sandwich: Calories 500 (Calories from Fat 263); Total Fat 29g; Saturated Fat 12g; Trans Fat 0g; Cholesterol 99mg; Sodium 845mg; Total Carbohydrate 28g; Dietary Fiber 0g; Sugars 5g; Protein 28g

CHICKEN AND SPINACH BISCUIT GYROS

Craving gyros? Try this 30-minute take using home-style biscuits and premade tzatziki.

PREP TIME: 30 MINUTES
TOTAL TIME: 30 MINUTES

MAKES 8 SERVINGS

Bethany Perry, Largo, Florida
Bake-Off® Contest 46, 2013

1 box (9 oz) frozen chopped spinach

1 lb ground chicken

2 teaspoons finely chopped garlic

1 teaspoon salt

1 can Pillsbury™ Grands!™ Homestyle refrigerated buttermilk biscuits (8 ct)

1 small red onion, thinly sliced

1 large tomato, cut in half, sliced

1 container (12 oz) tzatziki

1. Microwave frozen spinach as directed on box, 3 to 4 minutes to thaw. Squeeze dry with paper towels. In medium bowl, mix spinach, ground chicken, garlic and salt. Shape into 8 (6x1-inch) logs. Heat 12-inch skillet over medium-low heat. Cook logs 5 minutes; turn. Cover and reduce heat to low; cook 10 minutes. Uncover; cook 5 minutes longer or until thermometer inserted in center of logs reads 165°F and meat is browned.

2. Meanwhile, spray 11-inch griddle or 12-inch skillet with no-stick cooking spray; heat over medium-low heat until hot. Separate dough into 8 biscuits. Place 2 biscuits on waxed paper; flatten slightly. Cover with waxed paper; roll each biscuit into 8x4½-inch oval. Place on griddle. Cook 2 to 4 minutes per side or until golden brown and no longer doughy. Repeat with remaining biscuits. Cover with foil and keep warm.

3. Place chicken log in center of each biscuit flatbread. Top with onion slices, tomato slices and sauce. Fold flatbread around filling.

CLEVER IDEAS:

- *Tzatziki is a yogurt sauce mixed with cucumbers. If you can't find tzatziki look for Greek yogurt veggie dip containing cucumber, dill and feta at your grocery store.*

- *Moisten hands with water to easily shape chicken mixture into logs.*

1 Serving: Calories 280 (Calories from Fat 110); Total Fat 12g; Saturated Fat 4.5g; Trans Fat 0g; Cholesterol 35mg; Sodium 690mg; Total Carbohydrate 30g; Dietary Fiber 2g; Sugars 3g; Protein 12g

CHICKEN AND SPINACH BISCUIT GYROS *(opposite)*

CHICKEN FLORENTINE PANINI *(page 172)*

CHICKEN FLORENTINE PANINI

Pillsbury™ refrigerated pizza crust goes panini when it combines with ever-popular chicken breasts.

PREP TIME: 35 MINUTES
TOTAL TIME: 1 HOUR

MAKES 4 SERVINGS

Denise Yennie, Nashville, Tennessee
Bake-Off® Contest 40, 2002 Grand Prize Winner

1 (13.8-oz.) can Pillsbury™ refrigerated classic pizza crust

1 (9-oz.) pkg. frozen chopped spinach

¼ cup light mayonnaise

1 garlic clove, minced

1 tablespoon olive oil

1 cup chopped red onion

1 tablespoon sugar

1 tablespoon vinegar (cider, red wine or balsamic)

2 boneless skinless chicken breast halves

½ teaspoon dried Italian seasoning

1 garlic clove, minced

4 (4-inch) slices provolone cheese

1. Heat oven to 375°F. Unroll dough; place in ungreased 15x10x1-inch baking pan. Starting at center, press out dough to edges of pan. Bake at 375°F for 10 minutes. Cool 15 minutes or until completely cooled.

2. Meanwhile, cook spinach as directed on package. Drain well; squeeze dry with paper towels.

3. In small bowl, combine mayonnaise and 1 of the garlic cloves; mix well. Refrigerate.

4. Heat oil in small saucepan over medium-high heat until hot. Add onion; cook and stir 2 to 3 minutes or until crisp-tender. Add sugar and vinegar. Reduce heat to low; simmer 3 to 5 minutes or until most of liquid has evaporated, stirring occasionally.

5. To flatten each chicken breast half, place, boned side up, between 2 pieces of plastic wrap or waxed paper. Working from center, gently pound chicken with flat side of meat mallet or rolling pin until about ¼ inch thick; remove wrap. Sprinkle chicken with Italian seasoning and minced garlic.

6. Spray large skillet with nonstick cooking spray. Heat over medium-high heat until hot. Add chicken; cook 8 minutes or until browned, fork-tender and juices run clear, turning once.

7. Cut cooled pizza crust into 4 rectangles. Remove rectangles from pan; spread each with 1 tablespoon mayonnaise mixture. Top 2 rectangles with chicken, spinach, onion mixture, cheese and remaining crust rectangles, mayonnaise side down.

8. Heat large skillet or cast iron skillet over medium heat until hot. Place sandwiches in skillet. Place smaller skillet on sandwiches to flatten slightly. Cook about 1 to 2 minutes or until crisp and heated, turning once. Cut each warm sandwich into quarters.

1 Serving: Calories 523 (Calories from Fat 171); Total Fat 19g; Saturated Fat 7g; Trans Fat 0g; Cholesterol 59mg; Sodium 1182mg; Total Carbohydrate 59g; Dietary Fiber 4g; Sugars 12g; Protein 30g

A Peek Inside the Bake-Off® Contest:

Many of the recipes in this book are heirloom recipes, passed down from parent to child over many generations. However, many of us aren't lucky enough to have our own family recipes. Dorothy Wagoner had the idea of inventing her own heirloom recipe, describing the effort as "searching for a flavor to match a memory."

"My father came to this country [from Germany] when he was a young man, and I was never to meet any of his family," Dorothy said. "Dad had a vivid memory, and through the stories of his childhood I could picture Grandmother's kitchen, the many wonderful things she baked and the dark, luxurious pastries that were Dad's favorite." Dorothy tried different flavor combinations, and then decided to make her dessert a pie, combining her own memories of her mother's cooking—her mother died when Dorothy was twelve—with her father's memories of his mother's pastries. "My mother was a wonderful cook, and loved to bake. Saturday was baking day, and our big old kitchen would be filled with the fragrance of bread and sweet rolls, and always pie." Through long experimentation Dorothy came up with her Vienna Chocolate Pie—a true labor of love. Since the 1959 Bake-Off® Contest, Dorothy's pie has become an heirloom recipe for families nationwide.

CUBAN-STYLE SANDWICH POCKETS

Not your ordinary ham and cheese. Delve into these flaky crescent pockets for some seriously good eats.

PREP TIME: 25 MINUTES

TOTAL TIME: 45 MINUTES

MAKES 6 SERVINGS

Courtney Sawyer, Bellingham, Washington
Bake-Off® Contest 47, 2014

3 tablespoons coarse-grained mustard

¼ teaspoon ground cumin

2 cans Pillsbury™ Crescent Recipe Creations™ refrigerated seamless dough sheet

8 oz ground pork

6 slices (¾ oz each) cooked ham from deli

6 slices (¾ oz each) Swiss cheese

18 dill pickle chips

1. Heat oven to 400°F. Spray large cookie sheet with no-stick cooking spray.

2. In small bowl, mix mustard and cumin. Unroll dough sheets on work surface. Cut each sheet into thirds. Press each third into 7½x4½-inch rectangle. Spread mustard mixture evenly over each rectangle to within ½ inch of edges.

3. Shape pork into 6 (3-inch) squares; place over mustard on each rectangle. Top each pork patty with 1 slice ham, 1 slice cheese and 3 pickle chips. Fold dough over filling; press edges firmly with fork to seal. Prick top of each pocket 3 times with fork. Place pockets 2 inches apart on cookie sheet.

4. Bake 15 to 18 minutes or until golden brown and meat thermometer inserted in center of pockets reads 145°F.

1 Serving: Calories 440 (Calories from Fat 2200); Total Fat 25g; Saturated Fat 11g; Trans Fat 0g; Cholesterol 55mg; Sodium 1460mg; Total Carbohydrate 35g; Dietary Fiber 0g; Sugars 1g; Protein 20g

THAI CHICKEN BURGERS

Make a grand burger, Thai style, with a spicy peanut butter sauce and lots of crunchy greens.

PREP TIME: 20 MINUTES
TOTAL TIME: 30 MINUTES

MAKES 8 SERVINGS

Angie Pieropoulos, Downers Grove, Illinois
Bake-Off® Contest 46, 2013

1 can Pillsbury™ Grands!™ Homestyle refrigerated buttermilk biscuits (8 ct)

1 cup fresh bean sprouts

⅔ cup sliced green onions

1½ lbs ground chicken

1 teaspoon salt

½ teaspoon pepper

½ cup water

1 cup crunchy peanut butter

4½ teaspoons hot chili sauce

1½ cups shredded Chinese (napa) cabbage

1. Heat oven to 350°F. Bake biscuits as directed on can; keep warm.

2. Meanwhile, finely chop ½ cup of the bean sprouts; place in large bowl. Add ⅓ cup of the green onions, ground chicken, 1 teaspoon salt and ½ teaspoon pepper; mix well. Shape mixture into 8 patties, 3½ inches in diameter.

3. In 12-inch nonstick skillet, cook patties over medium-high heat 5 to 7 minutes, turning once, until thermometer inserted in center of patties reads 165°F.

4. In 1-quart saucepan, mix the water and remaining ½ cup bean sprouts. Bring to a boil; lower heat, simmer 2 minutes or until sprouts are thoroughly cooked and no longer crisp. Stir in peanut butter and hot chili sauce; cook over medium-low heat, stirring constantly, until thoroughly heated. Remove from heat. Stir in remaining ⅓ cup green onions.

5. Split biscuits; place burgers on bottom of each biscuit. Spoon 2 tablespoons peanut butter mixture over burgers; top with cabbage and biscuit tops. Serve with remaining peanut butter mixture. Garnish with green onions, if desired.

1 Serving: Calories 500 (Calories from Fat 270); Total Fat 30g; Saturated Fat 7g; Trans Fat 0g; Cholesterol 50mg; Sodium 1060mg; Total Carbohydrate 36g; Dietary Fiber 3g; Sugars 1g; Protein 22g

SPICY ASIAN LETTUCE WRAPS

Asian dinner made easy with frozen stir-fry meal starter. Enjoy these spicy chicken and lettuce wraps— a flavorful skillet dish.

PREP TIME: 50 MINUTES
TOTAL TIME: 50 MINUTES

MAKES 8 SERVINGS

Maria Baldwin, Mesa, Arizona
Bake-Off® Contest 40, 2002

2 tablespoons vegetable oil

2 tablespoons chili-garlic sauce

2 tablespoons soy sauce

2 cloves garlic, finely chopped

1 tablespoon sugar

2 tablespoons peanut butter

2 tablespoons water

1 lb boneless skinless chicken breast halves, cut into 1-inch pieces

1 bag (19 oz) frozen stir-fry lo mein meal starter

8 large leaves Bibb lettuce

1½ cups grated carrots

⅓ cup chopped peanuts

¼ cup finely chopped green onions

2 tablespoons finely chopped fresh cilantro, if desired

1. In small bowl, mix 1 tablespoon of the oil, the chili-garlic sauce, soy sauce, garlic, sugar, peanut butter and water until smooth. Set aside.

2. In 12-inch nonstick skillet, heat remaining 1 tablespoon oil over medium-high heat until hot. Add chicken; cook 5 to 6 minutes, stirring frequently, until chicken is no longer pink in center. Remove chicken from skillet; cover to keep warm.

3. In same skillet, heat soy sauce mixture over medium-high heat until hot. Add contents of bag of meal starter; cook 6 to 8 minutes, stirring frequently, until vegetables are crisp-tender. Add chicken; stir to coat. Remove from heat.

4. Pat lettuce dry with paper towel; arrange on part of large serving platter. Spoon carrots onto platter next to lettuce. Arrange chicken mixture on platter. Sprinkle with peanuts, onions and cilantro.

5. To serve, top each lettuce leaf with chicken-vegetable mixture and carrots. Wrap lettuce around filling.

1 Serving: Calories 240 (Calories from Fat 100); Total Fat 11g; Saturated Fat 2g; Trans Fat 0g; Cholesterol 35mg; Sodium 630mg; Total Carbohydrate 18g; Dietary Fiber 2g; Sugars 7g; Protein 18g

SWEET 'N SOUR CHICKEN WRAPS

You'll like the subtle honey-and-soy-flavored filling in these quick and easy sand-wiches. Serve them at your next luncheon or shower.

PREP TIME: 30 MINUTES
TOTAL TIME: 30 MINUTES

MAKES 8 SERVINGS

Carol Winder, Murray, Utah
Bake-Off® Contest 35, 1992

1 cup chopped cooked chicken

2 tablespoons chopped green onion, including tops

1 tablespoon canned crushed pineapple, well drained

2 tablespoons honey

1 tablespoon soy sauce

2 tablespoons prepared mustard

1 (8-oz.) can refrigerated crescent dinner rolls

1 egg beaten

2 teaspoons sesame seed, toasted

Green onions, if desired

1. Heat oven to 375°F. In small bowl, combine chicken, 2 table-spoons green onions and pineapple; mix well. In another small bowl, combine honey, soy sauce and mustard; blend well. Pour over chicken mixture; stir to coat.

2. Separate dough into 4 rectangles; firmly press perforations to seal. Cut each rectangle in half crosswise. Spoon 1 round tablespoon of chicken filling onto center of each square. To make each wrap, pull 4 corners of dough to center of filling; twist ends and pinch seams to seal. Brush wraps with egg; sprinkle with sesame seed. Place on ungreased cookie sheet.

3. Bake at 375°F for 10 to 15 minutes or until deep golden brown. Arrange on serving platter; garnish with whole green onions.

> **CLEVER IDEA:** *To toast sesame seed, spread in baking pan; bake at 350°F for 6 to 8 minutes or until light golden brown, stirring occasionally. Or place seeds in a skillet; stir over medium heat for 8 to 10 minutes or until light golden brown.*

1 Serving: Calories 170 (Calories from Fat 70); Total Fat 8g; Saturated Fat 2.5g; Trans Fat 1.5g; Cholesterol 40mg; Sodium 400mg; Total Carbohydrate 16g; Dietary Fiber 0g; Sugars 7g; Protein 9g

CHINESE ROAST PORK BUNS

Biscuit dough is wrapped around a barbecue filling to make a Chinese treat known in China as bau buns.

PREP TIME: 25 MINUTES
TOTAL TIME: 1 HOUR 35 MINUTES

MAKES 8 SERVINGS

Wayne Hu, West Bloomfield, Michigan
Bake-Off® Contest 36, 1994

ROAST PORK

¼ cup firmly packed brown sugar

¼ cup ketchup

2 tablespoons soy sauce

2 tablespoons hoisin sauce

1 tablespoon dry sherry

1 garlic clove, minced

1½ lb. pork steaks (½ inch thick)

SAUCE

1 tablespoon cornstarch

1 tablespoon dry sherry

1 tablespoon peanut oil or vegetable oil

½ cup chopped onion

½ cup chopped water chestnuts

1 tablespoon soy sauce

1 tablespoon hoisin sauce

½ cup chicken broth

PASTRY

1 (1 lb. 0.3-oz.) can large refrigerated buttermilk biscuits

GLAZE

1 teaspoon sugar

1 teaspoon water

1 egg white

1. Heat oven to 375°F. Line broiler pan with foil. In blender container or food processor bowl with metal blade, combine all roast pork ingredients except pork; blend until smooth. Generously brush both sides of the pork steaks, reserving remaining basting sauce. Place pork steaks on foil-lined broiler pan.

2. Bake at 375°F for 30 minutes. Remove pork from oven. Brush both sides of steaks with remaining basting sauce. Bake an additional 10 to 20 minutes or until no longer pink in the center. Remove from oven; cool (leave the oven on). Remove meat from bone; finely chop. Set aside.

3. In small bowl, combine cornstarch and 1 tablespoon sherry; blend well. Heat oil in wok or large skillet over high heat. Add onion and water chestnuts; cook and stir 2 to 3 minutes or until onion begins to brown. Add 1 tablespoon soy sauce and 1 tablespoon hoisin sauce; stir to coat. Add broth. Stir in cornstarch mixture; cook and stir until mixture begins to thicken. Remove from heat; stir in pork.

4. Separate dough into 8 biscuits. On lightly floured surface, press or roll each biscuit into 5-inch circle. Place about $1/3$ cup pork mixture in center of each biscuit. Gathering up edges, twist and pinch to seal. Place seam side down on ungreased cookie sheet. In small bowl, beat glaze ingredients until well blended; brush over buns.

5. Bake at 375°F for 14 to 18 minutes or until golden brown.

CLEVER IDEAS:

- *Mixture also can be blended in small bowl with wire whisk.*

- *After step 3, pork mixture can be covered and refrigerated. Heat until warm before making sandwiches.*

1 Serving: Calories 365 (Calories from Fat 120); Total Fat 13g; Saturated Fat 4.5g; Trans Fat 0.5g; Cholesterol 50mg; Sodium 1227mg; Total Carbohydrate 40g; Dietary Fiber 2g; Sugars 14g; Protein 21g

ITALIAN SAUSAGE CRESCENT SANDWICHES

PREP TIME: 25 MINUTES
TOTAL TIME: 45 MINUTES

MAKES 8 SANDWICHES

Cecilia V. Lagerak, Westminster, Colorado
Bake-Off® Contest 26, 1975

1 lb. bulk Italian sausage, crumbled

½ cup chopped green bell pepper

⅓ cup chopped onion

1 can (16-oz.) pizza sauce

2 cans (8-oz. each) Pillsbury™ refrigerated crescent dinner rolls

1 package (6-oz.) mozzarella cheese slices, halved, folded

1. Heat oven to 375°F. In 10-inch skillet, cook sausage, bell pepper and onion over medium-high heat, stirring frequently, until sausage is no longer pink and vegetables are tender; drain. Add 3 tablespoons of the pizza sauce; mix well.

2. Separate dough into 8 rectangles. Firmly press perforations to seal. Place about ¼ cup sausage mixture and ½ slice cheese, folded, on one end of each rectangle. Fold dough in half over filling; press edges with fork to seal. Place on ungreased cookie sheet.

3. Bake 15 to 18 minutes or until golden brown. Meanwhile, in 1-quart saucepan, heat remaining pizza sauce over low heat until hot. Serve sandwiches with warm pizza sauce.

1 Serving: Calories 400 (Calories from Fat 200); Total Fat 22g; Saturated Fat 7g; Trans Fat 3g; Cholesterol 30mg; Sodium 1013mg; Total Carbohydrate 30g; Dietary Fiber 1g; Sugars 6g; Protein 20g

SWISS HAM RING-A-ROUND

PREP TIME: 20 MINUTES
TOTAL TIME: 50 MINUTES

MAKES 8 SERVINGS

Mrs. Lyman Francis, Cheshire, Connecticut
Bake-Off® Contest 20, 1969

1 tablespoon butter or margarine, softened

¼ cup chopped fresh parsley or 2 tablespoons dried parsley flakes

2 tablespoons finely chopped onion or 1½ teaspoons dried minced onion

2 tablespoons yellow mustard

1 teaspoon lemon juice

1½ cups shredded Swiss cheese (6 oz.)

1 cup chopped fresh broccoli or frozen chopped broccoli, cooked, drained

1 cup diced cooked ham

1 can (8 oz) Pillsbury™ refrigerated crescent dinner rolls

1. Heat oven to 350°F. Grease large cookie sheet. In large bowl, mix butter, parsley, onion, mustard, and lemon juice. Add cheese, cooked broccoli and ham; mix lightly. Set aside.

2. Unroll dough into 8 triangles. Arrange triangles on cookie sheet with shortest sides toward center, overlapping in wreath shape and leaving a 3-inch round opening in center.

3. Spoon ham filling on widest part of dough. Pull end points of triangles over filling and tuck under dough to form a ring.

4. Bake 25 to 30 minutes or until golden brown.

1 Serving: Calories 257 (Calories from Fat 144); Total Fat 16g; Saturated Fat 7g; Trans Fat 0g; Cholesterol 40mg; Sodium 646mg; Total Carbohydrate 14g; Dietary Fiber 1g; Sugars 2g; Protein 13g

CRISPY DELI WRAPS

Crushed corn snacks are the secret to the crispy crust in these hearty sandwiches.

PREP TIME: 15 MINUTES
TOTAL TIME: 45 MINUTES
MAKES 4 SERVINGS

Bobbie Keefer, Byers, Colorado
Bake-Off® Contest 42, 2006

WRAPS

- 1 box (9 oz) frozen chopped spinach
- 2 cups Bugles™ original corn snacks
- ¼ cup butter or margarine, melted
- 16 thin slices cooked ham or turkey (about ½ lb)
- 4 sticks (1 oz each) mozzarella string cheese
- 1 can (8 oz) Pillsbury™ refrigerated crescent dinner rolls or 1 can (8 oz) Pillsbury™ Crescent Recipe Creations™ refrigerated seamless dough sheet

DIPPING SAUCE, IF DESIRED

- ⅓ cup mayonnaise or salad dressing
- ⅓ cup Dijon mustard
- ⅓ cup honey

1. Heat oven to 375°F. Line large cookie sheet with cooking parchment paper. Remove frozen spinach from pouch; place in colander. Rinse with warm water until thawed; drain well. Squeeze spinach dry with paper towel; divide evenly into 4 portions. Set aside.

2. Meanwhile, place corn snacks in re-sealable food-storage plastic bag; seal bag. With rolling pin, finely crush snacks; pour into shallow dish or pie plate. In another shallow dish or pie plate, place melted butter; set aside.

3. If using crescent rolls: Unroll dough; separate into 4 rectangles. Press each into 6x4-inch rectangle, firmly pressing perforations to seal. If using dough sheet: Unroll dough; cut into 4 rectangles. Press each into 6x4-inch rectangle.

4. Arrange ham in 4 stacks with 4 slices each. Top each stack with 1 portion of spinach, spreading spinach evenly over ham. Place 1 stick of cheese on one short side of spinach-topped ham. Roll up each stack.

5. Place 1 filled ham roll on one long side of each dough rectangle. Fold sides of dough up over ham roll, and roll to opposite long side; press edge and ends to seal and completely cover ham roll. Roll each in butter, then in crushed corn snacks to coat; place seam side down on cookie sheet.

6. Bake 20 to 28 minutes or until deep golden brown. Meanwhile, in small bowl, mix sauce ingredients with wire whisk. Serve warm wraps with sauce for dipping.

1 Serving: Calories 560 (Calories from Fat 330); Total Fat 36g; Saturated Fat 19g; Trans Fat 4g; Cholesterol 75mg; Sodium 1520mg; Total Carbohydrate 32g; Dietary Fiber 2g; Sugars 5g; Protein 26g

CRUNCHY CRESCENT HAMWICHES

PREP TIME: 20 MINUTES

TOTAL TIME: 40 MINUTES

MAKES 8 SANDWICHES

Ann Van Dorin, Webster, New York

Bake-Off® Contest 26, 1975

1 package (3-oz.) cream cheese, softened

2 tablespoons mayonnaise or salad dressing

½ teaspoon ground mustard

¼ teaspoon celery salt

1 cup diced cooked ham

½ cup frozen whole kernel corn (from 1-lb bag), thawed

¼ cup shredded Swiss or Monterey Jack cheese (1-oz.)

2 teaspoons chopped onion or ½ teaspoon dried minced onion

1 can (8-oz.) Pillsbury™ refrigerated crescent dinner rolls

1 tablespoon butter or margarine, melted

¼ to ½ cup finely crushed corn or potato chips

1. Heat oven to 375°F. In medium bowl, mix cream cheese, mayonnaise, mustard and celery salt until smooth; stir in ham, corn, cheese and onion. Separate crescent dough into 4-inch squares. Spoon about $1/4$ cup ham mixture onto center of each square. Pull 4 corners of dough to top center of filling; twist firmly and pinch corners to seal. Brush each with butter; sprinkle with chips. Place on ungreased large cookie sheet.

2. Bake 15 to 20 minutes or until golden brown. Serve immediately. Cover and refrigerate any remaining hamwiches.

1 Serving: Calories 261 (Calories from Fat 160); Total Fat 18g; Saturated Fat 6g; Trans Fat 0g; Cholesterol 36mg; Sodium 664mg; Total Carbohydrate 16g; Dietary Fiber 1g; Sugars 3g; Protein 9g.

BACON AND GOAT CHEESE SALAD ON WALNUT FLATBREAD

How can you go wrong with this combo? Smoky bacon, goat cheese, a raspberry jam surprise and crescents!

PREP TIME: 30 MINUTES
TOTAL TIME: 30 MINUTES
MAKES 4 SERVINGS

Frances Pietsch, Flower Mound, Texas
Bake-Off® Contest 46, 2013

1 can Pillsbury™ Grands!™ Big & Flaky refrigerated crescent dinner rolls

½ cup chopped walnuts

8 slices thick-sliced applewood-smoked bacon

¼ cup seedless red raspberry jam

1 tablespoon balsamic vinegar

4 cups baby salad greens

4 oz crumbled goat cheese (1 cup)

1. Heat oven to 350°F. Unroll dough; separate into 4 rectangles. Firmly press perforations to seal. Sprinkle 2 tablespoons walnuts on each rectangle; press firmly into dough. Place on large nonstick cookie sheet. Bake 10 to 12 minutes or until golden brown. Cool slightly.

2. Meanwhile, in 12-inch skillet, cook bacon over medium-high heat 5 minutes or until crisp. Remove from skillet; drain on paper towels.

3. In large bowl, beat jam and vinegar with wire whisk until well blended. Add salad greens; toss to coat.

4. Place 2 flatbreads walnut sides up. Top each with bacon slices, salad greens and goat cheese. Top with remaining flatbreads, walnut sides down. Cut each sandwich in half.

1 Serving: Calories 650 (Calories from Fat 350); Total Fat 39g; Saturated Fat 15g; Trans Fat 0g; Cholesterol 40mg; Sodium 1190mg; Total Carbohydrate 56g; Dietary Fiber 3g; Sugars 2g; Protein 19g

BACON AND GOAT CHEESE SALAD ON WALNUT FLATBREAD *(page 185)*

BACON, CAESAR, AND MOZZARELLA PANINI *(opposite)*

BACON, CAESAR, AND MOZZARELLA PANINI

An ordinary BLT won't stand a chance once you've tried a grilled sandwich on a freshly baked crust.

PREP TIME: 40 MINUTES
TOTAL TIME: 50 MINUTES
MAKES 4 SERVINGS

Carole Strachan, Houston, Texas
Bake-Off® Contest 43, 2008

1 can (13.8 oz) Pillsbury™ refrigerated classic pizza crust

4 teaspoons basil pesto

¼ cup Caesar dressing (creamy or vinaigrette style)

8 oz water-packed fresh mozzarella cheese, drained and cut into 8 slices, or

8 slices (1 oz each) regular mozzarella cheese

¼ teaspoon freshly ground pepper

12 slices cooked bacon

2 plum (Roma) tomatoes, each cut into 4 slices

8 large fresh basil leaves

¼ cup butter or margarine

1. Heat oven to 375°F. Spray large cookie sheet with no-stick cooking spray. Unroll pizza crust dough on cookie sheet; press dough into 16x11-inch rectangle, pulling dough gently if necessary. Bake 9 to 16 minutes or until light brown. Cool about 15 minutes or until cool enough to handle.

2. Cut cooled pizza crust in half lengthwise and crosswise to make 4 rectangles. Remove rectangles from cookie sheet; cut each rectangle in half crosswise for a total of 8 squares.

3. On each of 4 crust slices, spread 1 teaspoon pesto; set aside. On each of remaining 4 slices, spread 1 tablespoon Caesar dressing. Place 2 cheese slices on each crust slice with Caesar dressing. Top cheese with pepper, 3 bacon slices, 2 tomato slices and 2 basil leaves. Top with remaining crust slices, pesto sides down.

4. Heat 12-inch skillet or cast-iron skillet over medium heat until hot. Melt 2 tablespoons of the butter in skillet. Place 2 sandwiches in skillet. Place smaller skillet or saucepan on sandwiches to flatten slightly; keep skillet on sandwiches while cooking. Cook 1 to 2 minutes on each side or until bread is golden brown and crisp and fillings are heated. Remove from skillet; cover with foil to keep warm. Repeat with remaining 2 tablespoons butter and sandwiches.

1 Serving: Calories 760 (Calories from Fat 420); Total Fat 47g; Saturated Fat 20g; Trans Fat 1g; Cholesterol 90mg; Sodium 1840mg; Total Carbohydrate 51g; Dietary Fiber 0g; Sugars 8g; Protein 32g

TUNA CHEESE FLIPS

This creamy tuna sandwich with a crunchy potato chip coating was added to the list of America's favorites in 1976, our bicentennial year.

PREP TIME: 20 MINUTES
TOTAL TIME: 45 MINUTES
MAKES 10 SERVINGS

Marilyn Belschner, Amherst, Nebraska
Bake-Off® Contest 35, 1992

2 (6-oz.) cans tuna, drained, flaked

⅛ teaspoon lemon pepper seasoning

⅓ cup sliced ripe or green olives, drained

⅓ cup mayonnaise or salad dressing

2 oz. (½ cup) shredded Monterey Jack or Cheddar cheese

1 (12-oz.) can refrigerated flaky biscuits

1 egg, beaten, or 2 tablespoons milk

1 cup crushed potato chips

Heat oven to 375°F. In small bowl, combine tuna, lemon pepper seasoning, olives, mayonnaise and cheese. Separate dough into 10 biscuits. Press or roll out each to 5-inch circle. Spoon about ¼ cup tuna mixture onto center of each circle. Fold dough in half over filling; press edges with fork to seal. Brush both sides of each sandwich with egg; press both sides in chips. Place on ungreased cookie sheet. With sharp knife make two or three ½-inch slits in top of each sandwich. Bake at 375°F for 18 to 24 minutes or until deep golden brown.

1 Serving: Calories 274 (Calories from Fat 140); Total Fat 15g; Saturated Fat 3.5g; Trans Fat 1g; Cholesterol 40mg; Sodium 596mg; Total Carbohydrate 21g; Dietary Fiber 1g; Sugars 2g; Protein 12g

FISH AND CRESCENT ROLL-UPS

Looking for delicious sandwiches? Then check out these crescent bread sticks spooned with tartar sauce roll-ups made using Pillsbury™ refrigerated crescent dinner rolls.

PREP TIME: 10 MINUTES
TOTAL TIME: 25 MINUTES

MAKES 8 SERVINGS

Louise K. Ross, Sonora, California
Bake-Off® Contest 26, 1975

3 tablespoons tartar sauce

2 teaspoons finely chopped onion

1 can (8 oz) Pillsbury™ refrigerated crescent dinner rolls

8 frozen breaded fish sticks

1 tablespoon butter or margarine, melted

Sesame seed

1. Heat oven to 375°F. In small bowl, mix tartar sauce and onion.

2. Separate dough into 8 triangles. Place 1 fish stick on shortest side of each triangle. Spoon 1 teaspoon tartar sauce mixture onto each fish stick.

3. Roll up each, starting at shortest side of triangle and rolling to opposite point. (Fish sticks will not be completely covered.) Place roll-ups, point side down, on ungreased cookie sheet. Brush each with butter. Sprinkle with sesame seed.

4. Bake 11 to 13 minutes or until golden brown.

1 Serving: Calories 190 (Calories from Fat 110); Total Fat 13g; Saturated Fat 3.5g; Trans Fat 2g; Cholesterol 10mg; Sodium 330mg; Total Carbohydrate 16g; Dietary Fiber 0g; Sugars 3g; Protein 4g

EASY EATS PIZZAS, BURGERS, SANDWICHES AND SALADS

PHILLY CHEESESTEAK ONION SOUP

Slices of fresh-baked Pillsbury™ crusty French loaf top a beefy onion soup in a classic twist for two.

PREP TIME: 10 MINUTES

TOTAL TIME: 35 MINUTES

MAKES 2 SERVINGS

Anne Johnson, Vincent, Ohio
Bake-Off® Contest 42, 2006

1 can (11 oz) Pillsbury™ refrigerated crusty French loaf

½ teaspoon butter or margarine

1 boneless beef rib-eye steak (½ lb), trimmed of fat, cut into bite-size strips

¼ teaspoon salt

Dash pepper

1 can (18.5 oz) French onion soup

1 can (4 oz) mushroom pieces and stems, drained

½ cup shredded provolone cheese (2 oz)

3 tablespoons chopped green bell pepper

1. Heat oven to 350°F. Bake French loaf as directed on can. Meanwhile, in 2-quart saucepan, melt butter over medium heat. Add beef strips; sprinkle with salt and pepper. Cook and stir until browned. Stir in soup; heat to boiling. Reduce heat to medium-low; simmer uncovered 20 minutes.

2. Stir mushrooms into soup; cook until thoroughly heated. Cut 2 (1-inch-thick) diagonal slices from warm loaf; reserve remaining loaf to serve with soup.

3. Set oven control to broil. Ladle soup into 2 (15-oz) ovenproof bowls. Sprinkle 2 tablespoons of the cheese onto each serving. Top each with bread slice. Sprinkle bell pepper and remaining cheese evenly over each.

4. Place bowls on cookie sheet; broil 4 to 6 inches from heat 1 to 2 minutes or until cheese is bubbly and bread is toasted. Serve soup with remaining slices of loaf.

1 Serving: Calories 730 (Calories from Fat 210); Total Fat 23g; Saturated Fat 10g; Trans Fat 2g; Cholesterol 75mg; Sodium 2720mg; Total Carbohydrate 83g; Dietary Fiber 4g; Sugars 13g; Protein 48g

SOUTHWEST TORTELLINI CHOWDER

Enjoy a sumptuous dinner tonight with this southwestern style frozen veggies and pasta chowder that's ready in just 25 minutes!

PREP TIME: 25 MINUTES
TOTAL TIME: 25 MINUTES
MAKES 6 SERVINGS

Loanne Chiu, Fort Worth, Texas
Bake-Off® Contest 37, 1996

3 cans (10½ oz each) condensed chicken broth

1½ cups mild chunky-style salsa or picante

½ teaspoon grated orange peel

2 packages (9 oz each) refrigerated meat-filled or cheese-filled tortellini

2 cups frozen cut broccoli (from 1-lb bag)

1 cup frozen whole kernel corn (from 1-lb bag)

½ cup coarsely chopped red bell pepper

1 can (5 oz) evaporated milk

Dash salt

¼ cup chopped fresh cilantro

1. In Dutch oven or 4-quart saucepan, heat broth, salsa and orange peel to boiling. Reduce heat to low; simmer 3 minutes.

2. Stir in tortellini and vegetables; cook over medium heat 6 to 8 minutes or until tortellini and vegetables are tender.

3. Stir in milk and salt; cook 1 to 2 minutes or just until hot, stirring occasionally. DO NOT BOIL. Top each serving of chowder with cilantro. Serve immediately.

CLEVER IDEA: *One 16-oz package frozen tortellini can be substituted for both packages of refrigerated tortellini. Add frozen tortellini to simmered broth mixture; cook 4 minutes. Add vegetables; cook an additional 6 to 8 minutes or until tortellini and vegetables are tender.*

1 Serving: Calories 400 (Calories from Fat 90); Total Fat 10g; Saturated Fat 4.5g; Trans Fat 0g; Cholesterol 40mg; Sodium 1670mg; Total Carbohydrate 56g; Dietary Fiber 5g; Sugars 10g; Protein 23g

ENCHILADA PASTA SOUP

Homemade soup in minutes!
You CAN do it!

Barbara Catlin Craven, Kerrville, Texas
Bake-Off® Contest 40, 2002

PREP TIME: 20 MINUTES
TOTAL TIME: 20 MINUTES

MAKES 6 SERVINGS

SOUP

5¼ cups chicken broth (from two 32-oz. cartons)

2 (14.75-oz.) cans cream style sweet corn

2 (10-oz.) cans red enchilada sauce

1 (4.5-oz.) can chopped green chiles

1 (10-oz.) can chunk white and dark chicken in water, undrained

1 (5-oz.) pkg. uncooked vermicelli, broken into pieces

1½ teaspoons cumin

½ teaspoon salt

½ teaspoon onion powder

½ teaspoon dried oregano leaves, crushed

GARNISH, IF DESIRED

1 medium onion, chopped

12 oz. (3 cups) shredded Colby-Monterey Jack cheese blend

1. In Dutch oven or large saucepan, combine broth, corn, enchilada sauce and chiles; mix well. Bring to a boil over medium-high heat. Add all remaining soup ingredients; mix well.

2. Reduce heat to low; simmer 8 minutes or until vermicelli is tender, stirring occasionally. Ladle soup into individual bowls. Garnish each serving with onion and cheese.

1 Serving: Calories 591 (Calories from Fat 283); Total Fat 31g; Saturated Fat 17g; Trans Fat 0g; Cholesterol 116mg; Sodium 1979mg; Total Carbohydrate 48g; Dietary Fiber 3g; Sugars 9g; Protein 30g

BARBECUE BLACK BEAN CHILI

Chili meat is replaced with sassy barbecue pork or chicken in this updated version of a classic.

PREP TIME: 30 MINUTES
TOTAL TIME: 30 MINUTES

MAKES 6 SERVINGS

Paula Murphy, Richmond, Virginia
Bake-Off® Contest 41, 2004

CHILI

1 container (18 oz) refrigerated original barbecue sauce with shredded pork or chicken

2 cans (15 oz each) black beans, drained, rinsed

1 can (28 oz) organic diced tomatoes, undrained

1 can (14 oz) beef broth

1 package (1 oz) taco seasoning mix

1 teaspoon ground cumin

1 teaspoon chili powder

TOPPINGS, IF DESIRED

Sour cream

Grated cheese (such as Colby-Monterey Jack or Cheddar)

Salsa

Pickled jalapeño slices and/or chopped green chiles

Red pepper sauce

Tortilla chips

1. In 4½-quart Dutch oven or 4-quart saucepan, mix all chili ingredients. Heat over medium-high heat to boiling, stirring occasionally.

2. Reduce heat; simmer uncovered 20 minutes, stirring occasionally. Serve with choice of toppings.

CLEVER IDEA: *For a thicker consistency and more flavor, simmer longer. If time does not permit longer cooking, mix 1 tablespoon cornstarch and ¼ cup cold water until blended. Stir into chili; return to boiling and cook until desired consistency.*

1 Serving: Calories 275 (Calories from Fat 33); Total Fat 4g; Saturated Fat 1g; Trans Fat 0g; Cholesterol 25mg; Sodium 1937mg; Total Carbohydrate 42g; Dietary Fiber 7g; Sugars 18g; Protein 17g

WHITE CHILI WITH SALSA VERDE

PREP TIME: 45 MINUTES
TOTAL TIME: 1 HOUR 15 MINUTES

MAKES 8 SERVINGS
(1¼ CUPS EACH)

Reta M. Smith, Libertyville, Illinois
Bake-Off® Contest 35, 1992

SALSA VERDE

- 2 cups coarsely chopped fresh tomatillos or 2 cans (11-oz. each) tomatillos, chopped, well drained
- ½ cup chopped onion
- ½ cup chopped fresh cilantro
- 2 to 3 tablespoons lime juice
- ½ teaspoon lemon-pepper seasoning
- ½ teaspoon dried oregano leaves
- ½ teaspoon adobo seasoning or garlic powder
- 1 pickled jalapeño chili, chopped

CHILI

- 2½ cups water
- 1 teaspoon lemon-pepper seasoning
- 1 teaspoon cumin seed
- 4 bone-in chicken breasts (about 1½ lb.), skin removed
- 1 clove garlic, finely chopped
- 1 cup chopped onions
- 2 boxes (9-oz. each) frozen shoepeg white corn, thawed
- 2 cans (4.5-oz. each) chopped green chiles, undrained
- 1 teaspoon ground cumin
- 2 to 3 tablespoons lime juice
- 2 cans (15.5-oz. each) great northern beans, undrained
- ⅔ cup crushed tortilla chips
- ½ cup shredded reduced-fat Monterey Jack cheese (2-oz.)

1. In medium bowl, mix salsa verde ingredients. Refrigerate 30 minutes to blend flavors.

2. Meanwhile, in 4-quart saucepan, heat water, 1 teaspoon lemon-pepper seasoning and cumin seed to boiling. Add chicken. Reduce heat to low; cover and simmer 20 to 28 minutes or until chicken is fork-tender and juices run clear. Remove chicken from bones; cut into 1-inch pieces. Return chicken to saucepan.

3. Spray 8-inch skillet with cooking spray. Heat over medium heat until hot. Add 1 clove garlic; cook and stir 1 minute. Remove from skillet; add to chicken mixture.

4. Add 1 cup onions to skillet; cook and stir until tender. Add cooked onions, corn, chiles, cumin and 2 to 3 tablespoons lime juice to chicken mixture. Heat to boiling. Add beans; cook until hot.

5. To serve, place about 1 tablespoon each of tortilla chips and cheese in each of 8 individual soup bowls; ladle soup over cheese and serve with salsa verde.

CLEVER IDEAS:

- *If desired, substitute one 16-oz. jar salsa verde (green salsa).*

- *If fresh or canned tomatillos are not available, 2 cups coarsely chopped green tomatoes can be substituted.*

- *Adobo is a specialty seasoning available in Hispanic grocery stores.*

1 Serving: Calories 352 (Calories from Fat 60); Total Fat 6g; Saturated Fat 2g; Trans Fat 0g; Cholesterol 49mg; Sodium 445mg; Total Carbohydrate 48g; Dietary Fiber 9g; Sugars 5g; Protein 27g

A Peek Inside the Bake-Off® Contest:

About one month before the Pillsbury Bake-Off® Contest, finalists receive a letter with travel information and suggestions about what to pack. In the 1949 letter, Ann Pillsbury wrote: "You might want to bring a housedress of some kind that you like to cook in, but you won't need an apron because Pillsbury will furnish all the contestants with aprons that they may keep for souvenirs." And the tradition continues: The apron for the 43rd contest was designed with the Dallas location in mind. The dark brown apron features khaki-colored Western accent stitching and a blue jeans-style pocket.

A Peek Inside the Bake-Off® Contest:

Sharing her experiences with earning the $25,000 grand prize at the 1972 Bake-Off® Contest, Isabelle Collins says, "We were in the process of a little do-it-yourself project at the time I won." In reality, Isabelle and her family were building a new home, and she was so busy, "I couldn't even remember the recipe that I submitted."

She's still amazed that her easy-to-make Quick and Chewy Crescent Bars won the top prize. "You just press out the crescent rolls," she says. "It's so simple."

For Isabelle, winning couldn't have come at a better time. "There were a lot of hidden expenses on the house that we weren't expecting, and we were about $1,000 behind on our bills." When a contest photographer came to take her picture, the family was living in the basement of the unfinished home, with no kitchen. Isabelle had to run over to a neighbor's house to bake her bars for the photo.

Winning the Bake-Off® Contest changed that whole picture. The money allowed Isabelle to finish the house, put in a garage, sidewalks and draperies, and purchase a pickup truck. It also enabled her to be a stay-at-home mom. "It was really a godsend," Isabelle said. "It landed in our laps at a time when we really needed it."

BLACK BEAN-CHORIZO SOUP
IN TORTILLA BOWLS

Chorizo sausage adds heat to vegetable soup for two served in baked tortilla bowls.

PREP TIME: 25 MINUTES
TOTAL TIME: 25 MINUTES
MAKES 2 SERVINGS

Sita Lepczyk Williams, Blacksburg, Virginia
Bake-Off® Contest 42, 2006

2 flour tortillas (8 to 10 inch)

5 oz smoked chorizo sausage links, coarsely chopped

1 large clove garlic, finely chopped

⅓ cup dry sherry or chicken broth

½ teaspoon chili powder

1 can (19 oz) hearty black bean soup

1 can (4.5 oz) chopped green chiles

⅓ cup shredded Mexican 4-cheese blend (1⅓ oz)

2 tablespoons sour cream

2 tablespoons chopped fresh cilantro

1. Place oven rack in bottom rack position; heat oven to 350°F. Spray 2 (10-oz) ovenproof custard cups with cooking spray; place on cookie sheet.

2. Place tortillas on microwavable plate; cover with microwavable plastic wrap. Microwave on High 45 to 60 seconds, turning after 30 seconds, until very soft. Center tortillas over cups, press into cups so top edges are even. Press tortilla folds against side of each cup to make bowl as large as possible.

3. Bake on bottom oven rack 8 to 10 minutes or until tortillas are stiff enough to hold their shape. Remove tortilla bowls from cups; place on cookie sheet. Return to middle oven rack in oven; bake 5 to 7 minutes longer or until browned and stiff. Remove tortilla bowls from cookie sheet; place on wire rack.

4. Meanwhile, heat 10-inch regular or cast iron skillet over high heat. Add sausage; cook and stir about 30 seconds or until browned. Add garlic; cook and stir 30 to 60 seconds longer. Remove skillet from heat; stir in sherry. Return skillet to high heat; cook and stir 2 to 3 minutes or until liquid has almost evaporated. Stir in chili powder, soup and green chiles. Reduce heat to medium-low; cook, stirring occasionally, until thoroughly heated.

5. Place tortilla bowls on individual plates. Divide soup evenly among bowls. Top each with cheese, sour cream and cilantro. Serve immediately.

1 Serving: Calories 740 (Calories from Fat 360); Total Fat 40g; Saturated Fat 16g; Trans Fat 1g; Cholesterol 85mg; Sodium 2250mg; Total Carbohydrate 62g; Dietary Fiber 10g; Sugars 5g; Protein 34g

SPICY SAUSAGE-CRANBERRY-BAKED BEAN RAGOUT

Looking for a hearty skillet dinner using green chiles? Then check out this spicy ragout featuring sausage, cranberries and beans.

PREP TIME: 25 MINUTES
TOTAL TIME: 25 MINUTES

MAKES 4 SERVINGS

Marta Rallis, Los Angeles, California
Bake-Off® Contest 38, 1998

- 1 to 3 teaspoons oil
- 1 cup chopped onions
- 1 lb fully cooked smoked sausage links, skin removed if desired, cut into ½-inch slices
- 2 teaspoons cumin seed
- 1 can (28 oz) baked beans
- 1 can (4.5 oz) chopped green chiles
- ⅔ cup canned whole berry cranberry sauce
- ⅓ cup sweetened dried cranberries
- 1 chipotle chile in adobo sauce (from 11 oz can), chopped, or ¼ teaspoon crushed red pepper flakes
- Fresh cilantro sprigs, if desired

1. Heat oil in 12-inch skillet over medium-high heat until hot. Add onions and smoked sausage; cook 7 to 10 minutes or until sausage is browned and onions are tender, stirring frequently. Add cumin seed; cook 1 minute. Drain.

2. Add beans, green chiles, cranberry sauce, dried cranberries and chipotle chile; mix well. Reduce heat to low; cover and cook 5 to 7 minutes or until thoroughly heated, stirring occasionally.

3. To serve, spoon into serving bowl. Garnish with cilantro. If desired, serve with French bread.

1 Serving: Calories 671 (Calories from Fat 300); Total Fat 33g; Saturated Fat 11g; Trans Fats 0g; Cholesterol 80mg; Sodium 1980mg; Total Carbohydrate 85g; Dietary Fiber 14g; Sugars 43g; Protein 29g

CREAMY BEAN SOUP
WITH TAQUITO DIPPERS

*Cheese-filled tortillas are
the perfect match for a
quick, easy and hearty soup.*

PREP TIME: 30 MINUTES
TOTAL TIME: 30 MINUTES

MAKES 4 SERVINGS

Sheila Suhan, Scottdale, Pennsylvania
Bake-Off® Contest 43, 2008

1 can (16 oz) traditional refried beans

1 can (14.5 oz) petite diced tomatoes, undrained

1 cup chicken broth

½ cup (from 14-oz can) unsweetened coconut milk (not cream of coconut)

1 can (4.5 oz) chopped green chiles

1 package (1 oz) taco seasoning mix

6 sticks (0.75 oz each) sharp Cheddar or chipotle Cheddar cheese

1 package (10.5 oz) flour tortillas for soft tacos & fajitas (12 tortillas)

2 tablespoons vegetable oil

¼ cup chopped fresh cilantro, if desired

4 medium green onions, sliced (¼ cup), if desired

1. Heat oven to 450°F. Line cookie sheet with foil.

2. In 2-quart saucepan, stir refried beans, tomatoes, broth, coconut milk, green chiles and taco seasoning mix; heat to boiling. Reduce heat to low; simmer uncovered about 20 minutes.

3. Meanwhile, cut each cheese stick in half lengthwise to make 2 thin sticks. Place 1 cheese stick on one edge of each tortilla; roll tortilla tightly around cheese. Brush edges of tortillas with water to seal. Place taquitos, seam sides down, on cookie sheet. Brush each lightly with oil. Bake 5 to 7 minutes or until edges of tortillas are golden brown and cheese is melted.

4. Pour soup into serving bowls; garnish with cilantro or onions. Serve with taquitos for dipping.

1 Serving: Calories 660 (Calories from Fat 280); Total Fat 31g; Saturated Fat 14g; Trans Fat 2.5g; Cholesterol 45mg; Sodium 2460mg; Total Carbohydrate 71g; Dietary Fiber 9g; Sugars 8g; Protein 23g

CREAMY BROCCOLI AND WILD RICE SOUP

Dinner ready in 25 minutes!
Enjoy this hearty broccoli,
veggies and rice soup sprin-
kled with paprika.

PREP TIME: 25 MINUTES
TOTAL TIME: 25 MINUTES

MAKES 4 SERVINGS

Pat Bradley, Rohnert Park, California
Bake-Off® Contest 35, 1992

1 box (10 oz) frozen cut broccoli in a cheese flavored sauce

1 box (10 oz) frozen white and wild rice

2 tablespoons butter or margarine

½ cup chopped onion (1 medium)

½ cup chopped celery

½ cup sliced almonds

¼ lb cooked ham, cubed (¾ cup)

½ teaspoon dried thyme leaves

½ teaspoon dried marjoram leaves

¼ teaspoon salt

⅛ teaspoon pepper

3 cups whole milk or half-and-half

Paprika

1. Cook broccoli with cheese sauce and rice as directed on boxes. Set aside.

2. Meanwhile, in 4-quart saucepan, melt butter over medium-high heat. Cook onion, celery and almonds in butter, stirring frequently, until vegetables are crisp-tender and almonds are lightly browned.

3. Stir in cooked broccoli with cheese sauce, cooked rice, ham, thyme, marjoram, salt and pepper. Stir in milk. Cook, stirring frequently, until hot. DO NOT BOIL. Sprinkle individual servings with paprika.

1 Serving: Calories 400 (Calories from Fat 210); Total Fat 23g; Saturated Fat 9g; Trans Fat 0.5g; Cholesterol 50mg; Sodium 1310mg; Total Carbohydrate 30g; Dietary Fiber 4g; Sugars 13g; Protein 18g

SOUPER SHRIMP BISQUE

Shrimp and cream dress up tomato soup to make a rich and elegant first-course bisque.

PREP TIME: 20 MINUTES
TOTAL TIME: 20 MINUTES

MAKES 4 SERVINGS

Nina Pajak, Longwood, Florida
Bake-Off® Contest 41, 2004

8 oz cooked deveined shelled shrimp, tail shells removed

1 can (19 oz) hearty tomato soup

2 teaspoons Worcestershire sauce

¾ teaspoon seafood seasoning

⅓ cup whipping cream

Purchased or homemade croutons, if desired

¼ to ⅓ cup chopped fresh basil, if desired

1. In blender, process half of the shrimp with on/off pulses until chopped. Add half of the soup; process until smooth. Pour into 2-quart saucepan. Repeat with remaining half of shrimp and soup.

2. Stir Worcestershire sauce and seafood seasoning into soup. Heat over medium heat to boiling. Reduce heat; simmer 2 to 3 minutes, stirring frequently, until thoroughly heated. Stir in cream. Heat about 1 minute or just until thoroughly heated.

3. Ladle soup into individual soup bowls. Top each with croutons and basil.

CLEVER IDEA: *To make homemade croutons, heat oven to 325°F. Trim crusts from 3 slices of white bread; cut bread into ¾-inch cubes. Place on ungreased cookie sheet. Bake at 325°F for 3 to 4 minutes or until crisp.*

1 Serving: Calories 199 (Calories from Fat 80); Total Fat 9g; Saturated Fat 5g; Trans Fat 0g; Cholesterol 147mg; Sodium 1223mg; Total Carbohydrate 15g; Dietary Fiber 2g; Sugars 5g; Protein 14g

CURRY-CRAB CHOWDER

Curry powder and crabmeat perk up this easy 30-minute chowder that's perfect for a tasty weeknight supper.

PREP TIME: 30 MINUTES
TOTAL TIME: 30 MINUTES

MAKES 6 SERVINGS

Nancy J. Peart, London, Ohio
Bake-Off® Contest 41, 2004

1 (8.25-oz.) box Betty Crocker™ Tuna Helper™ Creamy Pasta

1 (12-oz.) can evaporated milk

5 cups water

1 medium carrot, thinly sliced (¾ cup)

3 tablespoons clam juice

1 teaspoon salt

1 teaspoon curry powder

¼ teaspoon white pepper

1 (6-oz.) can lump crabmeat, drained

1 (4.5-oz.) jar sliced mushrooms, drained

1. In 4½-quart Dutch oven, mix uncooked Pasta and Sauce Mix, evaporated milk and water. Stir in all remaining ingredients.

2. Heat over medium-high heat to boiling, stirring occasionally. Reduce heat; simmer uncovered 10 to 13 minutes, stirring occasionally, until pasta and carrots are tender.

1 Serving: Calories 214 (Calories from Fat 12); Total Fat 1g; Saturated Fat 0g; Trans Fat 0g; Cholesterol 30mg; Sodium 1366mg; Total Carbohydrate 37g; Dietary Fiber 2g; Sugars 8g; Protein 14g

CALABACITA CHICKEN STEW

A sassy chicken stew packs a powerful vitamin punch.

PREP TIME: 50 MINUTES
TOTAL TIME: 50 MINUTES

MAKES 6 SERVINGS

Linda S. Brown, Dallas, Texas
Bake-Off® Contest 42, 2006

1 tablespoon extra-virgin olive oil

1½ lb uncooked chicken breast tenders (not breaded)

8 to 10 small to medium zucchini (2½ lb), peeled, thinly sliced (8 cups)

1 medium white onion, chopped (½ cup)

1 can (15.25 oz) whole kernel corn, undrained

1 can (14.5 oz) diced tomatoes with green pepper and onion, undrained

1 can (4.5 oz) chopped green chiles, undrained

1½ teaspoons garlic powder

½ teaspoon ground cumin

Salt and pepper, if desired

½ cup chopped fresh cilantro

1. In 5- to 6-quart saucepan or Dutch oven, heat oil over medium heat. Add chicken; cover and cook 4 to 6 minutes, stirring occasionally, until no longer pink in center.

2. Stir in remaining ingredients except cilantro. Heat to boiling. Reduce heat to medium-low; cover and simmer about 20 minutes, stirring occasionally, until zucchini is tender.

3. Stir in cilantro; cook 3 minutes longer, stirring occasionally.

1 Serving: Calories 270 (Calories from Fat 60); Total Fat 7g; Saturated Fat 1.5g; Trans Fat 0g; Cholesterol 70mg; Sodium 470mg; Total Carbohydrate 24g; Dietary Fiber 4g; Sugars 9g; Protein 28g

MEDITERRANEAN CORN SALAD

Mozzarella cheese, olives, basil and garlic are ingredients commonly used in Mediterranean cuisine. You'll enjoy their combined flavors in this salad.

PREP TIME: 15 MINUTES
TOTAL TIME: 1 HOUR 15 MINUTES

MAKES 8 (½-CUP) SERVINGS

Ellen Nishimura, Fair Oaks, California
Bake-Off® Contest 34, 1990

SALAD

1 (15.25-oz.) can whole kernel corn, drained

8 oz. mozzarella cheese, cut into ¼-inch pieces

1 (2¼-oz.) can sliced ripe olives, drained

1 large tomato, seeded, cut into ½-inch pieces

¼ cup chopped fresh basil leaves

¼ cup chopped fresh parsley

DRESSING

¼ cup olive oil

3 tablespoons cider vinegar

1 teaspoon grated lemon peel

1 large garlic clove, minced

Salt

Pepper

Fresh spinach leaves, if desired

Toasted pine nuts, if desired

In large bowl, combine all salad ingredients; mix well. In small bowl using wire whisk, blend olive oil, vinegar, lemon peel and garlic. Pour over corn mixture; toss gently. Salt and pepper to taste. Refrigerate 1 to 2 hours to blend flavors. Serve on spinach-lined plates. Sprinkle each serving with pine nuts.

CLEVER IDEA: *To toast pine nuts, spread evenly in shallow pan; bake at 375°F for 3 to 5 minutes or until light golden brown, stirring occasionally.*

1 Serving: Calories 190 (Calories from Fat 130); Total Fat 14g; Saturated Fat 5g; Trans Fat 0g; Cholesterol 20mg; Sodium 240mg; Total Carbohydrate 10g; Dietary Fiber 1g; Sugars 2g; Protein 8g

A Peek Inside the Bake-Off® Contest:

If anyone ever asks you what it was like to live richly through the twentieth century, direct them to the story of Birdie Casement. "I married Russ," Birdie says, "then World War II changed our lives. We found ourselves wrestling with gas rationing, sugar stamps, tire shortages, among other shortages, and two wee tots. . . . The following years were a merry-go-round of PTA, fund-raising, cake bakes, Brownies, Cub Scouts, car pooling, measles, trips to the zoo, picnics and all the fun, tears, brawls and challenges that go hand in hand with parenthood. Time flies, and soon no one was hurrying home for that noontime sandwich." Birdie became a kindergarten teacher and was nominated for Colorado teacher of the year. At the Bake-Off® Contest, she wowed everybody with her ebullience, her wisdom and, of course, her Cabbage Salad Vinaigrette with Crunchy Noodles.

NUTTY CHICKEN DINNER SALAD

Strips of crunchy granola-coated chicken, juicy raspberries and toasted pecans over leafy greens combine in this refreshing meal.

PREP TIME: 40 MINUTES
TOTAL TIME: 40 MINUTES

MAKES 4 SERVINGS

Holly Young, Bountiful, Utah
Bake-Off® Contest 42, 2006

1 bag (10 oz) organic frozen raspberries

½ cup oil and vinegar dressing

¼ cup chopped pecans

1 tablespoon packed brown sugar

2 tablespoons mayonnaise or salad dressing

2 tablespoons maple-flavored syrup or real maple syrup

4 cinnamon crunchy granola bars (2 pouches from 8.9-oz box), finely crushed (¾ cup)

1 egg

1 lb uncooked chicken breast tenders (not breaded)

½ teaspoon salt

⅛ teaspoon pepper

3 tablespoons vegetable oil

1 bag (10 oz) or 2 bags (5 oz each) mixed baby salad greens

½ cup thinly sliced red onion

2 slices (¾ to 1 oz each) Swiss cheese, cut into thin julienne strips

¼ cup pecan halves, toasted or glazed

1. Spread frozen raspberries on paper towel; let stand to thaw while making dressing and salad. In small bowl, mix dressing, chopped pecans, brown sugar, mayonnaise and syrup with wire whisk until well blended. Refrigerate until serving time.

2. Place finely crushed granola bars on paper plate or in pie plate. In shallow bowl or another pie plate, beat egg with fork. Sprinkle chicken with salt and pepper.

3. In 12-inch nonstick skillet, heat oil over medium heat. Add chicken to beaten egg; stir to coat. Dip each chicken strip lightly into crushed granola bars; add to skillet. Cook 6 to 8 minutes, turning once, until chicken is no longer pink in center and browned on all sides. Remove from skillet; drain on paper towels.

4. In large serving bowl, mix salad greens, onion, cheese and thawed raspberries. Toss, adding only enough dressing to evenly coat ingredients. Arrange greens mixture on individual plates. Place chicken evenly over greens. Arrange pecan halves on top. Drizzle with remaining dressing.

CLEVER IDEAS:

- *To crush granola bars, unwrap and place in small re-sealable food-storage plastic bag; use rolling pin to finely crush bars.*

- *To toast pecans, bake uncovered in ungreased shallow pan in 350°F oven about 10 minutes, stirring occasionally, until golden brown.*

1 Serving: Calories 750 (Calories from Fat 440); Total Fat 8g; Saturated Fat 8g; Trans Fat 0g; Cholesterol 140mg; Sodium 810mg; Total Carbohydrate 44g; Dietary Fiber 9g; Sugars 22g; Protein 35g

BALSAMIC CHICKEN CRANBERRY PANZANELLA

Pizza crust bakes up to become the crusty bread in this easy flavorful take on Italian bread salad.

PREP TIME: 20 MINUTES
TOTAL TIME: 30 MINUTES
MAKES 4 SERVINGS

Kalani Allred, Looms, California
Bake-Off® Contest 46, 2013

1 can Pillsbury™ refrigerated classic pizza crust

3 tablespoons extra virgin olive oil

4 uncooked chicken breast tenders, cut into bite-size pieces (about 6 oz)

1 small yellow onion, halved and thinly sliced

¾ teaspoon salt

½ teaspoon pepper

¾ cup sweetened dried cranberries

4 cups shredded romaine lettuce

¼ cup balsamic dressing

1. Heat oven to 400°F. Line large cookie sheet with parchment paper. Unroll dough on cookie sheet. Bake 14 to 16 minutes or until crust is golden brown. Remove to cooling rack; cool 5 minutes. Tear crust into bite-size pieces; set aside.

2. Meanwhile, in 12-inch nonstick skillet, heat 1 tablespoon of the oil over medium-high heat. Add chicken, onion, ½ teaspoon of the salt and ¼ teaspoon of the pepper; cook 5 to 7 minutes, stirring occasionally or until chicken is no longer pink in center and onion starts to caramelize. Stir in cranberries; cook an additional 2 to 3 minutes. Place chicken mixture in large serving bowl. Keep warm. Wipe out skillet.

3. In same skillet, add remaining 2 tablespoons oil; heat over medium heat. Add bread pieces; sprinkle with the remaining salt and pepper. Cook 2 to 5 minutes, stirring frequently until golden brown and toasted.

4. Add romaine, bread pieces and dressing to chicken mixture; toss well.

1 Serving: Calories 530 (Calories from Fat 170); Total Fat 19g; Saturated Fat 3g; Trans Fat 0g; Cholesterol 25mg; Sodium 1320mg; Total Carbohydrate 70g; Dietary Fiber 4g; Sugars 18g; Protein 18g

MANGO-JALAPEÑO CHICKEN SALAD IN CUMIN TORTILLA BOWLS

Enjoy an old favorite with a whole new twist—spicy, fruity chicken salad served in flavored tortilla bowls.

PREP TIME: 50 MINUTES
TOTAL TIME: 50 MINUTES
MAKES 4 SERVINGS

Frances Pietsch, Flower Mound, Texas
Bake-Off® Contest 43, 2008

VINAIGRETTE

½ cup cubed peeled mango

2 tablespoons mango nectar (from 12.5-oz can)

2 tablespoons white wine vinegar

1 tablespoon fresh lime juice

1 tablespoon fresh orange juice

1 tablespoon honey

⅓ cup canola oil

BOWLS

4 flour tortillas for burritos (from 11-oz package)

½ teaspoon ground cumin

½ teaspoon salt

SALAD

4 cups cubed cooked chicken breast

1⅓ cups cubed peeled mango

1 tablespoon fresh lime juice

1½ cups cubed peeled avocado (from 2 medium)

½ cup finely chopped red bell pepper

½ cup finely chopped red onion

¼ cup finely chopped seeded jalapeño chiles (2 medium)

¼ cup chopped fresh cilantro

1 cup shredded iceberg lettuce

½ teaspoon salt

1. Heat oven to 400°F. Spray insides of 4 ovenproof 2-cup soup bowls with no-stick cooking spray. Set aside.

2. In food processor bowl with metal blade or blender, place all vinaigrette ingredients except oil. Cover; process until smooth. With food processor running, slowly pour oil through feed tube until mixture is thickened. Set aside.

3. Spray 1 side of each tortilla with no-stick cooking spray. Sprinkle cumin and ½ teaspoon salt evenly over sprayed sides of tortillas. Press tortillas, seasoned sides up, in bowls. Place bowls in 15x10x1-inch pan. Bake 5 to 7 minutes or until edges are golden brown. Remove tortillas from bowls; place upside down on cooling rack. Cool completely.

4. In large bowl, mix chicken and 1⅓ cups mango. In small bowl, mix 1 tablespoon lime juice and the avocado. Add avocado and remaining salad ingredients to chicken mixture; mix well. Add vinaigrette; mix well.

5. To serve, spoon chicken salad into tortilla bowls. (Bowls will be full.) Serve immediately.

CLEVER IDEAS:

- *One large mango provides enough mango for both the vinaigrette and salad.*

- *Foil balls can be used instead of bowls. Cut 4 (25x12-inch) pieces of foil. Slightly crush each to make 4-inch ball; flatten slightly. Place on ungreased cookie sheet. Spray and season tortillas as directed; gently shape to fit over each foil ball, seasoned side toward foil. Bake as directed.*

1 Serving: Calories 740 (Calories from Fat 360); Total Fat 40g; Saturated Fat 5g; Trans Fat 1g; Cholesterol 115mg; Sodium 1000mg; Total Carbohydrate 48g; Dietary Fiber 6g; Sugars 18g; Protein 47g

ITALIAN CHOPPED SALAD PIZZAS

In a twist on a bread bowl salad, crunchy greens and toppings are piled high on a cheesy pizza "plate."

PREP TIME: 40 MINUTES
TOTAL TIME: 55 MINUTES

MAKES 4 SERVINGS

Bob Gadsby, Great Falls, Montana
Bake-Off® Contest 43, 2008

2 tablespoons olive oil

Cornmeal, if desired

3 oz thickly sliced pancetta, chopped (¾ cup)

5 cups chopped iceberg or romaine lettuce

1½ cups (½-inch cubes) skinned rotisserie chicken breast

¾ cup cubed fresh mozzarella cheese

2 plum (Roma) tomatoes, chopped (¾ cup)

½ cup sun-dried tomatoes in oil, drained and chopped

3 tablespoons fresh basil leaves, thinly sliced

1 can (13.8 oz) Pillsbury™ refrigerated classic pizza crust

2 teaspoons Italian seasoning

½ cup shredded Asiago cheese (2 oz)

½ to ¾ cup red wine vinaigrette dressing

¼ cup crumbled sweet or regular Gorgonzola cheese, if desired

Basil sprigs

1. Heat oven to 425°F. Lightly brush large cookie sheet with 1 tablespoon of the oil; sprinkle with cornmeal. In 8-inch skillet, cook pancetta over medium-high heat, stirring occasionally, until crisp; drain.

2. In large bowl, mix lettuce, chicken, mozzarella cheese, plum tomatoes, sun-dried tomatoes, sliced basil and pancetta; set aside.

3. Unroll pizza crust dough; cut into 4 rectangles, using pizza cutter. Place rectangles on cookie sheet. Press each rectangle into 8x6-inch oval, folding over edges of dough to form a rim. Brush remaining 1 tablespoon oil over dough ovals; sprinkle evenly with Italian seasoning and Asiago cheese. Bake 11 to 13 minutes or until crusts are golden brown and cheese is melted.

4. Pour dressing over salad mixture; toss to mix. Mound about 2 cups of the salad mixture onto each pizza crust; sprinkle with Gorgonzola cheese. Garnish with basil sprigs.

1 Serving: Calories 690 (Calories from Fat 320); Total Fat 35g; Saturated Fat 11g; Trans Fat 0g; Cholesterol 85mg; Sodium 1810mg; Total Carbohydrate 55g; Dietary Fiber 2g; Sugars 12g; Protein 37g

SESAME-CROUTON ASIAN CHICKEN SALAD

Turn refrigerated bread-sticks into crunchy sesame croutons to toss with an easy and flavorful main-dish chicken salad.

PREP TIME: 45 MINUTES
TOTAL TIME: 45 MINUTES
MAKES 8 SERVINGS

Katie Long, Summerfield, North Carolina
Bake-Off® Contest 44, 2010

½ cup sesame seed
¼ cup butter, softened
½ cup soy sauce, room temperature
2 teaspoons freshly grated gingerroot
1 can (11 oz) Pillsbury™ refrigerated original breadsticks (12 breadsticks)
2½ cups cubed cooked chicken
2½ cups broccoli slaw or shredded broccoli

1 cup chopped cucumber
¾ cup julienne carrots (from 10-oz bag)
½ cup chopped fresh cilantro
¼ cup finely chopped red onion
¼ cup cashews, halves and pieces, coarsely chopped
½ cup olive oil
⅓ cup cider vinegar
½ to 1 teaspoon sesame oil
3 tablespoons sugar

1. In 10-inch skillet, cook sesame seed over medium-high heat 3 to 5 minutes, stirring constantly, until lightly toasted. Remove from skillet to plate to cool.

2. Heat oven to 375°F. In small bowl, beat butter, 1 tablespoon of the soy sauce, 1 teaspoon of the gingerroot and 2 tablespoons of the sesame seed with electric mixer on low speed until blended. Carefully unroll dough into 2 rectangles. On each of 2 ungreased cookie sheets with sides, place 1 rectangle; press into 8x6-inch rectangle. Spread with butter mixture. Using pizza cutter, cut each rectangle lengthwise into 6 breadsticks, then cut each breadstick crosswise into 8 pieces.

3. Bake 8 to 12 minutes, rotating cookie sheets halfway through baking, until crisp. Remove from cookie sheet to cooling rack; cool.

4. Meanwhile, in large bowl, toss chicken, broccoli slaw, cucumber, carrots, cilantro, onion and cashews. In container with tight-fitting lid, shake olive oil, vinegar, sesame oil, sugar and remaining soy sauce, gingerroot and sesame seed until well blended. Just before serving, pour dressing over chicken mixture; toss to coat. Add croutons; stir lightly.

1 Serving: Calories 500 (Calories from Fat 290); Total Fat 32g; Saturated Fat 9g; Trans Fat 0g; Cholesterol 55mg; Sodium 1270mg; Total Carbohydrate 31g; Dietary Fiber 2g; Sugars 9g; Protein 20g

CABBAGE SALAD VINAIGRETTE WITH CRUNCHY NOODLES

Ingredients for this salad are available year-round, so you can make this colorful side dish often.

PREP TIME: 20 MINUTES
TOTAL TIME: 2 HOURS
MAKES 16 (½-CUP) SERVINGS

Birdie Casement, Denver, Colorado
Bake-Off® Contest 34, 1990

SALAD

- 4½ cups (1 medium head) shredded red or green cabbage
- 5 green onions, thinly sliced (including tops)
- 1 (11-oz.) can vacuum-packed whole kernel corn, drained
- 1½ cups frozen sweet peas (from 1-lb. pkg.) cooked, drained
- 1 (4.5-oz.) jar sliced mushrooms, undrained

DRESSING

- 1 (3-oz.) pkg. instant Oriental noodles with chicken-flavor seasoning packet
- ¼ cup tarragon vinegar
- ¼ cup oil
- 3 tablespoons sugar
- ½ teaspoon pepper
- ½ cup slivered almonds, toasted
- 2 tablespoons sesame seed, toasted

1. In large bowl, combine all salad ingredients. In small bowl, combine contents of seasoning packet from noodles, vinegar, oil, sugar and pepper; blend well. Pour dressing over salad ingredients; toss to coat. Refrigerate at least 2 hours to chill.

2. Break noodles into ¾-inch pieces. Before serving, stir noodles, almonds and sesame seed into salad mixture. Store in refrigerator.

CLEVER IDEA: *To toast almonds, spread on cookie sheet; bake at 375°F for 5 to 7 minutes or until light golden brown. Or spread in medium skillet and stir over medium heat for 8 to 10 minutes or until light golden brown.*

1 Serving: Calories 151 (Calories from Fat 62); Total Fat 7g; Saturated Fat 1g; Trans Fat 0g; Cholesterol 0mg; Sodium 117mg; Total Carbohydrate 19g; Dietary Fiber 4g; Sugars 5g; Protein 3g

EASY VEGETABLE BULGUR SALAD

Enjoy the tender, nutty texture of nutritious bulgur in this colorful salad. Bulgur is kernels of whole wheat that have been steamed, dried and crushed.

PREP TIME: 15 MINUTES
TOTAL TIME: 2 HOURS
25 MINUTES

MAKES 6 (1-CUP) SERVINGS

Annette Erbeck, Mason, Ohio
Bake-Off® Contest 33, 1988

1 cup uncooked bulgur (cracked wheat)

2 cups boiling water

1 (1-lb) pkg. frozen broccoli, cauliflower and carrots

½ cup chopped fresh parsley

¼ cup sliced green onions

½ to 1 cup purchased Italian salad dressing

1. In medium bowl, combine bulgur and boiling water. Let stand 1 hour. Drain well.

2. Cook vegetables until crisp-tender as directed on package; cool 10 minutes.

3. In large bowl, combine softened bulgur, thawed vegetables, parsley, green onions and Italian dressing; blend well. Cover; refrigerate 1 to 2 hours to blend flavors. Store in refrigerator.

1 Serving: Calories 160 (Calories from Fat 40); Total Fat 4.5g; Saturated Fat 0.5g; Trans Fat 0g; Cholesterol 0mg; Sodium 230mg; Total Carbohydrate 25g; Dietary Fiber 6g; Sugars 4g; Protein 4g

Main Event Entrees and Casseroles

Jackie Carioscia of Castle Rock, Colorado, prepares Marmalade Crab Crusted Salmon (page 275) for the 46th Bake-Off Contest held in Las Vegas.

WRAPPED TENDERLOIN WITH GORGONZOLA-MUSHROOM GRAVY

Refrigerated biscuits make a twist on Beef Wellington, an easy and special meal for two.

PREP TIME: 20 MINUTES
TOTAL TIME: 40 MINUTES

MAKES 2 SERVINGS

Kelly Lynne Baxter, Olympia, Washington
Bake-Off® Contest 42, 2006

2 tablespoons olive oil

2 beef tenderloin steaks, about 1 inch thick (4 oz each)

½ teaspoon Montreal steak seasoning

4 Pillsbury™ Grands!™ frozen buttermilk biscuits (from 25-oz bag)

1 egg yolk

1 tablespoon water

1 cup crumbled gorgonzola cheese (4 oz)

⅛ teaspoon pepper

½ cup whipping cream

½ teaspoon Worcestershire sauce

1 jar (4.5 oz) sliced mushrooms, drained

1½ teaspoons chopped fresh parsley

1. Heat oven to 400°F. In 8-inch skillet, heat oil over medium-high heat. Pat steaks dry with paper towel; sprinkle both sides with steak seasoning. Add steaks to skillet; cook 1 to 2 minutes on each side or until browned. Remove steaks from skillet; place on plate.

2. Place 2 biscuits on microwavable plate. Microwave on High 30 to 40 seconds, turning biscuits over halfway through microwave time, until soft enough to press into rounds. Repeat with remaining 2 biscuits.

3. Spray cookie sheet or 13x9-inch baking dish with cooking spray. On cookie sheet or in baking dish, roll or press 2 of the biscuits into 5- to 6-inch rounds. Place 1 steak on center of each flattened biscuit. Press remaining 2 biscuits into 5- to 6-inch rounds; place over steaks. Flute or crimp edges with fork to seal. In small bowl, beat egg yolk and water with fork until blended; brush over top biscuits. Bake 14 to 18 minutes or until golden brown.

4. Meanwhile, in 1-quart saucepan, mix cheese, pepper, whipping cream and Worcestershire sauce. Heat to boiling. Reduce heat to medium-low; simmer uncovered, stirring constantly, until cheese is melted. Stir in mushrooms. Keep warm over low heat.

5. Serve half of mushroom gravy over each wrapped steak; sprinkle with parsley.

1 Serving: Calories 1050 (Calories from Fat 660); Total Fat 74g; Saturated Fat 32g; Trans Fat 8g; Cholesterol 255mg; Sodium 2310mg; Total Carbohydrate 50g; Dietary Fiber 1g; Sugars 8g; Protein 47g

A Peek Inside the Bake-Off® Contest:

Cooks tend to be a generous lot, and Teresa Hannan Smith makes a point of sharing the bounty of her life not just with guests at her table but with four-legged folk wherever she is. "I carry three kinds of dog and cat food in my car and feed strays everywhere I go," she says. While she never gets the raves from her animal guests that she got from the 35th Bake-Off® Contest judges for her Deluxe Turkey Club Pizza, Teresa considers cats and dogs among the most gratifying of her diners.

FIESTA SPAGHETTI

Welcome a fiesta of flavor in ordinary spaghetti!

PREP TIME: 30 MINUTES
TOTAL TIME: 30 MINUTES
MAKES 8 SERVINGS

Michele C. Santos, Austin, Texas
Bake-Off® Contest 40, 2002

1 package (16 oz) spaghetti

2 tablespoons olive oil

½ cup chopped onion

1 medium red bell pepper, chopped

1 lb lean (at least 80%) ground beef

⅓ cup sugar

1 package (1 oz) taco seasoning mix

1 can (28 oz) diced tomatoes, undrained

1 can (8 oz) tomato sauce

1 can (11 oz) whole kernel corn with red and green peppers, drained

1 jar (4.5 oz) sliced mushrooms, drained

Grated Parmesan cheese, if desired

1. Cook spaghetti as directed on package. Drain; cover to keep warm.

2. Meanwhile, in 12-inch nonstick skillet, heat oil over medium heat. Add onion and bell pepper; cook 3 to 4 minutes, stirring occasionally, until tender. Remove from skillet. Add ground beef to same skillet; cook until thoroughly cooked, stirring frequently. Drain.

3. Add onion and bell pepper to ground beef; mix well. Add sugar, taco seasoning mix, tomatoes, tomato sauce, corn and mushrooms; mix well. Heat to boiling. Reduce heat to low; simmer 5 minutes, stirring occasionally. Serve over spaghetti. Sprinkle with cheese.

1 Serving: Calories 460 (Calories from Fat 91); Total Fat 10g; Saturated Fat 3g; Trans Fat 0g; Cholesterol 37mg; Sodium 861mg; Total Carbohydrate 69g; Dietary Fiber 4g; Sugars 17g; Protein 21g

BAKED STEAK BURRITOS

A spicy beef and bean filling is all bundled up in a south of the border burrito.

PREP TIME: 30 MINUTES
TOTAL TIME: 45 MINUTES

MAKES 6 SERVINGS

Becky Fuller, Westmont, Illinois
Bake-Off® Contest 40, 2002

- ½ cup butter
- 1 package (1 oz) taco seasoning mix
- 1½ lb boneless beef sirloin tip steak, cut into thin bite-sized strips
- 1 can (16 oz) refried beans
- 12 flour tortillas for soft tacos & fajitas (6 inch; from two 8.2-oz packages)

- 2 cups shredded Cheddar cheese (8 oz)
- 3 green onions, thinly sliced
- 1 can (10 oz) red enchilada sauce
- 1 cup shredded Mexican cheese blend (4 oz)

1. Heat oven to 400°F. Melt butter in large skillet over medium heat. Stir in taco seasoning mix. Add beef strips; cook and stir 5 to 6 minutes or until of desired doneness. Drain.

2. Meanwhile, place refried beans in microwave-safe dish. Microwave on High for 2 minutes, stirring once or twice.

3. Spread each tortilla with refried beans to within ¼ inch of edge. Top each with beef, Cheddar cheese and onions. Roll up, folding in sides. Place, seam side down, in ungreased 13x9-inch (3-quart) glass baking dish. Pour enchilada sauce over burritos. Sprinkle with Mexican cheese blend.

4. Bake at 400°F for 7 to 12 minutes or until burritos are thoroughly heated and cheese is melted.

1 Serving: Calories 854 (Calories from Fat 473); Total Fat 53g; Saturated Fat 29g; Trans Fat 0g; Cholesterol 190mg; Sodium 1763mg; Total Carbohydrate 49g; Dietary Fiber 6g; Sugars 4g; Protein 48g

BISCUIT TACO CASSEROLE

Stretch a half-pound of ground beef deliciously into eight hearty servings!

PREP TIME: 20 MINUTES
TOTAL TIME: 40 MINUTES

MAKES 8 SERVINGS

Louise V. Davis, Oakley, Michigan
Bake-Off® Contest 37, 1996

2 jars (8 oz each) Taco Sauce

1 (12-oz) can Pillsbury™ Grands!™ Jr. Golden Layers™ refrigerated buttermilk biscuits

4 to 6 oz. (1 to 1½ cups) shredded sharp Cheddar cheese

4 to 6 oz. (1 to 1½ cups) shredded mozzarella cheese

1 (2.25-oz.) can sliced ripe olives, drained

½ lb. lean ground beef

¼ cup chopped red bell pepper, if desired

¼ cup chopped green bell pepper, if desired

1 (4-oz.) can mushroom pieces and stems, drained, if desired

1. Heat oven to 400°F. Lightly grease 13x9-inch (3-quart) baking dish. Spread taco sauce evenly over bottom of greased dish.

2. Separate dough into 10 biscuits; cut each biscuit into 4 pieces. Place biscuit pieces in taco sauce; turn to coat. Sprinkle biscuits with ½ to 1 cup of the Cheddar cheese, ½ to 1 cup of the mozzarella cheese and the olives; mix gently. Bake at 400°F for 15 to 18 minutes or until bubbly.

3. Meanwhile, in large skillet, combine ground beef, bell peppers and mushrooms. Cook until beef is thoroughly cooked; drain.

4. Sprinkle remaining ½ cup Cheddar cheese and ½ cup mozzarella cheese over mixture in casserole; top with ground beef mixture. Bake an additional 5 to 7 minutes or until mixture bubbles vigorously around edges.

1 Serving: Calories 315 (Calories from Fat 148); Total Fat 16g; Saturated Fat 7g; Trans Fat 0g; Cholesterol 45mg; Sodium 1160mg; Total Carbohydrate 26g; Dietary Fiber 1g; Sugars 3g; Protein 19g

SUPERSPEEDWAY TACO PIE

Your family will race to the table when you serve this crescent-crusted taco pie in which crushed corn chips add just the right crunch!

PREP TIME: 15 MINUTES
TOTAL TIME: 40 MINUTES

MAKES 6 SERVINGS

Allegra Bernal, Sylmar, California
Bake-Off® Contest 21, 1970

1 to 1¼ lb. lean ground beef

1 (1-oz.) pkg. taco seasoning mix

½ cup water

⅓ cup sliced stuffed green olives or pitted ripe olives

1 (8-oz.) can Pillsbury™ refrigerated crescent dinner rolls

1½ to 2 cups crushed corn chips

1 (8-oz.) container (1 cup) sour cream

6 slices American cheese or 4 oz. (1 cup) shredded Cheddar cheese

Shredded lettuce, if desired

Avocado slices, if desired

1. Heat oven to 375°F. Cook ground beef in 10-inch skillet until thoroughly cooked, stirring frequently. Drain. Stir in taco seasoning mix, water and olives. Simmer 5 minutes.

2. Meanwhile, separate crescent dough into 8 triangles. Place triangles in ungreased 9 or 10-inch pie pan, pressing to form crust. Sprinkle 1 cup of the corn chips over bottom of crust.

3. Spoon beef mixture into corn chips in crust. Spread sour cream over beef mixture. Cover with cheese. Sprinkle with remaining ½ to 1 cup corn chips.

4. Bake at 375°F for 20 to 25 minutes or until crust is golden brown. Cut in wedges. Serve immediately with lettuce and avocado. Store in refrigerator.

CLEVER IDEA: *To make ahead, assemble pie and cover with foil; refrigerate up to 2 hours before baking. Uncover; bake as directed above. To reheat, bake, uncovered, at 350°F for 10 to 15 minutes or until hot. Substitution: If using Pillsbury™ Big & Flaky large refrigerated crescent dinner rolls, separate into 6 triangles and use 9-inch deep-dish pie pan. Continue as directed.*

1 Serving: Calories 585 (Calories from Fat 350); Total Fat 39g; Saturated Fat 15g; Trans Fat 1g; Cholesterol 90mg; Sodium 1286mg; Total Carbohydrate 35g; Dietary Fiber 2g; Sugars 6g; Protein 24g

SWEET AND SALSY MEATLOAF

Give meatloaf a sassy Mexican twist with cinnamon, cocoa and salsa!

PREP TIME: 15 MINUTES
TOTAL TIME: 1 HOUR 35 MINUTES

MAKES 6 SERVINGS

Betty Boyle, Monroeville, Pennsylvania
Bake-Off® Contest 39, 2000

1½ lb. meatloaf mix (beef, pork and veal) or lean ground beef

¾ cup plain bread crumbs

1 egg

1 cup salsa

1 (4.5-oz.) can chopped green chiles

2 tablespoons brown sugar

1 tablespoon chopped fresh cilantro

1 tablespoon chopped fresh parsley

1 teaspoon unsweetened cocoa

½ teaspoon salt

¼ teaspoon garlic powder

¼ teaspoon cumin

¼ teaspoon cinnamon

¼ teaspoon chili powder

1 teaspoon lemon juice

1. Heat oven to 350°F. In large bowl, combine meatloaf mix, bread crumbs and egg; mix well.

2. In medium bowl, combine all remaining ingredients; mix well. Add ³⁄₄ cup of the salsa mixture to meat mixture; mix well. In ungreased 1¹⁄₂ or 2-quart casserole or 9x5-inch loaf pan, shape meat mixture into loaf.

3. Bake at 350°F for 50 minutes. Remove from oven. Spoon remaining salsa mixture over top of loaf. Return to oven; bake an additional 20 to 30 minutes or until thoroughly cooked in center and meat thermometer registers 160°F.

1 Serving: Calories 290 (Calories from Fat 130); Total Fat 14g; Saturated Fat 5g; Trans Fat 0g; Cholesterol 110mg; Sodium 740mg; Total Carbohydrate 18g; Dietary Fiber 1g; Sugars 7g; Protein 22g

PICADILLO CHIMICHANGAS

Savory ingredients get a sweet touch from applesauce and raisins in a fabulous twist on a family favorite.

PREP TIME: 35 MINUTES
TOTAL TIME: 50 MINUTES
MAKES 8 SERVINGS

Sherry Roper, San Diego, California
Bake-Off® Contest 43, 2008

¼ cup canola oil

1 small onion, chopped (¼ cup)

1 clove garlic, finely chopped

1 lb lean (at least 80%) ground beef

1 large tomato, chopped (1 cup)

1 can (4.5 oz) chopped green chiles

1 package (1 oz) taco seasoning mix

½ cup cinnamon applesauce or plain applesauce

¼ cup raisins

⅓ cup sliced almonds

½ cup pimiento-stuffed green olives, coarsely chopped

1 package (11 oz) flour tortillas for burritos (8 tortillas)

1 cup sour cream

4 medium green onions, chopped (¼ cup)

¼ cup chopped fresh cilantro

1. Heat oven to 475°F. Brush large cookie sheet with 1 tablespoon of the oil.

2. In 10-inch skillet, heat 2 tablespoons of the oil over medium heat. Add onion and garlic; cook 1 to 2 minutes, stirring occasionally, until onion is tender. Stir in beef; cook 8 to 10 minutes, stirring occasionally, until beef is thoroughly cooked; drain.

3. Reduce heat to medium-low. Stir in tomato, chiles, taco seasoning mix, applesauce and raisins; cook 10 minutes, stirring occasionally. Stir in almonds and olives; cook 1 to 2 minutes or until thoroughly heated.

4. For each chimichanga, spoon ½ cup beef mixture down center of each tortilla. Fold sides of each tortilla toward center; fold ends up. Place seam sides down on cookie sheet. Brush tops and sides of chimichangas with remaining 1 tablespoon oil.

5. Bake 6 to 8 minutes or until golden brown. Cool on cookie sheet 5 minutes.

6. Meanwhile, in small bowl, stir sour cream, green onions and 2 tablespoons of the cilantro.

7. To serve, top each chimichanga with 2 tablespoons sour cream mixture and remaining cilantro.

1 Serving: Calories 430 (Calories from Fat 240); Total Fat 26g; Saturated Fat 8g; Trans Fat 1.5g; Cholesterol 55mg; Sodium 970mg; Total Carbohydrate 33g; Dietary Fiber 2g; Sugars 7g; Protein 15g

HUNGRY BOYS' CASSEROLE

This hearty casserole was inspired by the contestant's three hungry boys.

PREP TIME: 40 MINUTES
TOTAL TIME: 1 HOUR 5 MINUTES

MAKES 8 SERVINGS

Mira Walilko, Detroit, Michigan
Bake-Off® Contest 15, 1963 Grand Prize Winner

CASSEROLE

1½ lb. ground beef

1 cup chopped celery

½ cup chopped onion

½ cup chopped green bell pepper

1 garlic clove, minced

1 (6-oz.) can tomato paste

¾ cup water

1 teaspoon paprika

½ teaspoon salt

1 (16-oz.) can baked beans, undrained

2 cups chickpeas (garbanzo beans), drained (from 19-oz can)

BISCUITS

1½ cups Pillsbury™ BEST™ All Purpose or Unbleached Flour

2 teaspoons baking powder

½ teaspoon salt

¼ cup margarine or butter

½ to ¾ cup milk

2 tablespoons sliced stuffed green olives

1 tablespoon slivered almonds

1. In 12-inch skillet, combine ground beef, celery, onion, bell pepper and garlic. Cook over medium-high heat until beef is browned and thoroughly cooked and vegetables are crisp-tender, stirring frequently. Drain. Reduce heat to low. Stir in tomato paste, water, paprika and ½ teaspoon salt. Add baked beans and garbanzo beans; simmer while preparing biscuits, stirring occasionally.

2. Heat oven to 425°F. Lightly spoon flour into measuring cup; level off. In large bowl, combine flour, baking powder and ½ teaspoon salt; mix well. With pastry blender or fork, cut in margarine until mixture resembles coarse crumbs. Gradually stir in enough milk until mixture leaves sides of bowl and forms a soft, moist dough.

3. On floured surface, gently knead dough 8 times. Roll dough to ¼-inch thickness. Cut with floured 2½-inch doughnut cutter. Reserve dough centers. Reroll dough to cut additional biscuits.

4. Reserve ½ cup of beef mixture. Pour remaining hot beef mixture into ungreased 13x9-inch (3-quart) glass baking dish. Arrange biscuits without centers over hot beef mixture. Stir olives and almonds into reserved ½ cup beef mixture; spoon into center of each biscuit. Top each with biscuit centers.

5. Bake at 425°F for 15 to 25 minutes or until biscuits are golden brown.

1 Serving: Calories 451 (Calories from Fat 151); Total Fat 17g; Saturated Fat 5g; Trans Fat 2g; Cholesterol 55mg; Sodium 1098mg; Total Carbohydrate 49g; Dietary Fiber 7g; Sugars 10g; Protein 28g

BEEF AND BEANS
WITH CHEESY BISCUITS

*Try this updated version of a
favorite recipe from the 22nd
Bake-Off® Contest.*

PREP TIME: 15 MINUTES
TOTAL TIME: 40 MINUTES

MAKES 5 SERVINGS

O. A. Creed, Florissant, Missouri
Bake-Off® Contest 22, 1971

1 lb lean (at least 80%)
ground beef

½ cup chopped onion

1 can (16 oz) barbecue
beans or pork and beans
with molasses

1 can (10¾ oz) condensed
tomato soup

1 teaspoon chili powder

¼ teaspoon garlic powder

1 can (7.5 oz) Pillsbury™
refrigerated buttermilk
biscuits

1 cup shredded Cheddar or
American cheese (4 oz)

1. Heat oven to 375°F. In 10-inch skillet, cook beef and onion over medium-high heat, stirring frequently, until beef is thoroughly cooked; drain.

2. Stir in beans, soup, chili powder and garlic powder. Heat to boiling. Reduce heat; simmer 5 minutes.

3. Separate dough into 10 biscuits. Spoon hot beef mixture into ungreased 8-inch square (2-quart) glass baking dish or 2-quart casserole. Arrange biscuits over hot mixture. Sprinkle with cheese.

4. Bake 20 to 25 minutes or until mixture is bubbly and biscuits are golden brown and no longer doughy.

CLEVER IDEA: *Add an extra
kick when you top the casserole
with Monterey Jack cheese with
peppers.*

1 Serving: Calories 480 (Calories from Fat 180);
Total Fat 20g; Saturated Fat 9g; Trans Fat 1g;
Cholesterol 80mg; Sodium 1570mg;
Total Carbohydrate 44g; Dietary Fiber 5g;
Sugars 10g; Protein 30g

CHEESEBURGER CASSEROLE

Tasty cheeseburger casserole ready in 45 minutes! Serve your family this beef and veggie dish arranged by cheese-filled biscuits.

PREP TIME: 25 MINUTES
TOTAL TIME: 45 MINUTES

MAKES 5 SERVINGS

Richard Klecka, Tinley Park, Illinois
Bake-Off® Contest 14, 1962

1 lb lean (at least 80%) ground beef

⅓ cup chopped onion

½ teaspoon salt

⅛ teaspoon pepper

1 can (10¾ oz) condensed tomato soup

1 cup frozen sweet peas (from 12-oz bag)

½ cup water

1 can (7.5 oz) Pillsbury™ refrigerated buttermilk or Country™ biscuits

3 oz American or Cheddar cheese, cut into ten ¾-inch cubes

1. Heat oven to 400°F. In 10-inch skillet, cook beef, onion, salt and pepper over medium-high heat 5 to 7 minutes, stirring frequently, until beef is thoroughly cooked; drain.

2. Stir in soup, peas and water. Heat to boiling, about 3 minutes. Reduce heat to low; simmer 5 minutes, stirring occasionally.

3. Meanwhile, separate dough into 10 biscuits. Wrap biscuit around each cheese cube, pinching edges to seal.

4. Place beef mixture in ungreased 1½-quart round casserole. Arrange cheese-filled biscuits, seam side down, in single layer over hot mixture.

5. Bake 13 to 18 minutes or until biscuits are golden brown.

1 Serving: Calories 400 (Calories from Fat 160); Total Fat 18g; Saturated Fat 7g; Trans Fat 1g; Cholesterol 70mg; Sodium 1310mg; Total Carbohydrate 34g; Dietary Fiber 2g; Sugars 9g; Protein 24g

CHUCK WAGON CHEESEBURGER SKILLET

Enjoy this delicious ground beef and bacon skillet covered with Pillsbury™ Grands!™ Biscuits and baked to a hearty casserole dinner.

PREP TIME: 15 MINUTES
TOTAL TIME: 40 MINUTES

MAKES 5 SERVINGS

Rosemary Warmuth, Wheeling, West Virginia
Bake-Off® Contest 40, 2002

4 slices bacon

1 lb. lean ground beef

3 tablespoons chopped onion

3 tablespoons oil

2½ cups frozen hash-brown potatoes, thawed

1 (11-oz.) can whole kernel corn, red and green peppers, drained

1 (4.5-oz.) can chopped green chiles, drained

½ cup barbecue sauce

8 oz. (2 cups) shredded Cheddar cheese

¼ teaspoon salt, if desired

¼ teaspoon pepper, if desired

1 (16.3-oz.) can Pillsbury™ Grands!™ Refrigerated Buttermilk, Southern Style or Reduced-Fat Buttermilk Biscuits

1. Heat oven to 400°F. Cook bacon until crisp; drain on paper towel. Crumble bacon; set aside.

2. In 12-inch cast iron or ovenproof skillet, cook ground beef and onion over medium heat until beef is thoroughly cooked, stirring frequently. Drain. Place beef mixture in medium bowl; cover to keep warm.

3. Add oil to same skillet. Heat over medium-high heat until hot. Add potatoes; cook 3 to 5 minutes or until browned, stirring constantly. Add cooked ground beef mixture, corn, chiles, barbecue sauce, cheese, salt and pepper; mix well. Cook until thoroughly heated, stirring occasionally. Sprinkle with bacon.

4. Separate dough into 8 biscuits. Arrange biscuits over hot mixture.

5. Bake at 400°F for 16 to 24 minutes or until biscuits are deep golden brown and bottoms are no longer doughy.

1 Serving: Calories 840 (Calories from Fat 403); Total Fat 45g; Saturated Fat 21g; Trans Fat 1g; Cholesterol 105mg; Sodium 1952mg; Total Carbohydrate 28g; Dietary Fiber 5g; Sugars 24g; Protein 40g

ZESTY ITALIAN CRESCENT CASSEROLE

Here's a casserole classic!
The beefy, cheesy filling is
topped with flaky crescents.

PREP TIME: 20 MINUTES

TOTAL TIME: 45 MINUTES

MAKES 6 SERVINGS

Hall of Fame

Madella Bathke, Wells, Minnesota
Bake-Off® Contest 28, 1978 Hall of Fame

1 lb. lean ground beef

½ cup chopped onion

1 cup tomato pasta sauce

6 oz. (1½ cups) shredded
   mozzarella or Monterey
   Jack cheese

½ cup sour cream

1 (8-oz.) can Pillsbury™
   refrigerated crescent
   dinner rolls

⅓ cup grated Parmesan
   cheese

2 tablespoons butter or
   margarine, melted

1. Heat oven to 375°F. In large skillet, cook ground beef and onion over medium heat for 8 to 10 minutes or until beef is thoroughly cooked, stirring frequently. Drain. Stir in pasta sauce; cook until thoroughly heated.

2. Meanwhile, in medium bowl, combine mozzarella cheese and sour cream; mix well.

3. Pour hot beef mixture into ungreased 9½- or 10-inch glass deep-dish pie pan or 11x7-inch (2-quart) glass baking dish. Spoon cheese mixture over beef mixture.

4. Unroll dough over cheese mixture. In small bowl, mix Parmesan cheese and butter. Spread evenly over dough.

5. Bake at 375°F for 18 to 25 minutes or until deep golden brown.

CLEVER IDEA: *If using a pie pan, separate dough into 8 triangles. Arrange points toward center over cheese mixture, crimping outside edges if necessary.*

1 Serving: Calories 490 (Calories from Fat 275); Total Fat 33g; Saturated Fat 14g; Trans Fat 1g; Cholesterol 94mg; Sodium 780mg; Total Carbohydrate 21g; Dietary Fiber 1g; Sugars 5g; Protein 27g

MEATBALL MINESTRONE BAKE

It's Italian night! Canned minestrone soup and Pillsbury™ crescents give a jump start to an easy dinner bake.

PREP TIME: 25 MINUTES
TOTAL TIME: 1 HOUR 20 MINUTES
MAKES 8 SERVINGS

Dinah Surh, Staten Island, New York
Bake-Off® Contest 45, 2012

¾ teaspoon oregano leaves

¼ teaspoon basil leaves

¼ teaspoon garlic powder

¼ teaspoon lemon peel

¼ teaspoon ground black pepper

1½ lb extra lean (at least 90%) ground beef

¾ cup Italian style bread crumbs

¼ cup chopped onion

¾ cup milk

1 egg

1 teaspoon kosher (coarse) salt

1 can (19 oz) minestrone soup

2 tablespoons grated Parmesan cheese

1 can Pillsbury™ Place 'n Bake™ refrigerated crescent rounds

1 tablespoon 100% extra virgin olive oil

2 cups shredded Italian cheese blend (8 oz)

1. Heat oven to 400°F. In small bowl, stir together oregano, basil, garlic powder, lemon peel and black pepper. Reserve ¾ teaspoon of mixture; set aside. In large bowl, mix ground beef, bread crumbs, onion, milk, egg, salt and remaining seasoning mix until thoroughly combined. Form into sixteen 2-inch meatballs. Pour soup into ungreased 13x9-inch (3-quart) glass baking dish; top with meatballs.

2. Bake 35 minutes or until bubbly.

3. Meanwhile, in small bowl, mix reserved ¾ teaspoon seasoning mixture and Parmesan cheese. Unroll each crescent round to make a strip; place strips on piece of foil. Brush strips with olive oil; sprinkle generously with Parmesan cheese mixture.

4. Remove baking dish from oven. Reduce oven temperature to 350°F. Sprinkle meatballs with Italian cheese. Place seasoned crescent strips in a diagonal pattern on top of cheese, cutting to fit if necessary and not crisscrossing the strips.

5. Bake an additional 20 to 24 minutes or until cheese is melted and strips are golden brown. Serve in bowls.

1 Serving: Calories 480 (Calories from Fat 230); Total Fat 26g; Saturated Fat 11g; Trans Fat 2.5g; Cholesterol 120mg; Sodium 1270mg; Total Carbohydrate 27g; Dietary Fiber 2g; Sugars 6g; Protein 35g

CRAFTY CRESCENT LASAGNA

Looking for a casserole dinner made with Pillsbury™ crescent dinner rolls? Then check out this cheesy pork sausage and ground beef lasagna flavored with herbs—a rich meal.

PREP TIME: 30 MINUTES
TOTAL TIME: 60 MINUTES

MAKES 8 SERVINGS

Betty Taylor, Dallas, Texas
Bake-Off® Contest 19, 1968

MEAT FILLING

½ lb bulk pork sausage

½ lb lean (at least 80%) ground beef

¾ cup chopped onions

1 tablespoon dried parsley flakes

½ teaspoon dried basil leaves

½ teaspoon dried oregano leaves

1 small clove garlic, finely chopped

Dash pepper

1 can (6 oz) tomato paste

CHEESE FILLING

¼ cup grated Parmesan cheese

1 cup small-curd cottage cheese

1 egg

CRUST

2 cans (8 oz each) Pillsbury™ refrigerated crescent dinner rolls or 2 cans (8 oz each) Pillsbury™ Crescent Recipe Creations™ refrigerated seamless dough sheet

2 (7x4-inch) slices mozzarella cheese

1 tablespoon milk

1 tablespoon sesame seed

1. In 10-inch skillet, cook sausage and beef until thoroughly cooked and no longer pink, stirring frequently; drain. Stir in remaining meat filling ingredients; cook 5 minutes, stirring occasionally, until thoroughly heated.

2. Meanwhile, heat oven to 375°F. In small bowl, mix cheese filling ingredients. Unroll both cans of dough. Place dough rectangles side by side, on ungreased cookie sheet (if using crescent dough, firmly press edges and perforations to seal). Press to form 15x13-inch rectangle.

3. Spoon half of meat filling in 6-inch wide strip lengthwise down center of dough to within 1 inch of short sides. Spoon cheese filling over meat filling; spoon remaining meat filling evenly over cheese filling. Arrange mozzarella cheese slices over filling.

4. Fold short sides of dough 1 inch over filling. Fold long sides of dough tightly over filling, overlapping edges in center ¼ inch; firmly pinch center seam and ends to seal. Brush with milk; sprinkle with sesame seed.

5. Bake 23 to 27 minutes or until deep golden brown.

1 Serving: Calories 410 (Calories from Fat 220); Total Fat 24g; Saturated Fat 9g; Trans Fat 3.5g; Cholesterol 65mg; Sodium 920mg; Total Carbohydrate 29g; Dietary Fiber 1g; Sugars 8g; Protein 20g

POPPIN' FRESH™ BARBECUPS

Refrigerated biscuits become the edible bowls in this zesty, cheese-topped winner.

PREP TIME: 20 MINUTES
TOTAL TIME: 35 MINUTES

MAKES 10 SERVINGS

Hall of Fame

Peter Russell, Topanga, California
Bake-Off® Contest 19, 1968 Hall of Fame

1 lb lean (at least 80%) ground beef

½ cup barbecue sauce

¼ cup chopped onion

1 to 2 tablespoons packed brown sugar

1 can (12 oz) Pillsbury™ Grands!™ Jr. Golden Layers™ Refrigerated Buttermilk or Flaky Biscuits

½ cup shredded Cheddar or American cheese (2 oz)

1. Heat oven to 400°F. Spray 10 regular-size muffin cups with no-stick cooking spray, or grease with shortening. In 10-inch skillet, cook beef over medium heat 8 to 10 minutes, stirring occasionally, until thoroughly cooked; drain. Stir in barbecue sauce, onion and brown sugar. Cook 1 minute to blend flavors, stirring constantly.

2. Separate dough into 10 biscuits. Place 1 biscuit in each muffin cup. Firmly press in bottom and up sides, forming ¼-inch rim over edge of cup. Spoon about ¼ cup beef mixture into each biscuit-lined cup. Sprinkle each with cheese.

3. Bake 10 to 12 minutes or until edges of biscuits are golden brown. Cool 1 minute; remove from muffin cups.

1 Serving: Calories 268 (Calories from Fat 131), Total Fat 15g; Saturated Fat 6g; Trans Fat 1g; Cholesterol 38mg; Sodium 576mg; Total Carbohydrate 22g; Dietary Fiber 1g; Sugars 8g; Protein 11g

SNAPPY JOES ON TEXAS TOAST

Make sloppy joes with pizzazz—sweet-hot additions served open-faced on fresh-baked bread make them anything but ordinary.

PREP TIME: 35 MINUTES
TOTAL TIME: 45 MINUTES

MAKES 6 SERVINGS

Devon Delaney, Princeton, New Jersey
Bake-Off® Contest 44, 2010

¼ cup butter, softened

2 tablespoons chopped fresh Italian (flat-leaf) parsley

1 clove garlic, finely chopped

¼ cup chopped fresh chives

1 can (11 oz) Pillsbury™ refrigerated crusty French loaf

1 tablespoon light olive oil

1½ lb extra-lean (at least 90%) ground beef

½ cup pickled jalapeño chiles, drained, chopped and 2 tablespoons liquid reserved

1 teaspoon ancho chili or chili powder

1 can (8 oz) tomato sauce

¼ cup seedless blackberry jam

1 tablespoon Dijon mustard

¼ teaspoon coarse (kosher or sea) salt

¼ teaspoon black pepper

½ cup sour cream

1. Heat oven to 350°F. In small bowl, mix butter, parsley, garlic and 2 tablespoons of the chives; set aside.

2. Bake French loaf as directed on can. Cool 5 minutes; cut into 12 (1-inch) slices. Spread butter mixture on one side of each slice.

3. While bread is baking, in 10-inch skillet, heat oil over medium heat. Add beef; cook 8 to 10 minutes, stirring occasionally, until thoroughly cooked; drain. Stir in chiles, reserved chile liquid, chili powder, tomato sauce, jam, mustard, salt and pepper; heat to simmering. Reduce heat to low; cover and cook 5 minutes.

4. For each serving, place 2 bread slices on each plate; top each slice with heaping ¼ cup beef mixture, dollop of sour cream and some of remaining chives.

1 Serving: Calories 480 (Calories from Fat 220);
Total Fat 25g; Saturated Fat 11g; Trans Fat 1g;
Cholesterol 100mg; Sodium 790mg;
Total Carbohydrate 38g; Dietary Fiber 1g;
Sugars 11g; Protein 27g

MAIN DISH CRESCENT REUBENS

Reuben sandwich made with sauerkraut and beef is perfect for a hearty dinner—ready in 55 minutes.

PREP TIME: 20 MINUTES
TOTAL TIME: 55 MINUTES

MAKES 6 SERVINGS

Annette Erbeck, Mason, Ohio
Bake-Off® Contest 28, 1978

1 (8-oz.) can Pillsbury™ Refrigerated Crescent Dinner Rolls

3 (7x4-inch) slices Swiss or mozzarella cheese

1 (12-oz.) can corned beef, chopped

1 (14-oz.) can sauerkraut, well drained

3 eggs, slightly beaten

¾ cup milk

1 tablespoon instant minced onion or ¼ cup chopped onion

1 teaspoon dried parsley flakes

¼ teaspoon salt

1. Heat oven to 425°F. Unroll dough into 2 long rectangles. Place in ungreased 13x9-inch pan; press over bottom and ½ inch up sides to form crust. Press perforations to seal.

2. Arrange cheese slices over dough. Spoon corned beef and sauerkraut over cheese. In medium bowl, combine all remaining ingredients; mix well. Pour over sauerkraut.

3. Bake at 425°F for 25 to 35 minutes or until filling is set and crust is deep golden brown. Cool 5 minutes. Cut into squares.

CLEVER IDEAS:

- *Corned beef starts out as fresh brisket or round. The beef is cured with spices in salt brine.*

- *Six ounces of shredded Swiss or mozzarella cheese can be used in place of the sliced cheese.*

- *If you want to tame the flavor of sauerkraut, rinse it thoroughly with water and drain it completely. This treatment will also remove some of the sodium.*

1 Serving: Calories 395 (Calories from Fat 190); Total Fat 21g; Saturated Fat 9g; Trans Fat 0g; Cholesterol 170mg; Sodium 1349mg; Total Carbohydrate 24g; Dietary Fiber 2g; Sugars 8g; Protein 27g

WEEKNIGHT BEEF BURGUNDY

Beef Burgundy in 30 minutes? With the help of instant rice and a hearty steak soup, dinner's ready in no time.

PREP TIME: 30 MINUTES
TOTAL TIME: 30 MINUTES
MAKES 6 SERVINGS

Sue O'Connor, Tequesta, Florida
Bake-Off® Contest 41, 2004

RICE

3 cups uncooked instant white rice

3 cups water

BEEF BURGUNDY

6 tablespoons butter or margarine

1½ cups (4 oz.) sliced fresh mushrooms

½ cup chopped onion (1 medium)

⅓ cup finely chopped fresh parsley

2 cans (18.8 oz each) sirloin steak & vegetables soup

⅔ cup dry red wine

2½ tablespoons cornstarch

⅛ teaspoon pepper

1 (14.5-oz.) can sliced carrots, drained

1. Cook rice in water as directed on package.

2. Meanwhile, in 12-inch nonstick skillet, melt 6 tablespoons butter over medium-high heat. Add mushrooms, onion and parsley; cook 7 to 10 minutes, stirring frequently, until vegetables are tender.

3. Stir in both cans of soup. Reduce heat to low; cook, stirring occasionally, until thoroughly heated.

4. In small bowl, mix wine, cornstarch and pepper until smooth. Increase heat to high; stir wine mixture into vegetables, cooking and stirring until mixture boils. Reduce heat to medium; cook about 1 minute, stirring constantly, until mixture thickens slightly. Add carrots; cook 1 to 2 minutes, stirring frequently, until mixture is well blended and hot. Serve over rice.

1 Serving: Calories 460 (Calories from Fat 140); Total Fat 16g; Saturated Fat 9g; Trans Fat 0g; Cholesterol 45mg; Sodium 864mg; Total Carbohydrate 69g; Dietary Fiber 5g; Sugars 5g; Protein 14g

CALIFORNIA CASSEROLE

When old-fashioned comfort food calls, try a casserole that's got it all, a winner in the Pillsbury Bake-Off® Contest.

PREP TIME: 60 MINUTES
TOTAL TIME: 1 HOUR 25 MINUTES
MAKES 10 SERVINGS

Margaret Hatheway, Santa Barbara, California
Bake-Off® Contest 8, 1956 Grand Prize Winner

CASSEROLE

- ⅓ cup Pillsbury™ BEST™ All Purpose or Unbleached Flour
- 1 teaspoon paprika
- 2 lb. boneless veal, cut into 1-inch pieces
- ¼ cup oil
- ½ teaspoon salt
- ⅛ teaspoon pepper
- 1 cup water
- 1 (10¾-oz.) can condensed cream of chicken soup
- 1½ cups water
- 1 (16-oz.) jar (1½ cups) small onions, drained

DUMPLINGS

- 2 cups Pillsbury™ BEST™ All Purpose or Unbleached Flour
- 4 teaspoons baking powder
- 1 tablespoon poppy seed, if desired
- 1 teaspoon instant minced onion
- 1 teaspoon celery seed
- 1 teaspoon poultry seasoning
- ¼ teaspoon salt
- ¼ cup oil
- ¾ to 1 cup milk
- 2 tablespoons margarine or butter, melted
- ½ cup plain bread crumbs

SAUCE

- 1 (10¾-oz.) can condensed cream of chicken soup
- 1 (8-oz.) container sour cream
- ¼ cup milk

1. In small bowl or plastic bag, combine ⅓ cup flour and paprika; mix well. Add veal; coat well with flour mixture.

2. Heat ¼ cup oil in 12-inch skillet over medium-high heat until hot. Add veal; cook until browned. Add ½ teaspoon salt, pepper and 1 cup water. Bring to a boil. Reduce heat; simmer uncovered 30 minutes or until veal is tender, stirring occasionally. Transfer veal mixture to ungreased 13x9-inch (3-quart) glass baking dish or 3-quart casserole.

3. In same skillet, combine 1 can cream of chicken soup and 1½ cups water; blend well. Bring to a boil, stirring constantly. Pour over veal mixture in baking dish. Add onions; mix well.

4. Heat oven to 425°F. In large bowl, combine 2 cups flour, baking powder, poppy seed, minced onion, celery seed, poultry seasoning and ¼ teaspoon salt; mix well. Add ¼ cup oil and enough milk so that, when stirred, dry ingredients are just moistened.

5. In small bowl, combine margarine and bread crumbs; mix well. Drop rounded tablespoons of dough into crumb mixture; roll to coat well. Arrange dumplings over warm veal mixture. Bake at 425°F for 20 to 25 minutes or until dumplings are deep golden brown.

6. Meanwhile, in medium saucepan, combine all sauce ingredients; blend well. Bring just to a boil. Reduce heat; simmer 2 to 3 minutes or until thoroughly heated, stirring frequently. Serve sauce with casserole and dumplings.

1 Serving: Calories 476 (Calories from Fat 235); Total Fat 30g; Saturated Fat 8g; Trans Fat 1g; Cholesterol 91mg; Sodium 1154mg; Total Carbohydrate 36g; Dietary Fiber 2g; Sugars 5g; Protein 23g

BREADED CHICKEN WITH EDAMAME SUCCOTASH

Tender baked chicken gets a kick from a salsa-spiked succotash.

PREP TIME: 30 MINUTES
TOTAL TIME: 1 HOUR 15 MINUTES
MAKES 6 SERVINGS

Rebecca R. Saulsbury, Lakeland, Florida
Bake-Off® Contest 42, 2006

1¼ cups organic medium chipotle salsa

¼ cup orange marmalade

5 tablespoons lime juice

Salt and pepper, if desired

6 boneless skinless chicken breasts (1¾ lb)

¾ cup garlic herb bread crumbs

¼ cup grated Parmesan cheese

2 tablespoons chopped fresh cilantro

2 cups organic frozen sweet corn (from 16-oz bag), thawed

1 bag (10 oz) organic frozen shelled edamame, thawed

1 teaspoon ground cumin

Fresh cilantro sprigs, if desired

1. In small bowl, mix ½ cup of the salsa, the marmalade and 4 tablespoons of the lime juice; season with salt and pepper. Pour into large resealable food-storage plastic bag. Add chicken; seal bag. Turn bag several times to coat chicken. Refrigerate 30 minutes.

2. Heat oven to 375°F. In another large resealable food-storage plastic bag, mix bread crumbs, cheese and chopped cilantro. Remove 1 chicken breast at a time from marinade; shake off excess marinade. Place in bag of bread crumbs; seal bag and shake to coat with crumb mixture. Place chicken on nonstick cookie sheet. Discard any remaining marinade and crumb mixture.

3. Bake uncovered 20 to 25 minutes, turning once, until juice of chicken is clear when center of thickest part is cut (170°F). Meanwhile, in 2-quart saucepan, place corn and edamame; add enough water to just cover vegetables. Heat to boiling over medium-high heat. Reduce heat to medium-low; cook uncovered 5 to 6 minutes or just until edamame is tender. Drain; stir in remaining ¾ cup salsa, the cumin and remaining tablespoon lime juice. Season to taste with salt and pepper. Cook over medium-low heat 1 to 3 minutes, stirring occasionally, until thoroughly heated.

4. Serve chicken with succotash; garnish with cilantro sprigs.

1 Serving: Calories 370 (Calories from Fat 68); Total Fat 8g; Saturated Fat 1.5g; Trans Fat 0g; Cholesterol 88mg, Sodium 768mg; Total Carbohydrate 36g; Dietary Fiber 4g; Sugars 14g; Protein 38g

BAKED CHICKEN AND SPINACH STUFFING

An old-fashioned chicken dinner is updated for two, with a surprising ingredient that makes the spinach stuffing extra special.

PREP TIME: 35 MINUTES
TOTAL TIME: 60 MINUTES

MAKES 2 SERVINGS

Anna Ginsberg, Austin, Texas
Bake-Off® Contest 42, 2006 Grand Prize Winner

3 tablespoons maple-flavored syrup

2 tablespoons peach preserves

½ teaspoon Worcestershire sauce

2 bone-in skin-on chicken breasts (1 lb)

¼ teaspoon salt

¼ teaspoon pepper

4 frozen plain or buttermilk waffles

1 tablespoon butter or margarine

½ cup chopped onion (1 medium)

¼ cup chicken broth

½ teaspoon poultry seasoning

½ teaspoon chopped fresh sage

1 tablespoon beaten egg white

1 box (9 oz) frozen chopped spinach, thawed, drained (about 1 cup)

1 tablespoon chopped pecans

1. Heat oven to 350°F. Spray 9-inch glass pie plate or 8-inch square pan with cooking spray. In small bowl, mix syrup, preserves and Worcestershire sauce. Place chicken, skin side up, in pie plate; sprinkle with salt and pepper. Spoon syrup mixture over chicken.

2. Bake uncovered 40 to 45 minutes. Meanwhile, toast waffles until golden brown. Cool slightly, about 2 minutes. Cut waffles into ³⁄₄-inch cubes; set aside. Spray 1-quart casserole with cooking spray (or use 9x5-inch nonstick loaf pan; do not spray). In 10-inch nonstick skillet, melt butter over medium heat. Add onion; cook and stir about 2 minutes or until tender. Stir in waffle pieces and broth, breaking up waffle pieces slightly to moisten. Sprinkle with poultry seasoning and sage. Remove from heat; cool about 5 minutes. Stir in egg white and spinach. Spoon stuffing into casserole. Sprinkle pecans over top.

3. Twenty minutes before chicken is done, place casserole in oven next to chicken in pie plate. Spoon syrup mixture in pie plate over chicken. Bake chicken and stuffing uncovered 20 to 25 minutes longer or until juice of chicken is clear when thickest part is cut to bone (170°F) and stuffing is thoroughly heated. Spoon remaining syrup mixture in pie plate over chicken. Serve chicken with stuffing.

1 Serving: Calories 758 (Calories from Fat 294); Total Fat 33g; Saturated Fat 8g; Trans Fat 1.5g; Cholesterol 141mg; Sodium 1140mg; Total Carbohydrate 68g; Dietary Fiber 5g; Sugars 28g; Protein 42g

CHICKEN PICADILLO PIE

Subtle, spicy flavors characterize a Cuban classic.

PREP TIME: 30 MINUTES
TOTAL TIME: 1 HOUR 15 MINUTES

MAKES 8 SERVINGS

Nina Reyes, Miami, Florida
Bake-Off® Contest 32, 1986

CRUST

1 (15-oz.) pkg. refrigerated pie crusts

FILLING

3 tablespoons margarine or butter

1 tablespoon cornstarch

⅛ teaspoon ginger

Dash pepper

1 tablespoon prepared mustard

1 tablespoon soy sauce, if desired

1 tablespoon Worcestershire sauce

1 cup orange juice

2 tablespoons margarine or butter

2 large whole chicken breasts, skinned, boned, cut into bite-size pieces

1 cup finely chopped onions

¼ cup finely chopped green bell pepper

2 garlic cloves, minced

½ cup coconut

¼ cup slivered almonds

¼ cup raisins

¼ to ½ cup chopped pimiento-stuffed green olives

2 tablespoons capers, if desired

1. Prepare pie crust according to package directions for two-crust pie using 9-inch pie pan. Heat oven to 400°F.

2. Melt 1 tablespoon margarine in small saucepan. Blend in cornstarch, ginger, pepper, mustard, soy sauce and Worcestershire sauce. Gradually add orange juice. Bring to a boil; cook until mixture thickens, stirring constantly. Set aside.

3. Melt 2 tablespoons margarine in large skillet. Cook chicken, onions, bell pepper and garlic over medium heat until chicken is completely cooked. Sir in coconut, almonds, raisins, olives, capers and the orange sauce. Continue to cook until thoroughly heated, stirring occasionally. Spoon into pie crust-lined pan. Top with second crust and flute; cut slits in several places.

4. Bake at 400°F for 30 to 40 minutes or until golden brown. Cover edge of crust with strips of foil after 15 to 20 minutes of baking to prevent excessive browning. Let stand 5 minutes before serving.

1 Serving: Calories 470 (Calories from Fat 238); Total Fat 26g; Saturated Fat 9g; Trans Fat 2g; Cholesterol 44mg; Sodium 765mg; Total Carbohydrate 37g; Dietary Fiber 2g; Sugars 9g; Protein 16g

CHICKEN AND BROCCOLI CAVATAPPI

This pasta dish is quick to prepare, and with its sun-dried tomatoes and creamy sauce, it's fancy enough for company.

PREP TIME: 30 MINUTES
TOTAL TIME: 30 MINUTES
MAKES 6 SERVINGS

Joni Busch, Rogers, Minnesota
Bake-Off® Contest 41, 2004

8 oz. (2⅔ cups) uncooked cavatappi pasta (thin, ridged spiral macaroni)

1 tablespoon oil (from jar of sun-dried tomatoes)

1 lb. chicken tenderloins, cut in half crosswise

2 tablespoons finely chopped green onions (2 medium)

3 teaspoons dry ground mustard

2 teaspoons minced garlic

¼ cup chopped drained oil-packed sun-dried tomatoes (from 7-oz. jar)

1 (24-oz.) bag frozen broccoli & three cheese sauce

1 (6.5-oz.) pkg. garlic-and-herb cream cheese spread

¼ cup milk

Salt and pepper to taste, if desired

1. In 4½- or 5-quart Dutch oven, cook pasta as directed on package. Drain; rinse well. Return to Dutch oven; cover to keep warm.

2. Meanwhile, in 12-inch skillet, heat oil over medium-high heat until hot. Add chicken; cook and stir 2 to 4 minutes or until chicken is beginning to brown. Stir in onions, mustard and garlic. Cook until garlic is softened. Stir in tomatoes until blended. Cook 2 to 3 minutes, stirring occasionally, until chicken is no longer pink in center. If necessary, drain off any liquid.

3. Add frozen broccoli with sauce chips; cook about 4 minutes, stirring occasionally, until sauce chips have melted. Stir in cream cheese spread. Add milk; cook about 2 minutes, stirring constantly, until well blended and thoroughly heated.

4. Gently stir broccoli mixture into cooked pasta to coat. Salt and pepper to taste. Pour into serving bowl.

1 Serving: Calories 441 (Calories from Fat 168); Total Fat 19g; Saturated Fat 12g; Trans Fat 0g; Cholesterol 95mg; Sodium 751mg; Total Carbohydrate 39g; Dietary Fiber 4g; Sugars 6g; Protein 32g

CHICK 'N CORN MINI PIES

Pillsbury™ Grands!™ Flaky Biscuits provide a great base and topping for these mini pies that are filled with chicken and canned corn and peppers—perfect for dinner.

PREP TIME: 20 MINUTES
TOTAL TIME: 35 MINUTES

MAKES 8 SERVINGS

Priscilla Yee, Concord, California
Bake-Off® Contest 31, 1984

1 (3-oz.) pkg. cream cheese, softened

2 tablespoons mayonnaise or salad dressing

¾ cup chopped cooked chicken

¼ cup chopped onion

2 oz. (½ cup) shredded Cheddar cheese

1 (11-oz.) can whole kernel corn, red and green peppers, drained

1 (16.3-oz.) can Pillsbury™ Grands!™ Refrigerated Flaky Biscuits

Sesame seed

1. Heat oven to 375°F. Lightly grease 8 muffin cups. In medium bowl, blend cream cheese and mayonnaise until smooth. Stir in chicken, onion, cheese and corn.

2. Separate dough into 8 biscuits. Separate each biscuit into 2 parts by removing the top ⅓ of each biscuit. Place bottom ⅔ piece of each biscuit in greased muffin cup; firmly press in bottom and up sides, forming ¼-inch rim. Spoon about ⅓ cup chicken mixture into each cup. Top each with remaining ⅓ biscuit, stretching slightly to fit. Press edges to seal. Sprinkle with sesame seed.

3. Bake at 375°F for 15 to 20 minutes or until golden brown.

1 Serving: Calories 340 (Calories from Fat 170); Total Fat 19g; Saturated Fat 7g; Trans Fat 4g; Cholesterol 35mg; Sodium 750mg; Total Carbohydrate 30g; Dietary Fiber 1g; Sugars 5g; Protein 11g

SALSA COUSCOUS CHICKEN

There will be no more complaints about plain old chicken! Fruit, nuts and spice make a honey of a main dish.

PREP TIME: 30 MINUTES
TOTAL TIME: 30 MINUTES
MAKES 4 SERVINGS

Ellie Mathews, Seattle, Washington
Bake-Off® Contest 38, 1998 Grand Prize Winner

3 cups hot cooked couscous or rice

1 tablespoon oil

¼ cup coarsely chopped almonds

2 garlic cloves, minced

8 chicken thighs, skin removed

1 cup salsa

¼ cup water

2 tablespoons dried currants or raisins

1 tablespoon honey

¾ teaspoon cumin

½ teaspoon cinnamon

1. Cook couscous as directed on package.

2. Meanwhile, heat oil in large skillet over medium-high heat until hot. Add almonds; cook 1 to 2 minutes or until golden brown. Remove from skillet; set aside.

3. Add garlic and chicken to skillet; cook 4 to 5 minutes until chicken is browned, turning once.

4. In small bowl, combine salsa and all remaining ingredients; mix well. Add to chicken. Reduce heat to medium; cover and cook 20 minutes or until chicken is no longer pink, stirring occasionally.

5. Stir in almonds. Serve over couscous.

1 Serving: Calories 417 (Calories from Fat 115); Total Fat 19g; Saturated Fat 13g; Trans Fat 0g; Cholesterol 131mg; Sodium 540mg; Total Carbohydrate 45g; Dietary Fiber 3g; Sugars 11g; Protein 34g

CHICK-N-BROCCOLI POT PIES

Biscuits make a flaky home-style crust for a popular pot pie with chicken in a creamy, cheesy sauce.

PREP TIME: 20 MINUTES
TOTAL TIME: 45 MINUTES

MAKES 10 SERVINGS

Linda Wood, Indianapolis, Indiana
Bake-Off® Contest 28, 1978 Grand Prize Winner

1 can (12 oz) Pillsbury™ Grands!™ Jr. Golden Layers™ refrigerated biscuits

⅔ cup shredded Cheddar or American cheese

⅔ cup crisp rice cereal

2 cups frozen broccoli cuts, thawed

1 cup cubed cooked chicken or turkey

1 can (10¾ oz) reduced-sodium condensed cream of chicken or mushroom soup

⅓ cup slivered or sliced almonds

1. Heat oven to 375°F. Separate dough into 10 biscuits. Place 1 biscuit in each ungreased muffin cup; firmly press in bottom and up sides, forming ½-inch rim over edge of muffin cup. Spoon about 1 tablespoon each of cheese and cereal into each biscuit-lined cup. Press mixture into bottom of each cup.

2. Cut large pieces of broccoli in half. In large bowl, combine broccoli, chicken and soup; mix well. Spoon about ⅓ cup of chicken mixture over cereal. Cups will be full. Sprinkle with almonds.

3. Bake at 375°F for 20 to 25 minutes or until edges of biscuits are deep golden brown.

CLEVER IDEA: *To make ahead, prepare, cover and refrigerate up to 2 hours; bake as directed above. To reheat, wrap loosely in foil; heat at 375°F for 18 to 20 minutes.*

1 Serving: Calories 220 (Calories from Fat 100); Total Fat 11g; Saturated Fat 3g; Trans Fat 0g; Cholesterol 25mg; Sodium 600mg; Total Carbohydrate 20g; Dietary Fiber 1g; Sugars 3g; Protein 10g

MEDITERRANEAN CHICKEN VEGETABLE GALETTE

Fill up flaky pastry with veggies, two cheeses and chicken for a new take on "dinner's in the oven in minutes."

PREP TIME: 15 MINUTES
TOTAL TIME: 55 MINUTES
MAKES 8 SERVINGS

Dinah Surh, Staten Island, New York
Bake-Off® Contest 46, 2013

1 bag (11.8 oz) frozen Mediterranean blend

1 cup ricotta cheese

¼ cup grated Parmesan cheese

1 to 1½ teaspoons grated lemon peel

1 teaspoon salt

¼ teaspoon pepper

1 Pillsbury™ refrigerated pie crust, softened as directed on box

2 cups cooked roasted chicken breast strips (9 oz)

1 egg, beaten

1. Heat oven to 375°F. Spray large cookie sheet with no-stick cooking spray. Microwave frozen vegetables as directed on bag.

2. Meanwhile, in small bowl, mix ricotta cheese, 3 tablespoons of the Parmesan cheese, ½ to 1 teaspoon of the lemon peel, ½ teaspoon of the salt and ⅛ teaspoon of the pepper.

3. Unroll pie crust on cookie sheet. Spread cheese mixture over crust to within 1¼ inches of edge.

4. In large bowl, mix chicken strips and remaining ½ teaspoon lemon peel, remaining ½ teaspoon salt and remaining ⅛ teaspoon pepper. Add cooked vegetables; mix well. Spoon over cheese.

5. Fold edge of crust over filling, pleating crust as necessary. Brush crust edge with egg. Sprinkle crust edge and filling with remaining 1 tablespoon Parmesan cheese.

6. Bake 25 to 35 minutes or until crust is golden brown. Let stand 5 minutes.

1 Serving: Calories 260 (Calories from Fat 120); Total Fat 13g; Saturated Fat 5g; Trans Fat 0g; Cholesterol 65mg; Sodium 878mg; Total Carbohydrate 19g; Dietary Fiber 0g; Sugars 0g; Protein 16g

CHICKEN AND WHITE BEAN BRUSCHETTA BAKE

The flavors of Italy fill this baked main dish that is best served in shallow soup bowls.

PREP TIME: 15 MINUTES
TOTAL TIME: 45 MINUTES
MAKES 4 SERVINGS

Shannon Kohn, Simpsonville, South Carolina
Bake-Off® Contest 42, 2006

1 can (19 oz) cannellini (white kidney) beans, drained, rinsed

1 can (14.5 oz) organic diced tomatoes with Italian herbs, drained

1 package (6 oz) refrigerated cooked Italian-style chicken breast strips, cut into 1-inch pieces

1 tablespoon balsamic vinegar

½ teaspoon salt

1 can (11 oz) Pillsbury™ refrigerated original breadsticks

2 cups shredded 6-cheese Italian cheese blend (8 oz)

½ teaspoon dried basil leaves, crushed

1 tablespoon chopped fresh parsley, if desired

1. Heat oven to 375°F. Spray 13x9-inch (3-quart) glass baking dish with cooking spray. In large bowl, mix beans, tomatoes, chicken, vinegar and salt.

2. Unroll dough; separate into 12 breadsticks. Cut each breadstick into 4 equal pieces. Stir ¼ of breadstick pieces at a time into bean mixture. Stir in 1 cup of the cheese. Spoon into baking dish, gently smoothing top. Top evenly with remaining 1 cup cheese; sprinkle with basil.

3. Bake 25 to 30 minutes or until bubbly and top is golden brown. To serve, spoon into individual shallow soup bowls; sprinkle with parsley.

1 Serving: Calories 630 (Calories from Fat 180); Total Fat 20g; Saturated Fat 10g; Trans Fat 1g; Cholesterol 80mg; Sodium 1880mg; Total Carbohydrate 73g; Dietary Fiber 8g; Sugars 10g; Protein 40g

CHICKEN-BROCCOLI AU GRATIN

Chicken bites and broccoli in a creamy cheese sauce are topped with flaky crescents in a casserole just for two.

PREP TIME: 20 MINUTES
TOTAL TIME: 45 MINUTES

MAKES 2 SERVINGS

Kibby Jackson, Gray, Georgia
Bake-Off® Contest 42, 2006

1 tablespoon olive oil

1 cup sliced fresh mushrooms

1 small onion, sliced (½ cup)

1 box (10 oz) frozen broccoli & zesty cheese sauce

⅔ cup ricotta cheese

1 cup chopped cooked chicken

1 can (4 oz) Pillsbury™ refrigerated crescent dinner rolls (4 rolls)

1. Heat oven to 375°F. In 10-inch skillet, heat oil over medium-high heat. Add mushrooms and onion; cook 5 to 7 minutes, stirring frequently, until tender. Meanwhile, microwave broccoli with cheese sauce as directed on box.

2. Spread ⅓ cup ricotta cheese in bottom of each of 2 ungreased 2-cup au gratin dishes or individual casseroles. Top each evenly with chicken, mushroom mixture and broccoli with cheese sauce.

3. Unroll dough; separate into 2 rectangles. Place 1 rectangle over top of each dish, tucking corners into dish as needed.

4. Place dishes on cookie sheet; bake 20 to 25 minutes or until tops are golden brown and edges are bubbly.

> **CLEVER IDEA:** *Recipe can be made in ungreased 8-inch square (2-quart) glass baking dish. Spread ricotta cheese in dish; top with chicken, mushroom mixture and broccoli with cheese sauce. Arrange dough rectangles over top. Bake as directed.*

1 Serving: Calories 560 (Calories from Fat 240); Total Fat 27g; Saturated Fat 7g; Trans Fat 3g; Cholesterol 70mg; Sodium 1170mg; Total Carbohydrate 43g; Dietary Fiber 3g; Sugars 16g; Protein 38g

DEEP-DISH CHICKEN CORDON BLEU

Check out this family-friendly dinner casserole that includes delicious layers of chicken, ham and cheese.

PREP TIME: 30 MINUTES
TOTAL TIME: 50 MINUTES

MAKES 12 SERVINGS

Amy Warren, Maineville, Ohio
Bake-Off® Contest 44, 2010

1 can (8 oz) Pillsbury™ refrigerated crescent dinner rolls (8 rolls)

2 tablespoons unsalted or salted butter

1 tablespoon 100% extra virgin olive oil or pure olive oil

1 medium onion, thinly sliced

1 clove garlic, finely chopped

1 box (13.25 oz) frozen baked honey-battered chicken tenders, thawed, cut into ½-inch pieces, or 1 deli rotisserie chicken (2 to 2½ lb), shredded

16 slices (1 oz each) Muenster cheese

¼ cup grated Parmesan cheese

¼ cup mayonnaise or salad dressing

2 tablespoons Dijon mustard

2 teaspoons lemon juice

1 teaspoon honey

1 teaspoon horseradish sauce or cream-style prepared horseradish

½ teaspoon chopped fresh thyme leaves or ⅛ teaspoon dried thyme leaves

1 lb shaved cooked brown-sugar or maple-glazed ham (from deli)

1. Heat oven to 375°F. Spray 13x9-inch (3-quart) glass baking dish with no-stick cooking spray. Unroll crescent rolls in baking dish; press perforations to seal. Bake 10 to 13 minutes or until light golden brown.

2. Meanwhile, in 10-inch skillet, heat butter and oil over medium heat. Add onion and garlic; cook 2 to 3 minutes, stirring frequently, until softened. Remove from heat; stir in cut-up chicken tenders.

3. Place 8 slices of the Muenster cheese over baked crust. In small bowl, stir Parmesan cheese, mayonnaise, mustard, lemon juice, honey, horseradish sauce and thyme until well blended. Spoon half of the mayonnaise mixture evenly over cheese on crust.

4. Spoon chicken mixture evenly over mayonnaise mixture on crust. Spoon remaining mayonnaise mixture evenly over chicken. Cover chicken evenly with ham. Top with remaining 8 slices Muenster cheese.

5. Bake 15 to 20 minutes longer or until cheese is melted and filling is thoroughly heated.

1 Serving: Calories 420 (Calories from Fat 250); Total Fat 28g; Saturated Fat 12g; Trans Fat 1.5g; Cholesterol 100mg; Sodium 1170mg; Total Carbohydrate 10g; Dietary Fiber 0g; Sugars 3g; Protein 31g

CRUNCHY BISCUIT CHICKEN CASSEROLE

Enjoy this hearty chicken casserole packed with vegetables and baked with Pillsbury™ Grands!™ biscuits—a delicious dinner.

PREP TIME: 15 MINUTES

TOTAL TIME: 40 MINUTES

MAKES 6 SERVINGS

Martin Miller, Waunakee, Wisconsin
Bake-Off® Contest 27, 1976

- 2 (5-oz.) cans chunk chicken or 2 cups cubed cooked chicken
- 1 (10¾-oz.) can condensed cream of chicken soup
- 1 (8.25-oz.) can sliced green beans, drained
- 1 (2.5-oz.) jar sliced mushrooms, undrained
- 4 oz. (1 cup) shredded Cheddar or American cheese
- ½ cup mayonnaise or salad dressing
- 1 teaspoon lemon juice
- 1 (16.3-oz.) can Pillsbury™ Grands!™ Refrigerated Buttermilk Biscuits
- 1 to 2 tablespoons margarine or butter, melted
- ¼ to ½ cup crushed Cheddar cheese flavor or seasoned croutons

1. Heat oven to 375°F. In medium saucepan, combine chicken, soup, green beans, mushrooms, cheese, mayonnaise and lemon juice. Bring to a boil, stirring occasionally. Pour hot chicken mixture into ungreased 13x9-inch baking dish.

2. Separate dough into 8 biscuits; arrange over hot chicken mixture. Brush each biscuit with margarine; sprinkle with crushed croutons.

3. Bake at 375°F for 23 to 27 minutes or until deep golden brown.

1 Serving: Calories 565 (Calories from Fat 317); Total Fat 35g; Saturated Fat 12g; Trans Fat 0g; Cholesterol 65mg; Sodium 1739mg; Total Carbohydrate 9g; Dietary Fiber 2g; Sugars 8g; Protein 23g

QUICK-TOPPED VEGETABLE CHICKEN CASSEROLE

As Americans began to eat less red meat in the 1980s, many excellent chicken recipes became Bake-Off® winners. The new twist for this old-fashioned chicken and vegetable pie is the spoon-on crust made with pancake mix.

PREP TIME: 20 MINUTES
TOTAL TIME: 45 MINUTES

MAKES 6 SERVINGS

Bernice Malinowski, Custer, Wisconsin
Bake-Off® Contest 31, 1984

CASSEROLE

1 (10¾-oz.) can condensed cream of chicken soup

1 (3-oz.) pkg. cream cheese, softened

½ cup milk

½ cup chopped celery

½ chopped onion

½ cup grated Parmesan cheese

¼ cup chopped green bell pepper

¼ cup shredded carrot

2 to 3 cups cubed cooked chicken

1 (9-oz.) pkg. frozen cut broccoli in a pouch, cooked, drained

TOPPING

1 cup complete or buttermilk pancake mix

¼ cup slivered almonds

4 oz. (1 cup) shredded Cheddar cheese

¼ cup milk

1 tablespoon oil

1 egg, slightly beaten

1. Heat oven to 375°F. In large saucepan, combine soup, cream cheese, $1/2$ cup milk, celery, onion, Parmesan cheese, bell pepper and carrot. Cook over medium heat until mixture is hot and cream cheese is melted, stirring frequently. Stir in chicken and broccoli. Pour into ungreased 2-quart casserole or 12 x 8-inch (2-quart) baking dish.

2. In medium bowl, combine all topping ingredients; blend well. Spoon tablespoonfuls of topping over hot chicken mixture.

3. Bake at 375°F for 20 to 30 minutes or until topping is golden brown and chicken mixture bubbles around edges.

1 Serving: Calories 510 (Calories from Fat 230); Total Fat 28g; Saturated Fat 11g; Trans Fat 0g; Cholesterol 142mg; Sodium 1018mg; Total Carbohydrate 29g; Dietary Fiber 3g; Sugars 7g; Protein 35g

TURKEY-SWEET POTATO POT PIES

Sweet potatoes and curry give this comfort food a new twist.

PREP TIME: 15 MINUTES
TOTAL TIME: 55 MINUTES

MAKES 4 SERVINGS

Dolly Craig, Denver, Colorado
Bake-Off® Contest 41, 2004

1 can (15 oz) sweet potatoes, drained, cut into bite-size pieces (2 cups)

1½ cups cubed cooked turkey or chicken

1 cup frozen sweet peas, thawed, drained

3 tablespoons chopped sweet yellow onion

3 teaspoons curry powder

Salt and pepper to taste, if desired

1 can (18.6 oz) chicken pot pie style soup

1 box Pillsbury™ refrigerated pie crusts, softened as directed on box

1. Heat oven to 400°F. In large bowl, mix all ingredients except pie crust. Divide mixture evenly into 4 (1¼- to 2-cup) ungreased individual ramekins.

2. Unroll pie crust on cutting board. Cut crust into 4 wedge-shaped pieces. Top each filled ramekin with 1 crust piece. With kitchen scissors or knife, trim crust edges. Pinch and flute edge, filling in areas with trimmed pie crust pieces where needed. With knife, cut several small slits in crusts for steam to escape. Place ramekins on cookie sheet.

3. Bake 25 to 33 minutes or until filling is bubbly and crust is deep golden brown. During last 10 to 15 minutes of baking, cover crust edge with strips of foil to prevent excessive browning. Cool 5 minutes before serving.

CLEVER IDEAS:

- *To quickly thaw frozen peas, place in colander or strainer; rinse with warm water until thawed. Drain well.*

- *A 1¼- to 1½-quart casserole can be substituted for the ramekins. Place whole crust over filled casserole.*

1 Serving: Calories 520 (Calories from Fat 160); Total Fat 18g; Saturated Fat 7g; Trans Fat 0g; Cholesterol 65mg; Sodium 840mg; Total Carbohydrate 67g; Dietary Fiber 6g; Sugars 23g; Protein 23g

TEX-MEX PASTA

Salsa and sausage kick up the heat in this pasta toss.

PREP TIME: 25 MINUTES
TOTAL TIME: 25 MINUTES

MAKES 6 SERVINGS

Karen Wetch, Santa Rosa, California
Bake-Off® Contest 40, 2002

2⅔ cups uncooked penne pasta (8 oz)

1 lb bulk Italian turkey sausage

1 medium onion, chopped

1 medium red bell pepper, chopped

1 small zucchini, chopped

2 cups frozen corn

1 cup thick 'n chunky salsa

1 can (14.5 oz) organic diced tomatoes, undrained

¾ teaspoon dried oregano leaves

1½ cups reduced-fat shredded Cheddar cheese (6 oz)

½ cup fresh cilantro, chopped

1. Cook penne as directed on package. Drain; cover to keep warm.

2. Meanwhile, spray nonstick wok or 12-inch skillet with non-stick cooking spray; heat over medium-high heat. Add sausage; cook 5 minutes, stirring frequently, until no longer pink and thoroughly cooked. Drain.

3. Add onion, bell pepper, zucchini, corn, salsa, tomatoes and oregano; mix well. Heat to boiling. Cook 5 minutes, stirring occasionally.

4. Reserve ½ cup cheese and 2 tablespoons cilantro. Add remaining 1 cup cheese and cilantro to mixture in wok; mix well. Add cooked penne; toss to mix. Spoon mixture onto serving platter. Garnish with reserved cheese and cilantro.

1 Serving: Calories 425 (Calories from Fat 110); Total Fat 12g; Saturated Fat 4g; Trans Fat 0g; Cholesterol 50mg; Sodium 1040mg; Total Carbohydrate 51g; Dietary Fiber 5g; Sugars 9g; Protein 28g

SPICY SWEET TURKEY ROLLS

Create baked, not fried, meat and veggie rolls with a warm sweet-and-sour sauce.

PREP TIME: 25 MINUTES
TOTAL TIME: 45 MINUTES

MAKES 5 SERVINGS

Margaret Martinez, Westminster, Colorado
Bake-Off® Contest 46, 2013

½ cup coarsely chopped orange bell pepper

1 can (8 oz) pineapple chunks in juice, drained, juice reserved

5 tablespoons red wine vinegar

¾ cup plus 2 tablespoons orange marmalade

⅛ teaspoon salt

¼ teaspoon ground red pepper (cayenne)

10 oz ground turkey

¼ teaspoon salt

¼ teaspoon ground black pepper

1 can Pillsbury™ Grands!™ Homestyle refrigerated buttermilk biscuits (5 ct)

1. Heat oven to 350°F. Line large cookie sheet with parchment paper. In food processor, place bell pepper and pineapple chunks. Cover; process with on-and-off pulses until finely chopped. Stop machine and scrape sides of bowl, if necessary.

2. In 1-quart saucepan, mix reserved pineapple juice, 4 tablespoons of the vinegar, ¾ cup of the marmalade, ⅛ teaspoon salt and ⅛ teaspoon of the cayenne pepper. Bring to a boil over medium-high heat. Reduce heat to low; simmer 15 minutes or until sauce thickens and is reduced to 1 cup.

3. Meanwhile, in 10-inch skillet, mix pineapple mixture, turkey, ¼ teaspoon salt, ¼ teaspoon pepper and remaining ⅛ teaspoon cayenne pepper. Cook over medium heat 5 minutes, stirring occasionally, or until turkey is no longer pink. Add remaining 1 tablespoon of the red wine vinegar and remaining 2 tablespoons of the marmalade. Cook 2 to 4 minutes longer or until most of the liquid is evaporated. Cool 5 minutes.

4. Separate dough into 5 biscuits; pat each biscuit into 7½ x 4½-inch oval. Spoon turkey mixture down center of each biscuit. Bring long sides of biscuit over filling, overlapping slightly in center. Fold up short sides to enclose filling; pinch edges to seal. Place seam side down 2 inches apart on cookie sheet. Prick tops 3 times with toothpick.

5. Bake 15 to 20 minutes or until golden brown. Serve with sauce.

1 Serving: Calories 427 (Calories from Fat 94); Total Fat 14g; Saturated Fat 3.5g; Trans Fat 0g; Cholesterol 45mg; Sodium 790mg; Total Carbohydrate 45g; Dietary Fiber 0g; Sugars 45g; Protein 13g

BISCUIT STUFFIN' ATOP CHOPS

Contestants in 1971 got the bonus of the trip to Hawaii when Honolulu was selected as the Bake-Off® site. The innovative idea of turning refrigerated biscuits into a golden-brown stuffing to dress up baked pork chops won the trip for this contestant.

PREP TIME: 20 MINUTES
TOTAL TIME: 1 HOUR 15 MINUTES
MAKES 6 SERVINGS

Marion Ohl, Clyde, Ohio
Bake-Off® Contest 22, 1971

1 tablespoon oil
6 (½-inch-thick) pork loin chops
1 (10¾-oz.) can condensed cream of chicken soup
1 cup chopped celery
1 cup chopped onions

1 egg
¼ teaspoon pepper
⅛ teaspoon poultry seasoning
1 (7.5-oz.) can Pillsbury™ Refrigerated Buttermilk Biscuits

1. Heat oven to 350°F. Heat oil in large skillet over medium heat until hot. Add pork chops; cook until browned on both sides. Place pork chops in ungreased 13x9-inch pan.

2. In medium bowl, combine soup, celery, onions, egg, pepper and poultry seasoning; mix well.

3. Separate dough into 10 biscuits; cut each into 8 pieces. Stir biscuit pieces into soup mixture. Spoon over pork chops.

4. Bake at 350°F for 45 to 55 minutes or until biscuit pieces are golden brown and no longer doughy in center.

CLEVER IDEA: *This is a nice home-style dish to serve on a cool evening. If you need to substitute for the poultry seasoning, use ⅛ teaspoon ground sage and a dash of ground thyme. No thyme? Use all ground sage, and it will still be tasty.*

1 Serving: Calories 427 (Calories from Fat 155); Total Fat 17g; Saturated Fat 4g; Trans Fats 2g; Cholesterol 158mg; Sodium 860mg; Total Carbohydrate 21g; Dietary Fiber 1g; Sugars 4g; Protein 45g

WILD RICE AND HAM COUNTRY TART

Looking for a dinner made using Pillsbury™ refrigerated pie crusts and sliced mushrooms? Then check out this wonderful rice and ham tart.

PREP TIME: 30 MINUTES
TOTAL TIME: 1 HOUR 5 MINUTES
MAKES 8 SERVINGS

Robert Holt, Mendota Heights, Minnesota
Bake-Off® Contest 34, 1990

1 box Pillsbury™ refrigerated pie crusts, softened as directed on box

FILLING

1 cup cubed cooked ham

½ cup cooked wild rice (from 15-oz can)

⅓ cup finely chopped red bell pepper

¼ cup thinly sliced green onion tops

1 jar (4.5 oz) sliced mushrooms, well drained

CUSTARD

3 eggs

1 cup sour cream

1 tablespoon country-style Dijon mustard

½ teaspoon salt

⅛ teaspoon pepper

TOPPING

2 cups shredded Swiss cheese (8 oz)

11 pecan halves

1. Heat oven to 425°F. Make pie crust as directed on box for One-Crust Baked Shell, using 10-inch tart pan with removable bottom or 9-inch pie plate. Place crust in pan; press in bottom and up sides of pan. Trim edges if necessary. Do not prick crust. Bake 10 to 12 minutes or until crust is very light golden brown. Remove from oven. Reduce heat to 400°F.

2. In medium bowl, stir together filling ingredients; set aside. In small bowl, beat eggs until blended. Stir in remaining custard ingredients.

3. Sprinkle 1 cup of the cheese over bottom of baked shell. Spread filling mixture over cheese. Pour custard mixture over filling; sprinkle with remaining 1 cup cheese. Arrange pecan halves on top.

4. Bake 30 to 35 minutes or until knife inserted in center comes out clean. Let stand 10 minutes before serving.

1 Serving: Calories 360 (Calories from Fat 220); Total Fat 25g; Saturated Fat 12g; Trans Fat 0g; Cholesterol 135mg; Sodium 780mg; Total Carbohydrate 19g; Dietary Fiber 1g; Sugars 2g; Protein 16g

BALSAMIC ROASTED TOMATO-SPINACH-BACON PIE

Bring out the natural sweetness of plum tomatoes when you roast them, then add to a scrumptious main-dish pie.

PREP TIME: 35 MINUTES
TOTAL TIME: 1 HOUR 20 MINUTES

MAKES 8 SERVINGS

Allison Foley, Greenwich, Connecticut
Bake-Off® Contest 44, 2010

1 Pillsbury™ refrigerated pie crust, softened as directed on box

9 medium plum (Roma) tomatoes, halved lengthwise, seeded

2 cloves garlic, finely chopped

½ teaspoon Italian seasoning

⅛ teaspoon salt

⅛ teaspoon black pepper

2 tablespoons balsamic vinegar

2 tablespoons olive oil

3 eggs

½ cup mascarpone cheese (4 oz), softened

1 box (9 oz) frozen chopped spinach, thawed, squeezed to drain

1 cup grated Parmesan cheese

2 or 3 dashes ground red pepper (cayenne), if desired

¼ teaspoon salt

½ teaspoon black pepper

6 slices bacon, cooked, crumbled

1. Heat oven to 425°F. Place pie crust in 9-inch glass pie plate as directed on box for One-Crust Filled Pie; flute edge. Bake 6 to 8 minutes or until just beginning to brown. Remove from oven.

2. Line 15x10-inch pan (with sides) with foil. Arrange tomatoes, cut sides up, in single layer in pan. Sprinkle tomatoes with garlic, Italian seasoning and ⅛ teaspoon each salt and black pepper. Drizzle with vinegar and oil. Roast 25 to 30 minutes or until tomatoes are very tender. Remove from oven; reduce oven temperature to 375°F.

3. Meanwhile, in medium bowl, beat eggs with wire whisk. Add mascarpone cheese; beat until well blended. Stir in spinach, ½ cup of the Parmesan cheese, red pepper, ¼ teaspoon salt and ½ teaspoon black pepper. Spread mixture evenly in partially baked crust.

4. Arrange tomatoes, overlapping slightly, in single layer on spinach mixture. Sprinkle with remaining ½ cup Parmesan cheese and bacon.

5. Bake at 375°F 25 to 35 minutes, covering edge of crust with strips of foil after 10 to 15 minutes, until filling is set in center and crust is golden brown. Let stand 10 minutes before serving.

1 Serving: Calories 300 (Calories from Fat 180); Total Fat 20g; Saturated Fat 8g; Trans Fat 0g; Cholesterol 95mg; Sodium 630mg; Total Carbohydrate 17g; Dietary Fiber 1g; Sugars 2g; Protein 11g

CAJUN RED BEANS AND RICE

Red beans and rice is a traditional Southern favorite made with a spicy heavily smoked sausage of French origin called andouille.

PREP TIME: 35 MINUTES
TOTAL TIME: 35 MINUTES

MAKES 6 SERVINGS

Del Tinsley, Nashville, Tennessee
Bake-Off® Contest 35, 1992

¾ lb. finely chopped hickory-smoked andouille sausage, skinned, or cooked hot Italian sausage

1 cup chopped onions

2 (15.5-oz.) cans red beans, drained

1 (8-oz.) can tomato sauce

½ cup diced green bell pepper

½ cup diced yellow bell pepper

2 garlic cloves, minced

1 teaspoon dried oregano leaves

1 teaspoon dried thyme leaves

1 tablespoon dry sherry, if desired

6 cups hot cooked rice

⅓ cup sliced green onions

Hot pepper sauce

In large skillet, brown sausage and onions over medium-high heat for 3 minutes, stirring frequently; drain. Stir in beans, tomato sauce, bell peppers, garlic, oregano and thyme. Reduce heat to low; simmer 15 minutes, stirring occasionally. Stir in sherry. Serve over rice; garnish with green onions. Serve with hot pepper sauce.

1 Serving: Calories 470 (Calories from Fat 80); Total Fat 8g; Saturated Fat 3g; Trans Fat 0g; Cholesterol 33mg; Sodium 858mg; Total Carbohydrate 85g; Dietary Fiber 8g; Sugars 6g; Protein 18g

BAKED CHORIZO CHILI QUESADILLA

Lots of melty cheese makes this Mexican-style meat pie a family favorite!

PREP TIME: 30 MINUTES
TOTAL TIME: 1 HOUR 25 MINUTES

MAKES 8 SERVINGS

Laura Ware, Fort Worth, Texas
Bake-Off® Contest 46, 2013

- 1 box (10 oz) frozen corn & butter sauce
- 10 oz ground pork chorizo
- ½ cup chopped onion
- ¼ cup tomato paste
- 1 can (15 oz) black beans, drained, rinsed
- 1 box Pillsbury™ refrigerated pie crusts, softened as directed on box
- 2 cups shredded pepper Jack cheese (8 oz)

1. Heat oven to 375°F. Microwave corn as directed on box. Set aside.

2. Meanwhile, heat 12-inch skillet over medium-high heat. Add chorizo, onion and tomato paste; cook 6 to 8 minutes, stirring frequently, or until thoroughly cooked. Add corn and beans; cook 2 to 3 minutes longer, stirring occasionally, until thoroughly heated.

3. Unroll one pie crust on large ungreased or parchment-lined cookie sheet; sprinkle ²/₃ cup of the cheese over crust to within 1 inch of edge. Top with chorizo mixture and ²/₃ cup of the remaining cheese.

4. Moisten edge of crust with water. Top with second crust; roll edge inward, pressing to seal. Cut 3 slits in top crust. Bake 30 to 40 minutes or until golden brown. Remove from oven; sprinkle with remaining ²/₃ cup cheese. Bake 3 to 4 minutes or until cheese is melted. Let stand 10 minutes.

1 Serving: Calories 523 (Calories from Fat 320); Total Fat 35g; Saturated Fat 16g; Trans Fat 0g; Cholesterol 86mg; Sodium 963mg; Total Carbohydrate 42g; Dietary Fiber 5g; Sugars 2g; Protein 20g

EASY CAPRESE PIZZA BAKE

Surprise! There's ooey, gooey melty cheese inside each baked biscuit. Sweet sausage, rich tomato sauce, fresh basil—that's Italian!

PREP TIME: 20 MINUTES
TOTAL TIME: 40 MINUTES

MAKES 5 SERVINGS

Sheila Suhan, Scottdale, Pennsylvania
Bake-Off® Contest 46, 2013

- 3 teaspoons 100% extra virgin olive oil
- 1 lb bulk sweet Italian sausage
- 4 cups pizza sauce
- ¼ cup water
- ½ cup fresh basil leaves, chopped
- 1 can Pillsbury™ Grands!™ Jr. Golden Layers™ refrigerated buttermilk biscuits
- 20 fresh mozzarella ciliegine (cherry-size) cheese balls (from 8 oz container)
- ¼ cup shredded Parmesan cheese (1 oz)

1. Heat oven to 400°F. In 12-inch skillet, heat 1 teaspoon of the oil over medium heat. Add sausage; cook 4 to 5 minutes, stirring frequently, until browned. Stir in pizza sauce, water, and ¼ cup of the basil leaves; cook over medium-low heat, 2 to 3 minutes or until thoroughly heated.

2. Meanwhile, separate dough into 10 biscuits; separate each biscuit into 2 layers to create 20 biscuits. Place 1 cheese ball in center of each biscuit. Carefully stretch dough around cheese; pinch edges to seal completely.

3. Pour meat sauce into ungreased 13x9-inch (3-quart) glass baking dish. Place biscuits, seam sides down, on top of sauce. Brush tops of biscuits with remaining oil. Bake 13 to 20 minutes or until biscuits are golden brown and sauce is bubbly. Sprinkle with shredded cheese and remaining ¼ cup basil.

1 Serving: Calories 700 (Calories from Fat 370); Total Fat 42g; Saturated Fat 17g; Trans Fat 0g; Cholesterol 75mg; Sodium 2140mg; Total Carbohydrate 50g; Dietary Fiber 4g; Sugars 5g; Protein 31g

FRANK AND BEAN BISCUIT CASSEROLE

Looking for a delicious baked casserole? Then check out this frank and beans dish, arranged over biscuits and sprinkled with corn chips and cheese.

PREP TIME: 20 MINUTES
TOTAL TIME: 45 MINUTES

MAKES 8 SERVINGS

Dennis Batich, Garwood, New Jersey
Bake-Off® Contest 23, 1972

2 tablespoons butter or margarine

½ cup chopped onion or 2 tablespoons dried minced onion

¾ cup chopped green bell pepper

1 lb hot dogs, sliced

⅓ cup chili sauce

⅓ cup ketchup

1 to 2 tablespoons packed brown sugar, if desired

1 can (15 oz) baked beans or pork and beans, undrained

1 can (7.5 oz) Pillsbury™ refrigerated buttermilk or Country™ biscuits

¾ cup shredded Cheddar cheese (3 oz)

1 cup corn chips, crushed

3 tablespoons grated Romano or Parmesan cheese

1. Heat oven to 375°F. In 10-inch skillet, melt 1 tablespoon of the butter over medium-high heat. Add onion and bell pepper; cook and stir until tender.

2. Add hot dogs, chili sauce, ketchup, brown sugar and beans; stir gently to mix. Reduce heat; simmer 2 minutes. Spoon hot mixture into ungreased 11x7- or 12x8-inch (2-quart) glass baking dish.

3. Separate dough into 10 biscuits. Separate each biscuit into 2 layers. Arrange 10 biscuit layers over hot dog mixture. Sprinkle with Cheddar cheese. Arrange remaining biscuit layers on top to cover.

4. In small bowl, mix corn chips and Romano cheese. Sprinkle over biscuits. Dot with remaining tablespoon butter.

5. Bake 20 to 25 minutes or until biscuits are golden brown.

1 Serving: Calories 470 (Calories from Fat 260); Total Fat 29g; Saturated Fat 11g; Trans Fat 0.5g; Cholesterol 55mg; Sodium 1600mg; Total Carbohydrate 37g; Dietary Fiber 5g; Sugars 11g; Protein 14g

SAVORY MASHED POTATO PIE

While savory vegetable pies are not as well known in this country as meat pies, they offer a creative way to dress up everyday foods. Serve a wedge of this attractive tomato-topped pie as a side dish for a company dinner or as a light luncheon main dish.

PREP TIME: 35 MINUTES
TOTAL TIME: 60 MINUTES
MAKES 8 SERVINGS

Christina Hurst, Atlanta, Georgia
Bake-Off® Contest 37, 1996

PIE

- 1 box Pillsbury™ refrigerated pie crusts, softened as directed on box
- 2 cups water
- 3 tablespoons butter or margarine
- ½ teaspoon salt, if desired
- ½ teaspoon garlic powder
- ⅛ teaspoon white pepper
- 2½ cups mashed potato flakes
- ½ cup sour cream
- ¼ cup real bacon bits, or 4 slices bacon, cooked, crumbled
- ½ cup thinly sliced green onions (about 8 medium)
- 1 cup shredded Cheddar cheese (4 oz)
- 2 small tomatoes, thinly sliced
- 1 tablespoon olive or vegetable oil

GARNISH

- 2 tablespoons thinly sliced green onions (2 medium)
- ½ cup sour cream

1. Heat oven to 450°F. Make pie crust as directed on box for One-Crust Baked Shell using 9-inch deep-dish glass pie pan or 9-inch glass pie pan. Bake 9 to 11 minutes or until light golden brown. Cool while making mashed potatoes.

2. Meanwhile, in 3-quart saucepan, mix water, butter, salt, garlic powder and pepper. Heat to boiling. Remove from heat. Stir in potato flakes, ½ cup sour cream and the bacon bits.

3. Sprinkle ½ cup onions in bottom of cooled baked shell; sprinkle with cheese. Spoon and spread potato mixture evenly over cheese. Arrange tomato slices around edge, overlapping if necessary. Brush potato mixture and tomatoes with oil.

4. Reduce oven temperature to 400°F; bake 15 to 20 minutes or until thoroughly heated in center. Cool 5 minutes. To serve, sprinkle with 2 tablespoons onions. Cut into wedges; top each serving with 1 tablespoon sour cream.

1 Serving: Calories 370 (Calories from Fat 210); Total Fat 23g; Saturated Fat 12g; Trans Fat 0g; Cholesterol 50mg; Sodium 410mg; Total Carbohydrate 32g; Dietary Fiber 1g; Sugars 2g; Protein 8g

MARMALADE CRAB CRUSTED SALMON

*Make salmon simply sensa-
tional! Top and bake it with
a sassy crab and marma-
lade mix.*

PREP TIME: 20 MINUTES

TOTAL TIME: 40 MINUTES

MAKES 4 SERVINGS

Jackie Carioscia, Castle Rock, Colorado
Bake-Off® Contest 46, 2013

¼ cup Pillsbury™ BEST™ All Purpose Flour

4 medium green onions, finely chopped (¼ cup)

¼ cup sweet orange marmalade

2 cans (6 oz each) crab meat, drained

2 teaspoons salt-free onion & herb seasoning blend

6 tablespoons plus 4 teaspoons mayonnaise

2 salmon fillets (12 oz each), skin removed, each cut into 2 pieces

¼ teaspoon salt

⅛ teaspoon pepper

1. Heat oven to 375°F. Spray 15x10-inch baking pan with sides with no-stick cooking spray.

2. In 12-inch nonstick skillet, cook flour over medium heat 2 to 3 minutes, stirring occasionally, or until light brown. In medium bowl, mix flour, green onions, marmalade, crab, seasoning blend and 6 tablespoons of the mayonnaise.

3. Place salmon on cookie sheet; spread each fillet with 1 teaspoon of the remaining mayonnaise. Sprinkle with the salt and pepper. Spread crab mixture over fillets.

4. Bake 20 to 25 minutes or until crab mixture browns and salmon flakes easily with fork.

1 Serving: Calories 540 (Calories from Fat 280); Total Fat 31g; Saturated Fat 6g; Trans Fat 0g; Cholesterol 155mg; Sodium 610mg; Total Carbohydrate 20g; Dietary Fiber 0g; Sugars 0g; Protein 44g

CHEESY TUNA TATER PIE

This savory pie is easy to make, thanks to refrigerated pie crust.

PREP TIME: 20 MINUTES
TOTAL TIME: 50 MINUTES

MAKES 6 SERVINGS

Mabel Simmons, Chattanooga, Tennessee
Bake-Off® Contest 27, 1976

CRUST

1 box Pillsbury™ refrigerated pie crusts, softened as directed on box

FILLING

¾ cup mashed potato flakes

1½ cups shredded Cheddar cheese (6 oz)

2 tablespoons chopped pimiento-stuffed green olives

1 can (10¾ oz) condensed cream of mushroom soup

1 can (5 oz) tuna in water, drained, flaked

1 egg

½ cup canned French fried onions, if desired

1. Heat oven to 400°F. Make pie crust as directed on box for One-Crust Baked Shell using 9-inch glass pie pan. Bake 5 minutes.

2. Meanwhile, in medium bowl, mix potato flakes, 1 cup of the cheese, the olives, soup, tuna and egg until well mixed.

3. Remove partially baked shell from oven. Spoon filling into shell. Return to oven; bake 15 minutes longer.

4. Sprinkle top of pie with French fried onions and remaining ½ cup cheese. Bake 10 to 15 minutes longer or until cheese is melted and onions begin to brown. Let stand 5 minutes before serving.

1 Serving: Calories 370 (Calories from Fat 200); Total Fat 22g; Saturated Fat 10g; Trans Fat 0g; Cholesterol 80mg; Sodium 770mg; Total Carbohydrate 27g; Dietary Fiber 0g; Sugars 1g; Protein 16g

ZESTY LIME-FISH TACOS

Fresh Pillsbury™ Grands!™ biscuits fold around seasoned fish fillets topped with kicky salsa in this Bake-Off® recipe that makes an easy gourmet meal in less than an hour.

PREP TIME: 40 MINUTES

TOTAL TIME: 40 MINUTES

MAKES 8 SERVINGS

Kellie White, St. Louis, Missouri
Bake-Off® Contest 44, 2010

1 lb tilapia fillets (about 4)

½ cup fresh lime juice (2 to 3 limes)

3 cloves garlic, finely chopped

¼ cup Pillsbury™ BEST™ All Purpose Flour

¼ cup yellow cornmeal

1 can (16.3 oz) Pillsbury™ Grands!™ Homestyle refrigerated buttermilk biscuits (8 biscuits)

6 tablespoons canola oil

1½ tablespoons chipotle chiles in adobo sauce (from 7-oz can), finely chopped

½ teaspoon salt

¼ teaspoon black pepper

½ cup salsa

½ cup sour cream

1½ cups shredded cabbage

1. Heat oven to 200°F. Cut each fish fillet lengthwise into 4 strips. In shallow glass dish, mix 7 tablespoons of the lime juice and garlic. Add fish; turn to coat. Let stand while preparing biscuits.

2. On work surface, mix flour and cornmeal. Separate dough into 8 biscuits. Press both sides of each biscuit into flour mixture, then press or roll into 6- to 7-inch round.

3. In 12-inch nonstick skillet, heat 1½ tablespoons of the oil over medium heat. Add 2 biscuit rounds; cook about 1 minute on each side or until golden brown and cooked through. Place on cookie sheet; keep warm in oven. Cook remaining rounds, adding 1½ tablespoons oil to skillet for each batch. Wipe skillet clean.

4. Heat same skillet over medium-high heat. Add fish and lime juice mixture, chiles, salt and pepper; cook about 5 minutes, turning fish once, until fish flakes easily with fork.

5. In small bowl, mix salsa, sour cream and remaining 1 tablespoon lime juice.

6. Using slotted spoon, remove fish and divide evenly among biscuit rounds. Top each with cabbage and 1 to 2 tablespoons salsa mixture. Fold biscuit rounds in half over filling. Serve with any remaining salsa mixture. Garnish with lime wedges, if desired.

1 Serving: Calories 400 (Calories from Fat 200); Total Fat 22g; Saturated Fat 4.5g; Trans Fat 2g; Cholesterol 40mg; Sodium 860mg; Total Carbohydrate 35g; Dietary Fiber 1g; Sugars 6g; Protein 15g

ZESTY LIME–FISH TACOS *(page 277)*

CRAVIN' CRAB ENCHILADAS *(opposite)*

CRAVIN' CRAB ENCHILADAS

Elevate enchiladas to a new level with a crab filling and a creamy sauce.

PREP TIME: 45 MINUTES
TOTAL TIME: 1 HOUR 25 MINUTES
MAKES 10 SERVINGS

Sharon Chittock, Grass Valley, California
Bake-Off® Contest 43, 2008

ENCHILADAS

- 1 can (19 oz) mild enchilada sauce
- 1 cup whipping (heavy) cream
- 2 tablespoons olive oil
- 1 small onion, coarsely chopped (¼ cup)
- 1 box (10 oz) frozen corn & butter sauce, thawed
- 1 can (4.5 oz) chopped green chiles
- ½ cup lightly packed fresh cilantro, stems removed, coarsely chopped
- ¼ cup dry sherry or apple juice
- 1 can (1 lb) pasteurized crabmeat or 3 cans (6 oz each) lump crabmeat, drained
- 10 soft flour tortillas (from 10.5-oz package)
- 4 cups shredded Cheddar-Monterey Jack or Colby-Monterey Jack cheese blend (1 lb)
- ½ cup chopped green onions (about 8 medium)
- 1 package (2 oz) slivered blanched almonds

GARNISHES

- ⅔ cup sour cream
- Lime wedges

1. Heat oven to 350°F. Spray 13x9-inch (3-quart) glass baking dish with no-stick cooking spray.

2. In 2-quart saucepan, heat enchilada sauce and whipping cream to boiling over medium heat, stirring occasionally. Reduce heat to low; simmer uncovered 7 to 10 minutes, stirring occasionally, until sauce is reduced and slightly thickened.

3. Meanwhile, in 12-inch skillet, heat oil over medium-high heat until hot. Add onion; cook 2 to 3 minutes, stirring occasionally, until softened and translucent (do not brown). Stir in corn, chiles, ¼ cup of the cilantro, the sherry and crabmeat until well mixed. Remove from heat.

4. Spoon slightly less than ½ cup crabmeat mixture down center of each tortilla; top each with ¼ cup of the cheese. Roll up tortillas; place seam sides down in baking dish. Add remaining cheese sauce mixture over enchiladas.

5. Bake 30 to 35 minutes or until bubbly around edges. Sprinkle with remaining ¼ cup cilantro, the green onions and almonds. Serve with sour cream and lime wedges.

1 Serving: Calories 530 (Calories from Fat 320); Total Fat 35g; Saturated Fat 17g; Trans Fat 1.5g; Cholesterol 130mg; Sodium 990mg; Total Carbohydrate 26g; Dietary Fiber 2g; Sugars 6g; Protein 26g

SPICY CITRUS SHRIMP AND BLACK BEAN TACOS

Toss an easy and refreshing salsa to top sizzling shrimp in crisp taco shells.

PREP TIME: 45 MINUTES
TOTAL TIME: 45 MINUTES

MAKES 4 SERVINGS

Karen Gulkin, Simpsonville, South Carolina
Bake-Off® Contest 43, 2008

2 tablespoons blackened seasoning (from 2.5-oz container)

1 tablespoon 100% olive oil

¼ cup sweet orange marmalade

1 lb uncooked medium shrimp (about 32 shrimp), thawed if frozen, peeled and deveined, tails removed

2 ripe medium avocados, pitted, peeled and cut into ½-inch pieces

1 small orange, peeled, chopped

1 small jalapeño chile, seeded, finely chopped

¼ cup chopped red onion

2 tablespoons chopped fresh cilantro

1 can (15 oz) black beans, drained, rinsed

1 teaspoon ground cumin

1 tablespoon fresh lime juice

8 Old El Paso Stand™ 'N Stuff Taco Shells (from 4.7-oz box)

2 cups shredded Cheddar-Monterey Jack cheese blend (8 oz)

1. Reserve 1 teaspoon of the blackened seasoning. In large resealable food-storage plastic bag, place oil, marmalade and remaining blackened seasoning; seal bag and shake. Add shrimp; seal bag and mix well. Refrigerate at least 30 minutes but no longer than 24 hours.

2. Meanwhile, in medium bowl, gently toss avocados, orange, chile, onion and cilantro until mixed. Cover; set aside.

3. In food processor bowl with metal blade, place reserved 1 teaspoon blackened seasoning, the black beans, cumin and lime juice. Cover; process with on-and-off pulses until mixed and beans are coarsely chopped.

4. Heat oven to 350°F. Place taco shells on cookie sheet. Divide bean mixture evenly among shells. Sprinkle with cheese. Bake 6 to 8 minutes or until cheese is melted.

5. Meanwhile, spray large skillet with no-stick cooking spray; heat over medium-high heat. Add shrimp; cook 3 to 5 minutes, turning once, until pink. Remove taco shells from oven; place 4 cooked shrimp in each shell. Top with avocado salsa.

1 Serving: Calories 830 (Calories from Fat 390); Total Fat 43g; Saturated Fat 16g; Trans Fat 2.5g; Cholesterol 220mg; Sodium 950mg; Total Carbohydrate 68g; Dietary Fiber 18g; Sugars 14g; Protein 43g

SMOKY SHRIMP WITH CREAMY GRITS

Chipotle chiles are dried smoked jalapeño chiles. Their presence gives this dish the smoky and hot spicy flavor, which is nicely balanced by the creamy grits.

PREP TIME: 30 MINUTES
TOTAL TIME: 30 MINUTES

MAKES 4 SERVINGS

Lillian Jagendorf, New York, New York
Bake-Off® Contest 42, 2006

3 cups water

1 to 2 teaspoons salt

1 can (14.75 oz) cream style sweet corn

¾ cup uncooked quick-cooking corn grits

½ cup finely chopped green onions (8 medium)

2 oz cream cheese

¼ cup butter or margarine

1 large clove garlic, finely chopped

1½ lb uncooked deveined peeled large shrimp

1 teaspoon seafood seasoning (from 6-oz container)

1 teaspoon chipotle chiles in adobo sauce (from 7-oz can), finely chopped

1 can (14.5 oz) organic fire roasted diced tomatoes, drained

1. In 3-quart saucepan, heat water, salt and corn to boiling. With wire whisk, gradually beat in grits. Return to boiling, beating constantly. Reduce heat to low; cover and simmer 5 to 7 minutes, stirring occasionally, until thickened. Remove from heat. Stir in onions and cream cheese until well combined. Cover; keep warm.

2. Meanwhile, in 10-inch heavy skillet, melt butter over medium-high heat. Add garlic; cook and stir about 2 minutes or until lightly browned. Add shrimp; cook and stir 4 to 6 minutes or just until shrimp are pink. Stir in seafood seasoning, chipotle chiles and tomatoes. Reduce heat to medium; simmer uncovered 2 to 3 minutes or until tomatoes are thoroughly heated.

3. Divide grits mixture evenly among individual large soup bowls; spoon shrimp mixture evenly over top.

1 Serving: Calories 500 (Calories from Fat 170); Total Fat 19g; Saturated Fat 11g; Trans Fat 0.5g; Cholesterol 290mg; Sodium 2388mg; Total Carbohydrate 49g; Dietary Fiber 3g; Sugars 8g; Protein 33g

CREAMY SPINACH AND TORTELLINI

For Florentine flair, pair cheese tortellini with spinach, tomato and basil in a creamy sauce.

PREP TIME: 25 MINUTES
TOTAL TIME: 25 MINUTES
MAKES 4 SERVINGS

Jeanine Alfano, Montauk, New York
Bake-Off® Contest 34, 1990

- 2 (9-oz.) pkg. refrigerated or 1 (19-oz.) pkg. frozen cheese-filled tortellini
- 2 tablespoons olive or vegetable oil
- ½ cup chopped onion
- 3 garlic cloves, minced
- 1 (9-oz.) pkg. frozen chopped spinach, thawed, undrained
- 1 cup cubed seeded tomato
- ¼ cup chopped fresh basil
- ½ teaspoon salt
- ½ teaspoon pepper
- 1 cup whipping cream
- ¼ cup grated Parmesan or Romano cheese

1. Cook tortellini to desired doneness as directed on package. Drain; cover to keep warm.

2. Meanwhile, heat oil in large skillet over medium heat until hot. Add onion and garlic; cook about 4 minutes or until tender and lightly browned, stirring occasionally. Add spinach, tomato, basil, salt and pepper; cook 5 minutes, stirring occasionally. Stir in whipping cream and cheese. Cook until mixture just comes to a boil.

3. Reduce heat to low; stir in cooked tortellini. Cook an additional 4 to 5 minutes or until thoroughly heated. If desired, serve with additional Parmesan cheese.

CLEVER IDEA: *To quickly thaw spinach, cut small slit in center of pouch; microwave on High for 2 to 3 minutes or until thawed.*

1 Serving: Calories 730 (Calories from Fat 360); Total Fat 40g; Saturated Fat 20g; Trans Fat 1g; Cholesterol 155mg; Sodium 970mg; Total Carbohydrate 70g; Dietary Fiber 5g; Sugars 7g; Protein 23g

BROCCOLI-CAULIFLOWER TETRAZZINI

Veggies rule in this twist on an old favorite.

PREP TIME: 30 MINUTES

TOTAL TIME: 50 MINUTES

MAKES 8 SERVINGS

Barbara Van Itallie, Poughkeepsie, New York
Bake-Off® Contest 33, 1988 Hall of Fame

8 oz. uncooked spaghetti, broken into thirds

1 (1-lb.) pkg. frozen broccoli, carrots and cauliflower

2 tablespoons butter or margarine

3 tablespoons all-purpose flour

2 cups skim milk

½ cup grated Parmesan cheese

Dash pepper

1 (4.5-oz.) jar sliced mushrooms, drained

2 tablespoons grated Parmesan cheese

1. Cook spaghetti as directed on package. Drain; rinse with hot water. Cover to keep warm; set aside. Cook vegetables until crisp-tender as directed on package. Drain; set aside.

2. Meanwhile, heat oven to 400°F. Grease 13x9-inch (3-quart) glass baking dish. Melt butter in medium saucepan over medium heat. Stir in flour until smooth. Gradually add milk, cooking and stirring until well blended. Cook 6 to 10 minutes or until mixture boils and thickens, stirring constantly. Stir in ½ cup Parmesan cheese and the pepper.

3. Spoon cooked spaghetti into greased baking dish. Top with cooked vegetables and sliced mushrooms. Pour milk mixture over mushrooms. Sprinkle with 2 tablespoons Parmesan cheese.

4. Bake at 400°F for 15 to 20 minutes or until mixture bubbles around edges and is thoroughly heated.

1 Serving: Calories 225 (Calories from Fat 55); Total Fat 6g; Saturated Fat 3g; Trans Fat 0g; Cholesterol 15mg; Sodium 229mg; Total Carbohydrate 32g; Dietary Fiber 3g; Sugars 5g; Protein 11g

BEAN PICADILLO TORTILLAS

These Spanish-inspired tortillas contain many favorite flavors of picadillo stew, such as tomato, raisins, onions and olives.

PREP TIME: 35 MINUTES
TOTAL TIME: 35 MINUTES

MAKES 6 SERVINGS

Gilbert J. Soucy, Lowell, Massachusetts
Bake-Off® Contest 35, 1992

6 (6- or 8-inch) corn tortillas or 8-inch flour tortillas

PICADILLO

2 tablespoons margarine or butter

½ cup finely chopped onion

1 (15.5-oz.) can light red kidney beans, drained, slightly mashed

1 (15.5-oz) can pinto beans, drained, slightly mashed

½ cup picante salsa

1 teaspoon chili powder

¼ teaspoon cumin

Dash cinnamon

¼ cup raisins

SALSA

1½ cups chunky-style salsa

1 cup frozen whole kernel corn (from 1-lb. pkg.), thawed, drained

GARNISH

6 pitted ripe olives, sliced

1 tomato, cut into 6 wedges

1. Heat oven to 350°F. Wrap tortillas in foil; heat at 350°F for 15 minutes. Meanwhile, melt margarine in large skillet over medium heat. Add onion; cook and stir until tender, about 5 minutes. Stir in all remaining picadillo ingredients. Bring to a boil. Reduce heat to low; cover and simmer 12 minutes or until thoroughly heated, stirring occasionally.

2. In small saucepan, combine salsa ingredients; bring to a boil. Reduce heat to low; cover and simmer 10 minutes or until thoroughly heated, stirring occasionally.

3. To serve, spread ½ cup hot picadillo on each tortilla to within 1 inch of edges; roll up, enclosing filling. Top with hot salsa mixture. Garnish with sliced ripe olives and tomato wedges.

1 Serving: Calories 248 (Calories from Fat 51); Total Fat 7g; Saturated Fat 1g; Trans Fat 1g; Cholesterol 0mg; Sodium 956mg; Total Carbohydrate 43g; Dietary Fiber 9g; Sugars 10g; Protein 10g

ITALIAN ZUCCHINI CRESCENT PIE

Whether you have a bounty of zucchini from your garden or you pick up a few from the supermarket, this savory pie is a winner!

PREP TIME: 30 MINUTES
TOTAL TIME: 55 MINUTES
MAKES 6 SERVINGS

Hall of Fame

Millicent (Caplan) Nathan, Boca Raton, Florida
Bake-Off® Contest 29, 1980 Grand Prize Winner and Hall of Fame

2 tablespoons butter or margarine

4 cups thinly sliced zucchini

1 cup chopped onions

2 tablespoons dried parsley flakes

½ teaspoon salt

½ teaspoon pepper

¼ teaspoon garlic powder

¼ teaspoon dried basil leaves

¼ teaspoon dried oregano leaves

2 eggs, well beaten

2 cups shredded Muenster or mozzarella cheese (8 oz)

1 can (8 oz) Pillsbury™ refrigerated crescent dinner rolls

2 teaspoons yellow mustard

1. Heat oven to 375°F. In 12-inch skillet, melt butter over medium-high heat. Add zucchini and onions; cook 6 to 8 minutes, stirring occasionally, until tender. Stir in parsley flakes, salt, pepper, garlic powder, basil and oregano.

2. In large bowl, mix eggs and cheese. Add cooked vegetable mixture; stir gently to mix.

3. Separate dough into 8 triangles. Place in ungreased 10-inch glass pie plate, 12x8-inch (2-quart) glass baking dish or 11-inch quiche pan; press over bottom and up sides to form crust. Firmly press perforations to seal. Spread crust with mustard. Pour egg mixture evenly into crust-lined pie plate.

4. Bake 18 to 22 minutes or until knife inserted near center comes out clean. If necessary, cover edge of crust with strips of foil during last 10 minutes of baking to prevent excessive browning. Let stand 10 minutes before serving.

1 Serving: Calories 370 (Calories from Fat 230); Total Fat 25g; Saturated Fat 13g; Trans Fat 2.5g; Cholesterol 115mg; Sodium 810mg; Total Carbohydrate 21g; Dietary Fiber 1g; Sugars 6g; Protein 15g

ITALIAN ZUCCHINI CRESCENT PIE (*opposite*)

PINEAPPLE-BLACK BEAN ENCHILADAS (*page 288*)

PINEAPPLE-BLACK BEAN ENCHILADAS

Traditional enchiladas take a healthful vegetarian twist in a sassy dish filled with fruity flavors.

PREP TIME: 30 MINUTES
TOTAL TIME: 1 HOUR 10 MINUTES

MAKES 8 SERVINGS

Mary Iovinelli Buescher, Bloomington, Minnesota
Bake-Off® Contest 42, 2006

2 teaspoons vegetable oil

1 large yellow onion, chopped (about 1 cup)

1 medium red bell pepper, chopped (about 1 cup)

1 can (20 oz) pineapple tidbits in juice, drained, ⅓ cup juice reserved

1 can (15 oz) black beans, drained, rinsed

1 can (4.5 oz) chopped green chiles

1 teaspoon salt

½ cup chopped fresh cilantro

3 cups shredded reduced-fat Cheddar cheese (12 oz)

1 can (10 oz) mild enchilada sauce

8 whole wheat flour tortillas (8 or 9 inch)

½ cup reduced-fat sour cream

8 teaspoons chopped fresh cilantro

1. Heat oven to 350°F. Spray 13x9-inch (3-quart) glass baking dish with cooking spray. In 12-inch nonstick skillet, heat oil over medium heat. Add onion and bell pepper; cook 4 to 5 minutes or until softened. Stir in pineapple, beans, green chiles and salt. Cook and stir until thoroughly heated. Remove skillet from heat. Stir in ½ cup cilantro and 2 cups of the cheese.

2. Spoon and spread 1 tablespoon enchilada sauce onto each tortilla. Spoon about ¾ cup vegetable mixture over sauce on each. Roll up tortillas; place seam side down in baking dish.

3. In small bowl, mix reserved ⅓ cup pineapple juice and remaining enchilada sauce; pour over entire surface of enchiladas in dish. Sprinkle with remaining 1 cup cheese. Spray sheet of foil large enough to cover baking dish with cooking spray; place sprayed side down over baking dish and seal tightly.

4. Bake 35 to 40 minutes, removing foil during last 5 to 10 minutes of baking, until cheese is melted and sauce is bubbly. Top each baked enchilada with 1 tablespoon sour cream and 1 teaspoon cilantro.

1 Serving: Calories 382 (Calories from Fat 138); Total Fat 15g; Saturated Fat 7.5g; Trans Fat 0g; Cholesterol 29mg; Sodium 1412mg; Total Carbohydrate 43g; Dietary Fiber 7g; Sugars 10g; Protein 19g

CORN AND CHEESE-STUFFED PEPPERS

Polenta and corn combine with cheese to make a flavorful filling for colorful bell peppers.

PREP TIME: 15 MINUTES
TOTAL TIME: 1 HOUR 10 MINUTES

MAKES 4 SERVINGS

Gloria Rendon, Murray, Utah
Bake-Off® Contest 41, 2004

4 large red, green and/or yellow bell peppers, tops cut off, seeds and membranes removed

12 oz. polenta (from 18-oz. roll), cut into ¼-inch pieces (2 cups)

1 (11-oz.) can whole kernel corn, red and green peppers, drained

3 oz. (¾ cup) shredded Monterey Jack cheese

3 oz. (¾ cup) shredded provolone cheese

Salt and pepper to taste, if desired

1 cup light sour cream, if desired

1. Heat oven to 350°F. If necessary, cut thin slice off bottom of each bell pepper so peppers stand upright.

2. In medium bowl, mix polenta pieces, corn, and half of each of the cheeses. Salt and pepper to taste. Spoon polenta mixture into bell peppers; sprinkle with remaining cheese. Place filled peppers in ungreased 8-inch square (2-quart) glass baking dish. Fill dish halfway with water. Spray 12-inch square piece of foil with cooking spray; cover dish tightly.

3. Carefully place dish in oven. Bake at 350°F for 30 minutes.

4. Remove foil; bake an additional 15 to 20 minutes or until bell peppers are crisp-tender and filling is thoroughly heated. Cool 5 minutes. Carefully remove bell peppers from dish. Garnish each with sour cream.

1 Serving (without sour cream): Calories 312 (Calories from Fat 118); Total Fat 14g; Saturated Fat 8g; Trans Fat 0g; Cholesterol 35mg; Sodium 728mg; Total Carbohydrate 33g; Dietary Fiber 4g; Sugars 11g; Protein 15g

POBLANOS FLORENTINE CASSEROLE

Serve your family a casserole with a kick—they'll never miss the meat in this hearty dish.

PREP TIME: 45 MINUTES
TOTAL TIME: 2 HOURS 5 MINUTES

MAKES 9 SERVINGS

Gloria Felts, Indianapolis, Indiana
Bake-Off® Contest 43, 2008

5 fresh poblano chiles (4½ x 3 inch)

1½ cups shredded Chihuahua or Monterey Jack cheese (6 oz)

1 cup shredded Mexican cheese blend (4 oz)

⅓ cup ricotta cheese

2 cloves garlic, finely chopped

½ teaspoon ground cumin

1 box (9 oz) frozen chopped spinach, thawed, squeezed to drain

1 can (12 oz) Pillsbury™ Grands!™ Jr. Golden Layers™ Butter Tastin'™ refrigerated biscuits (10 biscuits)

1 can (10 oz) mild enchilada sauce

2 plum (Roma) tomatoes, chopped, if desired

½ cup fresh guacamole, if desired

½ cup sour cream, if desired

1. Set oven control to broil. On cookie sheet, broil chiles with tops 2 inches from heat about 10 minutes, turning frequently with tongs, until all sides are blackened and blistered. Place chiles in paper bag; seal bag. Let chiles steam 15 minutes.

2. Heat oven to 350°F. Lightly spray 8-inch square (2-quart) glass baking dish with no-stick cooking spray.

3. In medium bowl, mix Chihuahua cheese and Mexican cheese blend; reserve ¾ cup for topping. In another medium bowl, mix ricotta cheese, garlic, cumin and spinach. Stir in remaining shredded cheeses. Set aside.

4. Wearing food-safe plastic gloves, peel blackened skin from chiles. Cut open chiles; remove stems, seeds and membranes. Cut each chile in half lengthwise into 2 pieces; pat dry.

5. Separate dough into 10 biscuits. Separate each biscuit into 2 thin layers; flatten slightly.

6. Pour half of the enchilada sauce over bottom of baking dish. Place 10 biscuit layers on sauce, cutting biscuits if necessary to fit into dish. Top with 5 chile halves; spread spinach mixture over chiles. Top with remaining 5 chile halves and remaining 10 biscuit layers. Pour remaining enchilada sauce over biscuits.

7. Spray sheet of foil with cooking spray. Cover baking dish with foil, sprayed side down. Bake 55 to 60 minutes or until thoroughly heated and bubbly around edges.

8. Sprinkle with reserved ³/₄ cup shredded cheeses. Bake uncovered 5 to 8 minutes longer or until cheese is melted. Cool 10 minutes before cutting. Top each serving with tomatoes, guacamole and sour cream.

1 Serving: Calories 290 (Calories from Fat 150); Total Fat 16g; Saturated Fat 8g; Trans Fat 2g; Cholesterol 30mg; Sodium 790mg; Total Carbohydrate 23g; Dietary Fiber 1g; Sugars 4g; Protein 12g

Baked Goodies, Cookies and Bars

Robin Janine Peterson of Peoria, Arizona, prepares Mock Lemon Meringue Bars (page 322) at the 42nd Bake-Off Contest held in Orlando, Florida.

LAZY DAISIES

Blooming beautifully for a spring or summer occasion, a whole batch of these cute cookies can be mixed and baked in just over an hour.

PREP TIME: 45 MINUTES
TOTAL TIME: 1 HOUR 15 MINUTES

MAKES 44 SERVINGS

Luella E. Maki, Ely, Minnesota
Bake-Off® Contest 12, 1960

½ cup sugar

½ cup butter or margarine, softened

1 tablespoon grated lemon peel

1 tablespoon lemon juice

1 egg

1¾ cups all-purpose flour

1 teaspoon baking powder

¼ teaspoon salt

21 small pastel-colored gumdrops or spice drops (about 2½ oz), cut in half

1. In large bowl, beat sugar and butter with electric mixer on medium speed until well blended. Beat in lemon peel, lemon juice and egg. With spoon, stir in flour, baking powder and salt until dough forms. Remove dough from bowl; place on large sheet of plastic wrap. Flatten dough into 6-inch round; wrap in plastic wrap. Refrigerate 30 minutes for easier handling.

2. Heat oven to 350°F. Work with half of dough at a time; refrigerate remaining dough until needed. Shape dough into 1-inch balls; place 2 inches apart on ungreased cookie sheets. With floured scissors and starting at top of each ball, snip each in half, without cutting through bottom. Snip each half into thirds. Gently open cookie balls to form 6 petals. Place gumdrop half in center of each.

3. Bake 8 to 11 minutes or until edges of cookies are light golden brown. Cool 1 minute; remove from cookie sheets.

CLEVER IDEA: *Vary the appearance and flavor of these cookies by substituting candied cherry halves, nut pieces, chocolate chips or candy-coated chocolate pieces for the gumdrops.*

1 Serving: Calories 60 (Calories from Fat 20); Total Fat 2.5g; Saturated Fat 1g; Trans Fat 0g; Cholesterol 10mg; Sodium 45mg; Total Carbohydrate 8g; Dietary Fiber 0g; Sugars 4g; Protein 0g

CHERRY WINKS

Looking for a dessert using cherries? Then check out these awesome tasting cookies.

PREP TIME: 1 HOUR 20 MINUTES
TOTAL TIME: 1 HOUR 20 MINUTES
MAKES 60 SERVINGS

Ruth Derousseau, Rice Lake, Wisconsin
Bake-Off® Contest 2, 1950

1 cup sugar

¾ cup shortening

2 tablespoons milk

1 teaspoon vanilla

2 eggs

2¼ cups all-purpose flour

1 teaspoon baking powder

½ teaspoon baking soda

½ teaspoon salt

1 cup chopped pecans

1 cup chopped dates

⅓ cup chopped maraschino cherries, patted dry with paper towels

1½ cups coarsely crushed corn flakes cereal

15 maraschino cherries, quartered

1. In large bowl, beat sugar and shortening with electric mixer on medium speed, scraping bowl occasionally, until well blended. Beat in milk, vanilla and eggs. On low speed, beat in flour, baking powder, baking soda and salt, scraping bowl occasionally, until dough forms. Stir in pecans, dates and ⅓ cup chopped cherries. If necessary, cover with plastic wrap and refrigerate 15 minutes for easier handling.

2. Heat oven to 375°F. Spray cookie sheets with cooking spray. Drop dough by rounded teaspoonfuls into cereal; coat thoroughly. Shape into balls. Place 2 inches apart on cookie sheets. Lightly press maraschino cherry quarter into top of each ball.

3. Bake 10 to 15 minutes or until light golden brown. Cool 1 minute; remove from cookie sheets to cooling racks.

CLEVER IDEA: *Chop the maraschino cherries, then drain them on paper towels to eliminate excess moisture.*

1 Serving: Calories 80 (Calories from Fat 35); Total Fat 4g; Saturated Fat 1g; Trans Fat 0g; Cholesterol 5mg; Sodium 45mg; Total Carbohydrate 11g; Dietary Fiber 0g; Sugars 6g; Protein 1g

LEMON-GO-LIGHTLY COOKIES

Potato flakes are the secret ingredient in these soft, chewy, delicately flavored cookies.

PREP TIME: 1 HOUR 15 MINUTES
TOTAL TIME: 1 HOUR 15 MINUTES

MAKES 72 SERVINGS
(1 COOKIE PER SERVING)

Margaret Conway, Oceano, California
Bake-Off® Contest 27, 1976

- 2 cups all-purpose flour
- 2 cups mashed potato flakes
- 1 cup sugar
- 1 cup firmly packed brown sugar
- ½ to ¾ cup finely chopped nuts
- 1 teaspoon baking soda
- ¾ cup margarine or butter, melted
- 1 teaspoon grated lemon peel
- 2 eggs
- ¼ cup sugar

1. Heat oven to 350°F. In large bowl, combine all ingredients except ¼ cup sugar; blend well. (Mixture will be crumbly.) Firmly press into 1-inch balls; roll in ¼ cup sugar. Place 2 inches apart on ungreased cookie sheets.

2. Bake at 350°F for 9 to 12 minutes or until golden brown. Cool 1 minute; remove from cookie sheets.

CLEVER IDEA: *To melt caramels in microwave, place in small microwave-safe bowl with 1 tablespoon water. Microwave on High for 2 to 3 minutes, stirring occasionally.*

1 Serving: Calories 70 (Calories from Fat 23); Total Fat 3g; Saturated Fat 0.5g; Trans Fat 0g; Cholesterol 5mg; Sodium 45mg; Total Carbohydrate 11g; Dietary Fiber 0g; Sugars 7g; Protein 1g

ACCORDION TREATS

This uniquely shaped cookie is an old family recipe that originated in Alsace-Lorraine.

PREP TIME: 2 HOURS
TOTAL TIME: 2 HOURS
MAKES 48 SERVINGS

Gerda Roderer, Berkeley, California
Bake-Off® Contest 9, 1957 Grand Prize Winner

2 (1-yard) sheets heavy-duty foil

¾ cup margarine or butter, softened

¾ cup sugar

1 teaspoon vanilla

2 eggs

1 cup Pillsbury™ BEST™ All Purpose or Unbleached Flour

¼ teaspoon salt

½ cup chopped walnuts, if desired

1. Heat oven to 325°F. Fold 1 sheet of foil in half lengthwise. Fold the double-thickness foil crosswise into 1-inch pleats to make an "accordion-pleated" pan. Place on ungreased cookie sheet. Repeat with second sheet of foil.

2. In large bowl, combine margarine and sugar; beat until light and fluffy. Add vanilla and eggs; beat well. Lightly spoon flour into measuring cup; level off. Add flour and salt; mix well. Stir in walnuts. Drop rounded teaspoon of dough into each fold of foil. (Dough spreads during baking to form 4½ to 5-inch long cookies.)

3. Bake at 325°F for 18 to 26 minutes or until golden brown. Remove cookies from foil; cool completely. Turn foil over for second baking.

1 Serving: Calories 60 (Calories from Fat 35); Total Fat 4g; Saturated Fat 1g; Trans Fat 1g; Cholesterol 10mg; Sodium 45mg; Total Carbohydrate 5g; Dietary Fiber 0g; Sugars 3g; Protein 1g

SPLIT SECONDS

These jelly-filled sugar cookies are as pretty as thumbprints but much simpler to make.

This contestant learned to cook in Sweden, where she was born, and this was one of her mother's family recipes. You'll enjoy the unique method for making these delicious shortbread cookies. Choose your favorite flavor of jelly or preserves to make this Bake-Off® Contest classic.

PREP TIME: 1 HOUR 15 MINUTES
TOTAL TIME: 1 HOUR 15 MINUTES

MAKES 48 SERVINGS

Robert E. Fellows, Silver Spring, Maryland
Bake-Off® Contest 6, 1954

⅔ cup sugar

¾ cup butter or margarine, softened

2 teaspoons vanilla

1 egg

2 cups Pillsbury™ BEST™ all-purpose flour

½ teaspoon baking powder

½ cup red jelly or preserves

1. Heat oven to 350°F. In large bowl with electric mixer, beat sugar and butter on medium speed until light and fluffy. Beat in vanilla and egg until well blended. Add flour and baking powder; beat on low speed until dough forms.

2. Divide dough into 4 equal portions. On lightly floured surface, shape each portion into 12x³⁄₄-inch roll; place on ungreased cookie sheets. With handle of wooden spoon or finger, make indentation about ¹⁄₂ inch wide and ¹⁄₄ inch deep lengthwise down center of each roll. Fill each with 2 tablespoons jelly.

3. Bake 15 to 20 minutes or until light golden brown. Cool slightly, 3 to 5 minutes. Cut each baked roll diagonally into 12 cookies; remove from cookie sheets.

1 Serving: Calories 70 (Calories from Fat 25); Total Fat 3g; Saturated Fat 1.5g; Trans Fat 0g; Cholesterol 10mg; Sodium 25mg; Total Carbohydrate 9g; Dietary Fiber 0g; Sugars 4g; Protein 0g

HAWAIIAN COOKIE TARTS

These melt-in-your mouth cookies are perfect for party trays. They are like miniature pineapple pies.

PREP TIME: 30 MINUTES
TOTAL TIME: 1 HOUR 15 MINUTES

MAKES 36 SERVINGS
(1 COOKIE PER SERVING)

Elizabeth Zemelko, Knox, Indiana
Bake-Off® Contest 34, 1990

COOKIES

1¾ cups all-purpose flour
½ cup powdered sugar
2 tablespoons cornstarch
1 cup margarine or butter, softened
1 teaspoon vanilla

FILLING

1 cup pineapple preserves
½ cup sugar
1 egg
1½ cups coconut
Powdered sugar

1. Heat oven to 350°F. In large bowl, combine flour, ½ cup powdered sugar and cornstarch; blend well. Add margarine and vanilla. By hand, blend until soft dough forms. Shape dough into 1-inch balls. Place 1 ball in each of 36 ungreased miniature muffin cups; press in bottom and up sides of each cup.

2. Spoon 1 teaspoon pineapple preserves into each dough-lined cup. In small bowl, combine sugar and egg. Using fork, beat until well blended. Stir in coconut until coated with egg mixture. Spoon 1 teaspoon coconut mixture over pineapple preserves in each cup.

3. Bake at 350°F for 23 to 33 minutes or until crusts are very light golden brown. Cool 20 minutes. To release cookies from cups, hold muffin pan upside down at an angle over wire rack. Using handle of table knife, firmly tap bottom of each cup until cookie releases. Cool completely. Just before serving, sprinkle with powdered sugar.

CLEVER IDEA: *If only 1 muffin pan is available, keep remaining cookie dough refrigerated until ready to bake.*

1 Serving: Calories 130 (Calories from Fat 55); Total Fat 6g; Saturated Fat 2g; Trans Fat 1g; Cholesterol 5mg; Sodium 55mg; Total Carbohydrate 17g; Dietary Fiber 1g; Sugars 11g; Protein 1g

SO-EASY SUGAR COOKIES

The name says it all—and they're so good, they'll become a family favorite! Instead of rolling out the dough, it's baked in a pan, then cut into squares.

PREP TIME: 10 MINUTES
TOTAL TIME: 25 MINUTES

MAKES 48 SERVINGS
(1 COOKIE PER SERVING)

Kathryn Blackburn, National Park, New Jersey
Bake-Off® Contest 30, 1982

¾ cup sugar

⅓ cup margarine or butter, softened, or shortening

⅓ cup oil

1 tablespoon milk

1 to 2 teaspoons almond extract

1 egg

1½ cups all-purpose flour

1½ teaspoons baking powder

¼ teaspoon salt

1 tablespoon sugar

1. Heat oven to 375°F. In large bowl, beat ¾ cup sugar, margarine, oil, milk, almond extract and egg until light and fluffy. Stir in flour, baking powder and salt; blend well. Spread evenly in ungreased 15x10x1-inch baking pan; sprinkle with 1 tablespoon sugar.

2. Bake at 375°F for 10 to 12 minutes or until light golden brown. Cool 5 minutes. Cut into bars.

CLEVER IDEA: *Food Processor Directions: Place ¾ cup sugar, margarine, oil, milk, almond extract and egg in food processor bowl with metal blade. Cover; process until light and fluffy. Add flour, baking powder and salt. Cover; process using on/off turns just until flour is well blended. (Do not over-process or cookies will be tough.) Continue as directed above.*

1 Serving: Calories 50 (Calories from Fat 26); Total Fat 3g; Saturated Fat 0.5g; Trans Fat 0g; Cholesterol 4mg; Sodium 35mg; Total Carbohydrate 6g; Dietary Fiber 0g; Sugars 3g; Protein 1g

CRANBERRY QUICK COOKIES

Coconut adds tropical flavor to these tasty cranberries and oats cookies—a perfect dessert to treat your guests.

PREP TIME: 15 MINUTES
TOTAL TIME: 45 MINUTES

MAKES 36 SERVINGS

Arlene Kremblas, Cheektowaga, New York
Bake-Off® Contest 38, 1998

- 1 (15.6-oz.) pkg. Pillsbury™ Cranberry Quick Bread & Muffin Mix
- ¾ cup quick-cooking rolled oats
- ½ cup coconut
- ½ cup sweetened dried cranberries
- ½ teaspoon grated orange peel
- ½ cup oil
- 1 tablespoon water
- 2 eggs

1. Heat oven to 350°F. In large bowl, combine quick bread mix, oats, coconut, cranberries and orange peel; mix well. Add oil, water and eggs; mix well. Drop by heaping teaspoonfuls 2 inches apart onto ungreased cookie sheets.

2. Bake at 350°F for 10 to 13 minutes or until bottoms are golden brown. Remove from cookie sheets.

1 Serving: Calories 90 (Calories from Fat 35); Total Fat 4g; Saturated Fat 1g; Trans Fat 0g; Cholesterol 10mg; Sodium 55mg; Total Carbohydrate 13g; Dietary Fiber 1g; Sugars 7g; Protein 1g

PUMPKIN, RAISIN, AND GINGER COOKIES

Enjoy these flavorful pumpkin cookies that are made with raisins and ginger—perfect for dessert.

PREP TIME: 15 MINUTES
TOTAL TIME: 45 MINUTES

MAKES 20 SERVINGS

Kathy Ault, Edmond, Oklahoma
Bake-Off® Contest 39, 2000

1 (14-oz.) pkg. Pillsbury™ Pumpkin Quick Bread & Muffin Mix

½ cup cinnamon-covered raisins or plain raisins

¼ cup chopped crystallized ginger

½ cup butter or margarine, melted

1 egg

¼ cup sugar

1 teaspoon cinnamon

1. Heat oven to 350°F. In large bowl, combine quick bread mix, raisins and ginger; mix well. Add butter and egg; stir until dry particles are moistened. (Mixture may be crumbly.)

2. In small bowl, combine sugar and cinnamon; mix well. Shape dough into 1½-inch balls; roll in sugar-cinnamon mixture. Place 2 inches apart on ungreased cookie sheets.

3. Bake at 350°F for 12 to 15 minutes or until cookies are set. Remove from cookie sheets.

CLEVER IDEA: *For Banana, Raisin and Ginger Cookies, substitute one 14-oz. pkg. Pillsbury™ Banana Quick Bread & Muffin Mix.*

1 Serving: Calories 150 (Calories from Fat 50); Total Fat 6g; Saturated Fat 3g; Trans Fat 0g; Cholesterol 25mg; Sodium 65mg; Total Carbohydrate 23g; Dietary Fiber 1g; Sugars 15g; Protein 2g

COCONUT PECAN FLORENTINE SANDWICH COOKIES

Just 4 ingredients are all that's needed to make crispy chocolate cookies sandwiched together with a creamy mocha cappuccino hazelnut spread. Pair them with a fresh cup of coffee.

PREP TIME: 30 MINUTES
TOTAL TIME: 1 HOUR 15 MINUTES

MAKES 24 SERVINGS

Paula Mahagnoul, Sioux Falls, South Dakota
Bake-Off® Contest 46, 2013

1 roll Pillsbury™ refrigerated sugar cookie dough

1 can Pillsbury™ Creamy Supreme™ Coconut Pecan Frosting

⅔ cup old-fashioned oats

⅛ teaspoon salt

1 cup mocha cappuccino flavored hazelnut spread

1. Heat oven to 350°F. Line 2 large cookie sheets with parchment paper.

2. Let cookie dough stand at room temperature 10 minutes to soften. In large bowl, break up cookie dough. Add frosting, oats and salt. Beat with electric mixer on medium speed until well blended. Working with ½ of the dough, drop by tablespoonfuls to make 24 cookies. Place 3 inches apart on cookie sheets. (Cookies will spread.)

3. Bake 2 cookie sheets at a time, 10 to 14 minutes or until golden brown, turning cookie sheets halfway through bake time. While cookies are baking, drop remaining tablespoonfuls of dough onto parchment paper to make 24 additional cookies. Remove baked cookies and parchment paper to cooling rack. Cool completely, about 10 minutes. Repeat with remaining dough and parchment paper.

4. Spread 1 heaping teaspoon of the hazelnut spread onto bottom of 24 cookies. Top with remaining cookies bottom side down; press lightly. Store in covered container.

1 Serving: Calories 250 (Calories from Fat 120); Total Fat 14g; Saturated Fat 4.5g; Trans Fat 2g; Cholesterol 0mg; Sodium 105mg; Total Carbohydrate 30g; Dietary Fiber 1g; Sugars 22g; Protein 2g

PRALINE COOKIES

Cheryl Dean Matthews, Charlotte, North Carolina
Bake-Off® Contest 11, 1959

This contestant was a fourteen-year-old Junior Second Prize winner. She did her recipe testing on a range that her mother won as a finalist in the fourth Bake-Off® Contest! Praline, a mixture of pecans and caramelized sugar, flavors the frosting on these irresistible cookies.

PREP TIME: 1 HOUR
TOTAL TIME: 1 HOUR

**MAKES 36 SERVINGS
(1 COOKIE PER SERVING)**

COOKIES

1½ cups firmly packed brown sugar

½ cup margarine or butter, softened

1 teaspoon vanilla

1 egg

1½ cups all-purpose flour

1½ teaspoons baking powder

½ teaspoon salt

FROSTING

½ cup firmly packed brown sugar

¼ cup half-and-half

1 cup powdered sugar

½ cup coarsely chopped pecans

1. Heat oven to 350°F. Grease cookie sheets. In large bowl, beat 1½ cups brown sugar and margarine until light and fluffy. Add vanilla and egg; blend well. Stir in flour, baking powder and salt; mix well. Drop dough by rounded teaspoonfuls 2 inches apart onto greased cookie sheets.

2. Bake at 350°F for 10 to 12 minutes or until light golden brown. Cool 1 minute; remove from cookie sheets.

3. In small saucepan, combine ½ cup brown sugar and half-and-half. Bring to a boil over medium heat; boil 2 minutes, stirring constantly. Remove from heat. Stir in powdered sugar; beat until smooth. Place about ½ teaspoon of the pecans on each cookie; drizzle with frosting, covering pecans. Let stand until set.

1 Serving: Calories 120 (Calories from Fat 35); Total Fat 4g; Saturated Fat 1g; Trans Fat 1g; Cholesterol 6mg; Sodium 80mg; Total Carbohydrate 20g; Dietary Fiber 0g; Sugars 15g; Protein 1g

STARLIGHT MINT SURPRISE COOKIES

Treat your guests with these mint chocolate cookies—a flavorful dessert.

The idea for this cookie came to the originator when she was given a package of mint-flavored chocolate candies. Brown sugar cookie dough is pressed around each candy so each cookie has a surprise chocolate mint in the center.

PREP TIME: 60 MINUTES
TOTAL TIME: 3 HOURS

MAKES 60 SERVINGS

Laura Rott, Naperville, Illinois
Bake-Off® Contest 1, 1949

1 cup granulated sugar

½ cup packed brown sugar

¾ cup butter or margarine, softened

2 tablespoons water

1 teaspoon vanilla

2 eggs

3 cups Pillsbury™ BEST™ all-purpose flour

1 teaspoon baking soda

½ teaspoon salt

60 thin rectangular crème de menthe chocolate candies (from three 4.67-oz packages), unwrapped

60 walnut halves or pieces

1. In large bowl, beat sugars, butter, water, vanilla and eggs with electric mixer on medium speed, scraping bowl occasionally, until blended. On low speed, beat in flour, baking soda and salt until well blended. Cover with plastic wrap; refrigerate at least 2 hours for easier handling.

2. Heat oven to 375°F. Using about 1 tablespoon dough, press dough around each chocolate candy to cover completely. Place 2 inches apart on ungreased cookie sheets. Top each with walnut half.

3. Bake 7 to 9 minutes or until light golden brown. Immediately remove from cookie sheets to cooling rack.

1 Serving: Calories 110 (Calories from Fat 45); Total Fat 5g; Saturated Fat 2.5g; Trans Fat 0g; Cholesterol 15mg; Sodium 65mg; Total Carbohydrate 13g; Dietary Fiber 0g; Sugars 8g; Protein 2g

DOUBLE-DELIGHT PEANUT BUTTER COOKIES

It's a twist on the classic peanut butter cookie! Crunchy outside, creamy inside, with just a hint of cinnamon. A real winner!

PREP TIME: 45 MINUTES

TOTAL TIME: 45 MINUTES

MAKES 24 SERVINGS

Carolyn Gurtz, Gaithersburg, Maryland
Bake-Off® Contest 43, 2008 Grand Prize Winner

¼ cup dry roasted peanuts, finely chopped

¼ cup granulated sugar

½ teaspoon ground cinnamon

½ cup creamy peanut butter

½ cup powdered sugar

1 roll (16.5 oz) Pillsbury™ refrigerated peanut butter cookies, well chilled

1. Heat oven to 375°F. In small bowl, mix chopped peanuts, granulated sugar and cinnamon; set aside.

2. In another small bowl, stir peanut butter and powdered sugar until completely blended. Shape mixture into 24 (1-inch) balls.

3. Cut roll of cookie dough into 12 slices. Cut each slice in half crosswise to make 24 pieces; flatten slightly. Shape 1 cookie dough piece around 1 peanut butter ball, covering completely. Repeat with remaining dough and balls.

4. Roll each covered ball in peanut mixture; gently pat mixture completely onto balls. On ungreased large cookie sheets, place balls 2 inches apart. Spray bottom of drinking glass with no-stick cooking spray; press into remaining peanut mixture. Flatten each ball to ½-inch thickness with bottom of glass. Sprinkle any remaining peanut mixture evenly on tops of cookies; gently press into dough.

5. Bake 7 to 12 minutes or until edges are golden brown. Cool 1 minute; remove from cookie sheets to cooling rack. Store tightly covered.

1 Serving: Calories 150 (Calories from Fat 70); Total Fat 7g; Saturated Fat 1.5g; Trans Fat 0.5g; Cholesterol 0mg; Sodium 125mg; Total Carbohydrate 17g; Dietary Fiber 0g; Sugars 11g; Protein 3g

PEANUT BLOSSOMS

Peanut butter and chocolate come together in these classic cookies—a tasty dessert.

PREP TIME: 60 MINUTES
TOTAL TIME: 60 MINUTES

MAKES 48 SERVINGS

Hall of Fame

Freda Smith, Gibsonburg, Ohio
Bake-Off® Contest 9, 1957 Hall of Fame

1¾ cups all purpose flour
½ cup sugar
½ cup firmly packed brown sugar
1 teaspoon baking soda
½ teaspoon salt
½ cup shortening

½ cup peanut butter
2 tablespoons milk
1 teaspoon vanilla
1 egg
Sugar
48 Hershey's® Kisses® Brand milk chocolates, unwrapped

1. Heat oven to 375°F. In large bowl, combine flour, ½ cup sugar, brown sugar, baking soda, salt, shortening, peanut butter, milk, vanilla and egg; mix with electric mixer on low speed until stiff dough forms.

2. Shape dough into 1-inch balls; roll in sugar. Place 2 inches apart on ungreased cookie sheets.

3. Bake at 375°F for 10 to 12 minutes or until golden brown. Immediately top each cookie with 1 milk chocolate candy, pressing down firmly so cookie cracks around edge; remove from cookie sheets.

1 Serving: Calories 100 (Calories from Fat 45); Total Fat 5g; Saturated Fat 2g; Trans Fats 0g; Cholesterol 5mg; Sodium 70mg; Total Carbohydrate 12g; Dietary Fiber 0g; Sugars 8g; Protein 2g

BRAZILIAN JUBILEE COOKIES

A hint of chocolate flavor in the dough tastes terrific with chocolate and Brazil nuts.

PREP TIME: 1 HOUR 15 MINUTES
TOTAL TIME: 1 HOUR 15 MINUTES
MAKES 36 SERVINGS

F. H. Speers, Midland, Texas
Bake-Off® Contest 4, 1952

¾ cup granulated sugar

¼ cup packed brown sugar

½ cup shortening

2 teaspoons vanilla

1 egg

1½ cups all-purpose flour

1 to 2 tablespoons instant coffee granules or crystals

1 teaspoon baking powder

½ teaspoon salt

½ teaspoon ground cinnamon

1 cup chopped Brazil nuts

36 milk chocolate stars (from 14-oz bag)

Additional chopped Brazil nuts, if desired

1. Heat oven to 350°F. Grease cookie sheets with shortening or cooking spray. In large bowl, beat sugars and shortening with electric mixer on medium speed, scraping bowl occasionally, until well blended. Beat in vanilla and egg. On low speed, beat in flour, instant coffee, baking powder, salt, cinnamon and 1 cup nuts until dough forms.

2. Shape dough by tablespoonfuls into balls. Place 2 inches apart on cookie sheets.

3. Bake 12 to 15 minutes or until golden brown. Immediately top each cookie with 1 chocolate star. Remove from cookie sheets to cooling rack; cool 5 minutes (chocolate will soften). Spread chocolate over cookies to frost. Sprinkle with additional chopped nuts.

CLEVER IDEAS:

• *In place of the Brazil nuts, try almonds, pecans or macadamia nuts.*

• *To prevent Brazil nuts from becoming rancid, store them in the fridge.*

1 Serving: Calories 120 (Calories from Fat 60); Total Fat 7g; Saturated Fat 2g; Trans Fat 0g; Cholesterol 5mg; Sodium 50mg; Total Carbohydrate 13g; Dietary Fiber 0g; Sugars 8g; Protein 2g

CANDY BAR COOKIES

Enjoy this distinctive dessert—vanilla bar cookies topped with caramel-pecan filling and a rich chocolate frosting.

PREP TIME: 1 HOUR 15 MINUTES
TOTAL TIME: 1 HOUR 30 MINUTES

MAKES 40 SERVINGS

Alice Reese, Minneapolis, Minnesota
Bake-Off® Contest 13, 1961 Grand Prize Winner

BASE

¾ cup powdered sugar

¾ cup margarine or butter, softened

2 tablespoons whipping cream

1 teaspoon vanilla

2 cups all purpose or unbleached flour

FILLING

21 caramels, unwrapped

3 tablespoons whipping cream

3 tablespoons margarine or butter

¾ cup powdered sugar

¾ cup chopped pecans

GLAZE

⅓ cup semisweet chocolate chips

1 tablespoon whipping cream

2 teaspoons margarine or butter

3 tablespoons powdered sugar

1 teaspoon vanilla

40 pecan halves (½ cup), if desired

1. In large bowl, combine all base ingredients except flour; blend well. Lightly spoon flour into measuring cup; level off. Add flour; mix well. If necessary, cover dough with plastic wrap; refrigerate 1 hour for easier handling.

2. Heat oven to 325°F. On well-floured surface, roll out half of dough at a time into 10x8-inch rectangle. With pastry wheel or knife, cut into 2-inch squares. Place $\frac{1}{2}$ inch apart on ungreased cookie sheets.

3. Bake at 325°F for 10 to 13 minutes or until set. Remove from cookie sheets; place on wire racks. Cool 15 minutes or until completely cooled.

4. In medium saucepan, combine caramels, 3 tablespoons whipping cream and 3 tablespoons margarine; cook over low heat, stirring frequently, until caramels are melted and mixture is smooth. Remove from heat. Stir in $\frac{3}{4}$ cup powdered sugar and chopped pecans. (Add additional whipping cream a few drops at a time, if needed for desired spreading consistency.) Spread 1 teaspoon warm filling on each cookie square.

5. In small saucepan, combine chocolate chips, 1 tablespoon whipping cream and 2 teaspoons margarine. Cook over low heat, stirring frequently, until chocolate chips are melted and mixture is smooth. REMOVE FROM HEAT. Stir in 3 tablespoons powdered sugar and 1 teaspoon vanilla. Spread glaze evenly over caramel filling on each cookie. Top each with pecan half.

1 Serving: Calories 130 (Calories from Fat 70); Total Fat 8g; Saturated Fat 2g; Trans Fat 1g; Cholesterol 3mg; Sodium 65mg; Total Carbohydrate 14g; Dietary Fiber 1g; Sugars 9g; Protein 1g

SNAPPY TURTLE COOKIES

These rich brown sugar cookies resemble the well-known turtle-shape candies. This recipe has earned the rank of a Bake-Off® Contest classic.

PREP TIME: 1 HOUR 30 MINUTES
TOTAL TIME: 2 HOURS
45 MINUTES

MAKES 42 SERVINGS

Beatrice Harlib, Lincolnwood, Illinois
Bake-Off® Contest 4, 1952 Grand Prize Winner

COOKIES

½ cup firmly packed brown sugar

½ cup margarine or butter, softened

¼ teaspoon vanilla

⅛ teaspoon imitation maple flavor, if desired

1 egg

1 egg, separated

1½ cups all purpose or unbleached flour

¼ teaspoon baking soda

¼ teaspoon salt

1 cup pecan halves, split lengthwise

FROSTING

⅓ cup semisweet chocolate chips

3 tablespoons milk

1 tablespoon margarine or butter

1 cup powdered sugar

1. In large bowl, combine brown sugar and $\frac{1}{2}$ cup margarine; beat until light and fluffy. Add vanilla, maple flavor, 1 whole egg and 1 egg yolk; beat well.

2. Lightly spoon flour into measuring cup; level off. Stir in flour, baking soda and salt; mix well. Cover with plastic wrap; refrigerate about 1 hour for easier handling.

3. Heat oven to 350°F. Grease cookie sheets. Arrange pecan pieces in groups of 5 on greased cookie sheets to resemble head and legs of turtle. In small bowl, beat egg white. Shape dough into 1-inch balls. Dip bottoms in beaten egg white; press lightly onto pecans. (Tips of pecans should show.)

4. Bake at 350°F for 10 to 12 minutes or until edges are light golden brown. Immediately remove from cookie sheets. Cool 15 minutes or until completely cooled.

5. In small saucepan, combine chocolate chips, milk and 1 tablespoon margarine; cook over low heat, stirring constantly until melted and smooth. Remove from heat; stir in powdered sugar. If necessary, add additional powdered sugar for desired spreading consistency. Frost cooled cookies. Let frosting set before storing. Store in tightly covered container.

1 Serving: Calories 90 (Calories from Fat 45); Total Fat 5g; Saturated Fat 1g; Trans Fat 1g; Cholesterol 10mg; Sodium 55mg; Total Carbohydrate 10g; Dietary Fiber 0g; Sugars 6g; Protein 1g

CLEVER COOKIE IDEAS:

- Don't substitute a low-fat spread for butter or margarine or the cookies will tend to turn out dense and may not brown.

- Unbaked cookie dough can be wrapped in airtight, freezer-weight plastic or foil and frozen for up to 1 year.

- You can freeze cookies, wrapping them in airtight plastic or foil, for up to 4 months. For iced cookies, it's best to frost cookies after they've thawed.

- Always use the pan size specified for bar cookies. If the pan is too small, your cookies may end up gummy; if it is too big, they may turn out dry.

- Always preheat the oven for 10 to 15 minutes before baking cookies.

- Don't store soft and crisp cookies together; the crisp ones will get soft.

- Cookies have to be completely cool before you store them or they will "sweat" and get soggy.

NUTTY CHOCOLATE CHIP BISCOTTI

Wow! Coffee shop biscotti made with refrigerated cookie dough!

PREP TIME: 35 MINUTES
TOTAL TIME: 2 HOURS 40 MINUTES
MAKES 40 SERVINGS

Paula Consolini, Williamstown, Massachusetts
Bake-Off® Contest 41, 2004

1 roll (16.5 oz) Pillsbury™ refrigerated chocolate chip cookies

1½ teaspoons vanilla

½ teaspoon rum extract

1½ cups chopped almonds, hazelnuts (filberts) or pecans, lightly toasted

1 cup semisweet chocolate chips

1. Heat oven to 350°F. Grease with shortening and flour large cookie sheet. In large bowl, break up cookie dough. Sprinkle vanilla and rum extract over dough; mix well. Stir toasted almonds into dough.

2. Divide dough into 4 equal portions; shape each into 8x1-inch log. On cookie sheet, place logs 3 inches apart; flatten each log until about $1\frac{1}{2}$ inches wide.

3. Bake 15 to 20 minutes or until golden brown. Cool 15 minutes. Reduce oven temperature to 200°F.

4. With serrated knife, carefully cut each log into 10 ($\frac{3}{4}$-inch) slices. On same cookie sheet, place slices, cut side down.

5. Return to oven; bake 1 hour. Remove cookies from cookie sheet to cooling rack. Cool completely, about 20 minutes. Meanwhile, in small microwavable bowl, place chocolate chips. Microwave on High 1 minute. Stir; microwave 1 minute longer, stirring every 15 seconds.

6. Line cookie sheet with waxed paper. Dip ¼ of each cookie into melted chocolate; place on cookie sheet. Refrigerate until chocolate is set, about 10 minutes.

CLEVER IDEA: *To toast almonds, spread on cookie sheet; bake at 350°F for 5 to 7 minutes, stirring occasionally, until golden brown. Or spread almonds in thin layer in microwavable pie pan; microwave on High for 4 to 7 minutes, stirring frequently, until golden brown.*

1 Serving: Calories 100 (Calories from Fat 50); Total Fat 6g; Saturated Fat 1.5g; Trans Fat 0g; Cholesterol 0mg; Sodium 35mg; Total Carbohydrate 11g; Dietary Fiber 0g; Sugars 7g; Protein 2g

CHOCOLATE COCONUT CRUNCHERS

Looking for a crunchy dessert? Then check out these drop cookies that bring together chocolate, coconut, walnuts, corn flakes and oats, all in one decadent treat.

PREP TIME: 1 HOUR 10 MINUTES
TOTAL TIME: 1 HOUR 10 MINUTES

MAKES 60 SERVINGS

Betty Chromzack, Northlake, Illinois
Bake-Off® Contest 36, 1994

- 1 (15.25-oz.) pkg. Pillsbury™ Moist Supreme™ German Chocolate Cake Mix
- 1 cup margarine or butter, softened
- 2 eggs
- 1 cup coconut
- 1 cup chopped walnuts
- 1 cup crushed corn flakes cereal or other cereal flakes
- 1 cup rolled oats
- 1 (6-oz.) pkg. (1 cup) semisweet chocolate chips
- 1 to 2 tablespoons sugar

1. Heat oven to 350°F. In large bowl, combine cake mix, margarine and eggs; mix well. Add coconut, walnuts, corn flakes, rolled oats and chocolate chips; mix well. Drop dough by rounded teaspoonfuls 2 inches apart onto ungreased cookie sheets. Flatten with glass dipped in sugar.

2. Bake at 350°F for 8 to 10 minutes or until set. Cool 1 minute; remove from cookie sheets.

1 Serving: Calories 120 (Calories from Fat 60); Total Fat 7g; Saturated Fat 2g; Trans Fat 1g; Cholesterol 5mg; Sodium 110mg; Total Carbohydrate 12g; Dietary Fiber 1g; Sugars 7g; Protein 1g

PEANUTTY PIE CRUST CLUSTERS

Whip up a delicious treat with flaky pie crust squares, peanut butter and toffee.

PREP TIME: 30 MINUTES
TOTAL TIME: 45 MINUTES

MAKES 30 CLUSTERS

Beth Royals, Richmond, Virginia Grand Prize Winner
Bake-Off® Contest 47, 2014

1 Pillsbury™ refrigerated pie crust, softened as directed on box

1 bag (12 oz) white vanilla baking chips (2 cups)

1 tablespoon vegetable shortening

1 tablespoon creamy peanut butter

1 cup salted cocktail peanuts

⅔ cup toffee bits

1. Heat oven to 450°F. Line 2 cookie sheets with wax paper.

2. Unroll pie crust on work surface. With pizza cutter or knife, cut into 16 rows by 16 rows to make small squares. Arrange squares in single layer on large ungreased cookie sheet. Bake 6 to 8 minutes or until light golden brown. Remove squares from pan to cooling rack. Cool completely, about 5 minutes.

3. In large microwavable bowl, microwave baking chips, shortening and peanut butter uncovered on High 1 minute to 1 minute 30 seconds, stirring once, until chips can be stirred smooth. Add pie crust squares, peanuts and toffee bits; stir gently until evenly coated. Immediately drop by heaping tablespoonfuls onto lined cookie sheets. (If mixture gets too thick, microwave on High 15 seconds; stir.) Refrigerate about 15 minutes or until set. Store covered.

1 Serving: Calories 150 (Calories from Fat 90); Total Fat 10g; Saturated Fat 4.5g; Trans Fat 0g; Cholesterol 0mg; Sodium 100mg; Total Carbohydrate 14g; Dietary Fiber 0g; Sugars 7g; Protein 2g

FUDGY BONBONS

Looking for a chocolate dessert? Then check out these fudgy bonbons packed with candies—a delicious treat!

PREP TIME: 45 MINUTES
TOTAL TIME: 1 HOUR
MAKES 60 SERVINGS

Mary Anne Tyndall, Whiteville, North Carolina
Bake-Off® Contest 36, 1994 Grand Prize Winner

1 (12-oz.) pkg. (2 cups) semisweet chocolate chips

¼ cup margarine or butter

1 (14-oz.) can sweetened condensed milk (not evaporated)

2 cups all purpose or unbleached flour

½ cup finely chopped nuts, if desired

1 teaspoon vanilla

60 milk chocolate candy drops or pieces, unwrapped

2 oz. white chocolate baking bar or vanilla-flavored candy coating (almond bark)

1 teaspoon shortening or oil

1. Heat oven to 350°F. In medium saucepan, combine chocolate chips and margarine; cook and stir over very low heat until chips are melted and smooth. (Mixture will be stiff.) Add condensed milk; mix well.

2. Lightly spoon flour into measuring cup; level off. In large bowl, combine flour, nuts, chocolate mixture and vanilla; mix well. Shape 1 tablespoon dough (use measuring spoon) around each milk chocolate candy, covering completely. Place 1 inch apart on ungreased cookie sheets.

3. Bake at 350°F for 6 to 8 minutes. DO NOT OVERBAKE. Cookies will be soft and appear shiny but will become firm as they cool. Remove from cookie sheets. Cool 15 minutes or until completely cooled.

4. Meanwhile, in small saucepan, combine baking bar and shortening; cook and stir over low heat until melted and smooth. Drizzle over cooled cookies. Let stand until set. Store in tightly covered container.

1 Serving: Calories 120 (Calories from Fat 50); Total Fat 6g; Saturated Fat 3g; Trans Fat 0g; Cholesterol 5mg; Sodium 20mg; Total Carbohydrate 14g; Dietary Fiber 1g; Sugars 10g; Protein 2g

CHOCOLATE BUTTERSWEETS

Rich, buttery cookies hold a coconut-and-cream-cheese filling. A touch of chocolate on top adds even more decadent flavor!

PREP TIME: 1 HOUR 35 MINUTES
TOTAL TIME: 2 HOURS
15 MINUTES

MAKES 36 SERVINGS

Vance Fletcher, Indianapolis, Indiana
Bake-Off® Contest 16, 1964

COOKIES

½ cup butter or margarine, softened

½ cup powdered sugar

¼ teaspoon salt

1 teaspoon vanilla

1 to 1¼ cups all-purpose flour

FILLING

1 package (3 oz) cream cheese, softened

1 cup powdered sugar

2 tablespoons all-purpose flour

1 teaspoon vanilla

½ cup chopped walnuts

½ cup flaked coconut

FROSTING

½ cup semisweet chocolate chips

2 tablespoons butter or margarine

2 tablespoons water

½ cup powdered sugar

1 teaspoon vanilla

1. Heat oven to 350°F. In large bowl, beat ½ cup butter, ½ cup powdered sugar, the salt and 1 teaspoon vanilla with electric mixer on medium speed, scraping bowl occasionally, until blended. Gradually beat in 1 to 1¼ cups flour until soft dough forms.

2. Shape teaspoonfuls of dough into balls. On ungreased cookie sheets, place balls 2 inches apart. With thumb or handle of wooden spoon, make indentation in center of each.

3. Bake 12 to 15 minutes or until edges are lightly browned. Meanwhile, in small bowl, beat cream cheese, 1 cup powdered sugar, 2 tablespoons flour and 1 teaspoon vanilla on medium speed until well blended. Stir in walnuts and coconut.

4. Immediately remove cookies from cookie sheets to cooling racks. Spoon about ½ teaspoon filling into each cookie. Cool completely, about 30 minutes.

5. In 1-quart saucepan, heat chocolate chips, 2 tablespoons butter and the water over low heat, stirring occasionally, until chips are melted. Remove from heat. With spoon, beat in ½ cup powdered sugar and vanilla until smooth. Frost cooled cookies. Store covered in refrigerator.

CLEVER IDEAS:

- *To soften butter, microwave unwrapped butter in glass bowl or measuring cup uncovered on High 10 to 20 seconds.*

- *Use chopped pecans instead of the walnuts, if you prefer.*

1 Serving: Calories 110 (Calories from Fat 60); Total Fat 6g; Saturated Fat 3.5g; Trans Fat 0g; Cholesterol 10mg; Sodium 50mg; Total Carbohydrate 12g; Dietary Fiber 0g; Sugars 8g; Protein 0g

LEMON MARDI GRAS SQUARES

Pecans make it perfect in this Southern-style dessert, tart-sweet bar cookies loaded with lemon.

PREP TIME: 40 MINUTES
TOTAL TIME: 2 HOURS
15 MINUTES

MAKES 24 SERVINGS

Mrs. Joseph Negrotto, New Orleans, Louisiana
Bake-Off® Contest 4, 1952

BARS
1½ cups all-purpose flour
½ teaspoon salt
¼ teaspoon baking powder
1 cup powdered sugar
1 cup granulated sugar
½ cup butter or margarine, softened
3 eggs
⅓ cup lemon juice
½ cup chopped pecans
2 tablespoons grated lemon peel

FROSTING
1 cup powdered sugar
2 tablespoons butter or margarine, softened
1 tablespoon half-and-half or milk

GARNISH
¼ cup chopped pecans
Lemon slices, if desired

1. Heat oven to 400°F. Generously grease 13x9-inch pan with shortening; lightly flour or spray with cooking spray. In small bowl, stir together flour, salt and baking powder; set aside.

2. In large bowl, beat powdered sugar, granulated sugar and butter with electric mixer on medium speed, scraping bowl occasionally, until blended. Beat in 1 egg at a time until blended. Beat 1 minute longer. On low speed, beat in flour mixture alternately with lemon juice, beginning and ending with flour mixture, until well blended. Stir in ½ cup pecans and lemon peel. Pour into pan.

3. Bake 22 to 27 minutes or until golden brown. Meanwhile, in small bowl, beat frosting ingredients on low speed until smooth and spreadable.

4. Spread frosting over warm bars. Sprinkle with ¼ cup pecans. Cool completely in pan on cooling rack, about 1 hour. For bars, cut into 6 rows by 4 rows. Garnish with lemon slices.

CLEVER IDEAS:

- *Leave out the pecans if you like and sprinkle with coconut instead.*

- *Make these bars up to a day ahead; store in the refrigerator until ready to serve.*

1 Serving: Calories 180 (Calories from Fat 70); Total Fat 8g; Saturated Fat 3.5g; Trans Fat 0g; Cholesterol 40mg; Sodium 95mg; Total Carbohydrate 25g; Dietary Fiber 1g; Sugars 18g; Protein 2g

MOCK LEMON MERINGUE BARS

The difficulty of making and cutting through soft meringue in this classic bar has been eliminated! Try this variation and see.

PREP TIME: 15 MINUTES
TOTAL TIME: 2 HOURS 5 MINUTES

MAKES 24 SERVINGS

Robin Janine Peterson, Peoria, Arizona
Bake-Off® Contest 42, 2006

1 roll Pillsbury™ refrigerated sugar cookies

1 cup lemon curd (from 11¼- to 12-oz jar)

1 package (3 oz) cream cheese, softened

½ cup marshmallow creme

1 container (6 oz) 99% fat free French vanilla yogurt

1 cup frozen whipped topping, thawed

1. Heat oven to 350°F. Grease 13x9-inch pan with shortening or cooking spray. In pan, break up cookie dough. With floured fingers, press dough evenly in bottom of pan to form crust.

2. Bake 15 to 20 minutes or until edges are golden brown and center is set. Cool 30 minutes.

3. Spread lemon curd over cooled crust. In large bowl, beat cream cheese, marshmallow creme and yogurt with wooden spoon until well blended. Fold in whipped topping. Spread over lemon curd, swirling to look like meringue topping. Refrigerate at least 1 hour until serving time. For bars, cut into 6 rows by 4 rows. Store in refrigerator.

1 Serving: Calories 160 (Calories from Fat 60); Total Fat 7g; Saturated Fat 2.5g; Trans Fat 1g; Cholesterol 20mg; Sodium 80mg; Total Carbohydrate 25g; Dietary Fiber 0g; Sugars 18g; Protein 1g

PECAN PIE SURPRISE BARS

Enjoy these crunchy bars packed with pecans— a delightful dessert!

PREP TIME: 15 MINUTES
TOTAL TIME: 2 HOURS 40 MINUTES

MAKES 36 SERVINGS

Pearl Hall, Snohomish, Washington
Bake-Off® Contest 22, 1971 Grand Prize Winner

BASE

1 (15.25-oz.) pkg. Pillsbury™ Moist Supreme™ Classic Yellow or Golden Butter Recipe Yellow Cake Mix

⅓ cup margarine or butter, softened

1 egg

FILLING

Reserved ⅔ cup dry cake mix

½ cup firmly packed brown sugar

1½ cups dark corn syrup

1 teaspoon vanilla

3 eggs

1 cup chopped pecans

1. Heat oven to 350°F. Grease 13x9-inch pan. Reserve ⅔ cup of the dry cake mix for filling. In large bowl, combine remaining dry cake mix, margarine and 1 egg; beat at low speed until well blended. Press in bottom of greased pan. Bake at 350°F. for 15 to 20 minutes or until light golden brown.

2. Meanwhile, in large bowl, combine reserved ⅔ cup dry cake mix, brown sugar, corn syrup, vanilla and 3 eggs; beat at low speed until moistened. Beat 1 minute at medium speed or until well blended.

3. Remove pan from oven. Pour filling mixture over warm base. Sprinkle with pecans.

4. Return to oven; bake an additional 30 to 35 minutes or until filling is set. Cool 1½ hours or until completely cooled. Cut into bars. Store in refrigerator.

1 Serving: Calories 160 (Calories from Fat 50); Total Fat 6g; Saturated Fat 1g; Trans Fats 0g; Cholesterol 25mg; Sodium 149mg; Total Carbohydrate 26g; Dietary Fiber 1g; Sugars 13g; Protein 1g

QUICK CRESCENT PECAN PIE BARS

Refrigerated crescent dough makes this pecan bar recipe simple and quick to prepare.

PREP TIME: 10 MINUTES
TOTAL TIME: 1 HOUR 45 MINUTES
MAKES 24 SERVINGS

Albina Flieller, Floresville, Texas
Bake-Off® Contest 24, 1973 Grand Prize Winner

CRUST

1 can (8 oz) Pillsbury™ refrigerated crescent dinner rolls or 1 can (8 oz) Pillsbury™ Crescent Recipe Creations™ refrigerated seamless dough sheet

FILLING

½ cup chopped pecans

½ cup sugar

½ cup corn syrup

1 tablespoon butter or margarine, melted

½ teaspoon vanilla

1 egg, beaten

1. Heat oven to 350°F.

2. If using crescent rolls: Unroll dough; separate dough into 2 long rectangles. Place in ungreased 13x9-inch pan; press over bottom and ½ inch up sides to form crust. Firmly press perforations to seal. If using dough sheet: Unroll dough; cut into 2 long rectangles. Place in ungreased 13x9-inch pan; press over bottom and ½ inch up sides to form crust.

3. Bake 8 minutes. Meanwhile, in medium bowl, mix filling ingredients. Pour filling over partially baked crust.

4. Bake 18 to 22 minutes longer or until golden brown. Cool completely, about 1 hour. For bars, cut into 6 rows by 4 rows. Store at room temperature.

1 Serving: Calories 100 (Calories from Fat 40); Total Fat 4.5g; Saturated Fat 1g; Trans Fat 0.5g; Cholesterol 10mg; Sodium 85mg; Total Carbohydrate 14g; Dietary Fiber 0g; Sugars 8g; Protein 1g

PEANUT BRITTLE COOKIES

Cookie dough is easily pressed into a pan, baked and broken into pieces. The fabulous flavor of peanut brittle with less fuss!

PREP TIME: 25 MINUTES
TOTAL TIME: 50 MINUTES

MAKES 24 SERVINGS

Mrs. John Hamlon, Fergus Falls, Minnesota
Bake-Off® Contest 4, 1952

½ cup packed brown sugar

½ cup butter or margarine, softened

1 egg, beaten,
1 tablespoon reserved

1 teaspoon vanilla

1 cup all-purpose flour

¼ teaspoon baking soda

½ teaspoon ground cinnamon

½ cup salted peanuts, finely chopped

Reserved 1 tablespoon beaten egg

½ cup salted peanuts or nuts

1. Heat oven to 325°F. Grease large cookie sheet with shortening or cooking spray. In large bowl, beat brown sugar and butter with electric mixer on medium speed, scraping bowl occasionally, until well blended. Beat in 2 tablespoons beaten egg and the vanilla. On low speed, beat in flour, baking soda and cinnamon until dough forms. Stir in ½ cup finely chopped peanuts. Refrigerate dough 30 minutes.

2. Crumble chilled dough onto cookie sheet. With floured hands, press dough into 14x10-inch rectangle. Brush with reserved 1 tablespoon egg. Sprinkle with ½ cup peanuts; press into dough.

3. Bake 20 to 25 minutes or until dark golden brown. Cool 5 minutes; while warm, cut or break into 24 pieces.

CLEVER IDEAS:

- *Instead of greasing the cookie sheets, use cooking parchment paper.*

- *With all the great flavor of peanut brittle in an easy-to-make cookie, these cookies make fantastic gifts.*

1 Serving: Calories 110 (Calories from Fat 70); Total Fat 7g; Saturated Fat 3g; Trans Fat 0g; Cholesterol 20mg; Sodium 65mg; Total Carbohydrate 9g; Dietary Fiber 0g; Sugars 5g; Protein 3g

COCONUT-LEMON-CRESCENT BARS

Cookie and bar making has been revolutionized with the introduction of refrigerated dough products. In this recipe, lemon and coconut combine with an easy crescent crust to make these refreshing bars.

PREP TIME: 15 MINUTES
TOTAL TIME: 1 HOUR 5 MINUTES

MAKES 36 BARS

Ms. Marilyn Blankschien, Clintonville, Wisconsin
Bake-Off® Contest 30, 1982

CRUST

1 can (8-oz.) Pillsbury™ refrigerated crescent dinner rolls

FILLING

2 eggs, slightly beaten

1 cup sugar

1 cup flaked coconut

2 tablespoons Pillsbury™ BEST™ all-purpose flour

½ teaspoon baking powder

½ teaspoon grated lemon peel

¼ teaspoon salt

2 tablespoons lemon juice

2 tablespoons butter or margarine, melted

1. Heat oven to 375°F. Unroll dough into 2 long rectangles. Place in ungreased 13x9-inch pan; press in bottom and ½ inch up sides to form crust, firmly pressing perforations to seal.

2. Bake 5 minutes. Meanwhile, in medium bowl, mix all filling ingredients until well blended.

3. Pour filling over partially baked crust; bake 12 to 17 minutes longer or until light golden brown. Cool completely in pan on cooling rack, about 30 minutes. For bars, cut into 6 rows by 6 rows.

1 Bar: Calories 70 (Calories from Fat 25); Total Fat 3g; Saturated Fat 1.5g; Trans Fat 0g; Cholesterol 15mg; Sodium 85mg; Total Carbohydrate 9g; Dietary Fiber 0g; Sugars 7g; Protein 1g

SALTED PEANUT CHEWS

Easy Pillsbury™ cookie dough makes a luscious crust that holds a nutty, chewy filling.

PREP TIME: 35 MINUTES
TOTAL TIME: 1 HOUR 35 MINUTES
MAKES 36 SERVINGS

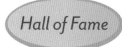

Gertrude M. Schweitzerhof, Cupertino, California
Bake-Off® Contest 29, 1980 Hall of Fame

BASE

1½ cups Pillsbury™ BEST™ all-purpose flour

⅔ cup packed brown sugar

½ teaspoon baking powder

½ teaspoon salt

¼ teaspoon baking soda

½ cup butter or margarine, softened

1 teaspoon vanilla

2 egg yolks

3 cups miniature marshmallows

TOPPING

⅔ cup corn syrup

¼ cup butter or margarine

2 teaspoons vanilla

1 bag (10-oz) peanut butter chips (1⅔ cups)

2 cups crisp rice cereal

2 cups salted peanuts

1. Heat oven to 350°F. In large bowl, beat all base ingredients except marshmallows with electric mixer on low speed until crumbly. Press mixture firmly in bottom of ungreased 13x9-inch pan.

2. Bake 12 to 15 minutes or until light golden brown. Immediately sprinkle marshmallows evenly over base; bake 1 to 2 minutes longer or until marshmallows just begin to puff. Cool while making topping.

3. In 3-quart saucepan, mix all topping ingredients except cereal and peanuts. Heat over low heat, stirring constantly, just until chips are melted and mixture is smooth. Remove from heat. Stir in cereal and peanuts. Immediately spoon warm topping over marshmallows; spread to cover. Refrigerate until firm, about 45 minutes. For bars, cut into 6 rows by 6 rows.

CLEVER IDEA: *Short on time? Using cookie dough as the crust makes preparation a snap.*

1 Serving: Calories 200 (Calories from Fat 100); Total Fat 11g; Saturated Fat 2.5g; Trans Fat 0.5g; Cholesterol 10mg; Sodium 100mg; Total Carbohydrate 22g; Dietary Fiber 1g; Sugars 13g; Protein 4g

CHOCOLATE CHIP, OATS, AND CARAMEL COOKIE SQUARES

A classic layered bar makes the perfect treat to tote to a get-together.

PREP TIME: 35 MINUTES
TOTAL TIME: 2 HOURS 40 MINUTES

MAKES 16 SERVINGS

Niela Frantellizzi, Boca Raton, Florida
Bake-Off® Contest 37, 1996

1 roll (16.5 oz) Pillsbury™ refrigerated chocolate chip cookies

1 cup quick-cooking oats

Dash salt, if desired

⅔ cup caramel ice cream topping

5 tablespoons Pillsbury™ BEST™ all-purpose flour

1 teaspoon vanilla

¾ cup chopped walnuts

1 cup semi-sweet baking chips (6 oz)

1. Heat oven to 350°F. In large bowl, break up cookie dough. Stir or knead in oats and salt. Reserve ½ cup dough for topping. In ungreased 9-inch square pan, press remaining dough mixture evenly in bottom to form crust.

2. Bake 10 to 12 minutes or until dough puffs and appears dry.

3. In small bowl, mix caramel topping, flour and vanilla until well blended. Sprinkle walnuts and baking chips evenly over crust. Drizzle evenly with caramel mixture. Crumble reserved ½ cup dough mixture over caramel.

4. Bake 20 to 25 minutes longer or until golden brown. Cool 10 minutes. Run knife around sides of pan to loosen bars. Cool completely, about 1 hour 30 minutes. For bars, cut into 4 rows by 4 rows. Store tightly covered.

CLEVER IDEAS:

- *Did you know? Pillsbury has a gluten free cookie dough.*

- *Totally totable, these classic layered bars are perfect for get-togethers with family and friends.*

1 Serving: Calories 280 (Calories from Fat 110); Total Fat 12g; Saturated Fat 4g; Trans Fat 1g; Cholesterol 5mg; Sodium 140mg; Total Carbohydrate 40g; Dietary Fiber 1g; Sugars 24g; Protein 4g

QUICK AND CHEWY CRESCENT BARS

Looking for a dessert made with Pillsbury™ crescent dinner rolls? Then check out these chewy coconut and pecan bars—a yummy treat.

PREP TIME: 40 MINUTES
TOTAL TIME: 1 HOUR 40 MINUTES
MAKES 48 SERVINGS

Isabelle Collins, Ramona, California
Bake-Off® Contest 23, 1972 Grand Prize Winner

½ cup all-purpose flour

1 cup coconut

¾ cup packed brown sugar

½ cup chopped pecans

¼ cup butter or margarine

1 can (8 oz) Pillsbury™ refrigerated crescent dinner rolls or 1 can (8 oz) Pillsbury™ Crescent Recipe Creations™ refrigerated seamless dough sheet

1 can (14 oz) sweetened condensed milk (not evaporated)

1. Heat oven to 400°F. In medium bowl, mix flour, coconut, brown sugar and pecans. Cut in butter, using pastry blender (or pulling 2 table knives through mixture in opposite directions), until mixture looks like coarse crumbs. Set aside.

2. If using crescent rolls: Unroll dough into 2 long rectangles. Place in ungreased 15x10x1-inch pan; gently press dough to cover bottom of pan. Firmly press perforations to seal. If using dough sheet: Unroll dough; cut into 2 long rectangles. Place in ungreased 15x10x1-inch pan; gently press dough to cover bottom of pan.

3. Pour condensed milk evenly over dough to within ½ inch of edges. Sprinkle coconut mixture over condensed milk; press in lightly.

4. Bake 12 to 15 minutes or until deep golden brown. Cool completely, about 1 hour. For bars, cut into 8 rows by 6 rows.

1 Serving: Calories 100 (Calories from Fat 40); Total Fat 4.5g; Saturated Fat 2g; Trans Fat 0g; Cholesterol 5mg; Sodium 65mg; Total Carbohydrate 13g; Dietary Fiber 0g; Sugars 10g; Protein 1g

QUICK CRESCENT BAKLAVA

This traditional nut and honey sweet treat is made remarkably easy when refrigerated crescent roll dough is used as its base.

PREP TIME: 25 MINUTES
TOTAL TIME: 2 HOURS 25 MINUTES

MAKES 36 SERVINGS

Annette Erbeck (Mrs. Gail), Mason, Ohio
Bake-Off® Contest 29, 1980

- 2 cans (8 oz each) Pillsbury™ refrigerated crescent dinner rolls or 2 cans (8 oz each) Pillsbury™ Crescent Recipe Creations™ refrigerated seamless dough sheet
- 3 to 4 cups walnuts, finely chopped

- ¾ cup sugar
- 1 teaspoon ground cinnamon
- ½ cup honey
- 2 tablespoons butter or margarine
- 2 teaspoons lemon juice

1. Heat oven to 350°F. Unroll 1 can of dough and separate into 2 long rectangles. Place in ungreased 13x9-inch pan; press in bottom and ½ inch up sides to form crust. (If using crescent rolls, firmly press perforations to seal.) Bake 5 minutes. Meanwhile, in large bowl, mix walnuts, ½ cup of the sugar and the cinnamon.

2. Spoon walnut mixture evenly over crust. Separate remaining can of dough into 2 long rectangles. Place over walnut mixture; press out to edges of pan. With tip of sharp knife, score dough with 6 lengthwise and 6 diagonal markings to form 36 diamond-shaped pieces, using dough edges and perforations as a guide.

3. In 1-quart saucepan, mix remaining ¼ cup sugar, the honey, butter and lemon juice. Heat to boiling. Remove from heat; spoon half of sugar mixture evenly over dough.

4. Bake 25 to 30 minutes longer or until golden brown. Spoon remaining sugar mixture evenly over hot baklava. Cool completely, about 1 hour. Refrigerate until thoroughly chilled, about 30 minutes. For diamond shapes, cut 6 straight parallel lines down length of pan; cut 6 diagonal lines across straight lines.

CLEVER IDEAS:

- *Baklava (bahk-lah-VAH) is a sweet dessert made with layers of butter-drenched pastry, spices and nuts. A honey-lemon syrup is poured over the baked warm pastry and left to soak.*

- *Feel free to use your favorite kind of nuts in this recipe.*

1 Serving: Calories 150 (Calories from Fat 90); Total Fat 10g; Saturated Fat 2g; Trans Fat 0.5g; Cholesterol 0mg; Sodium 105mg; Total Carbohydrate 14g; Dietary Fiber 0g; Sugars 9g; Protein 2g

CANDY BAR MELTAWAYS

Looking for an easy bar to tote to a potluck? Here's a winner, with just four simple steps.

PREP TIME: 15 MINUTES
TOTAL TIME: 55 MINUTES

MAKES 36 SERVINGS

Albert J. Miraglia, Medford, Massachusetts
Bake-Off® Contest 20, 1969

1 roll (16.5 oz) Pillsbury™ refrigerated chocolate chip cookies

13 bars (fun-size) milk chocolate-covered nougat and caramel candy, unwrapped, cut into ¼-inch-thick slices

½ cup crushed Golden Grahams™ cereal

½ cup chopped walnuts, pecans or peanuts

1. Heat oven to 375°F. In ungreased 13x9-inch pan, break up cookie dough. With floured fingers, press dough evenly in bottom of pan to form crust. Bake 12 to 15 minutes or until golden brown.

2. Arrange candy evenly over crust.

3. Bake 3 to 4 minutes longer or until candy softens. Meanwhile, in small bowl, mix cereal and walnuts.

4. With spatula or knife, quickly spread candy evenly over crust. Sprinkle evenly with cereal mixture; press in slightly. Cool completely, about 30 minutes. For bars, cut into 6 rows by 6 rows.

CLEVER IDEAS:

- *Any fun-size chocolate-covered candy bar with creamy filling can be used.*

- *Store the bars in a tightly sealed plastic container, and freeze them up to 3 months.*

1 Serving: Calories 110 (Calories from Fat 50); Total Fat 5g; Saturated Fat 2 g; Trans Fat 0.5g; Cholesterol 0mg; Sodium 60mg; Total Carbohydrate 14g; Dietary Fiber 0g; Sugars 9g; Protein 1g

CHOCOLATE CHERRY BARS

Enjoy the mouth-watering combination of chocolate and cherry in these lavish dessert bars.

Cake mix and cherry pie filling make this Silver Anniversary Grand Prize winner a quick and easy recipe. Very cakelike, this bar can also be served as a dessert square.

PREP TIME: 15 MINUTES
TOTAL TIME: 2 HOURS
MAKES 48 SERVINGS

Francis Jerzak, Porter, Minnesota
Bake-Off® Contest 25, 1974 Grand Prize Winner

CAKE BARS

- 1 (15.25-oz.) pkg. Pillsbury™ Moist Supreme™ Devil's Food Cake Mix
- 1 (21-oz.) can cherry pie filling
- 1 teaspoon almond extract
- 3 eggs, beaten

FROSTING

- 1 cup sugar
- ⅓ cup milk
- 5 tablespoons margarine or butter
- 1 (6-oz.) pkg. (1 cup) semisweet chocolate chips

1. Heat oven to 350°F. Grease and flour 15x10x1-inch baking pan or 13x9-inch pan. In large bowl, combine all cake bar ingredients; stir until well blended. Pour into greased and floured pan.

2. Bake at 350°F until toothpick inserted in center comes out clean. For 15x10x1-inch pan, bake 20 to 30 minutes; for 13x9-inch pan, bake 25 to 35 minutes.

3. In small saucepan, combine sugar, milk and margarine. Bring to a boil. Boil 1 minute, stirring constantly. Remove from heat; stir in chocolate chips until smooth. Pour and spread over warm bars. Cool 1¼ hours or until completely cooled. Cut into bars.

1 Serving: Calories 110 (Calories from Fat 35); Total Fat 5g; Saturated Fat 1g; Trans Fat 0g; Cholesterol 15mg; Sodium 105mg; Total Carbohydrate 18g; Dietary Fiber 1g; Sugars 14g; Protein 1g

CARAMEL LAYER CHOCO-SQUARES

Recipes using convenience products to achieve home-made results were especially popular in 1970. The cookie layer and topping for these luscious bars calls for chocolate cake mix. The easily made caramel filling uses caramel candies.

PREP TIME: 15 MINUTES
TOTAL TIME: 1 HOUR 40 MINUTES

**MAKES 36 SERVINGS
(1 BAR PER SERVING)**

Joan Adler, Marshfield, Wisconsin
Bake-Off® Contest 21, 1970

1 (5-oz.) can evaporated milk

1 (14-oz.) pkg. caramels, unwrapped

1 (1 lb. 2.25-oz.) pkg. pudding-included German chocolate cake mix

1 cup chopped nuts

½ cup margarine or butter, softened

1 (6-oz.) pkg. (1 cup) semi-sweet chocolate chips

1. Heat oven to 350°F. Reserve 2 tablespoons evaporated milk for cake mixture. In medium saucepan, combine caramels with remaining evaporated milk. Cook over low heat, stirring frequently, until caramels are melted and mixture is smooth. Remove from heat.

2. In large bowl, combine cake mix, nuts, margarine and reserved 2 tablespoons evaporated milk; mix at low speed until crumbly. Press half of dough mixture in bottom of ungreased 13 x 9-inch pan; reserve remaining dough mixture for topping.

3. Bake at 350°F for 8 minutes. Sprinkle chocolate chips evenly over partially baked crust. Carefully spread caramel mixture over chocolate chips. Crumble reserved dough mixture over caramel mixture. Return to oven; bake an additional 15 to 18 minutes or until filling is set. Cool completely; cut into bars.

1 Serving: Calories 164 (Calories from Fat 69); Total Fat 9g; Saturated Fat 2g; Trans Fat 1g; Cholesterol 2mg; Sodium 176mg; Total Carbohydrate 24g; Dietary Fiber 1g; Sugars 16g; Protein 2g

CARAMEL LAYER CHOCO-SQUARES *(opposite)*

CHEWY PEANUT BUTTER-CARAMEL BARS *(page 338)*

CHEWY PEANUT BUTTER-CARAMEL BARS

Pillsbury™ sugar cookies jump-start these ooey-gooey bars. A few additional ingredients create an awesome flavor combo!

PREP TIME: 20 MINUTES
TOTAL TIME: 2 HOURS
MAKES 36 SERVINGS

Sandra Hilbert, Fort Littleton, Pennsylvania
Bake-Off® Contest 45, 2012

1 package Pillsbury™ Ready to Bake!™ refrigerated sugar cookies

½ cup butter

1 can (14 oz) sweetened condensed milk

1 cup packed light brown sugar

1 cup granulated sugar

1¾ cups graham cracker crumbs

1 bag (11.5 oz) milk chocolate baking chips

½ cup creamy peanut butter

½ cup finely chopped dry roasted peanuts

1. Heat oven to 350°F. Spray 13x9-inch pan (dark pan not recommended) with no-stick cooking spray or line with nonstick foil. Evenly arrange cookie rounds in pan.

2. Bake 24 to 26 minutes or until light golden brown. Cool 15 minutes on cooling rack.

3. Meanwhile, in 2-quart heavy saucepan, melt butter over medium heat. Stir in condensed milk, brown sugar and granulated sugar until blended. Add graham cracker crumbs; mix well (mixture will be thick). Bring to a boil, stirring constantly. Reduce heat to low; cook 5 minutes, stirring constantly, or until slightly thickened. Pour caramel mixture over warm cookie crust, spreading evenly.

4. In medium microwavable bowl, microwave chocolate chips on High 1 minute to 1 minute 20 seconds, stirring every 30 seconds, until smooth. Stir in peanut butter until blended. Spread evenly over caramel layer. Sprinkle with chopped peanuts. Refrigerate 1 hour or until chocolate is set. For bars, cut into 6 rows by 6 rows. Store covered in refrigerator.

1 Serving: Calories 260 (Calories from Fat 110); Total Fat 12g; Saturated Fat 5g; Trans Fat 0g; Cholesterol 15mg; Sodium 130mg; Total Carbohydrate 35g; Dietary Fiber 1g; Sugars 29g; Protein 3g

TREASURE CHEST BARS

This recipe was developed by mistake by Mrs. Hammons. She was not having success with her usual cookie recipe and so decided to add fruit, nuts and candy to salvage the batter. She then baked the creation in a jelly-roll pan. The result is a delicious bar packed with a treasure of goodies!

PREP TIME: 25 MINUTES
TOTAL TIME: 1 HOUR 50 MINUTES

MAKES 48 SERVINGS
(1 BAR PER SERVING)

Marie Hammons, Shawnee, Kansas
Bake-Off® Contest 14, 1962

BARS

2 cups all-purpose flour

½ cup sugar

½ cup firmly packed brown sugar

1½ teaspoons baking powder

½ cup margarine or butter, softened

¾ cup milk

1 teaspoon vanilla

2 eggs

3 (1.45-oz.) bars milk chocolate candy, cut into small pieces

1 cup maraschino cherries, drained, halved

1 cup coarsely chopped mixed nuts

ICING

¼ cup butter

2 cups powdered sugar

½ teaspoon vanilla

2 to 3 tablespoons milk

1. Heat oven to 350°F. Grease and flour 15x10x1-inch baking pan. In large bowl, combine all bar ingredients except chocolate, cherries and nuts. Blend at medium speed until smooth, about 2 minutes. By hand, stir in chocolate, cherries and nuts; spread in greased and floured pan. Bake at 350°F for 25 to 30 minutes or until light golden brown.

2. In small heavy saucepan over medium heat, brown butter until light golden brown, stirring constantly. Remove from heat. Stir in powdered sugar and ½ teaspoon vanilla. Add 2 to 3 tablespoons milk; blend until smooth and of desired spreading consistency. Spread over warm bars. Cool completely.

1 Serving: Calories 120 (Calories from Fat 49); Total Fat 6g; Saturated Fat 2g; Trans Fat 0g; Cholesterol 11mg; Sodium 55mg; Total Carbohydrate 15g; Dietary Fiber 1g; Sugars 13g; Protein 2g

FUDGY CHOCOLATE HAZELNUT BARS

Try this delicious new way to get chocolate-drizzled, fudgy brownies with just six ingredients!

PREP TIME: 20 MINUTES
TOTAL TIME: 3 HOURS 10 MINUTES

MAKES 16 SERVINGS

Julie Pando, Watertown, Massachusetts
Bake-Off® Contest 46, 2013

1 can Pillsbury™ Creamy Supreme™ Chocolate Fudge Flavored Frosting

1 cup chocolate flavored hazelnut spread

3 eggs

¾ cup Pillsbury™ BEST™ All Purpose Flour

½ cup semisweet chocolate chips

½ cup chopped hazelnuts

1. Heat oven to 350°F. Line 9-inch square pan with foil, extending foil over 2 opposite sides of pan. Spray foil with no-stick cooking spray.

2. In large bowl, beat frosting and chocolate hazelnut spread with electric mixer on high speed 2 minutes until fluffy and light in color.

3. Reserve ¼ cup of the frosting mixture in small microwavable bowl; set aside. Add eggs and ¼ teaspoon salt to remaining frosting mixture; beat on high speed 1 minute until well mixed. Stir in flour and chocolate chips. Pour and spread batter into pan. Top with hazelnuts.

4. Bake 38 to 48 minutes or until center is set and slightly jiggly. Cool completely, about 2 hours.

5. Microwave reserved frosting mixture on High 15 seconds or until mixture is of drizzling consistency. Drizzle over brownies; let stand 5 minutes. Remove foil; using serrated knife cut into 4 rows by 4 rows.

1 Serving: Calories 300 (Calories from Fat 140); Total Fat 16g; Saturated Fat 4.5g; Trans Fat 1.5g; Cholesterol 35mg; Sodium 120mg; Total Carbohydrate 36g; Dietary Fiber 1g; Sugars 3g; Protein 4g

BLACK AND WHITE BROWNIES

Chewy brownies are topped with a creamy vanilla layer, then rich chocolate frosting. Yum!

PREP TIME: 15 MINUTES
TOTAL TIME: 2 HOURS
30 MINUTES

MAKES 36 SERVINGS

Hall of Fame

Penelope Weiss, Pleasant Grove, Utah
Bake-Off® Contest 35, 1992 Hall of Fame

BROWNIES

1 (18.4-oz.) pkg. Pillsbury™ Family Size Chocolate Fudge Brownie Mix

¼ cup water

½ cup oil

2 eggs

1½ cups chopped pecans

1 (6-oz.) pkg. (1 cup) semisweet chocolate chips

1 (12-oz.) pkg. (2 cups) white vanilla chips

FROSTING

2 cups powdered sugar

¼ cup unsweetened cocoa

3 to 4 tablespoons hot water

¼ cup butter or margarine, melted

1 teaspoon vanilla

½ to 1 cup pecan halves

1. Heat oven to 350°F. Grease bottom only of 13x9-inch pan. In large bowl, combine brownie mix, water, oil and eggs; beat 50 strokes with spoon. Add 1½ cups pecans, the chocolate chips and 1 cup of the vanilla chips; mix well. Spread in greased pan.

2. Bake at 350°F for 28 to 34 minutes or until center is set. Remove from oven; immediately sprinkle with remaining 1 cup vanilla chips. Return to oven for 1 minute to soften chips; spread evenly over brownies with back of spoon. Cool.

3. In small bowl, combine all frosting ingredients except pecan halves; beat until smooth. (Mixture will be thin.) Spoon over melted white vanilla chips; spread to cover. Arrange pecan halves over frosting. Cool 1½ hours or until completely cooled. Cut into bars.

1 Serving: Calories 230 (Calories from Fat 110); Total Fat 12g; Saturated Fat 5g; Cholesterol 15mg; Sodium 75mg; Total Carbohydrate 29g; Dietary Fiber 0g; Sugars 24g; Protein 2g

BLOND BROWNIE CARAMEL CUPS

These creative brownies are made in muffin cups. They're not only clever but decadent!

PREP TIME: 25 MINUTES
TOTAL TIME: 1 HOUR 45 MINUTES

**MAKES 16 SERVINGS
(1 BROWNIE PER SERVING)**

Alberta Richter, Lockport, Illinois
Bake-Off® Contest 34, 1990

CUPS

½ cup butter or margarine

1 cup firmly packed brown sugar

1 teaspoon vanilla

1 egg

1 cup all-purpose flour

1 teaspoon baking powder

¼ teaspoon salt

½ cup chopped nuts

TOPPING

20 caramels, unwrapped

1 tablespoon water

½ cup semi-sweet chocolate chips

¼ to ½ cup finely chopped nuts

1. Heat oven to 350°F. Line 16 muffin cups with foil or paper baking cups. Melt butter in medium saucepan over low heat. Remove from heat; stir in brown sugar. Add vanilla and egg; mix well. Add flour, baking powder and salt; blend well. Stir in ½ cup chopped nuts. Divide batter evenly into lined muffin cups. Bake at 350°F for 16 to 20 minutes or until golden brown.

2. Meanwhile, in small saucepan over low heat, melt caramels with water; stir constantly until smooth. Immediately after pans are removed from oven, place chocolate chips evenly into middle of each brownie. Spoon 1 scant tablespoon of caramel over chocolate chips in each cup. If necessary, stir additional water into melted caramels to maintain spoonable consistency. Sprinkle ¼ cup finely chopped nuts evenly over brownies. Cool completely. Store in tightly covered container.

CLEVER IDEA: *To melt caramels in microwave, place in small microwave-safe bowl with 1 tablespoon water. Microwave on High for 2 to 3 minutes, stirring occasionally.*

1 Serving: Calories 270 (Calories from Fat 110); Total Fat 14g; Saturated Fat 5.5g; Trans Fat 0g; Cholesterol 28mg; Sodium 140mg; Total Carbohydrate 33g; Dietary Fiber 1g; Sugars 25g; Protein 3g

PEANUT BUTTER CRUNCH BROWNIES

This bar is comprised of four delicious layers. Spread the caramel layer to within $\frac{1}{4}$ inch of the side of the pan. The bars are easier to remove when the caramel does not touch the side of the pan.

PREP TIME: 30 MINUTES
TOTAL TIME: 4 HOURS
10 MINUTES

MAKES 24 SERVINGS

Cindy Egersdorfer, Cuyahoga Falls, Ohio
Bake-Off® Contest 42, 2006

1 box (18.4 oz) Pillsbury™ Family Size Chocolate Fudge Brownie Mix

½ cup vegetable oil

¼ cup water

2 eggs

3 cups semisweet chocolate chips

1 bag (14 oz) caramels, unwrapped

¼ cup water

2 cups slightly broken pretzels (4½ oz)

¼ cup butter or margarine, melted

1 cup powdered sugar

1 jar (18 oz) crunchy peanut butter

2 cups Reese's™ Puffs™ cereal, slightly broken

1. Heat oven to 350°F (325°F for dark pan). Grease 13x9-inch pan with cooking spray or shortening. In large bowl, make brownie mix as directed on box using oil, water and eggs. Stir in 1 cup of the chocolate chips. Spread batter evenly in pan. Bake 28 to 30 minutes. Cool on wire rack while making topping.

2. In medium microwavable bowl, microwave caramels and water on High 1 minute. Stir; continue to microwave in 15-second increments, stirring after each, until caramels are completely melted and mixture is smooth. Stir in broken pretzels until well coated. Spoon and spread carefully over cooled brownie layer.

3. In large bowl, mix melted butter and powdered sugar until smooth. Stir in peanut butter. Stir in broken cereal until well blended. Spread or pat over caramel layer.

4. In small microwavable bowl, microwave remaining 2 cups chocolate chips on High 1 minute. Stir; continue to microwave in 15-second increments, stirring after each, until chocolate is melted. Spread over cereal layer. Refrigerate until chocolate is set and caramel mixture in center is firm, 2 to 3 hours. Let stand at room temperature 10 minutes before cutting. Cut into 6 rows by 4 rows.

CLEVER IDEAS:

- *To slightly break pretzels and cereal, place in separate re-sealable food-storage plastic bags; seal bags and break with rolling pin.*

- *To easily cut brownies, line pan with foil so foil extends over sides of pan; spray foil with cooking spray. When ready to cut, lift brownies from pan using foil.*

1 Serving: Calories 530 (Calories from Fat 250); Total Fat 28g; Saturated Fat 9g; Trans Fat 0g; Cholesterol 25mg; Sodium 340mg; Total Carbohydrate 61g; Dietary Fiber 4g; Sugars 41g; Protein 9g

ROCKY ROAD FUDGE BARS

These winning chocolate bars feature marshmallows and a rich chocolate icing.

PREP TIME: 25 MINUTES
TOTAL TIME: 2 HOURS 10 MINUTES
MAKES 48 SERVINGS

Mary Wilson, Leesburg, Georgia
Bake-Off® Contest 23, 1972

BASE

½ cup margarine or butter

1 oz. unsweetened chocolate, chopped

1 cup Pillsbury™ BEST™ All Purpose or Unbleached Flour

1 cup sugar

1 teaspoon baking powder

1 teaspoon vanilla

2 eggs

¾ cup chopped nuts

FILLING

1 (8-oz.) pkg. cream cheese, softened, reserving 2 oz. for frosting

¼ cup margarine or butter, softened

½ cup sugar

2 tablespoons Pillsbury™ BEST™ All Purpose or Unbleached Flour

½ teaspoon vanilla

1 egg

¼ cup chopped nuts

1 (6-oz.) pkg. (1 cup) semisweet chocolate chips

2 cups miniature marshmallows

FROSTING

¼ cup margarine or butter

¼ cup milk

1 oz. unsweetened chocolate, cut up

Reserved cream cheese

3 cups powdered sugar

1 teaspoon vanilla

1. Heat oven to 350°F. Grease and flour 13x9-inch pan. In large saucepan, melt $\frac{1}{2}$ cup margarine and 1 oz. unsweetened chocolate over low heat, stirring until smooth. Remove from heat. Lightly spoon flour into measuring cup; level off. Stir in 1 cup flour and all remaining base ingredients; mix well. Spread in greased and floured pan.

2. In small bowl, combine 6 oz. of the cream cheese, $\frac{1}{4}$ cup margarine, $\frac{1}{2}$ cup sugar, 2 tablespoons flour, $\frac{1}{2}$ teaspoon vanilla and 1 egg; beat 1 minute at medium speed until smooth and fluffy. Stir in $\frac{1}{4}$ cup nuts. Spread over chocolate mixture; sprinkle evenly with chocolate chips.

3. Bake at 350°F for 25 to 35 minutes or until toothpick inserted in center comes out clean. Remove from oven; immediately sprinkle with marshmallows. Return to oven; bake an additional 2 minutes.

4. While marshmallows are baking, in large saucepan, combine $\frac{1}{4}$ cup margarine, milk, 1 oz. unsweetened chocolate and reserved 2 oz. cream cheese. Cook over low heat, stirring until well blended. Remove from heat; stir in powdered sugar and 1 teaspoon vanilla until smooth. Immediately pour frosting over puffed marshmallows and lightly swirl with knife to marble. Refrigerate 1 hour or until firm. Cut into bars. Store in refrigerator.

1 Serving: Calories 170 (Calories from Fat 80); Total Fat 9g; Saturated Fat 3g; Trans Fat 1g; Cholesterol 20mg; Sodium 75mg; Total Carbohydrate 21g; Dietary Fiber 1g; Sugars 17g; Protein 2g

A Peek Inside the Bake-Off® Contest:

Anna Ginsberg won the 2006 Bake-Off® Contest million-dollar prize with her family-pleasing main dish. With its maple glaze and spinach-accented stuffing, the dish brings the usual—baked chicken—to new heights. But Anna's passion remains baking cookies. Nearly every day, Anna experiments with a new cookie recipe, testing and tinkering, then tasting to see if it meets her standards. Then Anna posts a photo of the day's cookie, along with her opinion of it, on her blog. Just as early Bake-Off® Contest finalists swapped recipe cards with their neighbors over the backyard fence, Anna is sharing recipes with friends, too, in today's style—around the world through the Internet.

CARAMEL GRAHAM FUDGE BROWNIES

Brownie doneness is often difficult to determine. Follow the recipe time range carefully and watch for the brownies to be "set" in the center. Usually the brownies will just begin to pull away from the sides of the pan when they're done. You'll enjoy the combination of ingredients in these rich, layered brownies.

PREP TIME: 30 MINUTES
TOTAL TIME: 2 HOURS
30 MINUTES

MAKES 24 SERVINGS
(1 BAR PER SERVING)

Kathy (Gardner) Herdman, Middleport, Ohio
Bake-Off® Contest 35, 1992

1 (1 lb. 3.5-oz.) pkg. fudge brownie mix

1½ cups graham cracker crumbs

½ cup sugar

½ cup margarine or butter, melted

1 (14-oz.) pkg. caramels, unwrapped

⅓ cup evaporated milk

¾ cup peanut butter chips

¾ cup semi-sweet chocolate chips

1 cup chopped pecans or walnuts

¼ cup water

¼ cup oil

1 egg

1. Heat oven to 350°F. In medium bowl, combine 1½ cups of the brownie mix, graham cracker crumbs, sugar and melted margarine; mix well. Press mixture in bottom of ungreased 13x9-inch pan.

2. In medium saucepan, combine caramels and evaporated milk. Cook over medium heat until caramels are melted, stirring constantly. Carefully spread melted caramel mixture over crust. Sprinkle with peanut butter chips, chocolate chips, and ¾ cup of the chopped pecans, reserving remaining ¼ cup pecans for topping.

3. In same medium bowl, combine remaining brownie mix, water, oil and egg. Beat 50 strokes by hand. Carefully spoon batter evenly over pecans. Sprinkle with remaining ¼ cup pecans.

4. Bake at 350°F for 33 to 38 minutes or until center is set. Cool completely. Cut into bars.

1 Serving: Calories 360 (Calories from Fat 158); Total Fat 17g; Saturated Fat 49; Trans Fat 1g; Cholesterol 10mg; Sodium 200mg; Total Carbohydrate 47g; Dietary Fiber 1g; Sugars 34g; Protein 4g

OATMEAL CARMELITAS

These rich, chewy bars have become a favorite of Pillsbury and are one of the most requested recipes ever. They will stay soft and delicious when stored tightly covered in the baking pan.

PREP TIME: 30 MINUTES
TOTAL TIME: 2 HOURS 55 MINUTES

MAKES 36 SERVINGS

Erlyce Larson, Kennedy, Minnesota
Bake-Off® Contest 18, 1967

CRUST

2 cups all-purpose flour

2 cups quick-cooking rolled oats

1½ cups firmly packed brown sugar

1 teaspoon baking soda

½ teaspoon salt

1¼ cups margarine or butter softened

FILLING

1 (12.5-oz.) jar (1 cup) caramel ice cream topping

3 tablespoons all-purpose flour

1 (6-oz.) pkg. (1 cup) semisweet chocolate chips

½ cup chopped nuts

1. Heat oven to 350°F. Grease 13x9-inch pan. In large bowl, blend all crust ingredients at low speed until crumbly. Press half of crumb mixture, about 3 cups, in bottom of greased pan. Reserve remaining crumb mixture for topping.

2. Bake at 350°F for 10 minutes. Meanwhile, in small bowl, combine caramel topping and 3 tablespoons flour. Remove partially baked crust from oven; sprinkle with chocolate chips and nuts. Drizzle evenly with caramel mixture; sprinkle with reserved crumb mixture.

3. Bake at 350°F for an additional 18 to 22 minutes or until golden brown. Cool completely. Refrigerate 1 to 2 hours until filling is set. Cut into bars.

1 Serving: Calories 200 (Calories from Fat 81); Total Fat 9g; Saturated Fat 2g; Trans Fat 1g; Cholesterol 0mg; Sodium 160mg; Total Carbohydrate 26g; Dietary Fiber 1g; Sugars 12g; Protein 2g

Sweet Treats Cakes, Pies and Desserts

Doris Wallace of Des Arc, Arizona, frosts her Cream-Filled Strawberry-Brownie Cake (page 382) at the 45th Bake-Off Contest in Orlando, Florida.

CHOCOLATE CHERRY SOUFFLÉ CUPCAKES

Cupcakes from sugar cookie dough? Yes! And they're super easy, super rich, and super surprising with preserves inside.

PREP TIME: 25 MINUTES
TOTAL TIME: 1 HOUR 30 MINUTES

MAKES 18 SERVINGS

Brenda Watts, Gaffney, South Carolina
Bake-Off® Contest 46, 2013

1 roll Pillsbury™ refrigerated sugar cookie dough

2 eggs, separated

½ cup chocolate flavored hazelnut spread

½ cup half-and-half

¾ cup red tart cherry preserves

1 can Pillsbury™ Creamy Supreme™ Milk Chocolate Frosting

18 maraschino cherries with stems

1. Heat oven to 350°F. Place paper baking cup in each of 18 regular-size muffin cups. Let cookie dough stand at room temperature for 10 minutes to soften.

2. In medium bowl, beat egg whites with electric mixer on medium-high speed 1 minute or until soft peaks form.

3. In large bowl, break up cookie dough. Add chocolate hazelnut spread, half-and-half and egg yolks. Beat with electric mixer on medium speed 1 minute or until well blended. Fold beaten egg whites into cookie mixture just until blended. Spoon batter into muffin cups, filling two-thirds full.

4. Bake 22 to 26 minutes or until toothpick inserted in center comes out clean. Cool in pans 3 minutes. Remove from pans to cooling rack. Cool completely, about 25 minutes.

5. Remove small 1-inch-deep circle from top center of each cupcake. Spoon about 2 teaspoons preserves in each cavity.

6. Pipe or spread frosting over top of each cupcake. Top each with maraschino cherry.

1 Serving: Calories 323 (Calories from Fat 131); Total Fat 15g; Saturated Fat 4.5g; Trans Fat 3g; Cholesterol 25mg; Sodium 121mg; Total Carbohydrate 43g; Dietary Fiber 0g; Sugars 37g; Protein 2g

BLACK BOTTOM CUPS

In this Bake-Off® Contest favorite, a delicate cream cheese filling is surrounded by moist and tender chocolate cake. For best results, bake these cupcakes in muffin cups lined with paper baking cups.

PREP TIME: 20 MINUTES
TOTAL TIME: 2 HOURS

MAKES 18 SERVINGS
(1 CUPCAKE PER SERVING)

Doris Geisert, Orange, California
Bake-Off® Contest 13, 1961

- 2 (3-oz.) pkg. cream cheese, softened
- ⅓ cup sugar
- 1 egg
- 1 (6-oz.) pkg. (1 cup) semisweet chocolate chips
- 1½ cups all-purpose flour
- 1 cup sugar
- ¼ cup unsweetened cocoa
- 1 teaspoon baking soda
- ½ teaspoon salt
- 1 cup water
- ⅓ cup oil
- 1 tablespoon vinegar
- 1 teaspoon vanilla
- ½ cup chopped almonds, if desired
- 2 tablespoons sugar, if desired

1. Heat oven to 350°F. Line 18 muffin cups with paper baking cups. In small bowl, combine cream cheese, ⅓ cup sugar and egg; mix well. Stir in chocolate chips; set aside. In large bowl, combine flour, 1 cup sugar, cocoa, baking soda and salt. Add water, oil, vinegar and vanilla; beat 2 minutes at medium speed. Fill paper-lined muffin cups ½ full. Top each with 1 tablespoon cream cheese mixture. Combine almonds and 2 tablespoons sugar; sprinkle evenly over cream cheese mixture.

2. Bake at 350°F for 20 to 30 minutes or until cream cheese mixture is light golden brown. Cool 15 minutes; remove from pans. Cool completely. Store in refrigerator.

1 Serving: Calories 250 (Calories from Fat 108); Total Fat 13g; Saturated Fat 4.5g; Trans Fat 0g; Cholesterol 21mg; Sodium 160mg; Total Carbohydrate 31g; Dietary Fiber 2g; Sugars 21g; Protein 3g

CARROT CUPCAKES
WITH COCONUT PECAN FROSTING

What a sweet and tasty way to get your veggies! Mix up 7 ingredients in 30 minutes to make easy cupcakes.

PREP TIME: 30 MINUTES
TOTAL TIME: 1 HOUR 30 MINUTES
MAKES 24 SERVINGS

Heidi Givler, Lenhartsville, Pennsylvania
Bake-Off® Contest 46, 2013

1 bag (11.8 oz) frozen honey Dijon carrots

1 box (15.25 oz) Pillsbury™ Classic Yellow Cake Mix

⅓ cup vegetable oil

3 eggs

1 cup water

½ cup golden raisins

¼ cup pecans, finely chopped

1 can Pillsbury™ Creamy Supreme™ Coconut Pecan Frosting

1. Heat oven to 375°F. Place paper baking cups in each of 24 regular-size muffin cups. Microwave frozen carrots as directed on bag 3 to 4 minutes to thaw. In food processor, place carrots. Cover; process until finely chopped.

2. In large bowl, beat cake mix, oil, eggs and water with electric mixer on low speed 30 seconds. Beat on high speed 2 minutes, scraping bowl occasionally, until blended. Fold in carrots, raisins and pecans. Spoon into muffin cups, filling three-fourths full.

3. Bake 23 to 25 minutes or until toothpick inserted in center comes out clean. Cool in pan 5 minutes; remove to cooling rack. Cool completely, about 30 minutes. Spread cupcakes with frosting.

1 Serving: Calories 230 (Calories from Fat 110); Total Fat 12g; Saturated Fat 3.5g; Trans Fat 1g; Cholesterol 25mg; Sodium 220mg; Total Carbohydrate 28g; Dietary Fiber 0g; Sugars 2g; Protein 2g

CRESCENT CARAMEL SWIRL

Here's a hot, chewy sweet roll made with easy refrigerated Crescents.

PREP TIME: 20 MINUTES
TOTAL TIME: 55 MINUTES

MAKES 12 SERVINGS

Hall of Fame

Lois Ann Groves, Greenwood Village, Colorado
Bake-Off® Contest 27, 1976 Grand Prize Winner and Hall of Fame

½ cup butter (do not use margarine)

½ cup chopped nuts

¾ cup packed brown sugar

1 tablespoon water

2 cans (8 oz each) Pillsbury™ refrigerated crescent dinner rolls or 2 cans (8 oz each) Pillsbury™ Crescent Recipe Creations™ refrigerated seamless dough sheet

1. Heat oven to 350°F. In 1-quart saucepan, melt butter. Coat bottom and sides of 12-cup fluted tube cake pan with 2 tablespoons of the melted butter; sprinkle pan with 3 tablespoons of the nuts. Add remaining nuts, brown sugar and water to remaining melted butter. Heat to boiling, stirring occasionally. Boil 1 minute, stirring constantly.

2. Remove dough from cans; do not unroll. Cut each long roll into 8 slices. Arrange 8 slices, cut side down, in nut-lined pan; separate layers of each pinwheel slightly. Spoon half of brown sugar mixture over dough. Place remaining 8 dough slices alternately over bottom layer. Spoon remaining brown sugar mixture over slices.

3. Bake 23 to 33 minutes or until deep golden brown. Cool 3 minutes. Turn upside down onto serving platter or waxed paper. Serve warm.

CLEVER IDEA: *If using Pillsbury™ Big & Flaky large refrigerated crescent dinner rolls, bake time will be closer to 33 minutes.*

1 Serving: Calories 300 (Calories from Fat 170); Total Fat 19g; Saturated Fat 8g; Trans Fat 2.5g; Cholesterol 20mg; Sodium 350mg; Total Carbohydrate 29g; Dietary Fiber 0g; Sugars 16g; Protein 3g

BANANA CRUNCH CAKE

Delicious ingredients come together in this crunchy banana cake—a wonderful dessert!

PREP TIME: 25 MINUTES
TOTAL TIME: 2 HOURS
40 MINUTES

MAKES 16 SERVINGS

Bonnie Brooks, Salisbury, Maryland
Bake-Off® Contest 24, 1973 Grand Prize Winner

½ cup all purpose or unbleached flour

1 cup coconut

1 cup rolled oats

¾ cup firmly packed brown sugar

½ cup chopped pecans

½ cup margarine or butter

1½ cups (2 large) sliced very ripe bananas

½ cup sour cream

4 eggs

1 (15.25-oz.) pkg. Pillsbury™ Moist Supreme™ Yellow Cake Mix

1. Heat oven to 350°F. Grease and flour 10-inch tube pan. Lightly spoon flour into measuring cup; level off. In medium bowl, combine flour, coconut, rolled oats, brown sugar and pecans; mix well. With fork or pastry blender, cut in margarine until mixture is crumbly. Set aside.

2. In large bowl, combine bananas, sour cream and eggs; beat at low speed until smooth. Add cake mix; beat 2 minutes at high speed. Spread ⅓ of batter in greased and floured pan; sprinkle with ⅓ of coconut mixture. Repeat layers 2 more times using remaining batter and coconut mixture, ending with coconut mixture.

3. Bake at 350°F for 50 to 60 minutes or until toothpick inserted near center comes out clean. Cool upright in pan 15 minutes. Remove cake from pan; place on serving plate, coconut side up. Cool 1 hour or until completely cooled.

1 Serving: Calories 314 (Calories from Fat 118); Total Fat 16g; Saturated Fat 5g; Trans Fat 1g; Cholesterol 55mg; Sodium 320mg; Total Carbohydrate 49g; Dietary Fiber 2g; Sugars 30g; Protein 5g

CRANBERRY-TOPPED CAKE

Bake this delicious cake topped with cranberry sauce and nuts—dessert ready in 1 hour 50 minutes.

PREP TIME: 30 MINUTES
TOTAL TIME: 1 HOUR 50 MINUTES
MAKES 9 SERVINGS

Joseph Serafino, Muskegon, Michigan
Bake-Off® Contest 1, 1949

TOPPING

⅔ cup canned jellied cranberry sauce (from 16-oz can)

⅓ cup chopped walnuts or pecans

3 tablespoons sugar

1 teaspoon grated lemon peel

¼ teaspoon ground cinnamon, if desired

CAKE

2 cups all-purpose flour

2 teaspoons baking powder

½ to 1 teaspoon salt

1 cup sugar

⅓ cup butter or margarine, softened

1 teaspoon lemon extract or grated lemon peel

2 eggs

¾ cup milk

1. Heat oven to 350°F. Generously grease 9-inch square pan with shortening; lightly flour. In medium bowl, mix all topping ingredients. Set aside.

2. In small bowl, mix flour, baking powder and salt. In large bowl, beat 1 cup sugar and the butter with electric mixer on medium speed until well blended. Add lemon extract and eggs; beat well. Alternately add flour mixture and milk to butter mixture, beating until well combined. Pour batter into pan.

3. Drop topping by teaspoonfuls evenly onto batter. Spread topping over batter.

4. Bake 42 to 47 minutes or until toothpick inserted in center comes out clean. Cool at least 30 minutes. Serve warm or cool.

CLEVER IDEA: *Do you have leftover jellied cranberry sauce from your turkey day dinner? Perfect! Use it for this tasty little cake. Serve with vanilla ice cream or frozen yogurt.*

1 Serving: Calories 370 (Calories from Fat 110); Total Fat 12g; Saturated Fat 3g; Trans Fat 1.5g; Cholesterol 50mg; Sodium 326mg; Total Carbohydrate 58g; Dietary Fiber 1g; Sugars 35g; Protein 6g

CARAMEL APPLE CAKE

In the 1970s, homespun desserts edged out earlier elaborate dessert entries. Caramel and apple was a popular flavor combination. This family-favorite apple-nut sheet cake shows why.

PREP TIME: 20 MINUTES
TOTAL TIME: 2 HOURS

MAKES 15 SERVINGS

Josephine DeMarco, Chicago, Illinois
Bake-Off® Contest 27, 1976

CAKE

1¾ cups all-purpose flour

1½ cups firmly packed brown sugar

½ teaspoon salt

½ teaspoon baking powder

½ teaspoon baking soda

1½ teaspoons cinnamon

1 teaspoon vanilla

¾ cup margarine or butter, softened

3 eggs

1½ cups (2 to 3 medium) finely chopped peeled apples

½ to 1 cup chopped nuts

½ cup raisins, if desired

FROSTING

2 cups powdered sugar

¼ teaspoon cinnamon

¼ cup margarine or butter, melted

½ teaspoon vanilla

4 to 5 teaspoons milk

1. Heat oven to 350°F. Grease and flour 13x9-inch pan. In large bowl, combine flour, brown sugar, salt, baking powder, baking soda, 1¹⁄₂ teaspoons cinnamon, 1 teaspoon vanilla, ³⁄₄ cup margarine and eggs; beat 3 minutes at medium speed. Stir in apples, nuts and raisins. Pour batter into greased and floured pan.

2. Bake at 350°F for 30 to 40 minutes or until toothpick inserted in center comes out clean. Cool completely.

3. In small bowl, blend all frosting ingredients, adding enough milk for desired spreading consistency. Spread over cooled cake.

1 Serving: Calories 390 (Calories from Fat 140); Total Fat 18g; Saturated Fat 2.5g; Trans Fat 3g; Cholesterol 37mg; Sodium 280mg; Total Carbohydrate 56g; Dietary Fiber 1g; Sugars 42g; Protein 4g

NUTTY GRAHAM PICNIC CAKE

This orange-flavored cake is topped with a brown sugar glaze for just the right touch.

PREP TIME: 30 MINUTES
TOTAL TIME: 2 HOURS
30 MINUTES
MAKES 16 SERVINGS

Esther Tomich, San Pedro, California
Bake-Off® Contest 28, 1978 Grand Prize Winner

CAKE

- 2 cups Pillsbury™ BEST™ All Purpose or Unbleached Flour
- 1 cup (14 squares) finely crushed graham crackers or graham cracker crumbs
- 1 cup firmly packed brown sugar
- ½ cup sugar
- 1 teaspoon baking powder
- 1 teaspoon baking soda
- 1 teaspoon salt
- ½ teaspoon cinnamon
- 1 cup margarine or butter, softened
- 1 cup orange juice
- 1 tablespoon grated orange peel
- 3 eggs
- 1 cup chopped nuts

GLAZE

- 2 tablespoons brown sugar
- 5 teaspoons milk
- 1 tablespoon margarine or butter
- ¾ cup powdered sugar
- ¼ cup chopped nuts

1. Heat oven to 350°F. Generously grease and flour 12-cup fluted tube cake pan or 10-inch tube pan. In large bowl, combine all cake ingredients except nuts; beat 3 minutes at medium speed. By hand, stir in 1 cup nuts. Pour batter into greased and floured pan.

2. Bake at 350°F for 40 to 60 minutes or until toothpick inserted in center comes out clean. Cool upright in pan 15 minutes; invert onto serving plate. Cool 1 hour or until completely cooled.

3. In small saucepan, combine 2 tablespoons brown sugar, milk and 1 tablespoon margarine; cook over low heat just until sugar is dissolved, stirring constantly. Remove from heat. Stir in powdered sugar; blend until smooth. Drizzle over cake; sprinkle with ¼ cup nuts.

1 Serving: Calories 390 (Calories from Fat 180); Total Fat 20g; Saturated Fat 3g; Trans Fat 3g; Cholesterol 40mg; Sodium 440mg; Total Carbohydrate 47g; Dietary Fiber 1g; Sugars 30g; Protein 5g

STREUSEL SPICE CAKE

Relish this spiced cake packed with coconut, chocolate, nuts and a hint of cinnamon— a lavish dessert.

PREP TIME: 30 MINUTES
TOTAL TIME: 3 HOURS 10 MINUTES
MAKES 16 SERVINGS

Rose DeDominicis, Verona, Pennsylvania
Bake-Off® Contest 23, 1972 Grand Prize Winner

CAKE

- 1 (15.25-oz.) pkg. Pillsbury™ Moist Supreme™ Yellow Cake Mix
- ¾ cup milk
- ½ cup margarine or butter, softened
- 5 eggs
- ¼ cup coconut
- ¼ cup chopped nuts
- 1 oz. unsweetened chocolate, melted

FILLING

- ½ cup coconut
- ½ cup chopped nuts
- ½ cup firmly packed brown sugar
- 2 tablespoons Pillsbury™ BEST™ All Purpose or Unbleached Flour
- 2 teaspoons cinnamon

GLAZE

- 1 cup powdered sugar
- 1 tablespoon margarine or butter, softened
- 2 to 3 tablespoons milk

1. Heat oven to 350°F. Grease and flour 10-inch tube or 12-cup fluted tube cake pan. In large bowl, combine cake mix, ¾ cup milk, ½ cup margarine and eggs; beat at low speed until moistened. Beat 2 minutes at high speed. Stir in ¼ cup coconut and ¼ cup nuts. With spoon, marble chocolate through batter. Pour half of batter (about 2 cups) into greased and floured pan.

2. In small bowl, combine all filling ingredients; reserve ½ cup filling. Sprinkle remaining filling over batter in pan. Cover with remaining batter; sprinkle with ½ cup reserved filling.

3. Bake at 350°F for 55 to 70 minutes or until toothpick inserted near center comes out clean. Cool upright in pan 30 minutes. Remove from pan. Cool 1 hour or until completely cooled.

4. In small bowl, blend all glaze ingredients until smooth, adding enough milk for desired drizzling consistency. Drizzle over cake.

1 Serving: Calories 310 (Calories from Fat 150); Total Fat 17g; Saturated Fat 5g; Trans Fat 1g; Cholesterol 65mg; Sodium 330mg; Total Carbohydrate 45g; Dietary Fiber 1g; Sugars 32g; Protein 5g

BROWN BUTTER APRICOT CAKE

To split the cake layers evenly, insert toothpicks around the middle as a cutting guide line and cut with a long-bladed sharp knife or a long piece of dental floss.

PREP TIME: 35 MINUTES
TOTAL TIME: 2 HOURS 5 MINUTES
MAKES 12 SERVINGS

Shirley Sauber, Indianapolis, Indiana
Bake-Off® Contest 32, 1986

CAKE

- 1 (1 lb. 2.25-oz.) pkg. pudding-included white cake mix
- 1¼ cups water
- ⅓ cup oil
- 1 tablespoon grated orange peel
- 1 teaspoon orange extract
- 3 egg whites

FROSTING AND FILLING

- ½ cup butter (do not use margarine)
- 3 to 4 cups powdered sugar
- ⅓ cup orange juice
- ⅔ cup apricot preserves
- ⅓ cup chopped walnuts or pecans

1. Heat oven to 350°F. Grease and flour two 8- or 9-inch round cake pans. In large bowl, combine all cake ingredients at low speed until moistened. Beat 2 minutes at high speed. Pour batter into greased and floured pans.

2. Bake at 350°F for 20 to 30 minutes or until toothpick inserted in center comes out clean. Cool 15 minutes; remove from pans. Cool completely.

3. Meanwhile, in small heavy saucepan over medium heat, brown butter until light golden brown, stirring constantly. Remove from heat; cool completely. In large bowl, combine browned butter, 3 cups powdered sugar and orange juice at low speed until moistened. Beat 2 minutes at medium speed or until smooth and well blended. Beat in up to 1 cup additional powdered sugar if necessary for desired spreading consistency.

4. To assemble cake, slice each cake layer in half horizontally; remove top half of each layer. Spread ⅓ cup of the preserves on bottom half of each layer; replace top half. Place 1 filled layer top side down on serving plate; spread with ½ cup of frosting mixture. Top with second layer, top side up. Frost sides and top of cake with remaining frosting. Sprinkle walnuts over cake. Refrigerate until serving time. Store in refrigerator.

1 Serving: Calories 540 (Calories from Fat 178); Total Fat 20g; Saturated Fat 7g; Trans Fat 0g; Cholesterol 20mg; Sodium 370mg; Total Carbohydrate 87g; Dietary Fiber 1g; Sugars 69g; Protein 3g

KENTUCKY BUTTER CAKE

This was the year the contest became popularly known simply as "The Bake-Off®." Old family recipes were still eligible, if they had a new twist. Here the idea was the hot butter sauce poured slowly over the buttermilk pound cake as it came from the oven.

PREP TIME: 20 MINUTES
TOTAL TIME: 3 HOURS 10 MINUTES

MAKES 12 SERVINGS

Nell Lewis, Platte City, Missouri
Bake-Off® Contest 15, 1963

CAKE

- 3 cups all-purpose flour
- 2 cups sugar
- 1 teaspoon salt
- 1 teaspoon baking powder
- ½ teaspoon baking soda
- 1 cup buttermilk
- 1 cup butter or margarine, softened
- 2 teaspoons vanilla or rum extract
- 4 eggs

BUTTER SAUCE

- ¾ cup sugar
- ⅓ cup butter or margarine
- 3 tablespoons water
- 1 to 2 teaspoons vanilla or rum extract

GARNISH

- 2 to 3 teaspoons powdered sugar

1. Heat oven to 325°F. Generously grease and lightly flour 12-cup Bundt pan or 10-inch tube pan. In large bowl, combine all cake ingredients; blend at low speed until moistened. Beat 3 minutes at medium speed. Pour batter into greased and floured pan.

2. Bake at 325°F for 55 to 70 minutes or until toothpick inserted in center comes out clean.

3. In small saucepan, combine all sauce ingredients; cook over low heat, stirring occasionally, until butter melts. DO NOT BOIL. Using long-tined fork, pierce cake 10 to 12 times. Slowly pour hot sauce over warm cake. Let stand 5 to 10 minutes or until sauce is absorbed. Invert cake onto serving plate. Allow to cool for 1½ hours. Just before serving, sprinkle with powdered sugar. Serve with whipped cream, if desired.

CLEVER IDEA: *To substitute for buttermilk, use 1 tablespoon vinegar or lemon juice plus milk to make 1 cup.*

1 Serving: Calories 510 (Calories from Fat 200); Total Fat 23g; Saturated Fat 13.5g; Trans Fat 1g; Cholesterol 117mg; Sodium 520mg; Total Carbohydrate 72g; Dietary Fiber 1g; Sugars 48g; Protein 6g

BUTTERCREAM POUND CAKE

Swirls of poppy seed add interest to this lemon pound cake. This recipe originally used a dry frosting mix that is no longer available. Our updated version has the delicious buttery flavor of the original recipe.

PREP TIME: 30 MINUTES
TOTAL TIME: 2 HOURS
55 MINUTES

MAKES 16 SERVINGS

Phyllis Lidert, Fort Lauderdale, Florida
Bake-Off® Contest 19, 1968 Grand Prize Winner

CAKE

- 1 lb. (2 cups) butter, softened (do not use margarine)
- 2½ cups powdered sugar
- 6 eggs
- 2 teaspoons grated lemon peel
- 3 tablespoons lemon juice
- 4 cups Pillsbury™ BEST™ All Purpose or Unbleached Flour
- 3 teaspoons baking powder
- 1 (12½-oz.) can poppy seed filling

GLAZE

- 1 cup powdered sugar
- 1 to 2 tablespoons lemon juice or milk

1. Heat oven to 350°F. Beat butter in large bowl until light and fluffy. Gradually add 2½ cups powdered sugar, beating until well combined. At medium speed, add eggs 1 at a time, beating well after each addition. Beat in lemon peel and 3 tablespoons lemon juice. Lightly spoon flour into measuring cup; level off. At low speed, gradually beat in flour and baking powder; blend well.

2. In medium bowl, combine 3 cups batter with poppy seed filling; blend well. Spread half of plain batter in bottom of ungreased 10-inch tube pan. Alternately add spoonfuls of poppy seed batter and remaining plain batter.

3. Bake at 350°F for 1 hour 15 minutes to 1 hour 25 minutes or until toothpick inserted near center comes out clean. Cool 15 minutes; remove from pan. Cool 1 hour or until completely cooled.

4. In small bowl, combine glaze ingredients, adding enough lemon juice for desired drizzling consistency; blend until smooth. Drizzle over cake.

1 Serving: Calories 520 (Calories from Fat 240);
Total Fat 27g; Saturated Fat 15g; Trans Fat 1g;
Cholesterol 140mg; Sodium 360mg;
Total Carbohydrate 62g; Dietary Fiber 3g;
Sugars 35g; Protein 7g

ALMOND-FILLED COOKIE CAKE

Grated lemon peel brings out the flavor of almonds in a moist filling of a sandwich cookie-like cake.

PREP TIME: 25 MINUTES
TOTAL TIME: 2 HOURS 55 MINUTES
MAKES 24 SERVINGS

Elizabeth Meijer, Tucson, Arizona
Bake-Off® Contest 30, 1982 Grand Prize Winner

CRUST

- 2⅔ cups Pillsbury™ BEST™ All Purpose or Unbleached Flour
- 1⅓ cups sugar
- 1⅓ cups butter, softened (do not use margarine)
- ½ teaspoon salt
- 1 egg

FILLING

- 1 cup finely chopped almonds
- ½ cup sugar
- 1 teaspoon grated lemon peel
- 1 egg, slightly beaten
- 4 whole blanched almonds

1. Heat oven to 325°F. Place cookie sheet in oven to preheat. Grease 10- or 9-inch springform pan. In large bowl, blend all crust ingredients at low speed until dough forms. If desired, refrigerate dough for easier handling. Divide dough in half. Spread half in bottom of greased pan to form crust.

2. In small bowl, combine all filling ingredients except whole almonds; blend well. Spread over crust to within ½ inch of sides of pan.

3. Between 2 sheets of waxed paper, press remaining dough to 10- or 9-inch round. Remove top sheet of waxed paper; place dough over filling. Remove waxed paper; press dough in place. Top with whole almonds.

4. Place cake on preheated cookie sheet. Bake at 325°F for 65 to 75 minutes or until top is light golden brown. Cool 15 minutes; remove sides of pan. Cool 1 hour or until completely cooled.

1 Serving: Calories 250 (Calories from Fat 130); Total Fat 14g; Saturated Fat 7g; Trans Fat 1g; Cholesterol 45mg; Sodium 145mg; Total Carbohydrate 27g; Dietary Fiber 1g; Sugars 16g; Protein 3g

MARDI GRAS PARTY CAKE

Let the good times roll with this scrumptious butterscotch/coconut-filled cake.

PREP TIME: 60 MINUTES
TOTAL TIME: 3 HOURS
MAKES 16 SERVINGS

Eunice Surles, Lake Charles, Louisiana
Bake-Off® Contest 11, 1959 Grand Prize Winner

CAKE

⅔ cup butterscotch chips

¼ cup water

2¼ cups Pillsbury™ BEST™ All Purpose or Unbleached Flour

1¼ cups sugar

1 teaspoon baking soda

1 teaspoon salt

½ teaspoon baking powder

1 cup buttermilk

½ cup shortening

3 eggs

FILLING

½ cup sugar

1 tablespoon cornstarch

½ cup half-and-half or evaporated milk

⅓ cup water

⅓ cup butterscotch chips

1 egg, slightly beaten

2 tablespoons margarine or butter

1 cup coconut

1 cup chopped nuts

SEAFOAM CREAM

1 cup whipping cream

¼ cup firmly packed brown sugar

½ teaspoon vanilla

1. Heat oven to 350°F. Generously grease and flour two 9-inch round cake pans. In small saucepan over low heat, melt $^2/_3$ cup butterscotch chips in $^1/_4$ cup water, stirring until smooth. Cool slightly.

2. Lightly spoon flour into measuring cup; level off. In large bowl, combine flour, all remaining cake ingredients and cooled butterscotch mixture; beat at low speed until moistened. Beat 3 minutes at medium speed. Pour batter into greased and floured pans.

3. Bake at 350°F for 20 to 30 minutes or until toothpick inserted in center comes out clean. Cool 10 minutes; remove from pans. Cool 30 minutes or until completely cooled.

4. In medium saucepan, combine $^1/_2$ cup sugar and cornstarch; stir in half-and-half, $^1/_3$ cup water, $^1/_3$ cup butterscotch chips and 1 egg. Cook over medium heat until mixture thickens, stirring constantly. Remove from heat. Stir in margarine, coconut and nuts; cool slightly.

5. In small bowl, beat whipping cream until soft peaks form. Gradually add brown sugar and vanilla, beating until stiff peaks form.

6. To assemble cake, place 1 cake layer, top side down, on serving plate. Spread with half of filling mixture. Top with second layer, top side up; spread remaining filling on top to within $^1/_2$ inch of edge. Frost sides and top edge of cake with seafoam cream. Refrigerate at least 1 hour before serving. Store in refrigerator.

CLEVER IDEAS:

- *To substitute for buttermilk, use 1 teaspoon vinegar or lemon juice plus milk to make 1 cup.*
- *Cake can be baked in 13x9-inch pan. Grease bottom only of pan. Bake at 350°F for 30 to 35 minutes or until toothpick inserted in center comes out clean. Cool completely. Spread top of cooled cake with filling mixture. Serve topped with seafoam cream.*

1 Serving: Calories 450 (Calories from Fat 230); Total Fat 25g; Saturated Fat 11g; Trans Fat 1g; Cholesterol 75mg; Sodium 300mg; Total Carbohydrate 51g; Dietary Fiber 1g; Sugars 36g; Protein 6g

"MY INSPIRATION" CAKE

This beautiful cake, layered with pecans and chocolate, looks as if it came straight from the gourmet bakery down the street.

PREP TIME: 25 MINUTES
TOTAL TIME: 2 HOURS
10 MINUTES

MAKES 16 SERVINGS

Lois Kanago, Denver, Colorado
Bake-Off® Contest 5, 1953 Grand Prize Winner

CAKE

- 1 cup chopped pecans
- 2¼ cups Pillsbury™ BEST™ All Purpose or Unbleached Flour
- 1½ cups sugar
- 4 teaspoons baking powder
- ½ teaspoon salt
- ⅔ cup shortening
- 1¼ cups milk
- 1 teaspoon vanilla
- 4 egg whites
- 2 oz. semisweet chocolate, grated

FROSTING

- ½ cup sugar
- 2 oz. unsweetened chocolate
- ¼ cup water
- ½ cup shortening
- 1 teaspoon vanilla
- 2¼ cups powdered sugar
- 1 to 2 tablespoons water

1. Heat oven to 350°F. Grease and flour two 9-inch round cake pans. Sprinkle pecans evenly in bottom of greased and floured pans.

2. Lightly spoon flour into measuring cup; level off. In large bowl, combine all remaining cake ingredients except egg whites and chocolate; beat 1½ minutes at medium speed. Add egg whites; beat 1½ minutes. Carefully spoon ¼ of batter into each pecan-lined pan. Sprinkle with grated chocolate. Spoon remaining batter over grated chocolate; spread carefully.

3. Bake at 350°F for 30 to 40 minutes or until cake is golden brown and top springs back when touched lightly in center. Cool 10 minutes; remove from pans. Cool 1 hour or until completely cooled.

4. Meanwhile, in small saucepan, combine ½ cup sugar, unsweetened chocolate and ¼ cup water; cook over low heat until melted, stirring constantly until smooth. Remove from heat; cool.

5. In small bowl, combine ½ cup shortening and 1 teaspoon vanilla. Gradually beat in 2 cups of the powdered sugar until well blended. Reserve ⅓ cup white frosting. To remaining frosting, add cooled chocolate, remaining ¼ cup powdered sugar and enough water for desired spreading consistency.

6. To assemble cake, place 1 layer, pecan side up, on serving plate. Spread with about ¹⁄₂ cup chocolate frosting. Top with second layer, pecan side up. Frost sides and ¹⁄₂ inch around top edge of cake with remaining chocolate frosting. If necessary, thin reserved white frosting with enough water for desired piping consistency; pipe around edge of nuts on top of cake.

CLEVER IDEA: *For easy removal, use parchment paper to prevent the cake from sticking to the pan. Cut rounds of parchment paper to fit the bottom of your cake pans. Simply loosen the baked cake around the edge with the tip of a sharp knife before turning the cake out onto a rack. Carefully peel back the parchment before assembling the cake.*

1 Serving: Calories 470 (Calories from Fat 210); Total Fat 23g; Saturated Fat 6g; Trans Fat 2g; Cholesterol 0mg; Sodium 210mg; Total Carbohydrate 61g; Dietary Fiber 2g; Sugars 45g; Protein 4g

PIÑA COLADA PARTY CAKE

Enjoy piña colada flavors in a cake!

PREP TIME: 30 MINUTES
TOTAL TIME: 1 HOUR 30 MINUTES
MAKES 12 SERVINGS

Jeanne Bruns, Tucson, Arizona
Bake-Off® Contest 30, 1982

CAKE

1 cup coconut

1 (1 lb. 2.25-oz.) pkg. pudding-included white cake mix

½ cup water

½ cup pineapple juice

⅓ cup oil

¼ cup rum

4 egg whites

½ cup pineapple juice

½ cup sugar

FROSTING

1 (16-oz.) can vanilla frosting

1 tablespoon rum or ½ teaspoon rum extract

½ cup reserved toasted coconut

1. Heat oven to 350°F. Sprinkle 1 cup coconut on cookie sheet. Bake at 350°F for 5 to 7 minutes or until toasted.

2. Meanwhile, grease and flour 13x9-inch pan. In large bowl, combine cake mix, water, ½ cup pineapple juice, oil, ¼ cup rum and egg whites; beat at low speed until moistened. Beat 2 minutes at high speed.

3. Stir in ½ cup of the toasted coconut; reserve remaining ½ cup for frosting. Pour into greased and floured pan.

4. Bake at 350°F for 25 to 35 minutes or until toothpick inserted in center comes out clean. Cool 10 minutes.

5. In small saucepan, combine ½ cup pineapple juice and sugar; bring to a boil. With long-tined fork, prick cake at ½-inch intervals. Pour hot pineapple mixture over cake. Cool 1 hour or until completely cooled.

6. In small bowl, combine frosting and 1 tablespoon rum; blend well. Frost cake. Sprinkle with reserved ½ cup coconut. Refrigerate until serving time.

CLEVER IDEA: *To substitute for rum, use ¼ cup water plus 1 teaspoon rum extract.*

1 Serving: Calories 488 (Calories from Fat 163); Total Fat 18g; Saturated Fat 5g; Trans Fat 0g; Cholesterol 0mg; Sodium 396mg; Total Carbohydrate 75g; Dietary Fiber 1g; Sugars 58g; Protein 3g

ORANGE KISS-ME CAKE

Looking for a tasty dessert? Then check out this orange cake packed with walnuts and raisins.

PREP TIME: 30 MINUTES
TOTAL TIME: 2 HOURS
15 MINUTES
MAKES 16 SERVINGS

Lily Wuebel, Redwood City, California
Bake-Off® Contest 2, 1950 Grand Prize Winner

CAKE

1 orange

1 cup raisins

⅓ cup walnuts

2 cups Pillsbury™ BEST™ All Purpose or Unbleached Flour

1 cup sugar

1 teaspoon baking soda

1 teaspoon salt

1 cup milk

½ cup margarine or butter, softened, or shortening

2 eggs

TOPPING

Reserved ⅓ cup orange juice

⅓ cup sugar

1 teaspoon cinnamon

¼ cup finely chopped walnuts

1. Heat oven to 350°F. Grease and flour 13x9-inch pan. Squeeze orange, reserving ⅓ cup juice for topping; remove seeds. In blender container, food processor bowl with metal blade or food mill, grind together orange peel and pulp, raisins and ⅓ cup walnuts. Set aside.

2. Lightly spoon flour into measuring cup; level off. In large bowl, combine flour and all remaining cake ingredients at low speed until moistened; beat 3 minutes at medium speed. Stir in orange-raisin mixture. Pour batter into greased and floured pan.

3. Bake at 350°F for 35 to 45 minutes or until toothpick inserted in center comes out clean. Drizzle reserved ⅓ cup orange juice over warm cake in pan.

4. In small bowl, combine ⅓ cup sugar and cinnamon; mix well. Stir in ¼ cup walnuts; sprinkle over cake. Cool 1 hour or until completely cooled.

1 Serving: Calories 270 (Calories from Fat 90); Total Fat 10g; Saturated Fat 2g; Trans Fat 1g; Cholesterol 30mg; Sodium 300mg; Total Carbohydrate 40g; Dietary Fiber 2g; Sugars 25g; Protein 4g

STARLIGHT DOUBLE-DELIGHT CAKE

Helen Weston's 1951 grand prize winner uses a unique technique: some of the frosting is blended with the cake batter before it's baked, yielding a superbly moist, rich cake.

PREP TIME: 25 MINUTES
TOTAL TIME: 2 HOURS 10 MINUTES
MAKES 12 SERVINGS

Helen Weston, La Jolla, California
Bake-Off® Contest 3, 1951 Grand Prize Winner

FROSTING

2 (3-oz.) pkg. cream cheese, softened

½ cup margarine or butter, softened

½ teaspoon vanilla

½ teaspoon peppermint extract

6 cups powdered sugar

¼ cup hot water

4 oz. semisweet chocolate, melted

CAKE

¼ cup margarine or butter, softened

3 eggs

2 cups Pillsbury™ BEST™ All Purpose or Unbleached Flour

1½ teaspoons baking soda

1 teaspoon salt

¾ cup milk

1. Heat oven to 350°F. Grease and flour two 9-inch round cake pans. In large bowl, combine cream cheese, ¹⁄₂ cup margarine, vanilla and peppermint extract; blend until smooth. Add powdered sugar alternately with hot water, beating until smooth. Add chocolate; blend well.

2. In another large bowl, combine 2 cups of the frosting mixture and ¹⁄₄ cup margarine; blend well. Beat in eggs 1 at a time, beating well after each addition. Lightly spoon flour into measuring cup; level off. Add flour, baking soda, salt and milk; beat until smooth. Pour batter evenly into greased and floured pans.

3. Bake at 350°F for 30 to 40 minutes or until toothpick inserted in center comes out clean. Cool 5 minutes; remove from pans. Cool 1 hour or until completely cooled.

4. To assemble cake, place 1 layer, top side down, on serving plate. Spread with about ¹⁄₄ of frosting. Top with second layer, top side up. Spread sides and top of cake with remaining frosting. Store in refrigerator.

1 Serving: Calories 550 (Calories from Fat 190); Total Fat 21g; Saturated Fat 8g; Trans Fat 3g; Cholesterol 70mg; Sodium 540mg; Total Carbohydrate 83g; Dietary Fiber 1g; Sugars 65g; Protein 6g

CHOCOLATE 'TATO CAKE

When convenience products were still new, a quick tip in the original 1961 recipe was to use reconstituted mashed potato flakes for the cooked fresh potato. Now they are included in the recipe, where they help keep this chocolate-glazed tube cake moist and delicious.

PREP TIME: 30 MINUTES
TOTAL TIME: 3 HOURS

MAKES 20 SERVINGS

Rosalie Giuffre, Milwaukee, Wisconsin
Bake-Off® Contest 13, 1961

CAKE

4 oz. semisweet chocolate
1 cup mashed potato flakes
1 cup boiling water
1¾ cups all-purpose flour
1¼ cups sugar
1¼ teaspoons baking soda
1 teaspoon salt
1 teaspoon vanilla
½ cup margarine, softened, or shortening
½ cup dairy sour cream
3 eggs
½ cup chopped pecans, if desired

GLAZE

4 oz. semisweet chocolate
1 tablespoon water
1 tablespoon margarine or butter
½ cup powdered sugar
½ teaspoon vanilla

1. Heat oven to 350°F. Generously grease 12-cup Bundt or 10-inch tube pan. Break 4 oz. chocolate into pieces; place in large bowl. Add potato flakes; pour boiling water over flakes and chocolate. Let stand 5 minutes or until potato flakes are softened and chocolate is melted; stir to combine.

2. Lightly spoon flour into a measuring cup; level off. Add flour and all remaining cake ingredients except pecans. Blend at low speed until moistened; beat 3 minutes at medium speed. Stir in pecans. Pour batter into greased pan.

3. Bake at 350°F for 45 to 60 minutes or until toothpick inserted near center comes out clean. Cool upright in pan 30 minutes; invert onto serving plate to cool completely.

4. In small saucepan over low heat, melt 4 oz. chocolate with water and 1 tablespoon margarine. Remove from heat. Add powdered sugar and ½ teaspoon vanilla, beating until smooth. Stir in additional water, a few drops at a time, if needed for desired glaze consistency. Immediately spoon glaze over cooled cake, allowing some to run down sides.

1 Serving: Calories 280 (Calories from Fat 120); Total Fat 13g; Saturated Fat 4g; Trans Fat 1g; Cholesterol 35mg; Sodium 260mg; Total Carbohydrate 37g; Dietary Fiber 1g; Sugars 26g; Protein 3g

TUNNEL OF FUDGE CAKE

This recipe, arguably the recipe most closely identified with the Bake-Off® Contest, mysteriously develops a "tunnel of fudge" filling as it bakes. Don't scrimp on the nuts, or it won't work!

PREP TIME: 35 MINUTES
TOTAL TIME: 4 HOURS
30 MINUTES

MAKES 16 SERVINGS

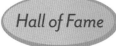
Hall of Fame

Ella Rita Helfrich, Houston, Texas
Bake-Off® Contest 17, 1966 Hall of Fame

CAKE

1¾ cups sugar

1¾ cups margarine or butter, softened

6 eggs

2 cups powdered sugar

2¼ cups Pillsbury™ BEST™ All Purpose or Unbleached Flour

¾ cup unsweetened cocoa

2 cups chopped walnuts

GLAZE

¾ cup powdered sugar

¼ cup unsweetened cocoa

4 to 6 teaspoons milk

1. Heat oven to 350°F. Grease and flour 12-cup fluted tube cake pan or 10-inch tube pan. In large bowl, combine sugar and margarine; beat until light and fluffy. Add eggs 1 at a time, beating well after each addition. Gradually add 2 cups powdered sugar; blend well. By hand, stir in flour and remaining cake ingredients until well blended. Spoon batter into greased and floured pan; spread evenly.

2. Bake at 350°F for 45 to 50 minutes or until top is set and edges are beginning to pull away from sides of pan. Cool upright in pan on wire rack 1½ hours. Invert onto serving plate; cool at least 2 hours.

3. In small bowl, combine all glaze ingredients, adding enough milk for desired drizzling consistency. Spoon over top of cake, allowing some to run down sides. Store tightly covered.

CLEVER IDEAS:

- *Nuts are essential for the success of this recipe.*

- *Since this cake has a soft filling, an ordinary doneness test cannot be used. Accurate oven temperature and baking times are essential.*

1 Serving: Calories 570 (Calories from Fat 290); Total Fat 32g; Saturated Fat 6g; Trans Fat 4g; Cholesterol 80mg; Sodium 260mg; Total Carbohydrate 62g; Dietary Fiber 3g; Sugars 43g; Protein 8g

CARAMEL IN-BETWEEN FUDGE CAKE

Enjoy this chocolate frosted fudge cake that's made using Pillsbury™ Moist Supreme™ cake mix with pudding and filled with caramels—a delicious dessert.

PREP TIME: 35 MINUTES
TOTAL TIME: 2 HOURS
20 MINUTES

MAKES 18 SERVINGS

Judee Disco, Norwich, Connecticut
Bake-Off® Contest 21, 1970

FILLING

28 caramels, unwrapped

1 tablespoon butter or margarine

1 can (14 oz) sweetened condensed milk (not evaporated)

CAKE

1 box Pillsbury™ Moist Supreme™ dark chocolate cake mix with pudding

1 cup water

3 eggs

FROSTING AND GARNISH

½ cup butter or margarine, softened

2 envelopes (1 oz each) pre-melted unsweetened baking chocolate

3 tablespoons half-and-half

1 teaspoon vanilla

2 cups powdered sugar

⅓ cup sliced almonds, toasted

1. Heat oven to 350°F. Grease bottom only of 13x9-inch pan with shortening; lightly flour. In 2-quart saucepan, cook and stir filling ingredients over medium-low heat until caramels are melted. Set aside.

2. In large bowl, beat cake ingredients with electric mixer on low speed 30 seconds. Beat on medium speed 2 minutes. Spread half of batter in pan. Bake 20 minutes. Spread filling over partially baked cake; cover with remaining batter. Bake 20 to 25 minutes or until toothpick inserted in center comes out clean. Cool completely.

3. In small bowl, beat ½ cup butter, the chocolate, half-and-half and vanilla with electric mixer on medium speed until well blended. Beat in powdered sugar until light and fluffy. Frost cooled cake; sprinkle with almonds.

CLEVER IDEA: *To toast almonds, bake uncovered in ungreased shallow pan in 350°F oven about 10 minutes, stirring occasionally, until golden brown.*

1 Serving: Calories 390 (Calories from Fat 130); Total Fat 14g; Saturated Fat 8g; Trans Fat 0.5g; Cholesterol 60mg; Sodium 360mg; Total Carbohydrate 60g; Dietary Fiber 2g; Sugars 45g; Protein 6g

MOLTEN MOCHA CAKES

Enjoy this delicious coffee-flavored chocolate cake that's garnished with strawberries and served with ice cream—a perfect dessert.

PREP TIME: 20 MINUTES
TOTAL TIME: 40 MINUTES

MAKES 12 SERVINGS

Janet Barton, Sandy, Utah
Bake-Off® Contest 40, 2002

1 cup semisweet chocolate chips

½ cup butter

3 eggs

3 egg yolks

1 (15.8-oz.) pkg. Pillsbury™ Chocolatier Collection™ Double Chocolate Premium Brownie Mix

2 tablespoons coffee-flavored liqueur or strong brewed coffee

12 fresh strawberries or 1 pint (2 cups) fresh raspberries

12 fresh mint sprigs

1 quart (4 cups) vanilla ice cream

1. Heat oven to 400°F. Grease 12 (2³⁄₄x1¹⁄₄-inch) nonstick muffin cups. In medium microwave-safe bowl, combine chocolate chips and butter. Microwave on High for 45 to 60 seconds or until melted, stirring every 15 seconds until smooth. Cool 5 minutes.

2. In large bowl, combine eggs and egg yolks; beat with electric mixer at high speed for 4 to 6 minutes or until foamy and doubled in size. Reserve chocolate syrup packet from brownie mix. Gradually add brownie mix to egg mixture, beating until well blended. Fold in melted chocolate chip mixture and liqueur. Divide batter evenly into greased muffin cups. (Cups will be full.)

3. Bake at 400°F for 10 to 14 minutes or until edges are set. DO NOT OVERBAKE. Centers will be soft. Cool 2 minutes.

4. While cakes are cooling, drizzle chocolate syrup from packet onto each individual serving plate. Run knife around edge of each cake to loosen. Invert warm cake over chocolate on each plate. Garnish each serving with strawberry and mint sprig. Serve with ice cream.

1 Serving: Calories 406 (Calories from Fat 177); Total Fat 23g; Saturated Fat 12g; Trans Fat 0g; Cholesterol 145mg; Sodium 230mg; Total Carbohydrate 51g; Dietary Fiber 1g; Sugars 37g; Protein 6g

PEPPERMINT SWIRL FUDGE NUT CAKE

Here's a chocolate cake that's made with white cake mix! The reason: with the addition of crème de menthe syrup, half the batter becomes the green peppermint swirl. The result: a picture-pretty cake that tastes as good as it looks.

PREP TIME: 20 MINUTES
TOTAL TIME: 2 HOURS 40 MINUTES

MAKES 16 SERVINGS

Elsie Wigahl, Ruthven, Iowa
Bake-Off® Contest 28, 1978

CAKE

1 (1 lb. 2.25-oz.) pkg. pudding-included white cake mix

1 (3-oz.) pkg. cream cheese, softened

½ cup water

¼ cup oil

3 eggs

¼ cup crème de menthe syrup

½ teaspoon peppermint extract

4 oz. (4 squares) semi-sweet chocolate, melted

3 tablespoons water

¼ cup finely chopped walnuts

GLAZE

1 oz. (1 square) semi-sweet chocolate

1 cup powdered sugar

2 to 3 tablespoons water

1. Heat oven to 350°F. Generously grease and flour 12-cup Bundt pan or 10-inch tube pan. In large bowl, combine cake mix, cream cheese, ½ cup water, oil and eggs at low speed until moistened; beat 2 minutes at high speed. Place 1½ cups batter in small bowl; stir in crème de menthe syrup and peppermint extract until well blended. Set aside. To remaining batter, add 4 oz. melted chocolate and 3 tablespoons water; blend well. Stir in walnuts. Spoon half of chocolate batter into greased and floured pan. Spoon peppermint batter randomly over chocolate batter; top with remaining chocolate batter. Pull knife through batter from top to bottom in a folding motion, turning pan while folding.

2. Bake at 350°F for 40 to 50 minutes or until cake springs back when touched lightly near center. Cool upright in pan 30 minutes; turn out onto serving plate. Cool completely.

3. In small saucepan, melt 1 oz. chocolate; stir in powdered sugar and enough water for desired drizzling consistency. Spoon glaze over cake allowing some to run down sides. Store in refrigerator.

1 Serving: Calories 310 (Calories from Fat 116); Total Fat 13g; Saturated Fat 4g; Trans Fat 0g; Cholesterol 41mg; Sodium 240mg; Total Carbohydrate 43g; Dietary Fiber 1g; Sugars 31g; Protein 4g

CHOCOLATE PRALINE LAYER CAKE

Created by a university professor of music, this easy-to-prepare cake is spectacular to serve and marvelous to eat! It's best if made a few hours ahead and refrigerated before serving.

PREP TIME: 25 MINUTES
TOTAL TIME: 2 HOURS 15 MINUTES
MAKES 16 SERVINGS

Hall of Fame

Julie Bengtson, Bemidji, Minnesota
Bake-Off® Contest 33, 1988 Grand Prize Winner and Hall of Fame

CAKE
- ½ cup butter or margarine
- ¼ cup whipping cream
- 1 cup firmly packed brown sugar
- ¾ cup coarsely chopped pecans
- 1 (15.25-oz.) pkg. Pillsbury™ Moist Supreme™ Devil's Food Cake Mix
- 1¼ cups water
- ⅓ cup oil
- 3 eggs

TOPPING
- 1¾ cups whipping cream
- ¼ cup powdered sugar
- ¼ teaspoon vanilla
- 16 pecan halves, if desired
- 16 chocolate curls, if desired

1. Heat oven to 325°F. In small heavy saucepan, combine butter, ¼ cup whipping cream and brown sugar. Cook over low heat just until butter is melted, stirring occasionally. Pour into two 9- or 8-inch round cake pans; sprinkle evenly with chopped pecans.

2. In large bowl, combine cake mix, water, oil and eggs; beat at low speed until moistened. Beat 2 minutes at medium speed. Carefully spoon batter over pecan mixture.

3. Bake at 325°F for 35 to 45 minutes or until cake springs back when touched lightly in center. Cool 5 minutes; remove from pans. Cool 1 hour or until completely cooled.

4. In small bowl, beat 1¾ cups whipping cream until soft peaks form. Add powdered sugar and vanilla; beat until stiff peaks form.

5. To assemble cake, place 1 layer on serving plate, praline side up. Spread with half of whipped cream. Top with second layer, praline side up; spread top with remaining whipped cream. Garnish with whole pecans and chocolate curls. Store in refrigerator.

1 Serving: Calories 408 (Calories from Fat 270); Total Fat 30g; Saturated Fat 13g; Trans Fat 1g; Cholesterol 95mg; Sodium 300mg; Total Carbohydrate 43g; Dietary Fiber 2g; Sugars 32g; Protein 4g

CREAM-FILLED STRAWBERRY-BROWNIE CAKE

Fudgy brownie meets strawberry cake in a layered extravaganza!

PREP TIME: 40 MINUTES
TOTAL TIME: 3 HOURS
20 MINUTES

MAKES 16 SERVINGS

Doris Wallace, Des Arc, Arkansas
Bake-Off® Contest 45, 2012

BROWNIE LAYER

1 box (18.4 oz) Pillsbury™ Family Size Chocolate Fudge Brownie Mix

⅔ cup vegetable oil

¼ cup water

3 eggs

CAKE LAYER

1 box Pillsbury™ Moist Supreme™ Strawberry Flavored Cake Mix

¾ cup water

⅓ cup vegetable oil

3 eggs

½ cup diced fresh strawberries

FILLING

1 package (8 oz) cream cheese, softened

½ cup butter, softened

3 cups powdered sugar

1 container (8 oz) frozen whipped topping, thawed

FROSTING AND GARNISH

1 container (16 oz) frozen whipped topping, thawed

⅔ cup powdered sugar

3 cups sliced fresh strawberries

1. Heat oven to 350°F. Spray 3 (9-inch) round cake pans with no-stick cooking spray. Line bottoms of pans with cooking parchment paper; spray paper with cooking spray. In medium bowl, stir all brownie layer ingredients 50 strokes with spoon. Spread about 1 cup batter in each of 3 pans.

2. In large bowl, beat all cake layer ingredients except diced strawberries with electric mixer on low speed 30 seconds. Beat on high speed 2 minutes or until blended. Fold in diced strawberries. Pour and spread about 1$\frac{1}{3}$ cups mixture evenly over brownie batter in each pan.

3. Bake 20 to 30 minutes or until toothpick inserted in center comes out clean. Cool in pans 10 minutes. Carefully invert cake layers from pans onto cooling racks; remove parchment paper. Cool completely, about 1 hour.

4. Meanwhile, to make filling, in medium bowl, beat cream cheese and butter with electric mixer on high speed until smooth and creamy. Beat in 3 cups powdered sugar until creamy. Carefully fold in 8 oz whipped topping.

5. To make frosting, in another medium bowl, beat 16 oz whipped topping and $\frac{2}{3}$ cup powdered sugar with electric mixer on low speed until blended.

6. To assemble cake, place 1 cake layer, brownie side down, on serving plate. Spread half of filling to within $\frac{1}{4}$ inch of edge; top with $\frac{3}{4}$ cup of the strawberry slices. Repeat with second layer, remaining filling and $\frac{3}{4}$ cup strawberry slices. Top with remaining cake layer, top side up. Frost sides and top of cake with frosting. Garnish with remaining 1$\frac{1}{2}$ cups strawberry slices. Refrigerate 1 hour before serving. Store in refrigerator.

CLEVER IDEA: *Whole strawberries dipped in chocolate can be substituted for the sliced strawberries.*

1 Serving: Calories 610 (Calories from Fat 330); Total Fat 37g; Saturated Fat 17g; Trans Fat 0g; Cholesterol 100mg; Sodium 360mg; Total Carbohydrate 65g; Dietary Fiber 1g; Sugars 47g; Protein 5g

UPSIDE-DOWN GERMAN CHOCOLATE CAKE

Next time you want a special cake-to-take, try this one. The cake and frosting bake all in one.

PREP TIME: 20 MINUTES
TOTAL TIME: 1 HOUR 20 MINUTES
MAKES 16 SERVINGS

Betty Nelson, Fridley, Minnesota
Bake-Off® Contest 27, 1976

TOPPING

¼ cup margarine or butter

¾ cup water

⅔ cup firmly packed brown sugar

1 cup coconut

1½ cups miniature marshmallows

½ cup chopped nuts

CAKE

1 (1 lb. 2.25-oz.) pkg. pudding-included German chocolate cake mix

1 cup water

½ cup dairy sour cream

⅓ cup oil

3 eggs

1. Heat oven to 350°F. In small saucepan over low heat, melt margarine with ¾ cup water. Stir in brown sugar. Pour into ungreased 13x9-inch pan. Sprinkle coconut, marshmallows and nuts evenly over top.

2. In large bowl, combine all cake ingredients at low speed until moistened; beat 2 minutes at high speed. Spoon batter evenly over topping mixture in pan. Bake at 350°F for 38 to 48 minutes or until toothpick inserted in center comes out clean. Cool slightly. To serve, cut into squares; transfer and invert onto individual plates. Serve warm or cool.

1 Serving: Calories 301 (Calories from Fat 128); Total Fat 17g; Saturated Fat 4.5g; Trans Fat 1g; Cholesterol 38mg; Sodium 339mg; Total Carbohydrate 42g; Dietary Fiber 1g; Sugars 28g; Protein 3g

CHOCOLATE MOUSSE FANTASY TORTE

Create a memory that lingers—an unforgettably fudgy, rich brownie topped with a luscious creamy chocolate mousse layer.

PREP TIME: 20 MINUTES
TOTAL TIME: 3 HOURS
35 MINUTES

MAKES 16 SERVINGS

Christine Vidra, Maumee, Ohio
Bake-Off® Contest 34, 1990

BASE

1 (1 lb. 3.5 oz.) pkg. fudge brownie mix

2 teaspoons instant coffee granules or crystals

½ cup butter or margarine, softened

2 tablespoons water

2 eggs

TOPPING

1½ cups semi-sweet chocolate chips

1 oz. unsweetened chocolate

1 teaspoon instant coffee granules or crystals

¼ cup water

2 tablespoons butter or margarine

1 cup whipping cream

½ oz. unsweetened chocolate, melted

1. Heat oven to 350°F. Grease 9- or 10-inch springform pan. In large bowl, combine all base ingredients; beat at medium speed 1 minute. Spread batter in greased pan. Bake at 350°F for 36 to 42 minutes or until set. Cool in pan on wire rack for 1 hour. Remove sides of pan; cool completely.

2. In small saucepan, combine chocolate chips, 1 oz. unsweetened chocolate, 1 teaspoon coffee granules, ¼ cup water and 2 tablespoons butter. Cook over low heat until mixture is smooth, stirring constantly. Remove from heat. Cool 15 minutes, stirring occasionally.

3. In small bowl, beat whipping cream until soft peaks form. Fold warm chocolate mixture into whipping cream. Using pastry tube fitted with decorative tip, pipe topping mixture evenly over cooled base. Or spread topping over base.

4. Drizzle ½ oz. melted unsweetened chocolate over topping. Refrigerate at least 1 hour or until topping is set. Let stand at room temperature about 30 minutes before serving. Store in refrigerator.

1 Serving: Calories 380 (Calories from Fat 212); Total Fat 23g; Saturated Fat 13g; Trans Fat 0g; Cholesterol 63mg; Sodium 180mg; Total Carbohydrate 40g; Dietary Fiber 1g; Sugars 26g; Protein 4g

FUDGY ORANGE CAPPUCCINO TORTE

This rich, indulgent torte is simple to make with brownie mix and is finished off with an orangey-chocolate filling and topping. It's a real show-stopper.

PREP TIME: 30 MINUTES
TOTAL TIME: 2 HOURS
40 MINUTES

MAKES 16 SERVINGS

Sharla Jack, Springfield, Oregon
Bake-Off® Contest 35, 1992

BROWNIE

1 (1 lb. 3.5-oz.) pkg. fudge brownie mix

½ cup oil

¼ cup water

¼ cup orange-flavored liqueur or orange juice

2 eggs

1 teaspoon grated orange peel

4 oz. sweet dark chocolate or semi-sweet baking chocolate, coarsely chopped

FILLING

1 cup sweetened condensed milk (not evaporated)

6 oz. sweet dark chocolate or semi-sweet baking chocolate, chopped

2 egg yolks, slightly beaten

2 tablespoons orange-flavored liqueur or orange juice

¾ cup finely chopped nuts

TOPPING

1½ cups whipping cream

¾ cup powdered sugar

⅓ cup unsweetened cocoa

2 tablespoons orange-flavored liqueur or orange juice

1 teaspoon grated orange peel

⅛ teaspoon salt

GARNISH, IF DESIRED

Orange slices, twisted

Orange leaves

1. Heat oven to 350°F. Grease bottom of 9- or 10-inch springform pan. In large bowl, combine all brownie ingredients except 4 oz. chocolate; beat 50 strokes by hand. Stir in chocolate. Spread in greased pan. Bake at 350°F for 40 to 45 minutes or until center is set. Cool completely.

2. In medium saucepan, combine condensed milk and 6 oz. chocolate. Cook over low heat, stirring constantly, until chocolate is melted and mixture is smooth. Remove from heat. Stir 2 tablespoons hot mixture into egg yolks. Gradually stir yolk mixture into hot mixture in saucepan. Cook over medium heat 3 minutes, stirring constantly. Remove from heat. Stir in 2 tablespoons liqueur and nuts. Refrigerate until just cool, about 25 minutes. Spread filling mixture over top of cooled brownies. Refrigerate at least 1 hour or until filling is set.

3. Run knife around sides of pan to loosen; remove sides of pan. To serve, place brownie on serving plate. In large bowl, beat all topping ingredients until stiff peaks form. Pipe or spoon topping mixture evenly over chilled filling. Garnish with orange slices and leaves. Store in refrigerator.

1 Serving: Calories 540 (Calories from Fat 285); Total Fat 30g; Saturated Fat 12g; Trans Fat 0g; Cholesterol 85mg; Sodium 160mg; Total Carbohydrate 60g; Dietary Fiber 2g; Sugars 42g; Protein 6g

A Peek Inside the Bake-Off® Contest:

A good number of the men who came to the Bake-Off® Contest did so from the army, or from a similar situation in which they'd been cooking for their coworkers. Firefighter Gil Soucy works "saving lives, saving homes, saving and helping my brother firefighters." But when times are quiet, Gil doesn't let them stay that way, spicing things up by cooking for the firemen at his station and trying new dishes on them. "It makes for great fun. One time I made some venison, telling them it was steak. It came out good, and I never told them what it was." His fellow firefighters may not always appreciate Gil's mischief, but they always come running when a lively dish like Bean Picadillo Tortillas is served.

TIRAMISU TOFFEE TORTE

PREP TIME: 35 MINUTES

TOTAL TIME: 2 HOURS 5 MINUTES

MAKES 12 SERVINGS

Christie Henson, Conway, Arkansas

Bake-Off® Contest 35, 1992

CAKE

1 box (15.25 oz.) Pillsbury™ Moist Supreme™ Classic White Cake Mix

1 cup strong brewed coffee, room temperature

4 egg whites

4 toffee candy bars (1.4 oz each), very finely chopped

FROSTING

⅔ cup sugar

⅓ cup chocolate-flavor syrup

4 oz. cream cheese, softened

2 cups whipping cream

2 teaspoons vanilla

1 cup strong brewed coffee, room temperature

GARNISH, IF DESIRED

Chopped toffee candy bars or chocolate curls

1. Heat oven to 350°F. Grease two 9- or 8-inch round cake pans; lightly flour. In large bowl, beat cake mix, 1 cup coffee and the egg whites with electric mixer on low speed about 30 seconds or until moistened. Beat on medium speed 2 minutes, scraping bowl occasionally. Fold in chopped toffee bars. Spread batter evenly in pans.

2. Bake 9-inch pans 20 to 30 minutes, 8-inch 30 to 40 minutes or until toothpick inserted in center comes out clean. Cool 10 minutes. Remove from pans to cooling racks. Cool completely, about 1 hour.

3. In medium bowl, beat sugar, chocolate syrup and cream cheese with electric mixer on medium speed until smooth. Add whipping cream and vanilla; beat until light and fluffy. Refrigerate until ready to use.

4. To assemble cake, cut each cake layer in half horizontally to make 4 layers. Drizzle each cut side with ¼ cup coffee. Place 1 cake layer, coffee side up, on serving plate; spread with ¾ cup frosting. Repeat with second and third layers. Top with remaining cake layer. Frost side and top of cake with remaining frosting. Garnish with chopped toffee bars. Cover and refrigerate torte.

1 Serving: Calories 448 (Calories from Fat 230); Total Fat 0.5g; Saturated Fat 13g; Trans Fat 1.5g; Cholesterol 60mg; Sodium 400mg; Total Carbohydrate 60g; Dietary Fiber 0g; Sugars 39g; Protein 4g

KEY LIME CREAM TORTE

The flavors of Key lime pie are combined in an impressive yet quick and easy torte that was developed by the contestant when visiting Key West.

PREP TIME: 35 MINUTES
TOTAL TIME: 4 HOURS
35 MINUTES

MAKES 12 SERVINGS

Joan Wittan, North Potomac, Maryland
Bake-Off® Contest 35, 1992

CAKE

1 (1 lb. 2.25-oz.) pkg. pudding-included butter flavor cake mix

2 tablespoons lime juice plus water to equal 1 cup

½ cup butter or margarine, softened

3 eggs

FILLING

1 (14-oz.) can sweetened condensed milk (not evaporated)

½ cup lime juice

2 cups whipping cream

GARNISH

Lime slices, if desired

1. Heat oven to 350°F. Grease and flour two 9- or 8-inch round cake pans. In large bowl, combine all cake ingredients at low speed until moistened; beat 2 minutes at high speed. Pour batter into greased and floured pans.

2. Bake at 350°F. Bake 9-inch pans 30 to 40 minutes, bake 8-inch pans 35 to 45 minutes, or until toothpick inserted in center comes out clean. Cool 15 minutes; remove from pans. Cool completely, about 1 hour.

3. In small bowl, combine sweetened condensed milk and ½ cup lime juice; mix well. In large bowl, beat whipping cream until stiff peaks form. Reserve 1 cup of whipped cream. Fold condensed milk mixture into remaining whipped cream just until blended.

4. To assemble cake, slice each cake layer in half horizontally to make 4 layers. Place 1 cake layer cut side up on serving plate; spread with ⅓ of whipped cream filling. Repeat with second and third cake layers. Top with remaining cake layer. Pipe in decorative pattern or spread reserved whipped cream over top of torte. Refrigerate 2 to 3 hours before serving. Garnish with lime slices. Store in refrigerator.

1 Serving: Calories 510 (Calories from Fat 276); Total Fat 29g; Saturated Fat 17g; Trans Fat 1g; Cholesterol 133mg; Sodium 430mg; Total Carbohydrate 56g; Dietary Fiber 0g; Sugars 37g; Protein 7g

MACADAMIA FUDGE TORTE

Enjoy these chocolate fudge tortes packed with macadamia nuts, served with caramel sauce—a delicious dessert!

PREP TIME: 30 MINUTES
TOTAL TIME: 3 HOURS

MAKES 12 SERVINGS

Kurt Wait, Redwood City, California
Bake-Off® Contest 37, 1996 Grand Prize Winner

FILLING

⅓ cup low-fat sweetened condensed milk (not evaporated)

½ cup semisweet chocolate chips

CAKE

1 (15.25-oz.) pkg. Pillsbury™ Moist Supreme™ Devil's Food Cake Mix

1½ teaspoons cinnamon

⅓ cup oil

1 (15-oz.) can sliced pears in light syrup, drained

3 eggs

⅓ cup chopped macadamia nuts or pecans

2 teaspoons water

SAUCE

1 (17-oz.) jar butterscotch caramel ice cream topping

⅓ cup milk

1. Heat oven to 350°F. Spray 9- or 10-inch springform pan with nonstick cooking spray. In small saucepan, combine filling ingredients; cook over medium-low heat until chocolate is melted, stirring occasionally.

2. In large bowl, combine cake mix, cinnamon and oil; blend at low speed for 20 to 30 seconds or until crumbly. (Mixture will be dry.)

3. Place pears in blender container or food processor bowl with metal blade; cover and blend until smooth.

4. In another large bowl, combine $2\frac{1}{2}$ cups of the cake mix mixture, pureed pears and eggs; beat at low speed until moistened. Beat 2 minutes at medium speed. Spread batter evenly in sprayed pan. Drop filling by spoonfuls over batter. Stir nuts and water into remaining cake mix mixture. Sprinkle over filling.

5. Bake at 350°F for 45 to 50 minutes or until top springs back when touched lightly in center. Cool 10 minutes. Remove sides of pan. Cool $1\frac{1}{2}$ hours or until completely cooled.

6. In small saucepan, combine sauce ingredients; cook over medium-low heat for 3 to 4 minutes or until well blended, stirring occasionally. Just before serving, spoon 2 tablespoons warm sauce onto each individual dessert plate. Top each with wedge of torte. If desired, serve with ice cream and garnish with chocolate curls.

1 Serving: Calories 460 (Calories from Fat 140); Total Fat 16g; Saturated Fat 5g; Trans Fat 0g; Cholesterol 55mg; Sodium 392mg; Total Carbohydrate 73g; Dietary Fiber 3g; Sugars 51g; Protein 6g

A Peek Inside the Bake-Off® Contest:

Carolyn Gurtz, of Gaithersburg, Maryland, was named the grand prize winner for her Double-Delight Peanut Butter Cookies in 2008. The contest judges agreed that Carolyn's recipe surpassed the 99 other competitors for its simplicity and approachability, allowing the home cook to take a convenience product and turn it into an unexpected cookie that bursts with layers of peanut butter flavor. In an interview following the contest, Carolyn said, "Just being a finalist was such a thrill for me, and then to have won the grand prize, I'm just flabbergasted. And then I started thinking that my recipe will be published as a grand prize winner for the Pillsbury Bake-Off® Contest. People will be making the cookie I created. I just can't believe it."

PISTACHIO MOUSSE BROWNIE TORTE

When the celebration calls for a stunning dessert, look no further than rich brownie layers filled with a nutty mousse.

PREP TIME: 60 MINUTES
TOTAL TIME: 2 HOURS 45 MINUTES

MAKES 16 SERVINGS

Jane Estrin, Gainesville, Florida
Bake-Off® Contest 43, 2008

CAKE

1 box (18.4 oz) Pillsbury™ Family Size Chocolate Fudge Brownie Mix

½ cup canola oil

¼ cup water

3 eggs

MOUSSE

1 box (4-serving size) pistachio instant pudding and pie filling mix

¾ cup cold whole milk

1 cup cold whipping (heavy) cream

½ cup pistachio nuts, coarsely chopped

GLAZE

½ cup whipping (heavy) cream

4 oz semisweet baking chocolate, finely chopped

1 teaspoon vanilla

1 teaspoon light corn syrup

GARNISH

½ cup whipping (heavy) cream

2 tablespoons powdered sugar

Reserved 1 tablespoon pistachio instant pudding and pie filling mix

1. Heat oven to 350°F. Lightly spray bottom of 2 (8-inch) round cake pans with no-stick cooking spray. Line bottoms of pans with cooking parchment paper; lightly spray paper with cooking spray.

2. In large bowl, stir brownie mix, oil, water and eggs 50 strokes with spoon. Spread half of batter (1½ cups) evenly in each pan.

3. Bake 27 to 30 minutes or until toothpick inserted 2 inches from edge of pan comes out clean. Cool in pans on cooling racks 10 minutes. Run knife around edge of pans to loosen. Place cooling rack upside down on 1 pan; turn rack and pan over. Remove pan and parchment paper. Repeat with second brownie layer. Place racks with brownie layers in refrigerator to cool completely, about 20 minutes.

4. Meanwhile, measure 1 tablespoon of the pudding mix; reserve for garnish. In large bowl, beat remaining pudding mix, the milk and 1 cup whipping cream with electric mixer on high speed about 2 minutes or until mixture is thick and creamy. Stir in nuts. Cover; refrigerate.

5. Carefully cut each brownie layer horizontally in half, using long serrated knife, to make 4 layers. On serving plate, place 1 brownie layer, cut side down. Spread ⅓ of the mousse (¾ cup) evenly to edge of brownie. Repeat layering twice, using 2 brownie layers (place cut sides down) and remaining mousse. Top with remaining brownie layer, cut side down. Refrigerate torte while making glaze.

6. In 1-quart saucepan, heat ½ cup whipping cream over medium heat, stirring occasionally, just until bubbles start to form at edge of saucepan. Remove from heat. Add chocolate; stir constantly until smooth. Stir in vanilla and corn syrup; let stand 10 minutes. Stir glaze; spoon over top of torte, allowing some to run down side. Return torte to refrigerator while making garnish.

7. In medium bowl, beat ½ cup whipping cream, the powdered sugar and reserved 1 tablespoon pudding mix on high speed until stiff peaks form. Spoon mixture into decorating bag fitted with star tip and pipe rosettes on top of torte, or spoon dollops of mixture on torte. Refrigerate at least 30 minutes before serving. Cover and refrigerate any remaining torte.

1 Serving: Calories 280 (Calories from Fat 210); Total Fat 23g; Saturated Fat 9g; Trans Fat 0g; Cholesterol 75mg; Sodium 120mg; Total Carbohydrate 15g; Dietary Fiber 0g; Sugars 12g; Protein 3g

HEAVENLY CHOCOLATE RASPBERRY TORTE

Dark chocolate is the perfect complement to subtle raspberry in this luscious dessert.

PREP TIME: 20 MINUTES
TOTAL TIME: 1 HOUR 50 MINUTES

MAKES 12 SERVINGS

Pat Freymuth, Colorado Springs, Colorado
Bake-Off® Contest 42, 2006

1 bag (12 oz) dark chocolate chips (2 cups)

1 container (6 oz) 99% fat free raspberry yogurt

6 roasted almond crunchy granola bars (3 pouches from 8.9-oz box), finely crushed (heaping 1 cup)

1 cup egg whites (about 7)

2 tablespoons plus 1 teaspoon fat-free half-and-half

2 teaspoons raspberry-flavored syrup (for coffee drinks) or red raspberry syrup (for pancakes)

¼ cup powdered sugar

Fresh raspberries, if desired

Fresh mint leaves, if desired

1. Heat oven to 350°F. Lightly spray bottom of 9-inch round cake pan with cooking spray; line bottom with parchment paper. Spray paper and side of pan with cooking spray.

2. Reserve ½ cup of the chocolate chips for glaze; place remaining chips in medium microwavable bowl (or place in top of double boiler). Stir in yogurt until chips are coated. Microwave on High in 1-minute increments, stirring after each, until chips are completely melted (or heat in double boiler over simmering water, stirring frequently, until melted). Stir in crushed granola bars and egg whites until well blended. Pour batter into pan.

3. Bake 20 to 30 minutes or until side of torte has risen and center is shiny but firm when touched (if center rises, torte has been overbaked). Cool in pan on wire rack, about 30 minutes (as torte cools, side will pull away from pan and torte will slightly sink). Refrigerate until chilled, about 1 hour.

4. In small microwavable bowl, microwave reserved ½ cup chocolate chips and the half-and-half on High in 30-second increments, stirring after each, until chips are melted. Cool slightly, about 2 minutes.

5. Place wire rack upside down over pan; turn rack and pan over. Remove pan and parchment paper. Pour chocolate mixture over torte; spread over top and side. Slide torte onto serving plate.

6. In small bowl, mix syrup and sugar. Place in small resealable food-storage plastic bag; seal bag and cut tiny hole in one bottom corner. Drizzle over top of torte in spiral pattern; gently run toothpick back and forth through spiral pattern to feather. Refrigerate until glaze is set and firm to the touch, about 20 minutes.

7. Before serving, garnish tray and/or individual dessert plates with raspberries and mint. Cut torte into wedges with warm, dry knife, cleaning knife between cuts. Store torte in refrigerator.

CLEVER IDEA: *To easily crush granola bars, do not unwrap; use rolling pin to crush bars.*

1 Serving: Calories 240 (Calories from Fat 90); Total Fat 10g; Saturated Fat 5g; Trans Fat 0g; Cholesterol 0mg; Sodium 90mg; Total Carbohydrate 31g; Dietary Fiber 2g; Sugars 24g; Protein 5g

PEANUT BUTTER TRUFFLE TART

Peanut butter and chocolate lovers have found a new favorite!

PREP TIME: 25 MINUTES
TOTAL TIME: 3 HOURS
MAKES 10 SERVINGS

Laura Stensberg, Marshfield, Wisconsin
Bake-Off® Contest 42, 2006

1 roll (16.5 oz) Pillsbury™ refrigerated peanut butter cookies

6 peanut butter crunchy granola bars (3 pouches from 8.9-oz box), crushed (1 heaping cup)

2 bags (12 oz each) semisweet chocolate chips (4 cups)

1 cup whipping cream

½ cup crunchy peanut butter

⅓ cup chopped peanuts or 1 package (2 oz) nut topping

1. Heat oven to 350°F. In large bowl, break up cookie dough. Stir or knead in crushed granola bars until well mixed. In 10-inch tart pan with removable bottom or 13x9-inch pan, press dough in bottom and up side. Bake 12 to 17 minutes or until light golden brown.

2. With back of spoon, press down crust on bottom and side; bake 3 to 5 minutes longer or until deep golden brown. Press down crust again with spoon. Cool 3 minutes.

3. Meanwhile, in large microwavable bowl, microwave chocolate chips and whipping cream on High 1 minute. Stir; microwave 1 to 2 minutes longer, stirring every 30 seconds to prevent chocolate from burning, until completely melted and smooth. In small microwavable bowl, microwave peanut butter on High 1 minute or until melted; stir.

4. Spread warm peanut butter in bottom of crust. Pour chocolate mixture over peanut butter mixture. Sprinkle peanuts evenly over top. Refrigerate at least 2 hours or until serving time. For easier cutting, let tart stand at room temperature 15 minutes before serving. Store in refrigerator.

CLEVER IDEA: *To easily crush granola bars, do not unwrap; use rolling pin to crush bars.*

1 Serving: Calories 500 (Calories from Fat 270); Total Fat 30g; Saturated Fat 13g; Trans Fat 1g; Cholesterol 20mg; Sodium 240mg; Total Carbohydrate 51g; Dietary Fiber 3g; Sugars 35g; Protein 8g

ROYAL MARBLE CHEESECAKE

Ribbons of dark chocolate are swirled throughout to produce this delectable creation. Placing a shallow pan half full of water on the bottom oven rack will help keep the surface of the cheesecake moist and prevent cracks.

PREP TIME: 35 MINUTES
TOTAL TIME: 12 HOURS

MAKES 16 SERVINGS

Dora Feinstein, Atlantic City, New Jersey
Bake-Off® Contest 16, 1964

CRUST
¾ cup all-purpose flour

2 tablespoons sugar

Dash salt

¼ cup margarine or butter

1 (6-oz.) pkg. (1 cup) semi-sweet chocolate chips, melted

FILLING
3 (8-oz.) pkg. cream cheese, softened

1 cup sugar

¼ cup all-purpose flour

2 teaspoons vanilla

6 eggs

1 cup dairy sour cream

1. Heat oven to 400°F. In small bowl, combine ¾ cup flour, 2 tablespoons sugar and salt. Using pastry blender or fork, cut in margarine until mixture resembles coarse crumbs. Stir in 2 tablespoons of the melted chocolate. Reserve remaining chocolate for filling. Press in bottom of ungreased 9-inch springform pan. Bake at 400°F for 10 minutes or until very light brown. Remove from oven. Reduce oven temperature to 325°F.

2. In large bowl, beat cream cheese and 1 cup sugar until light and fluffy. Add ¼ cup flour and vanilla; blend well. At low speed, add eggs 1 at a time, beating just until blended. Add sour cream; mix well. Place 1¾ cups filling mixture in medium bowl; stir in reserved melted chocolate. Pour half of filling over crust. Top with spoonfuls of half of the chocolate filling. Cover with remaining plain filling, then with spoonfuls of remaining chocolate filling. Using table knife, swirl chocolate filling through plain filling.

3. Bake at 325°F for 60 to 75 minutes or until center is almost set. Cool 10 minutes; remove sides of pan. Cool 2 to 3 hours. Refrigerate 8 hours or overnight before serving. Store in refrigerator.

1 Serving: Calories 359 (Calories from Fat 160); Total Fat 25g; Saturated Fat 4g; Trans Fat 0g; Cholesterol 25mg; Sodium 215mg; Total Carbohydrate 29g; Dietary Fiber 1g; Sugars 22g; Protein 7g

APPLE-CRESCENT CHEESECAKE

PREP TIME: 25 MINUTES
**TOTAL TIME: 4 HOURS
50 MINUTES**

MAKES 10 SERVINGS

Eugene Majewski, Elmhurst, Illinois
Bake-Off® Contest 22, 1971

⅓ cup sugar

½ teaspoon ground cinnamon

3 cups thinly sliced, peeled cooking apples (3 medium)

3 packages (3-oz. each) cream cheese, softened

¼ cup sugar

2 tablespoons milk

½ teaspoon vanilla

1 egg

1 can (8-oz.) refrigerated crescent dinner rolls

½ cup apricot preserves

1 tablespoon water

1. Heat oven to 400°F. In medium bowl, mix ⅓ cup sugar and the cinnamon. Stir in apples until coated; set aside.

2. In small bowl, beat cream cheese, ¼ cup sugar, the milk, vanilla and egg with electric mixer on medium speed until smooth; set aside.

3. Unroll dough; separate into 8 triangles. In ungreased 9-inch springform pan or 9-inch round cake pan, arrange triangles; press in bottom and about 1½ inches up side to make crust. Spoon cheese mixture into crust.

4. Drain any liquid from apples; arrange apples over cheese mixture. In small bowl, mix preserves and water; drizzle over apples.

5. Bake 20 minutes. Reduce oven temperature to 350°F; bake 30 to 35 minutes longer or until crust is deep golden brown and center is firm to the touch. Cool completely, about 30 minutes. Refrigerate at least 1 hour 30 minutes before serving.

1 Serving: Calories 420 (Calories from Fat 190); Total Fat 21g; Saturated Fat 8g; Trans Fat 2.5g; Cholesterol 20mg; Sodium 350mg; Total Carbohydrate 53g; Dietary Fiber 2g; Sugars 31g; Protein 5g

CRANBERRY CHEESECAKE TART

Add a luscious layer of zesty cranberries between the crust and the creamy cheesecake filling for a pie just right for the holidays (or any day!).

PREP TIME: 30 MINUTES
TOTAL TIME: 5 HOURS
30 MINUTES
MAKES 10 SERVINGS

James Sloboden, Puyallup, Washington
Bake-Off® Contest 34, 1990

CRUST

1 box Pillsbury™ refrigerated pie crusts, softened as directed on box

FILLING

1 can (16 oz) whole berry cranberry sauce

½ cup chopped pecans

6 tablespoons sugar

1 tablespoon cornstarch

12 oz cream cheese, softened

2 eggs

½ cup sugar

1 tablespoon milk

TOPPING

1 cup sour cream

½ teaspoon vanilla

2 tablespoons sugar

1. Heat oven to 450°F. Bake pie crust as directed on box for One-Crust Baked Shell, using 10-inch tart pan with removable bottom or 9-inch glass pie plate. Cool completely, about 15 minutes. Reduce oven temperature to 375°F.

2. In medium bowl, mix cranberry sauce, pecans, 6 tablespoons sugar and the cornstarch; spread in crust.

3. In medium bowl, beat cream cheese, eggs, ½ cup sugar and the milk with electric mixer on medium speed until smooth. Spoon evenly over cranberry mixture. Bake at 375°F for 25 to 30 minutes or until set.

4. In small bowl, mix topping ingredients. Spoon evenly over filling. Bake 5 minutes longer. Cool slightly. Refrigerate 3 to 4 hours or until set. Cover and refrigerate any remaining tart.

CLEVER IDEA: *You can replace the pecans with chopped toasted almonds for a different flavor twist.*

1 Serving: Calories 460 (Calories from Fat 230); Total Fat 26g; Saturated Fat 12g; Trans Fat 0g; Cholesterol 95mg; Sodium 260mg; Total Carbohydrate 51g; Dietary Fiber 1g; Sugars 39g; Protein 5g

CRANBERRY CHEESECAKE TART (*opposite*)

APPLE PIE '63 (*page 402*)

APPLE PIE '63

Perfect for large gatherings, this caramel, cream cheese and apple pie was a favorite of our taste panel testers.

PREP TIME: 45 MINUTES
TOTAL TIME: 1 HOUR 30 MINUTES

MAKES 18 SERVINGS

Julia Smogor, Cedar Rapids, Iowa
Bake-Off® Contest 14, 1962 Grand Prize Winner

CARAMEL SAUCE

28 caramels, unwrapped

½ cup half-and-half or evaporated milk

CRUST

2½ cups Pillsbury™ BEST™ All Purpose, Unbleached or Self Rising Flour

¼ cup sugar

1½ teaspoons salt

½ cup margarine or butter

¼ cup oil

¼ cup water

1 egg, beaten

APPLE FILLING

6 cups sliced peeled apples (about 6 medium)

1 cup sugar

⅓ cup Pillsbury™ BEST™ All Purpose or Unbleached Flour

1 to 2 teaspoons grated lemon peel

2 tablespoons lemon juice

TOPPING

1 (8-oz.) pkg. cream cheese, softened

⅓ cup sugar

1 egg

⅓ cup chopped nuts

1. Heat oven to 375°F. In small saucepan, combine caramels and half-and-half; cook over low heat, stirring occasionally, until caramels are melted. Keep warm.

2. Lightly spoon flour into measuring cup; level off. In large bowl, combine 2½ cups flour, ¼ cup sugar and salt. With pastry blender or fork, cut in margarine until mixture resembles coarse crumbs. Add oil, water and egg; mix well. Press crust mixture evenly in bottom and up sides of ungreased 15x10x1-inch baking pan.

3. In large bowl, combine all apple filling ingredients; toss lightly. Spoon into crust-lined pan. Drizzle warm caramel sauce over apples.

4. In small bowl, combine all topping ingredients except nuts; beat until smooth. Spoon over apples, spreading slightly. Sprinkle with nuts.

5. Bake at 375°F for 35 to 45 minutes or until light golden brown. Cool. Cut into squares. Store in refrigerator.

CLEVER IDEA: *If using self rising flour, omit salt.*

1 Serving: Calories 370 (Calories from Fat 150); Total Fat 17g; Saturated Fat 6g; Trans Fat 1g; Cholesterol 40mg; Sodium 320mg; Total Carbohydrate 49g; Dietary Fiber 2g; Sugars 31g; Protein 5g

APPLE DATE PIE

The contest was still called the Grand National in 1955. Most homemakers were still spending hours in the kitchen and pie was the favorite dessert. This spicy variation on apple pie still has lots of family appeal but today you can save time with ready-prepared pie crust.

PREP TIME: 20 MINUTES
TOTAL TIME: 2 HOURS

MAKES 8 SERVINGS

Susan Dunne, Summit, New Jersey
Bake-Off® Contest 7, 1955

1 (15-oz.) pkg. refrigerated pie crusts

FILLING

½ cup sugar

1 tablespoon all-purpose flour

½ teaspoon cinnamon

¼ teaspoon ginger

¼ teaspoon nutmeg

¼ teaspoon salt

1 teaspoon grated lemon peel

5 cups thinly sliced peeled apples (5 medium)

½ cup pitted dates, cut into pieces

1 teaspoon lemon juice

1 tablespoon margarine or butter

1. Prepare pie crust according to package directions for *two-crust pie* using 9-inch pie pan.

2. Heat oven to 425°F. In large bowl, combine sugar, flour, cinnamon, ginger, nutmeg, salt and lemon peel; mix well. Add apple slices and dates; mix well. Spoon into crust-lined pan. Sprinkle with lemon juice. Dot with margarine. Top with second crust; seal edges and flute. Cut slits in top crust.

3. Bake at 425°F for 35 to 40 minutes or until apples are tender and crust is golden brown. Cover edge of crust with strips of foil after 15 to 20 minutes of baking to prevent excessive browning.

1 Serving: Calories 370 (Calories from Fat 139); Total Fat 16g; Saturated Fat 6g; Trans Fat 0g; Cholesterol 6mg; Sodium 350mg; Total Carbohydrate 53g; Dietary Fiber 2g; Sugars 27g; Protein 2g

TOPSY-TURVY APPLE PIE

Brown sugar and pecans make the crust special. After baking, the pie gets a twist: it's turned upside down onto the serving plate, transforming the sticky bottom crust into a moist, nutty topping.

PREP TIME: 45 MINUTES
TOTAL TIME: 1 HOUR 30 MINUTES
MAKES 8 SERVINGS

Betty Cooper, Kensington, Maryland
Bake-Off® Contest 3, 1951

GLAZE AND CRUST

¼ cup packed brown sugar

1 tablespoon butter, melted

1 tablespoon corn syrup

½ cup pecan halves

1 box Pillsbury™ refrigerated pie crusts, softened as directed on box

FILLING

⅔ cup granulated sugar

2 tablespoons Pillsbury™ BEST™ all-purpose flour

½ teaspoon ground cinnamon

4 cups thinly sliced, peeled apples (4 medium)

TOPPING

Whipped cream, if desired

1. Heat oven to 425°F. In 9-inch glass pie plate, mix brown sugar, butter and corn syrup. Spread evenly in bottom of pie plate. Arrange pecans over mixture. Make pie crusts as directed on box for Two-Crust Pie, placing bottom crust over mixture in pan.

2. In small bowl, mix granulated sugar, flour and cinnamon. Arrange half of apple slices in crust-lined pie plate. Sprinkle with half of sugar mixture. Repeat with remaining apple slices and sugar mixture. Top with second crust; seal edge and flute. Cut slits in several places in top crust.

3. Place pie on sheet of foil on middle oven rack in oven; bake 8 minutes. Reduce oven temperature to 350°F; bake 35 to 45 minutes longer or until apples are tender and crust is golden brown. Immediately run knife around edge of pie to loosen. Place serving plate upside down over pie; turn serving plate and pie plate over. Remove pie plate. Serve warm or cool with whipped cream.

1 Serving: Calories 410 (Calories from Fat 160); Total Fat 18g; Saturated Fat 6g; Trans Fat 0g; Cholesterol 10mg; Sodium 270mg; Total Carbohydrate 59g; Dietary Fiber 1g; Sugars 30g; Protein 2g

APPLE NUT LATTICE TART

This elegant tart, adapted from several recipes, is a delicious contemporary variation of apple pie.

PREP TIME: 30 MINUTES
TOTAL TIME: 3 HOURS 25 MINUTES

MAKES 8 SERVINGS

Mary Lou Warren, Medford, Oregon
Bake-Off® Contest 32, 1986 Grand Prize Winner

CRUST

1 box Pillsbury™ refrigerated pie crusts, softened as directed on box

FILLING

3 to 3½ cups thinly sliced, peeled apples (3 to 4 medium)

½ cup granulated sugar

3 tablespoons golden raisins

3 tablespoons chopped walnuts or pecans

½ teaspoon ground cinnamon

¼ to ½ teaspoon grated lemon peel

2 teaspoons lemon juice

GLAZE

¼ cup powdered sugar

1 to 2 teaspoons lemon juice

1. Make pie crusts as directed on box for Two-Crust Pie using 10-inch tart pan with removable bottom or 9-inch glass pie pan. Place 1 crust in pan; press in bottom and up side of pan. Trim edge if necessary.

2. Place cookie sheet on middle oven rack in oven to preheat; heat oven to 400°F. In large bowl, mix filling ingredients to coat. Spoon into crust-lined pan.

3. To make lattice top, cut second crust into ¹/₂-inch-wide strips. Arrange strips in lattice design over filling. Trim and seal edge.

4. Place tart on preheated cookie sheet in oven; bake 40 to 55 minutes or until apples are tender and crust is golden brown. During last 10 to 15 minutes of baking, cover crust edge with strips of foil to prevent excessive browning. Remove from cookie sheet. Cool 1 hour.

5. In small bowl, blend glaze ingredients, adding enough lemon juice for desired drizzling consistency. Drizzle over slightly warm tart. Cool completely, about 1 hour. Remove sides of pan.

1 Serving: Calories 330 (Calories from Fat 120); Total Fat 14g; Saturated Fat 5g; Trans Fat 0g; Cholesterol 5mg; Sodium 260mg; Total Carbohydrate 49g; Dietary Fiber 1g; Sugars 22g; Protein 2g

SPICY APPLE TWISTS

These miniature pastries are a lighter version of old-fashioned apple dumplings.

PREP TIME: 45 MINUTES
TOTAL TIME: 1 HOUR 25 MINUTES

MAKES 16 SERVINGS

Dorothy DeVault, Delaware, Ohio
Bake-Off® Contest 10, 1958 Grand Prize Winner

TWISTS

2 large baking apples, peeled, cored

1½ cups Pillsbury™ BEST™ All Purpose, Unbleached or Self Rising Flour

½ teaspoon salt

½ cup shortening

4 to 6 tablespoons cold water

1 tablespoon margarine or butter, softened

TOPPING

¼ cup margarine or butter, melted

½ cup sugar

1 teaspoon cinnamon

1 cup water

1. Heat oven to 425°F. Cut each apple into 8 wedges. Lightly spoon flour into measuring cup; level off. In medium bowl, blend flour and salt. With pastry blender or fork, cut in shortening until mixture resembles coarse crumbs. Sprinkle flour mixture with water 1 tablespoon at a time, mixing lightly with fork until dough is just moist enough to hold together. Shape dough into ball.

2. On floured surface, roll dough lightly from center to edge into 12-inch square. Spread with 1 tablespoon softened margarine. Fold 2 sides to center. Roll to 16x10-inch rectangle. Cut crosswise into 16 (10-inch) strips. Wrap 1 strip around each apple wedge. Place ½ inch apart in ungreased 13x9-inch pan.

3. Brush each wrapped apple wedge with melted margarine. In small bowl, blend sugar and cinnamon; sprinkle over wrapped apples.

4. Bake at 425°F for 20 minutes. Pour water into pan. Bake an additional 12 to 17 minutes or until golden brown. Spoon sauce in pan over twists. Serve warm or cool, plain or with whipped cream.

CLEVER IDEA: *If using self rising flour, omit salt.*

1 Serving: Calories 170 (Calories from Fat 90); Total Fat 10g; Saturated Fat 2g; Trans Fat 2g; Cholesterol 0mg; Sodium 110mg; Total Carbohydrate 18g; Dietary Fiber 1g; Sugars 9g; Protein 1g

CARROT CAKE TART

Love carrot cake? Love pie? Bake them together in an ultimate dessert with cream cheese frosting and over-the-top caramel drizzle!

PREP TIME: 30 MINUTES
TOTAL TIME: 3 HOURS 10 MINUTES

MAKES 12 SERVINGS

Laura Majchrzak, Hunt Valley, Maryland
Bake-Off® Contest 45, 2012

TART

- 1 Pillsbury™ refrigerated pie crust, softened as directed on box
- ¼ cup unsalted butter, melted, cooled slightly
- 1 cup packed light brown sugar
- ⅓ cup light corn syrup
- 2 eggs
- ⅔ cup Pillsbury™ BEST™ All Purpose Flour
- 1 teaspoon ground cinnamon
- ½ teaspoon baking soda
- ½ teaspoon salt
- 1½ cups shredded carrots
- ½ cup raisins
- ½ cup chopped pecans

FROSTING

- 2 packages (3 oz each) cream cheese, softened
- 2 tablespoons unsalted butter, softened
- 1½ cups powdered sugar
- ½ teaspoon pure vanilla extract

GARNISH

- 12 whole praline pecans
- ½ cup caramel syrup
- 12 carrot curls, if desired

1. Heat oven to 350°F. Place large cookie sheet on middle oven rack. Unroll pie crust; place in ungreased 10-inch tart pan with removable bottom. Press crust firmly against bottom and side of pan; trim edges.

2. In large bowl, beat ¼ cup melted butter, brown sugar and corn syrup with electric mixer on medium speed until blended; beat in eggs until blended. Add flour, cinnamon, baking soda and salt; beat on low speed until blended. Stir in carrots, raisins and chopped pecans. Spread mixture evenly over bottom of crust-lined pan. Place tart on cookie sheet in oven.

3. Bake 30 to 40 minutes or until filling is set and deep golden brown. Cool completely on cooling rack, about 1 hour. Remove side of pan; place tart on serving plate.

4. In medium bowl, beat cream cheese and 2 tablespoons butter with electric mixer on high speed until smooth. Add powdered sugar and vanilla; beat on low speed until creamy. Frost cooled tart. Place praline pecans evenly around edge of tart. Refrigerate 1 hour.

5. To serve, cut into 12 wedges. Drizzle each serving with 2 teaspoons caramel syrup; garnish each with carrot curl. Store covered in refrigerator.

CLEVER IDEA: *To make carrot curls, cut thin strips of peeled, medium-size carrots with a vegetable peeler. Roll each strip and fasten with a toothpick. Chill in ice water 2 to 3 hours. Remove toothpicks before garnishing.*

1 Serving: Calories 500 (Calories from Fat 200); Total Fat 22g; Saturated Fat 9g; Trans Fat 0g; Cholesterol 70mg; Sodium 380mg; Total Carbohydrate 71g; Dietary Fiber 2g; Sugars 48g; Protein 4g

PEACHEESY PIE

This peachy pie, scented with pumpkin pie spice, is topped with a delectable mixture reminiscent of cheesecake.

PREP TIME: 30 MINUTES
TOTAL TIME: 2 HOURS 20 MINUTES

MAKES 8 SERVINGS

Janis Risley, Melbourne, Florida
Bake-Off® Contest 16, 1964 Grand Prize Winner

FILLING

½ cup sugar

2 tablespoons cornstarch

1 to 2 teaspoons pumpkin pie spice

2 tablespoons light corn syrup

2 teaspoons vanilla

1 can (28 oz) peach slices, drained, reserving 3 tablespoons liquid

TOPPING

⅓ cup sugar

1 tablespoon lemon juice

2 eggs, slightly beaten

½ cup sour cream

1 package (3 oz) cream cheese, softened

2 tablespoons butter or margarine

CRUST

1 box Pillsbury™ refrigerated pie crusts, softened as directed on box

1. In medium bowl, mix all filling ingredients except peach liquid; set aside.

2. In 1-quart saucepan, mix 2 tablespoons of the reserved peach liquid, $1/3$ cup sugar, the lemon juice and eggs. Cook over medium heat, stirring constantly, until mixture boils and thickens. Boil 1 minute, stirring constantly. Remove from heat.

3. In small bowl with electric mixer, beat sour cream and cream cheese on medium speed until smooth. Gradually beat in hot egg mixture until well blended; set aside.

4. Heat oven to 425°F. Place 1 pie crust in 9-inch glass pie pan as directed on box for One-Crust Filled Pie. Spoon filling into crust-lined pan. Dot with butter. Spoon topping mixture evenly over filling.

5. Remove second pie crust from pouch; place flat on work surface. With floured 3-inch round cutter, cut out 8 rounds from crust. Brush tops of rounds with remaining 1 tablespoon reserved peach liquid. Arrange pie crust rounds over topping.

6. Bake 10 minutes. Reduce oven temperature to 350°F; bake 35 to 40 minutes longer or until crust is golden brown. After 15 to 20 minutes of baking, cover crust edge with strips of foil to prevent excessive browning. Cool completely, about 1 hour. Store in refrigerator.

1 Serving: Calories 360 (Calories from Fat 150); Total Fat 17g; Saturated Fat 8g; Trans Fat 0g; Cholesterol 85mg; Sodium 220mg; Total Carbohydrate 47g; Dietary Fiber 1g; Sugars 30g; Protein 3g

FRESH FRUIT DEVONSHIRE PIE

Devonshire cream is a rich thickened cream tradition-ally served with scones and tea. In this pie, this creamy flavoring is combined with mixed fruit to create a per-fectly delectable pie!

PREP TIME: 60 MINUTES
TOTAL TIME: 4 HOURS

MAKES 8 SERVINGS

George H. Berggren, State College, Pennsylvania
Bake-Off® Contest 16, 1964

CRUST

1 box Pillsbury™ refrigerated pie crusts, softened as directed on box

FILLING

1 package unflavored gelatin

¼ cup water

⅓ cup sugar

⅛ teaspoon salt

1 cup sour cream

2 tablespoons milk

2 egg yolks, slightly beaten

1 cup whipping cream, whipped

TOPPING

1 medium peach, pitted, sliced

1 medium plum, pitted, sliced

½ cup fresh raspberries

½ cup fresh blackberries

1. Heat oven to 450°F. Make pie crust as directed on box for One-Crust Baked Shell using 9-inch glass pie pan. Bake 9 to 11 minutes or until light golden brown. Cool completely.

2. In small bowl, sprinkle gelatin over ¼ cup water; let stand to soften. In 2-quart saucepan, mix ⅓ cup sugar, the salt, sour cream, milk and egg yolks. Cook over medium heat 10 to 15 minutes, stirring constantly, until very hot; do not boil. Stir in softened gelatin. Cover surface with plastic wrap; refriger-ate until slightly thickened, 45 to 60 minutes.

3. Fold whipped cream into filling. Spoon into cooled baked shell. Refrigerate until set, about 2 hours.

4. Just before serving, arrange fruit over filling. Garnish as desired. Store in refrigerator.

1 Serving: Calories 424 (Calories from Fat 272); Total Fat 30g; Saturated Fat 15.5g; Trans Fat 0g; Cholesterol 105mg; Sodium 330mg; Total Carbohydrate 37g; Dietary Fiber 1g; Sugars 14g; Protein 4g

CRUNCHY CRUST BLUEBERRY SWIRL PIE

An ordinary can of pie filling becomes extraordinary in this beautiful dessert that's a breeze to make.

PREP TIME: 30 MINUTES
TOTAL TIME: 3 HOURS
30 MINUTES

MAKES 8 SERVINGS

Mrs. Richard Furry, La Mesa, California
Bake-Off® Contest 23, 1972

CRUST

½ cup butter or margarine

¾ cup all-purpose or self-rising flour

½ cup quick-cooking oats

½ cup chopped nuts

2 tablespoons sugar

FILLING

1 box (4-serving size) lemon-flavored gelatin

½ cup boiling water

1 can (21 oz) blueberry pie filling

½ cup sour cream

TOPPING, IF DESIRED

Whipped cream

1. Heat oven to 400°F. Butter 9-inch glass pie plate.

2. In 2½-quart microwavable bowl, microwave ½ cup butter uncovered on High 30 seconds, adding 10 seconds as needed until butter melts. Stir in flour, oats, nuts and sugar. Press in bottom and side of pie plate. Bake 11 to 13 minutes or until edges are golden brown.

3. Meanwhile, in 1½-quart bowl, dissolve gelatin in boiling water. Stir in pie filling. Refrigerate until thickened, about 1 hour.

4. Pour filling mixture into crust. Spoon sour cream by tablespoonfuls on top. Cut through sour cream and lightly fold filling over it, making swirls. Refrigerate 2 hours or until cold. Top individual servings with whipped cream. Cover and refrigerate any remaining pie.

CLEVER IDEA: *Make sure to use quick-cooking oats in this recipe. Instant or old-fashioned oats will not work.*

1 Serving: Calories 423 (Calories from Fat 172); Total Fat 19g; Saturated Fat 9g; Trans Fat 1g; Cholesterol 37mg, Sodium 181mg; Total Carbohydrate 60g; Dietary Fiber 3g; Sugars 42g; Protein 5g

CREAMY MOJITO PIE

Take a tropical turn with a cream pie made easily with an unroll, bake and fill pie crust.

PREP TIME: 15 MINUTES
TOTAL TIME: 1 HOUR 45 MINUTES

MAKES 8 SERVINGS

Ayofemi Wright, Atlanta, Georgia
Bake-Off® Contest 43, 2008

CRUST

1 box Pillsbury™ refrigerated pie crusts, softened as directed on box

FILLING

1 package (8 oz) cream cheese, softened

1 cup whole or 2% milk

1 box (4-serving size) vanilla instant pudding and pie filling mix

½ cup frozen (thawed) limeade concentrate

1½ teaspoons rum extract

TOPPING

1½ cups whipping (heavy) cream

¼ cup powdered sugar

¾ to 1½ teaspoons mint extract

GARNISHES, IF DESIRED

Fresh mint sprigs

Lime slices

1. Heat oven to 450°F. Make pie crust as directed on box for One-Crust Baked Shell using 9-inch glass pie plate. Bake 10 to 12 minutes or until light golden brown. Cool completely on cooling rack, about 15 minutes.

2. In large bowl, beat cream cheese with electric mixer on low speed until creamy. Add remaining filling ingredients; beat on low speed about 30 seconds or until blended. Beat on medium speed 2 minutes, scraping bowl occasionally, until thickened and creamy. Spoon filling evenly into pie crust; refrigerate while making topping.

3. In same bowl, beat topping ingredients on medium speed until stiff peaks form. Spread topping evenly over filling. Refrigerate about 1 hour or until set.

4. Garnish pie with mint sprigs and lime slices. Cover and refrigerate any remaining pie.

1 Serving: Calories 470 (Calories from Fat 280);
Total Fat 31g; Saturated Fat 17g; Trans Fat 1g;
Cholesterol 85mg; Sodium 430mg;
Total Carbohydrate 43g; Dietary Fiber 0g;
Sugars 24g; Protein 4g

CREAM CHEESE BROWNIE PIE

This fudgy top-prize winning dessert needs nothing more than an ice-cold glass of milk to make a perfect ending to any meal.

PREP TIME: 15 MINUTES
TOTAL TIME: 4 HOURS 5 MINUTES
MAKES 8 SERVINGS

Roberta Sonefeld, Hopkins, South Carolina
Bake-Off® Contest 39, 2000 Grand Prize Winner

CRUST

1 box Pillsbury™ refrigerated pie crusts, softened as directed on box

BROWNIE LAYER

1 box (15.8 oz) Pillsbury™ double chocolate brownie mix
¼ cup vegetable oil
1 tablespoon water
2 eggs

CREAM CHEESE LAYER

1 package (8 oz) cream cheese, softened
3 tablespoons sugar
1 teaspoon vanilla
1 egg
½ cup chopped pecans

TOPPING

Reserved chocolate syrup packet from brownie mix
3 tablespoons hot fudge topping

1. Heat oven to 350°F. Place pie crust in 9-inch glass pie plate as directed on box for One-Crust Filled Pie.

2. Reserve chocolate syrup packet from brownie mix for topping. In large bowl, place brownie mix, oil, water and eggs; beat 50 strokes with spoon. Set aside.

3. In medium bowl, beat cream cheese layer ingredients with electric mixer on medium speed until smooth.

4. Spread ½ cup brownie mixture in bottom of crust-lined pie plate. Spoon and carefully spread cream cheese mixture over brownie layer. Top with small spoonfuls of remaining brownie mixture; spread evenly. Sprinkle with pecans. Cover crust edge with 2- to 3-inch-wide strips of foil to prevent excessive browning; remove foil during last 15 minutes of bake time.

5. Bake 40 to 50 minutes or until center is puffed and crust is golden brown (pie may have cracks on surface).

6. In small bowl, mix chocolate syrup from packet and hot fudge topping. Place mixture in small resealable bag. Cut small hole off corner of bag. Drizzle topping over pie. Cool completely, about 3 hours, before serving. Cover and refrigerate any remaining pie.

1 Serving: Calories 630 (Calories from Fat 290); Total Fat 32g; Saturated Fat 10g; Trans Fat 0g; Cholesterol 115mg; Sodium 480mg; Total Carbohydrate 78g; Dietary Fiber 1g; Sugars 48g; Protein 8g

PINEAPPLE CRUNCH PIE

In the 1950s, when pie often was served as an everyday dessert, homemakers welcomed new recipes that would impress family or friends. This two-layer pineapple pie topped with a brown sugar-pecan layer still makes a big hit.

PREP TIME: 20 MINUTES
TOTAL TIME: 2 HOURS

MAKES 8 SERVINGS

June L. McVey, Lincoln, Nebraska
Bake-Off® Contest 3, 1951

1 (15-oz.) pkg. refrigerated pie crusts

FILLING

2 tablespoons cornstarch

2 tablespoons sugar

Dash salt

1 (20-oz.) can crushed pineapple in heavy syrup, undrained

1 tablespoon lemon juice

1 tablespoon margarine or butter

TOPPING

¼ cup firmly packed brown sugar

2 tablespoons margarine or butter

1 tablespoon corn syrup

½ cup chopped pecans

1. Prepare pie crust according to package directions for *two-crust filled pie* using 9-inch pie pan.

2. Heat oven to 425°F. In medium saucepan, combine cornstarch, sugar and salt; mix well. Stir in pineapple. Cook over medium heat until mixture thickens and boils, stirring constantly. Boil 1 minute. Remove from heat; stir in lemon juice and 1 tablespoon margarine. Pour into crust-lined pan. Top with second crust; seal edges and flute. Cut slits in top crust and bake at 425°F for 15 to 20 minutes or until light golden brown.

3. Meanwhile, in small heavy saucepan, combine all topping ingredients. Cook over low heat until sugar is dissolved, stirring constantly. Remove pie from oven.

4. Spoon and spread warm topping mixture evenly over top of pie. Cover edge of crust with strips of foil to prevent excessive browning. Bake at 425°F for an additional 10 to 15 minutes or until crust is deep golden brown. Cool completely.

> **CLEVER IDEA:** *One (20-oz.) can crushed pineapple in unsweetened juice, undrained, can be substituted for crushed pineapple in heavy syrup.*

1 Serving: Calories 430 (Calories from Fat 206); Total Fat 24g; Saturated Fat 7g; Trans Fat 1g; Cholesterol 6mg; Sodium 340mg; Total Carbohydrate 52g; Dietary Fiber 1g; Sugars 24g; Protein 3g

OPEN SESAME PIE

Heavy cream, sometimes labeled heavy whipping cream, has a slightly higher fat content than whipping cream, but either will work well in this recipe. Just don't substitute light cream or half-and-half: they won't whip up. For the best results, chill the bowl and beaters for at least an hour before whipping cream.

PREP TIME: 45 MINUTES
TOTAL TIME: 2 HOURS 45 MINUTES
MAKES 8 SERVINGS

Dorothy Koteen, Washington, D.C.
Bake-Off® Contest 6, 1954 Grand Prize Winner

CRUST

1 box Pillsbury™ refrigerated pie crusts, softened as directed on box

2 tablespoons sesame seed, toasted

FILLING

1 package unflavored gelatin

¼ cup cold water

1 package (8 oz) chopped dates (1¾ cups)

¼ cup sugar

¼ teaspoon salt

1 cup milk

2 egg yolks

1 teaspoon vanilla

1½ cups whipping cream

2 tablespoons sugar

⅛ to ¼ teaspoon nutmeg

1. Heat oven to 450°F. Make pie crust as directed on box for One-Crust Baked Shell using 9-inch glass pie pan. Press toasted seeds into bottom of crust-lined pan. Bake 9 to 11 minutes or until light golden brown. Cool completely, about 30 minutes.

2. Meanwhile, in small bowl, sprinkle gelatin over ¼ cup cold water; set aside to soften. In 2-quart saucepan, mix dates, ¼ cup sugar, the salt, milk and egg yolks. Cook over medium heat 10 to 12 minutes, stirring constantly, until mixture is slightly thickened. Remove from heat. Stir in softened gelatin and vanilla until gelatin is dissolved. Refrigerate, stirring occasionally, until date mixture is thickened and partially set.

3. In small bowl with electric mixer, beat whipping cream and 2 tablespoons sugar on high speed until stiff peaks form. Fold whipped cream into date mixture. Spoon filling into cooled baked shell; sprinkle with nutmeg. Refrigerate at least 2 hours before serving. Store in refrigerator.

CLEVER IDEA: *To toast sesame seed, spread on cookie sheet; bake at 375°F 3 to 5 minutes, stirring occasionally, until light golden brown. Or spread in 7-inch skillet; cook over medium heat about 5 minutes, stirring frequently, until light golden brown.*

1 Serving: Calories 529 (Calories from Fat 294); Total Fat 33g; Saturated Fat 17g; Trans Fat 0.5g; Cholesterol 105mg; Sodium 365mg; Total Carbohydrate 58g; Dietary Fiber 2g; Sugars 30g; Protein 5g

PENNSYLVANIA DUTCH CAKE AND CUSTARD PIE

Applesauce and sour cream add fresh flavor and a custard-like filling to this take-off of a shoofly pie.

PREP TIME: 25 MINUTES
TOTAL TIME: 1 HOUR 25 MINUTES

MAKES 10 SERVINGS

Gladys Fulton, Summerville, South Carolina
Bake-Off® Contest 35, 1992 Grand Prize Winner

CRUST

1 box Pillsbury™ refrigerated pie crusts, softened as directed on box

FILLING

⅓ cup granulated sugar

2 tablespoons Pillsbury™ BEST™ all-purpose flour

1 teaspoon apple pie spice

1 cup applesauce

⅔ cup sour cream

⅓ cup molasses

1 egg, beaten

CAKE

½ cup granulated sugar

¼ cup butter or margarine, softened

½ cup sour milk

1 egg

1 teaspoon vanilla

1¼ cups Pillsbury™ BEST™ all-purpose flour

1 teaspoon baking powder

½ teaspoon salt

¼ teaspoon baking soda

GLAZE

½ to ¾ cup powdered sugar

2 tablespoons brewed coffee

1. Place pie crust in 9-inch glass pie pan or 9-inch deep-dish glass pie pan as directed on box for One-Crust Filled Pie.

2. Heat oven to 350°F. In medium bowl, mix ⅓ cup granulated sugar, 2 tablespoons flour and the apple pie spice. Stir in remaining filling ingredients until well blended; set aside.

3. In small bowl with electric mixer, beat ½ cup granulated sugar and the butter on medium speed until well blended. Beat in sour milk, 1 egg and the vanilla (mixture will look curdled). On low speed, beat in flour, baking powder, salt and baking soda. Spoon into crust-lined pan. Carefully pour filling mixture over batter.

4. Bake 50 to 65 minutes or until center springs back when touched lightly and top is deep golden brown (filling will sink to bottom during baking).

5. In small bowl, mix powdered sugar and coffee until smooth and desired drizzling consistency. Drizzle over warm pie. Serve warm.

CLEVER IDEAS:

- *A mixture of ½ teaspoon ground cinnamon, ¼ teaspoon ground ginger, ⅛ teaspoon ground nutmeg and ⅛ teaspoon ground allspice can be substituted for the apple pie spice.*

- *To make sour milk, use 1 teaspoon lemon juice plus milk to make ½ cup; let stand 5 minutes.*

1 Serving: Calories 380 (Calories from Fat 130); Total Fat 14g; Saturated Fat 7g; Trans Fat 0g; Cholesterol 65mg; Sodium 380mg; Total Carbohydrate 58g; Dietary Fiber 1g; Sugars 32g; Protein 4g

CLEVER CAKE IDEAS:

- Don't fill your cake pans more than three-quarters full of batter; the batter may spill over as it expands during baking.

- Make sure there are at least 2 inches between cake pans in the oven, so air can circulate and cakes will be evenly baked.

- What makes a cake fall? Sudden changes in temperature or movement of the cake. Try not to open the oven during the first 15 minutes of baking, and not much after that, either. Close the oven door gently, if you do open it.

OATS AND HONEY GRANOLA PIE

Enjoy the old-fashioned flavors of oats, brown sugar and walnuts in a pie filling that goes together in minutes.

PREP TIME: 15 MINUTES
TOTAL TIME: 1 HOUR 35 MINUTES
MAKES 8 SERVINGS

Suzanne Conrad, Findlay, Ohio
Bake-Off® Contest 41, 2004 Grand Prize Winner

CRUST

1 box Pillsbury™ refrigerated pie crusts, softened as directed on box

FILLING

½ cup butter

½ cup packed brown sugar

¾ cup corn syrup

⅛ teaspoon salt

1 teaspoon vanilla

3 eggs, lightly beaten

4 crunchy granola bars (2 pouches from 8.9-oz. box), crushed (¾ cup)

½ cup chopped walnuts

¼ cup quick-cooking or old-fashioned oats

¼ cup semi-sweet or milk chocolate baking chips

Whipped cream or ice cream, if desired

1. Heat oven to 350°F. Place pie crust in 9-inch glass pie plate as directed on box for One-Crust Filled Pie.

2. In large microwavable bowl, microwave butter on High 50 to 60 seconds or until melted. Stir in brown sugar and corn syrup until blended. Beat in salt, vanilla and eggs. Stir crushed granola bars, walnuts, oats and baking chips into brown sugar mixture. Pour into crust-lined pan.

3. Bake 40 to 50 minutes or until filling is set and crust is golden brown. During last 15 to 20 minutes of baking, cover crust edge with strips of foil to prevent excessive browning. Cool at least 30 minutes before serving. Serve warm, at room temperature or chilled with whipped cream or ice cream. Cover and refrigerate any remaining pie.

CLEVER IDEA: *To easily crush granola bars, do not unwrap. Use rolling pin to crush bars.*

1 Serving: Calories 530 (Calories from Fat 250); Total Fat 28g; Saturated Fat 12g; Trans Fat 0g; Cholesterol 115mg; Sodium 340mg; Total Carbohydrate 64g; Dietary Fiber 1g; Sugars 31g; Protein 6g

OATS AND HONEY GRANOLA PIE (*opposite*)

MYSTERY PECAN PIE (*page 422*)

MYSTERY PECAN PIE

Solve the mystery when you taste the smooth cream cheese filling hiding under the rich pecan filling in this extra-special pie.

PREP TIME: 15 MINUTES
TOTAL TIME: 3 HOURS
MAKES 8 SERVINGS

Mary McClain, North Little Rock, Arkansas
Bake-Off® Contest 16, 1964

CRUST

1 box Pillsbury™ refrigerated pie crusts, softened as directed on box

FILLING

1 package (8 oz) cream cheese, softened

⅓ cup sugar

¼ teaspoon salt

1 teaspoon vanilla

1 egg

3 eggs

¼ cup sugar

1 cup corn syrup

1 teaspoon vanilla

1¼ cups chopped pecans

1. Place pie crust in 9-inch glass pie pan as directed on box for One-Crust Filled Pie.

2. Heat oven to 375°F. In small bowl with electric mixer, beat cream cheese, ⅓ cup sugar, the salt, 1 teaspoon vanilla and 1 of the eggs on low speed until smooth and well blended; set aside.

3. In another small bowl with electric mixer, beat remaining 3 eggs, ¼ cup sugar, the corn syrup and 1 teaspoon vanilla on medium speed until well blended. Spread cream cheese mixture in bottom of crust-lined pan. Sprinkle with pecans. Gently pour corn syrup mixture over pecans.

4. Bake 35 to 45 minutes or until center is set. After 15 to 20 minutes of baking, cover crust edge with strips of foil to prevent excessive browning. Cool completely, about 2 hours. Store in refrigerator.

1 Serving: Calories 560 (Calories from Fat 280); Total Fat 31g; Saturated Fat 10g; Trans Fat 0g; Cholesterol 140mg; Sodium 350mg; Total Carbohydrate 63g; Dietary Fiber 1g; Sugars 33g; Protein 7g

COCONUT PECAN CHOCOLATE FUDGE

Got frosting? Make fudge. It's the yummiest, easiest-ever candy you can mix up in minutes!

PREP TIME: 25 MINUTES
TOTAL TIME: 1 HOUR 55 MINUTES

MAKES 64 SERVINGS

Lesley Pew, Lynn, Massachusetts
Bake-Off® Contest 46, 2013

1 cup milk chocolate chips (6 oz)

1 can Pillsbury™ Creamy Supreme™ Milk Chocolate Frosting

2 teaspoons vanilla

2 cups chopped pecans, toasted

2 cups sweetened shredded coconut, toasted

1 cup white vanilla baking chips (6 oz)

1 can Pillsbury™ Creamy Supreme™ Coconut Pecan Frosting

1. Line 9-inch square pan with foil, extending foil over 2 opposite sides of pan. Spray foil with no-stick cooking spray.

2. In medium microwavable bowl, microwave chocolate chips on High 1 to 2 minutes, stirring every 30 seconds, until melted. Stir in milk chocolate frosting and 1 teaspoon of the vanilla. Reserve 2 tablespoons of the nuts and 2 tablespoons of the coconut. Stir half of the remaining nuts and half of the remaining coconut into the chocolate mixture. Spread in pan.

3. In medium microwavable bowl, microwave white vanilla chips on High 1 to 2 minutes, stirring every 30 seconds, until melted. Stir in coconut pecan frosting and remaining 1 teaspoon vanilla. Stir in remaining half of the nuts and coconut. Spread over chocolate mixture. Sprinkle reserved nuts and coconut over fudge.

4. Refrigerate 1½ hours or until firm. Remove foil; cut into 8 rows by 8 rows. Store covered in refrigerator.

CLEVER IDEAS:

To toast pecans, spread pecans in ungreased shallow pan. Bake at 350°F for 6 to 10 minutes, stirring occasionally, until light brown.

To toast coconut, spread coconut in ungreased shallow pan. Bake at 350°F for 5 to 7 minutes, stirring occasionally, until golden brown.

1 Serving: Calories 130 (Calories from Fat 70); Total Fat 8g; Saturated Fat 3.5g; Trans Fat 0.5g; Cholesterol 0mg; Sodium 45mg; Total Carbohydrate 13g; Dietary Fiber 0g; Sugars 4g; Protein 1g

COOKIE CRUST PECAN PIE

Ever-popular pecan pie is baked in a 13x9-inch pan for a new shape, and refrigerated cookie dough makes an unusual quick-to-prepare crust.

PREP TIME: 20 MINUTES
TOTAL TIME: 2 HOURS 15 MINUTES

MAKES 12 SERVINGS

Louise Schlinkert, China City, California
Bake-Off® Contest 20, 1969

1 (18-oz.) pkg. refrigerated sugar cookies

1 (3.4-oz.) pkg. instant butterscotch pudding and pie filling mix

Dash salt

¾ cup dark corn syrup

⅔ cup milk

½ teaspoon vanilla, if desired

1 egg

1½ cups pecan halves or pieces

1 cup whipped cream or 1 pint ice cream, if desired

1. Heat oven to 350°F. Slice cookie dough into ¼-inch slices. Press slices in bottom and 1 inch up sides of ungreased 13x9-inch pan to form crust. (Press dough as thin as possible on sides.) In medium bowl, combine pudding mix, salt, corn syrup, milk, vanilla and egg; blend well. Fold in pecans. Pour into crust-lined pan.

2. Bake at 350°F for 25 to 35 minutes or until edges are deep golden brown and filling is set. Cool completely; cut into squares. Serve with whipped cream or ice cream.

CLEVER IDEA: *For easier slicing of cookie dough, place in freezer 10 minutes before slicing.*

1 Serving: Calories 458 (Calories from Fat 245); Total Fat 27g; Saturated Fat 9g; Trans Fat 3g; Cholesterol 54mg; Sodium 320mg; Total Carbohydrate 53g; Dietary Fiber 1g; Sugars 37g; Protein 4g

COMPANY'S COMING CASHEW PIE

In this recipe from the first Bake-Off® Contest, cashew nuts are used instead of pecans to make a rich, decadent pie. Garnish each slice of pie with whipped cream and a whole cashew nut.

PREP TIME: 15 MINUTES
TOTAL TIME: 2 HOURS
MAKES 8 SERVINGS

Hazel Frost, Chicago, Illinois
Bake-Off® Contest 1, 1949

1 box Pillsbury™ refrigerated pie crusts (from 15-oz. pkg.)

FILLING

¾ cup firmly packed brown sugar

3 tablespoons margarine or butter, softened

¾ cup light corn syrup

1 teaspoon vanilla

3 eggs

1 cup chopped cashews

1. Prepare pie crust according to package directions for One-Crust Filled Pie using 9-inch pie pan.

2. Heat oven to 350°F. In large bowl, beat brown sugar and margarine at high speed until light and fluffy. Add corn syrup and vanilla; beat at medium speed until smooth. Beat in eggs 1 at a time, blending well after each addition. Stir in cashew nuts. Pour into crust-lined pan.

3. Bake at 350°F for 45 to 50 minutes or until top of pie is deep golden brown. Cover edge of crust with strips of foil after 15 or 20 minutes of baking to prevent excessive browning. Cool completely.

1 Serving: Calories 553 (Calories from Fat 249); Total Fat 28g; Saturated Fat 9g; Trans Fat 1g; Cholesterol 76mg; Sodium 478mg; Total Carbohydrate 75g; Dietary Fiber 1g; Sugars 46g; Protein 6g

CHOCOLATE SILK PECAN PIE

Enjoy this yummy chocolate and pecan filled pie made with Pillsbury™ refrigerated pie crusts—perfect for a dessert.

PREP TIME: 25 MINUTES
TOTAL TIME: 3 HOURS 50 MINUTES
MAKES 10 SERVINGS

Leonard Thompson, San Jose, California
Bake-Off® Contest 32, 1986

CRUST

1 box Pillsbury™ refrigerated pie crusts

PECAN FILLING

2 eggs

⅓ cup granulated sugar

½ cup dark corn syrup

3 tablespoons butter or margarine, melted

⅛ teaspoon salt, if desired

½ cup chopped pecans

CHOCOLATE FILLING

1 cup hot milk

¼ teaspoon vanilla

1 bag (12 oz) semisweet chocolate chips (2 cups)

TOPPING

1 cup whipping cream

2 tablespoons powdered sugar

¼ teaspoon vanilla

Chocolate curls, if desired

1. Heat oven to 350°F. Place pie crust in 9-inch glass pie plate as directed on box for One-Crust Filled Pie.

2. In small bowl, beat eggs with electric mixer on medium speed until well blended. Add granulated sugar, corn syrup, butter and salt; beat 1 minute. Stir in pecans. Pour into crust-lined pie plate. Cover crust edge with 2- to 3-inch-wide strips of foil to prevent excessive browning; remove foil during last 15 minutes of bake time.

3. Bake 40 to 55 minutes or until center of pie is puffed and golden brown. Cool 1 hour.

4. Meanwhile, in blender or food processor, place chocolate filling ingredients. Cover; blend about 1 minute or until smooth. Refrigerate until mixture is slightly thickened but not set, about 1 hour 30 minutes.

5. Gently stir chocolate filling; pour over cooled pecan filling in crust. Refrigerate at least 1 hour or until firm before serving.

6. Just before serving, in small bowl, beat whipping cream, powdered sugar and ¼ teaspoon vanilla with mixer on high speed until stiff peaks form. Spoon or pipe whipped cream over filling. Garnish with chocolate curls.

1 Serving: Calories 490 (Calories from Fat 250); Total Fat 28g; Saturated Fat 16g; Trans Fat 0g; Cholesterol 85mg; Sodium 170mg; Total Carbohydrate 54g; Dietary Fiber 2g; Sugars 35g; Protein 4g

VIENNA CHOCOLATE PIE

A Pillsbury Bake-Off®
Contest recipe from 1959,
this recipe is considered
a classic.

PREP TIME: 15 MINUTES
TOTAL TIME: 1 HOUR 45 MINUTES

MAKES 8 SERVINGS

Dorothy Wagoner, Lufkin, Texas
Bake-Off® Contest 11, 1959

- 1 box Pillsbury™ refrigerated pie crusts
- 1½ cups sugar
- 3 tablespoons all-purpose flour
- ¾ teaspoon instant coffee granules or crystals
- ¼ teaspoon ground cinnamon
- Dash salt
- 4 eggs
- ½ cup buttermilk
- 1½ teaspoons vanilla
- ½ cup butter or margarine, softened
- 2 oz unsweetened baking chocolate, melted
- ¼ cup slivered almonds

1. Heat oven to 400°F. Make pie crust as directed on box for One-Crust Filled Pie using 9-inch glass pie pan.

2. In medium bowl, mix sugar, flour, instant coffee, cinnamon and salt. In large bowl, beat eggs with electric mixer on high speed until light in color. Beat in sugar mixture. Beat in buttermilk, vanilla, butter and chocolate until well combined (filling may look curdled). Pour into crust-lined pan. Sprinkle with almonds.

3. Bake 25 to 30 minutes or until center is set and crust is deep golden brown. After 15 to 20 minutes of baking, cover edge of crust with strips of foil to prevent excessive browning. Cool completely, about 1 hour.

> **CLEVER IDEA:** *To substitute for buttermilk, use 1 teaspoon vinegar or lemon juice plus enough milk to make ½ cup.*

1 Serving: Calories 480 (Calories from Fat 230); Total Fat 26g; Saturated Fat 13g; Trans Fat 0g; Cholesterol 140mg; Sodium 280mg; Total Carbohydrate 56g; Dietary Fiber 1g; Sugars 39g; Protein 6g

FRENCH SILK CHOCOLATE PIE

French Silk Chocolate Pie—the ultimate in decadence—is easy with a classic recipe from the Bake-Off® Contest. It's one of our Top 10 Pies to Try!

PREP TIME: 50 MINUTES
TOTAL TIME: 2 HOURS
50 MINUTES

MAKES 10 SERVINGS

Hall of Fame

Betty Cooper, Kensington, Maryland
Bake-Off® Contest 3, 1951 Hall of Fame

CRUST

1 box Pillsbury™ refrigerated pie crusts, softened as directed on box

FILLING

3 oz unsweetened chocolate, cut into pieces

1 cup butter, softened (do not use margarine)

1 cup sugar

½ teaspoon vanilla

4 pasteurized eggs

TOPPING

½ cup sweetened whipped cream

Chocolate curls, if desired

1. Heat oven to 450°F. Make pie crust as directed on box for One-Crust Baked Shell, using 9-inch glass pie plate. Bake 9 to 11 minutes or until light golden brown. Cool completely, about 30 minutes.

2. In 1-quart saucepan, melt chocolate over low heat; cool. In small bowl with electric mixer, beat butter on medium speed until fluffy. Gradually beat in sugar until light and fluffy. Beat in cooled chocolate and vanilla until well blended.

3. Add eggs 1 at a time, beating on high speed 2 minutes after each addition; beat until mixture is smooth and fluffy. Pour into cooled baked shell. Refrigerate at least 2 hours before serving. Garnish with whipped cream and chocolate curls. Cover and refrigerate any remaining pie.

CLEVER IDEAS:

● *Did you know? Pillsbury has a gluten free pie and pastry dough.*

● *Use of pasteurized eggs eliminates food safety concerns and allows you to enjoy this Bake-Off® Contest favorite.*

1 Serving: Calories 430 (Calories from Fat 270); Total Fat 30g; Saturated Fat 18g; Trans Fat 0.5g; Cholesterol 135mg; Sodium 260mg; Total Carbohydrate 33g; Dietary Fiber 1g; Sugars 21g; Protein 4g

CARAMEL CANDY PIE

PREP TIME: 40 MINUTES
TOTAL TIME: 5 HOURS
15 MINUTES

MAKES 10 SERVINGS

Florence E. Ries, Sleepy Eye, Minnesota
Bake-Off® Contest 4, 1952

1 package unflavored gelatin

¼ cup cold water

1 bag (14 oz) caramels, unwrapped

1 cup milk

1 box Pillsbury™ refrigerated pie crusts, softened as directed on box

1½ cups whipping cream

¼ cup slivered almonds

2 tablespoons sugar

1. In small bowl, sprinkle gelatin over water; let stand to soften. In 2-quart saucepan, cook caramels and milk over medium-low heat, stirring occasionally, until caramels are melted and mixture is smooth. Stir in softened gelatin. Refrigerate until slightly thickened, stirring occasionally, 45 to 60 minutes.

2. Meanwhile, heat oven to 450°F. Make pie crust as directed on box for One-Crust Baked Shell using 9-inch glass pie plate. Bake 9 to 11 minutes or until lightly browned. Cool completely, about 30 minutes.

3. In large bowl, beat whipping cream with electric mixer on high speed until stiff peaks form. Fold thickened caramel mixture into whipped cream. Pour into cooled baked shell. Refrigerate at least 4 hours or overnight before serving.

4. Meanwhile, line cookie sheet with foil. In 7-inch skillet, cook almonds and sugar over medium-low heat, stirring constantly, until sugar is melted and almonds are golden brown. Immediately spread on cookie sheet. Cool completely, then break apart.

5. Just before serving, garnish pie with caramelized almonds. Store pie in refrigerator.

1 Serving: Calories 481 (Calories from Fat 261); Total Fat 29g; Saturated Fat 10g; Trans Fat 0g; Cholesterol 45mg; Sodium 230mg; Total Carbohydrate 45g; Dietary Fiber 0g; Sugars 23g; Protein 5g

PEACH ELIZABETH

A sunny peach filling is nestled between two spicy butter crunch layers— a dressed-up version of a fruit crisp.

PREP TIME: 20 MINUTES
TOTAL TIME: 1 HOUR 30 MINUTES
MAKES 9 SERVINGS

Rosemary H. Sport, Roxbury, Massachusetts
Bake-Off® Contest 7, 1955

½ cup butter or margarine, softened

½ cup firmly packed brown sugar

1 teaspoon grated lemon peel

1 teaspoon lemon juice

1 cup all-purpose flour

½ teaspoon baking soda

½ teaspoon salt

½ teaspoon cinnamon

¼ teaspoon nutmeg

½ cup crushed corn flakes or other flake cereal

9 fresh peach halves

1. Heat oven to 350°F. Generously grease 8-inch square pan. In large bowl, beat butter, brown sugar, lemon peel and lemon juice until light and fluffy.

2. Add flour, baking soda, salt, cinnamon and nutmeg to butter mixture; beat until well blended. Stir in cereal until mixture resembles coarse crumbs. Press half of mixture in bottom of greased pan. Arrange peach halves, cut side down, over crust. Sprinkle with remaining crumb mixture.

3. Bake at 350°F for 45 to 50 minutes or until golden brown. Serve warm or cold with cream or whipped cream.

CLEVER IDEA: *Canned peach halves can be substituted for fresh peaches.*

1 Serving: Calories 220 (Calories from Fat 94); Total Fat 10g; Saturated Fat 6.5g; Trans Fat 0g; Cholesterol 27mg; Sodium 350mg; Total Carbohydrate 31g; Dietary Fiber 2g; Sugars 18g; Protein 2g

SOUR CREAM APPLE SQUARES

Relish these nutty apple squares made distinctive with sour cream and a hint of cinnamon. A delicious dessert that you can serve with whipped cream or ice cream.

PREP TIME: 20 MINUTES
TOTAL TIME: 1 HOUR 30 MINUTES

MAKES 12 SERVINGS

Luella Maki, Ely, Minnesota
Bake-Off® Contest 26, 1975 Grand Prize Winner

2 cups all purpose or unbleached flour

2 cups firmly packed brown sugar

½ cup margarine or butter, softened

1 cup chopped nuts

1 to 2 teaspoons cinnamon

1 teaspoon baking soda

½ teaspoon salt

1 (8-oz.) container sour cream

1 teaspoon vanilla

1 egg

2 cups finely chopped, peeled apples

1. Heat oven to 350°F. In large bowl, combine flour, brown sugar and margarine; beat at low speed until crumbly. Stir in nuts. Press 2¾ cups crumb mixture in bottom of ungreased 13x9-inch pan.

2. To remaining mixture, add cinnamon, baking soda, salt, sour cream, vanilla and egg; mix well. Stir in apples. Spoon evenly over crumb mixture in pan.

3. Bake at 350°F for 30 to 40 minutes or until toothpick inserted in center comes out clean. Cool 30 minutes. Cut into squares. Serve warm or cool. If desired, serve with whipped cream or ice cream. Store in refrigerator.

1 Serving: Calories 404 (Calories from Fat 160); Total Fat 18g; Saturated Fat 4g; Trans Fat 0g; Cholesterol 25mg; Sodium 322mg; Total Carbohydrate 58g; Dietary Fiber 2g; Sugars 40g; Protein 5g

SWEDISH APPLE MINI-DUMPLINGS

Enjoy these baked Swedish-style mini apple dumplings for a delicious homemade dessert made using Pillsbury™ refrigerated pie crusts.

PREP TIME: 20 MINUTES
TOTAL TIME: 1 HOUR 10 MINUTES

MAKES 4 SERVINGS

Stella Riley Bender, Colorado Springs, Colorado
Bake-Off® Contest 36, 1994

½ cup packed brown sugar

½ teaspoon ground cinnamon

¼ teaspoon ground cardamom

2 teaspoons vanilla

1 box Pillsbury™ refrigerated pie crusts, softened as directed on box

1 tablespoon butter or margarine, softened

1 small Granny Smith apple, peeled, cored and cut into 8 slices

¼ cup raisins

1½ cups apple juice

3 tablespoons sugar

2 tablespoons red cinnamon candies

¼ cup half-and-half

1. Heat oven to 375°F. Spray 8-inch square (2-quart) glass baking dish with cooking spray. In small bowl, mix brown sugar, cinnamon, cardamom and vanilla; set aside.

2. Remove pie crust from pouch; unroll on work surface. Spread butter over crust; sprinkle with brown sugar mixture. Cut crust into 8 wedges; place apple slice crosswise in center of each wedge. Starting with pointed end, fold crust wedge over apple; fold corners of wide end of wedge over apple, forming dumpling and sealing completely. Place seam side down and sides touching in baking dish. Sprinkle with raisins.

3. In 1-quart saucepan, heat apple juice, sugar and cinnamon candies to boiling over medium heat. Cook 1 minute, stirring frequently, until candies are melted. Carefully pour over dumplings.

4. Bake 30 to 40 minutes or until crust is light golden brown, apples are tender and sauce thickens. Cool 10 minutes before serving. Spoon dumplings into serving dishes; spoon sauce over dumplings. Serve warm with half-and-half.

1 Serving: Calories 530 (Calories from Fat 150); Total Fat 17g; Saturated Fat 8g; Trans Fat 0g; Cholesterol 20mg; Sodium 300mg; Total Carbohydrate 90g; Dietary Fiber 1g; Sugars 60g; Protein 2g

PUMPKIN RAVIOLI WITH SALTED CARAMEL WHIPPED CREAM

Create a sweet new twist on pumpkin ravioli with flaky crescent dough, cream cheese and caramel sauce. Mmm.

PREP TIME: 1 HOUR 10 MINUTES
TOTAL TIME: 1 HOUR 10 MINUTES
MAKES 12 SERVINGS

Christina Verrelli, Devon, Pennsylvania
Bake-Off® Contest 45, 2012 Grand Prize Winner

- 4 tablespoons butter, melted
- 2 packages (3 oz each) cream cheese, softened
- ½ cup canned pumpkin
- 1 egg yolk
- ½ teaspoon pure vanilla extract
- ¼ cup sugar
- 5 tablespoons Pillsbury™ BEST™ All Purpose Flour
- ½ teaspoon pumpkin pie spice
- ⅓ cup chopped pecans, finely chopped
- 2 cans Pillsbury™ Crescent Recipe Creations™ refrigerated seamless dough sheet
- 1 cup heavy whipping cream
- ⅛ teaspoon salt
- 5 tablespoons caramel syrup
- 4 tablespoons cinnamon sugar

1. Heat oven to 375°F. Brush 2 large cookie sheets with 2 tablespoons of the melted butter. In large bowl, beat cream cheese and pumpkin with electric mixer on medium speed about 1 minute or until smooth. Add egg yolk, vanilla, sugar, 3 tablespoons of the flour and pumpkin pie spice; beat on low speed until blended. Reserve 4 teaspoons of the pecans; set aside. Stir remaining pecans into pumpkin mixture.

2. Lightly sprinkle work surface with 1 tablespoon of the flour. Unroll 1 can of dough on floured surface with 1 short side facing you. Press dough into 14x12-inch rectangle. With paring knife, lightly score the dough in half horizontally. Lightly score bottom half of dough into 12 squares (3x2¼-inch each). Spoon heaping tablespoon of the pumpkin filling onto center of each square. Gently lift and position unscored half of dough over filling. Starting at the top folded edge, press handle of wooden spoon firmly between mounds and along edges of pumpkin filling to seal. Using toothpick, poke small hole in top of each ravioli. Using a pizza cutter or sharp knife, cut between each ravioli; place 1 inch apart on cookie sheets. Repeat with remaining 1 tablespoon flour, dough sheet and filling. Brush ravioli with remaining 2 tablespoons melted butter.

3. Bake 9 to 14 minutes or until golden brown.

4. Meanwhile, in medium bowl, beat whipping cream and salt with electric mixer on high speed until soft peaks form. Beat in 2 tablespoons of the caramel syrup until stiff peaks form. Transfer to serving bowl; cover and refrigerate.

5. Remove ravioli from oven. Sprinkle ravioli with 2 tablespoons cinnamon sugar; turn. Sprinkle with remaining cinnamon sugar.

6. To serve, place 2 ravioli on each of 12 dessert plates. Drizzle each serving with scant teaspoon of the caramel syrup; sprinkle with reserved chopped pecans. With spoon, swirl remaining 1 tablespoon caramel syrup into bowl of whipped cream. Serve warm ravioli with whipped cream.

1 Serving: Calories 380 (Calories from Fat 220); Total Fat 25g; Saturated Fat 13g; Trans Fat 0.5g; Cholesterol 70mg; Sodium 440mg; Total Carbohydrate 35g; Dietary Fiber 1g; Sugars 16g; Protein 4g

PUMPKIN BREAD PUDDING WITH GINGER CREAM

Looking for a famous dessert using Progresso™ Plain Bread Crumbs? Then try this delicious pudding made with pumpkin and eggs and served with ginger cream.

PREP TIME: 15 MINUTES
TOTAL TIME: 1 HOUR 45 MINUTES

MAKES 9 SERVINGS

Candice Merrill, Pasadena, California
Bake-Off® Contest 38, 1998

PUDDING

3 eggs

1¼ cups sugar

1½ teaspoons cinnamon

½ to 1½ teaspoons nutmeg

¼ cup butter or margarine, melted

1½ teaspoons vanilla

1 (8-oz.) container (1¾ cups) Progresso™ Plain Bread Crumbs

2 cups milk

1 cup canned pumpkin

½ cup raisins

GINGER CREAM

1 cup whipping cream

3 tablespoons sugar

½ teaspoon ginger

1. Heat oven to 350°F. Spray 8- or 9-inch square pan with non-stick cooking spray. In large bowl, beat eggs until well blended. Add 1¼ cups sugar, cinnamon, nutmeg, butter and vanilla; beat well. Add bread crumbs, milk and pumpkin; mix well. Let stand 10 minutes.

2. Add raisins to batter; mix well. Spread evenly in sprayed pan. Bake at 350°F for 37 to 47 minutes or until knife inserted 1½ inches from edge comes out clean. Cool 30 minutes.

3. In small bowl, beat whipping cream, gradually adding 3 tablespoons sugar and ginger until soft peaks form. To serve, cut pudding into squares. Serve warm or cool topped with ginger cream. Store in refrigerator.

1 Serving: Calories 460 (Calories from Fat 170); Total Fat 19g; Saturated Fat 11g; Trans Fat 1g; Cholesterol 125mg; Sodium 300mg; Total Carbohydrate 62g; Dietary Fiber 2g; Sugars 42g; Protein 9g

RUBY RAZZ CRUNCH

PREP TIME: 25 MINUTES

TOTAL TIME: 1 HOUR 30 MINUTES

MAKES 9 SERVINGS

C. W. Myers, Fort Collins, Colorado
Bake-Off® Contest 8, 1956

FILLING

1 package (10-oz.) frozen raspberries with syrup, thawed, drained, reserving liquid

1 bag (16-oz.) frozen rhubarb, thawed, drained, reserving liquid

½ cup granulated sugar

3 tablespoons cornstarch

GARNISH

½ cup whipping cream, whipped

2 tablespoons granulated sugar

1 to 3 drops red food color, if desired

CRUST AND TOPPING

1¼ cups all-purpose flour

1 cup packed brown sugar

1 cup quick-cooking oats

1 teaspoon ground cinnamon

½ cup butter or margarine, melted

1. Heat oven to 325°F. Reserve 2 tablespoons raspberries for topping. In measuring cup, mix reserved raspberry and rhubarb liquids; if necessary, add water to make 1 cup.

2. In 2-quart saucepan, mix ½ cup granulated sugar and the cornstarch; stir in reserved liquids. Cook over medium heat, stirring constantly, until thickened. Remove from heat. Stir in remaining raspberries and rhubarb; set aside.

3. Line cookie sheet with waxed paper. In small bowl, gently mix whipped cream, 2 tablespoons granulated sugar, reserved raspberries and food color. Drop in 9 mounds onto lined cookie sheet; freeze until firm.

4. In large bowl, mix flour, brown sugar, oats and cinnamon. Stir in butter until crumbly. Press ⅔ of crumb mixture in bottom of ungreased 9-inch square pan. Spoon filling mixture over crust, spreading evenly. Sprinkle with remaining crumb mixture.

5. Bake 45 to 55 minutes or until topping is golden brown and filling bubbles around edges. Cool slightly, about 10 minutes, before serving with mounds of frozen garnish.

1 Serving: Calories 457 (Calories from Fat 143); Total Fat 16g; Saturated Fat 9.5g; Trans Fat 1g; Cholesterol 45mg; Sodium 112mg; Total Carbohydrate 76g; Dietary Fiber 3g; Sugars 44g; Protein 4g

TOFFEE MOCHA VELVET

Mix chocolate fudge frosting and toffee candy bars to make this creamy frozen dessert.

PREP TIME: 15 MINUTES
TOTAL TIME: 1 HOUR 15 MINUTES

MAKES 10 SERVINGS

Persis Schlosser, Denver, Colorado
Bake-Off® Contest 39, 2000

1 (16-oz.) can Pillsbury™ Creamy Supreme™ Chocolate Fudge Frosting

2 cups whipping cream

½ cup sweetened condensed milk (not evaporated)

2 tablespoons instant coffee granules or crystals

1 teaspoon vanilla

3 (1.4-oz.) milk chocolate English toffee candy bars, coarsely crushed

1. In large bowl, combine all ingredients except candy bars; beat at low speed until combined. Beat at high speed for 3 to 4 minutes or until mixture thickens and forms soft peaks.

2. Fold in crushed candy. Pour mixture into ungreased 13x9-inch (3-quart) glass baking dish. Freeze at least 1 hour for a soft set or 4 hours for a firm texture. To serve, spoon into bowls.

1 Serving: Calories 470 (Calories from Fat 280); Total Fat 31g; Saturated Fat 17g; Trans Fat 3g; Cholesterol 75mg; Sodium 170mg; Total Carbohydrate 44g; Dietary Fiber 1g; Sugars 39g; Protein 3g

MINI ICE CREAM COOKIE CUPS

An easy make-ahead recipe is a fun and impressive dessert for your next gathering.

PREP TIME: 20 MINUTES

TOTAL TIME: 45 MINUTES

MAKES 24 SERVINGS

Sue Compton, Delanco, New Jersey
Bake-Off® Contest 44, 2010 Grand Prize Winner

1 package (16 oz) Pillsbury™ Ready to Bake!™ refrigerated sugar cookies (24 cookies)

4 teaspoons sugar

⅓ cup chopped walnuts, finely chopped

½ cup semi-sweet chocolate baking chips

¼ cup seedless red raspberry jam

1½ cups vanilla bean ice cream, softened

24 fresh raspberries

1. Heat oven to 350°F. Spray 24 mini muffin cups with no-stick cooking spray. Place 1 cookie dough round in each muffin cup. Bake 15 to 20 minutes or until golden brown.

2. Place 2 teaspoons of the sugar in small bowl. Dip end of wooden spoon handle in sugar; carefully press into center of each cookie to make 1-inch-wide indentation. Cool completely in pan, about 20 minutes.

3. Meanwhile, in small bowl, mix walnuts and remaining 2 teaspoons sugar; set aside. In small microwavable bowl, microwave chocolate chips uncovered on High 30 to 60 seconds, stirring after 30 seconds, until smooth.

4. Run knife around edges of cups to loosen; gently remove from pan. Dip rim of each cup into melted chocolate, then into walnut mixture. Place walnut side up on cookie sheet with sides.

5. In another small microwavable bowl, microwave jam uncovered on High about 15 seconds until melted. Spoon ½ teaspoon jam into each cup. Freeze cups about 5 minutes or until chocolate is set.

6. Spoon ice cream into cups, using small cookie scoop or measuring tablespoon. Top each cup with fresh raspberry; serve immediately.

CLEVER IDEA: *Prepare cookie cups through step 5, omitting jam. Store covered up to two days at room temperature. When ready to serve, fill with jam, ice cream and top with raspberry.*

1 Serving: Calories 140 (Calories from Fat 60); Total Fat 7g; Saturated Fat 2.5g; Trans Fat 0g; Cholesterol 0mg; Sodium 55mg; Total Carbohydrate 19g; Dietary Fiber 0g; Sugars 13g; Protein 1g

Index

Underscored page references indicate boxed text. **Boldfaced** page references indicate photographs.

Conversion Chart

These equivalents have been slightly rounded to make measuring easier.

VOLUME MEASUREMENTS		
U.S.	Imperial	Metric
¼ tsp	–	1 ml
½ tsp	–	2 ml
1 tsp	–	5 ml
1 Tbsp	–	15 ml
2 Tbsp (1 oz)	1 fl oz	30 ml
¼ cup (2 oz)	2 fl oz	60 ml
⅓ cup (3 oz)	3 fl oz	80 ml
½ cup (4 oz)	4 fl oz	120 ml
⅔ cup (5 oz)	5 fl oz	160 ml
¾ cup (6 oz)	6 fl oz	180 ml
1 cup (8 oz)	8 fl oz	240 ml

WEIGHT MEASUREMENTS	
U.S.	Metric
1 oz	30 g
2 oz	60 g
4 oz (¼ lb)	115 g
5 oz (⅓ lb)	145 g
6 oz	170 g
7 oz	200 g
8 oz (½ lb)	230 g
10 oz	285 g
12 oz (¾ lb)	340 g
14 oz	400 g
16 oz (1 lb)	455 g
2.2 lb	1 kg

LENGTH MEASUREMENTS	
U.S.	Metric
1/4"	0.6 cm
1/2"	1.25 cm
1"	2.5 cm
2"	5 cm
4"	11 cm
6"	15 cm
8"	20 cm
10"	25 cm
12" (1')	30 cm

PAN SIZES	
U.S.	Metric
8" cake pan	20 × 4 cm sandwich or cake tin
9" cake pan	23 × 3.5 cm sandwich or cake tin
11" × 7" baking pan	28 × 18 cm baking tin
13" × 9" baking pan	32.5 × 23 cm baking tin
15" × 10" baking pan	38 × 25.5 cm baking tin (Swiss roll tin)
1½ qt baking dish	1.5 liter baking dish
2 qt baking dish	2 liter baking dish
2 qt rectangular baking dish	30 × 19 cm baking dish
9" pie plate	22 × 4 or 23 × 4 cm pie plate
7" or 8" springform pan	18 or 20 cm springform or loose-bottom cake tin
9" × 5" loaf pan	23 × 13 cm or 2 lb narrow loaf tin or pâté tin

TEMPERATURES		
Fahrenheit	Centigrade	Gas
140°	60°	–
160°	70°	–
180°	80°	–
225°	105°	¼
250°	120°	½
275°	135°	1
300°	150°	2
325°	160°	3
350°	180°	4
375°	190°	5
400°	200°	6
425°	220°	7
450°	230°	8
475°	245°	9
500°	260°	–